Casualty Care

in Mountain Rescue

Edited by John Ellerton

Commissioned by the
Mountain Rescue Council

Readers should be aware that the care of a casualty is continually changing as new techniques, equipment and drugs are developed. Research into the best type of treatment advances our knowledge and the recommendations in this book may, in time, become outdated. Every effort has been taken to ensure that the information given is up to date and accurate. However errors may still be present. Readers are urged to report any errors to the Medical Subcommittee of the Mountain Rescue Council.

Every effort has been made to check drug doses in this book. It is still possible that errors have been missed. Drug schedules are being continually revised and side effects recognised. For these reasons the reader is strongly urged to consult the drug companies' printed instructions before administering any of the drugs recommended in this book.

ISBN 0-9501765-7-5

978-0-9501765-7-4

Cover photo of the Cullin, Skye by Eric Shaw

Printed by REED'S LIMITED of Penrith, Cumbria

August 2006

Abbreviations

A, B, C, D, E, F	Airway; Breathing; Circulation; Disability; Exposure; Fractures
AED	Automatic external defibrillator
ALS	Advanced Life Support
AMPLE	Allergies; Medication; Past history; Last meal; Events
ARCC	Aeronautical Rescue Co-ordination Centre
AVPU	Alert; Verbal; Pain; Unresponsive
BASICS	British Association for Immediate Care
BLS	Basic Life Support
BMC	British Mountaineering Council
BP	Blood pressure
BSE	Bovine Spongiform Encephalitis ('Mad cow disease')
CPB	Cardiopulmonary bypass
CPR	Cardiopulmonary resuscitation
CT	Computer tomogram (xray)
DCS	Decompression sickness
DKA	Diabetic ketoacidosis
Doctor	Medically-qualified doctor
ECG	Electrocardiogram
EMD	Electromechanical dissociation (replaced by the term PEA)
EMS	Emergency Medical System
ET(T)	Endotracheal (tube)
ETCO$_2$	End tidal carbon dioxide concentration
GCS	Glasgow Coma Scale
GPS	Global Position System
GTN	Glyceral trinitrate
HIV	Human Immunodeficiency Virus
ICAR Medcom	International Commission for Mountain Emergency Medicine

IHD	Ischaemic heart disease
ILCOR	International Liaison Committee on Resuscitation
JRCALC	Joint Royal Colleges Ambulance Liaison Committee
LDSAMRA	Lake District Search and Mountain Rescue Association
LMA	Laryngeal Mask Airway
MI	Myocardial Infarction
MRC	Mountain Rescue Council and its trade name MR (England & Wales)
MRI	Magnetic Resonance Imaging (non-xray scan good for soft tissues)
MRT	Mountain Rescue Team
NSAID	Non-steroidal anti-inflammatory drug
PAD	Public access defibrillator
PEA	Pulseless electrical activity
PTSD	Post-traumatic Stress Disorder
RAF	Royal Air Force
SAH	Subarachnoid haemorrhage
SaO_2	Arterial oxygen saturation
SAR	Search and Rescue
SARDA	Search & Rescue Dog Association
SCUBA	Self contained underwater breathing apparatus
UKSAR	UK Search and Rescue Operators Group (a Governmental advisory group)
VF	Ventricular fibrillation

Units

l/min	litres per minute	mcg	micrograms
mg	milligrams	ml	millilitres
mm Hg	millimetres of mercury	mmol/l	millimoles per litre

References

References are written – Author(s). Title. *Journal* (year); volume: page range

DTB	Drug and Therapeutics Bulletin
NEJM	New England Journal of Medicine
BMJ	British Medical Journal
HABM	High Altitude Medicine & Biology
EMJ	Emergency Medicine Journal (Emerg Med J)

Positions

Abduction	move away from the mid line	Flexion	move forward
Adduction	move towards the mid line	Extend	move backward
External rotation	rotate outwards	Lateral	outside (edge)
Internal rotation	rotate inwards	Medial	inside (edge)
Proximal	nearer to the centre		

Glossary

ALS	Resuscitation with aids (and drugs)
Anaphylactoid	(Anaphylaxis) A reaction characterised by histamine release
Aneurysm	Dilation of an artery with the implication that it may burst.
Angio-oedema	Swelling of the tissues below the skin
Autopsy	(post-mortem) Examination to determine the cause of death
Arrhythmia	An abnormal electrical pattern of the heart
Asphyxia	The condition caused by a lack of oxygen
Asystole	No electrical activity of the heart
Barotrauma	damage resulting from exposure to a high external pressure
BLS	Cardiac compression and artificial breathing without aids
Bradycardia	A heart rate of <60/minute
Bronchoconstriction	Narrowing of the size of the bronchioles by muscle contraction
Diagnosis	Identification of a disease
Diuresis	Increased urine production
EMS	The infrastructure and operations designed to manage a casualty before arriving at hospital.
Haematoma	Collection of blood outside blood vessels
Heart block	Electrical activity of the heart is disrupted giving a slow heart rate
Hypotension	Low blood pressure causing symptoms
Hypothermia	Core body temperature <35°C
Hypoxia	An inadequate supply of oxygen
Intraluminal	Within the lumen of a tube-like structure
Ischaemia	Local reduction in blood supply due to arterial obstruction
Laryngospasm	Narrowing of the air passage between the vocal cords
Normothermic	Normal body temperature
No *'signs of life'*	No detectable breathing, circulation or brain response without using equipment (such as an ECG)
Oedema	Excessive accumulation of fluid
Pathology	Study of diseases
Physiology	Study of normal body function
Prehospital Critical Care	The following skills: Rapid sequence induction, controlled ventilation, pleural decompression, external haemorrhage control, long bone and pelvic fracture reduction and splinting, emergency iv analgesia and anaesthesia
Prognosis	Prediction as to the probable course and outcome of a condition
Surgical emphysema	Abnormal air in the body tissues
Syncope	Loss of consciousness from brain hypoxia
Tachycardia	A heart rate of >100/minute
Thrombus	Clot of blood formed in heart or blood vessel
Urticaria	Skin condition characterised by itchy wheals

Mountain rescue is nothing more than an extension of mountaineering. Rescuers must be totally at home in the environment in which they work. Of paramount importance is the safety of all concerned. Little can be achieved if a member of the rescue team is injured; it only adds to an already complicated situation. Casualty care, the diagnosis and treatment of the sick and injured, is a facet of mountain rescue and mountaineering. This book was commissioned by the Mountain Rescue Council (MRC) to focus on this important facet. In reality, casualty care is often only a small part of the total effort and rescuers need to consider a wide canvas to be competent.

The principles of first-aid treatment have been established since the beginning of the 20th century. These principles are illustrated well in West's Climbers' Pocket Book produced in about 1906. Though the equipment has changed the principles are largely the same. The development of mountain rescue has been hampered by unsuitable equipment. For example a padded box splint is woefully inadequate for splinting a fractured ankle when the evacuation involves carrying the casualty over rough terrain. We had to wait until 1936 for a suitable, robust stretcher. Transport of the injured is but a continuation of the treatment initiated at the incident site. Splinting, packaging and transporting casualties are essential components of mountain rescue.

In the late 1940s it was recognised that injuries on the mountains required special measures. In 1949 the MRC was granted a licence to hold stocks of morphia at its Posts. This is a very rare privilege.

The development of a first aid syllabus specific to mountain rescue had to wait until the 1960s. Dr. Ieuan Jones in Bangor, North Wales, developed one of the first courses. It showed, amongst other things, that a comprehensive physical examination, with a sound diagnosis, was the foundation of casualty care. During the 1970s and 80s the MRC looked at the needs for training its members in first-aid. Approaches to both St. John Ambulance and British Red Cross were made but faltered. The MRC was left to develop its own syllabus and issue its own certificates. In view of the special equipment as well as the long, protracted periods when the casualty is in the care of the rescuer, this was perhaps inevitable.

The aim of mountain rescue is to deliver a casualty in the best possible condition to hospital. This publication is a step in encouraging effective casualty care. May it be the first of a number of documents, commissioned by the MRC, setting out good practice in the other equally important facets of mountain rescue.

Dr. A S G Jones MBE

Vice chairman, Mountain Rescue Council

Editorial (First edition, 2000)

The aim of this book is to give mountain rescuers confidence to handle the problems they will encounter whilst rescuing injured casualties. There are many first aid books which deal with the core management of casualties; the editors of this book want to build on these texts and adapt the techniques used to the unique environment of the fell-side or crag. We have made the major assumption that the reader is already a competent first-aider well versed in the basic principles and practice of the delivery of emergency care to the ill and injured. In addition they must be familiar with the specific types and makes of equipment used by their own teams. We make no apologies for excluding some basic explanations but expect a modicum of experience and the capacity to seek the advice of individual Rescue Team Doctors and experienced rescuers.

Modern equipment and materials can give the impression that a casualty unit can be transferred to the hillside. However we feel this is, and will remain, an illusion. Mountain rescuers have to learn from other pre-hospital groups but at the same time adapt themselves to their own situations. We do not need to describe to any mountain rescuer why our environment is different from a roadside or sports-field accident. To the outsider however it must be hard to understand that the 'golden hour' has often passed long before we even arrive on scene; that the rescuer might have been at maximal exertion for a couple hours and be performing an assessment tied to a rope on a vertical face. Never mind the freezing temperatures and poor lighting, etc. Though many casualties have the advantage of a mountain rescue doctor, the majority (75%) do not. The percentage of incidents attended by a doctor varies from 6% to 85% in the different areas of England and Wales. Even when a doctor is attending, the nature of the service means that it is often the normal team member who arrives first and does the initial assessment and treatment of the casualty. Casualties remain in the care of the rescue team for hours rather than minutes. We recognise these facts in this book.

We see case histories as an important feature of this book. The aim is to highlight the dilemmas that occur between 'textbook' casualty care and practical mountain rescue. In each case the care may differ from generally accepted protocols. They are not excuses to ignore protocols, indeed they shouldn't be read until the reader is confident of the standard management presented in the text. Nor are they an excuse to use inappropriate equipment; muddling through by improvising splints does not feature. We hope, through the accompanying commentaries, to illustrate a flexibility in giving care. We want to introduce risk-benefit assessments to mountain rescuers and, most importantly, to encourage them to think about the care they give beyond protocols. We think a casualty with a number of significant injuries needs this dimension to his or her care. Each of the injuries may have its own protocol but what do you do when there is conflict in treatment between injuries? You can't divide the casualty in two! The cases have been chosen to reflect recurring problems in mountain rescue casualty care. They have been drawn from throughout England and Wales. The time and location of the incidents and the age and sex of the casualty have been changed to protect the identity of the casualty and team involved. We hope they give a flavour of real mountain rescue.

We aim to stimulate discussion of what we should be doing in mountain rescue. What techniques should become standard in the future? We hope, by highlighting these areas, that terms such as 'basic' and 'advanced' will not gain ground. We feel it is better to think of the whole casualty and what is best for him or her, rather than whether the casualty is being treated by a basic or advanced team member. We want to instil depth of knowledge and confidence into the rescuers.

The final aim of this book is encourage other specialist areas within the Mountain Rescue Council to produce supporting texts. There is a clear need for texts dealing with equipment and training. The medical care of the casualty can never be seen in isolation and the development of these texts would encourage all team members to acquire the necessary skills for safe and effective mountain rescue.

David Allan

Stuart Durham

John Ellerton

Simon Harvey

Simon Mardel

Stretcher evacuation, Patterdale MRT. (1992)

Editorial (Second edition)

Six years ago the first edition of Casualty Care in Mountain Rescue was distributed at the UK Millennium Mountain Rescue Conference in Lancaster. The aim was for every mountain rescuer to have a copy to mark the new century. I think we realised this goal - 2000 copies sold in the first weekend and the remaining 1200 copies 'selling out' in about one year. Copies reached all parts of the UK fairly equitably (at least based on the annual number of incidents). Of course, some books ventured much further, to South Africa, USA, Canada, Singapore and Kent! The feedback we received was encouraging; ten days after the launch, Nikki Wallis had a question about page 197 and interest from non-mountain rescue circles was high. The Mountain Rescue Council, who had paid for the printing of the book, just about broke even and had established a group of people (and a text) that would serve as a nucleus for further development.

Of course, at the millennium, we almost gave the book away. And, quite rightly, the English and the lack of an index and glossary were criticised. Doctors (and others) wanted more guidance and the wider outdoor establishment wanted copies. Well OK, it was the first attempt and we had made a commitment to keep the book up-to-date so a second edition could address these issues. Little did I realise that writing a second edition would be quite as difficult. As with the first edition, this book has been commissioned by the MRC; it is not the syllabus for MRC Casualty Care exam. This arrangement allows freedom for: teams to pitch the level of first aid to their environment; the MRC to set its exam; and the contributors to write down what they think is important. Sorry it's double the size of the first edition!

So what has changed?

The basic first aid is essentially the same but a surprising amount of the more advanced casualty care is different. Examples include the Basic Life Support and defibrillator protocol.

The apparent complexity of management has increased as the text has expanded into paramedical and medical treatments. I have tried to separate out the 'advanced' stuff by writing it in blue but I am not sure this has really helped. I have added 'The Basics' section for those wanting core information (equivalent to the current entry criteria for all MRC team members) and for those who find themselves first at an incident without the resources of a mountain rescue team. The first edition stimulated many teams to produce *aide memoirs* and I am relying on these to develop, as *Casualty Care in Mountain Rescue* becomes more of a reference book. Indeed references, chosen for their importance and Internet accessibility, have been included in many sections.

In a number of areas, the text exceeds what is commonly regarded as decisions for a non-medical professional. For example, stopping resuscitation in a cardiac arrest and when asphyxia appears to have occurred in avalanche incidents. These decisions should be taken in the context for which they were written. That is an isolated, hostile environment without timely professional help (whether in person or by radio). Individual rescuers and the MRC may not wish to take on this burden, which is quite understandable. But, I think, the text is a reflection of reality and a more humane type of rescue. The section on supportive care has been expanded and a new section on medical ethics added.

The intention of the book is to appeal to a wider outdoor audience. This edition costs more, a lot more. To compensate, the book is in full colour, an index is included and hopefully the English is better. However *Casualty Care* remains an amateur production and the pricing reflects this. There has been no payment of any kind to the contributors or myself; the MRC will make a few pounds profit for each book sold to further mountain rescue in general. I hope you find that acceptable.

As many of you know, my view of mountain rescue (a term that covers a whole host of outdoor activity) is that it provides a service to the activities we love. I would happily see no rescues and for this book to become redundant. Having gained experience of many of the world's rescue services through the International Commission for Alpine Rescue, I am surprised how this ethos pervades the governmental, paid services of other countries. So, hopefully you will forgive the calming pictures of mountaineering, recalling great days out often with fellow rescuers.

I wish you many great days out!

John Ellerton
ellerton@enterprise.net
June 2006

Acknowledgements

This book would not have been possible without the contributions of many people. The process of producing *Casualty Care in Mountain Rescue* has stretched over 11 years; it is certain that I have inadvertently missed acknowledging someone, for which I apologise. I received over 200 comments, corrections and questions following the publication of the first edition. All have been extremely helpful and I have tried to incorporate as many as possible into the second edition.

The text remains based on the first edition, so I have listed the original contributors below. Some of the contributors have provided an update of their work – others have lapsed!

David Allan (Head injury); Stuart Durham (Circulation and Extremities); Christine Ellerton (Eye injuries); John Frankland (Cave and Extended Rescue); Paul Goulding (A passing doctor's story); Mike Greene (Spinal injuries); Simon Harvey (Medical); Tony Jones MBE (Foreword); David Madley (Dental and Facial injuries); Simon Mardel (Breathing); John McCormick (Helicopters); Ann Pattinson (First Aid for dogs); John Williams (Airway).

The following people have provided additional content or extensively revised sections:

Elizabeth J. Allan BvetMed MRCVS (Treating sick or injured animals); Pete Allwright (caving picture); Dr. Werner Beikircher (C-clamp picture); Dr. Mike Brookes (Patient Assessment and Blast injury); Dr. Hermann Brugger (Avalanche); Ged Feeney (MRC Statistics Officer); Dr. David Hillebrandt (Frostbite); Mike Holman (SAR helicopters); Adam Marcinowicz (toes); Dr. Andy McAlea (Air Ambulances and pictures); Dr. Peter Paal (Breathing); Dr. Günther Suman (Fluid resuscitation); Nikki Wallis (Diabetes); Dr. Theo Weston (Case histories); Paul Witheridge (Suspension induced trauma); Brian Wright (Casualty Care exam); Dr. Venetia Young, GP and Family Therapist (Breaking bad news to children); Dr. Greg Zenruffinen (Crevasse rescue pictures).

As in the first edition, David Allan has provided many diagrams and cartoons, which greatly enhance the text. In addition he has provided some excellent clinical pictures to add to my own. His retirement from the NHS has been a godsend! The picture library of the Patterdale Mountain Rescue Team has also been invaluable.

Writing and editing is more than just sitting down at a keyboard. I would especially like to thank Paul Barker for correcting the grammar in the first edition and Peter G Baker (Penrith MRT) for proof reading this edition. My final thanks go to Dave Freeborn for his professional input at a number of crucial stages during the project.

About the Editor

John elected to work near the mountains. He started walking the long distance footpaths on the North York Moors while still at school. A 'double' White Rose walk one weekend left him with not enough money to get himself back to Middlesbrough. An extra three-mile walk to a phone box - no mobiles in those days - and a call home for a lift relieved anxious parents! From then on it was the trusted Mini 850 and trips to the Lake District, Arran and the Yorkshire Dales. Medical training in Cambridge then Oxford put pay to outdoor development but his first year of medicine saw him in Stoke-on-Trent where the Peak District and Wales occupied the few spare weekends. One weekend, when returning from a snowy grade two scramble on Helvellyn, a MR Landrover roared up with lights blazing. The team started jumping out and John muttered the fateful words to the then team leader - *"Can I help? I'm a Doctor."* A few glances between the team members and "OK, come along." And so started his career with the Patterdale Mountain Rescue Team. (The team knew that they were heading for a climber with serious pelvic and leg injuries who had fallen onto a small ledge!) The die was cast; a move to Lancaster then Penrith sealed it. In 1985 he joined the team as its Medical Officer, a post he still holds jointly with Dr. Theo Weston. The team has the *luxury* of 60 call-outs a year, so has provided a good grounding to mountain rescue.

After a period of emergency medicine, anaesthetic and Accident and Emergency training, John settled down as a General Practitioner. Until recently, he was an active BASICS Doctor attending many road traffic collisions.

John joined the MRC Medical Subcommittee in 1993 and became its chairman in 2002. He has attended the biannual ICAR Medcom meetings on behalf of England and Wales for the last three years. As one of the few native English speakers, he is often drafted in to compile the ICAR Medcom papers, which are then published in leading medical journals.

At times mountain rescue has pushed walking, cycling and climbing to the background - particularly in the last six months! But he still enjoys getting out once a fortnight for an easy climb, a moderate scramble or a frozen waterfall.

The Coach road, near Keswick. (2003)

The Basics

Objectives

To be able to carry out potentially life-saving procedures
(even if you have no equipment)
To perform a basic primary survey
(when you have first aid equipment with you)

Procedures to adopt when an accident occurs

Sending for help

When an accident takes place in a wild and remote place in the upland areas of the UK, there are a number of services that can help. Collect your thoughts - the emergency services will need to know what has happened, the nature of the injuries and the position of the incident including, if possible, the map reference. Mobile phone coverage is now good in most areas except in some of the deep valleys. If there is no signal, a reliable member of the party, with full information about the accident, should be sent to find the nearest telephone.

In the event of an accident, you need to consider whether you need an Ambulance, a Mountain Rescue Team or the Coast Guard. If you are short distance from a road, an ambulance is most appropriate. However, if the injured person is unable to walk or on dangerous terrain, a stretcher and a Mountain Rescue Team will be needed - dial the emergency number and ask for the Police. The Police will then notify the appropriate Mountain Rescue Team. Accidents on some large lakes, as well as the coastline, are coordinated by the Maritime Coast Guard Agency - dial the emergency number and ask for the Coast Guard.

Confused? Don't worry, make the call to any of the emergency services, and they will pass your information on to the service best placed to respond.

Lack of help

You have a difficult decision when the casualty is severely injured, possibly unconscious, and you are alone. You should try to summon help from nearby climbers or walkers by shouting, giving the distress call on a whistle (6 blasts repeated regularly), flashing a torch (6 flashes repeated regularly), or sending up a red flare. If there is no response, assess the relative dangers of leaving the casualty or of failing to get help, and then act decisively in the interest of the casualty.

General Treatment

While waiting for the emergency service, basic first-aid treatment should be given. Think 'Safety, A, B, C then D, E and F' (if appropriate).

Safety First

Are you and the casualty safe from further danger? If not, try to make yourselves safe either by moving or anchoring yourselves. Is the casualty responsive?

A - Is the casualty's airway open?

If necessary, open it by a simple jaw thrust or chin lift. An open airway is essential; if the casualty is unconscious or semiconscious, the tongue can fall back blocking the airway and cause death from asphyxia. After trauma, gently stabilise the neck in the straight-line (neutral) position with your hands. Try to avoid further movement of the neck. Continually check that the airway remains open, adjusting the casualty's position as required.

B - Is the casualty breathing?

Look, feel and listen for breathing. Basic Life Support should be started, if you are trained, when the casualty is unconscious and shows no signs of breathing, and it can be continued until help arrives, and where there is a chance of recovery (lightning, drowning, heart attack). It is usually futile in casualties with internal injuries and is probably best to defer in cases of severe exposure/hypothermia until expert help is available. An unconscious but breathing casualty should be put in the 'recovery position' if possible. In cases involving trauma take care that the neck remains in a neutral position. Check the airway is still open.

C - Is the circulation adequate?

Stop any bleeding from wounds by elevation and direct pressure with dressings or clothing. The pressure needs to be applied continuously for at least 10 minutes. Internal bleeding should be suspected if the casualty has sustained blows to the chest or abdomen or broken the thigh bone (femur). Loss of blood leads to shock; the casualty will be looking white, feel cold and be sweating. The pulse may be rapid and the casualty anxious. Lay the casualty down and possibly raise the legs. The condition often deteriorates and all steps should be taken to facilitate the rapid arrival of the emergency services and, if possible, a helicopter. A record of the pulse rate and conscious level is very helpful.

D - Is the casualty disabled due to damage to head or spine?

Record the casualty's conscious level - Alert, responsive to voice, responsive to pain or unresponsive? Has the spine been damaged? If so, do not move the casualty unless essential for safety reasons. Maintain the head in the normal straight (neutral) position with your hands.

E - Prevent exposure

Prevent exposure (hypothermia) by sheltering the casualty from the wind and rain. Wrap them in as many layers of clothing as possible and encase in a 'poly bag' or other impermeable barrier. Do not forget to insulate the head and underneath the casualty.

F - Check for fractures

If present, immobilise the limb by the simplest method available. In the case of the arm, pad it and bandage it to the chest, and in the case of the leg, pad it and bandage it to the other leg.

Communicate appropriate updates of the casualty's condition by phone, if possible, to the responding emergency service. You may need to be sensitive to what the casualty hears.

Further points to consider

Large, organised groups should bear in mind that Mountain Rescue Teams are a finite resource and it is wrong to assume their availability.

A helicopter may arrive before the Mountain Rescue Team. Extinguish all flames and secure all equipment. To attract the attention of the helicopter stand facing it with both arms up in the air making a 'Y' shape. The down draught can knock you over, so make sure you are in a safe position. Do not approach the helicopter until clearly signalled to do so by the pilot.

Prevention is better than First Aid! Most injuries are lower leg sprains and fractures; appropriate footwear is important. The majority of climbers killed in the Lake District as a result of a climbing accident die from a head injury. A helmet, whilst not being 100% effective, can make the difference between living and dying. GPS systems, whilst being useful, are no substitute for carrying a map and compass, and knowing how to use them.

The routine carrying of a suitable head-torch would save many needless call-outs. And finally, whilst mobile phones can be very useful in emergencies, any temptation to use them in the hills to call the emergency services in non-emergency circumstances should be resisted. If you are not sure whether it is an emergency or not, please investigate a little yourself first before reaching for your phone.

Mountain rescuers are unpaid volunteers and rely on charitable contributions. Your consideration and a 'Thank you' go a long way to ensure the service continues.

Jaw thrust

Chin lift

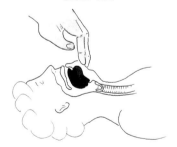

In-line manual immobilisation

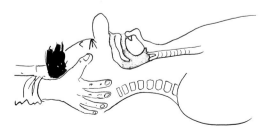

Casualty Care A, B, C and D cards

The MRC Medical Subcommittee developed Airway, Breathing, Circulation and Disability cards a few years ago to help team members quickly assess a casualty (both for real and during exams). The cards summarise the primary survey, which will be dealt with more fully in subsequent chapters. Reproducing them here will hopefully remind the team member of a basic assessment; unlike the preceding assessment 'Procedures to adopt when an accident occurs', there is the expectation that equipment, medical gases and drugs are available. This is the type of assessment expected when you arrive as a Casualty Care certified member of a rescue team! With practice, I would hope that you should be able to work through the cards in a few minutes, perhaps up to 15 minutes for the complete assessment including spinal immobilisation. A few sentences are in blue - these are largely for those team members with additional training, paramedics and doctors. If the casualty's condition starts to deteriorate, reassess the casualty by starting at 'A'. The cards are available on the MRC web site in black. Please print them off, enlarge them if necessary and carry them in the First Aid sacs.

Analgesia

"Analgesia at the scene of an accident is a human right"

Urs Wiget (Past President ICAR Medcom)

Giving pain relief is a fundamental part of mountain rescue. As a rescuer, you have to accept that a casualty's pain is subjective and treat what the casualty tells you. For example, some casualties with a dislocated shoulder are in agony and unable to move; others, with apparently the same injury, will walk off the hill and be driven to the nearest hospital without any analgesia! Think of the severity of pain and match it with the strength of the analgesic. Consider the options available: Entonox®; paracetamol; diclofenac; codeine and morphine, and exclude those that cannot be used in your casualty. For example, a significant chest injury and Entonox® or diclofenac and an allergy to NSAIDs. Always aim at maximising the non-drug treatments, such as splinting and reassurance, that reduce pain. *Mix and match* analgesics together to get more effect. In general, pre-hospital care providers under-treat pain perhaps because of fear of inducing side effects or masking injuries. Try to avoid this.

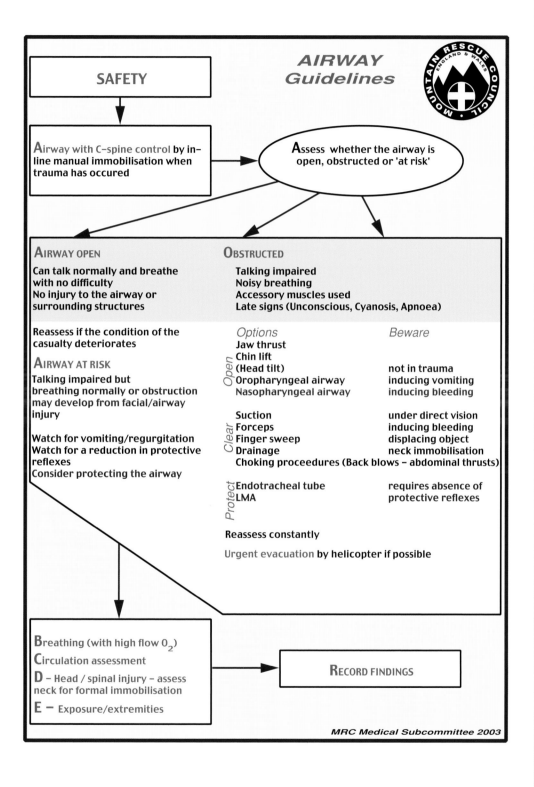

AIRWAY Guidelines

SAFETY

Airway with C–spine control by in-line manual immobilisation when trauma has occured

Assess whether the airway is open, obstructed or 'at risk'

AIRWAY OPEN

Can talk normally and breathe with no difficulty
No injury to the airway or surrounding structures

Reassess if the condition of the casualty deteriorates

AIRWAY AT RISK

Talking impaired but breathing normally or obstruction may develop from facial/airway injury

Watch for vomiting/regurgitation
Watch for a reduction in protective reflexes
Consider protecting the airway

OBSTRUCTED

Talking impaired
Noisy breathing
Accessory muscles used
Late signs (Unconscious, Cyanosis, Apnoea)

Options   *Beware*

Open
Jaw thrust
Chin lift
(Head tilt) — not in trauma
Oropharyngeal airway — inducing vomiting
Nasopharyngeal airway — inducing bleeding

Clear
Suction — under direct vision
Forceps — inducing bleeding
Finger sweep — displacing object
Drainage — neck immobilisation
Choking proceedures (Back blows – abdominal thrusts)

Protect
Endotracheal tube — requires absence of
LMA — protective reflexes

Reassess constantly

Urgent evacuation by helicopter if possible

Breathing (with high flow 0₂)
Circulation assessment
D – Head / spinal injury – assess neck for formal immobilisation
E – Exposure/extremities

RECORD FINDINGS

MRC Medical Subcommittee 2003

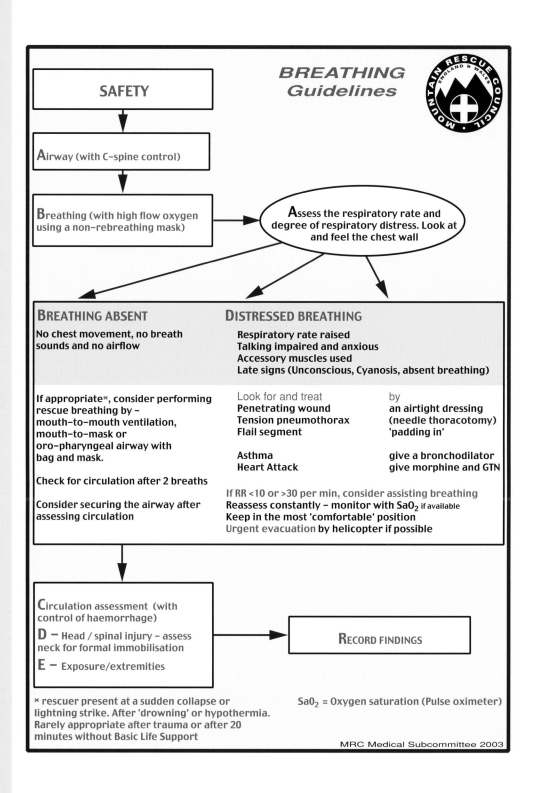

SAFETY

BREATHING
Guidelines

MOUNTAIN RESCUE COUNCIL · ENGLAND & WALES

Airway (with C–spine control)

Breathing (with high flow oxygen using a non–rebreathing mask)

Assess the respiratory rate and degree of respiratory distress. Look at and feel the chest wall

BREATHING ABSENT

No chest movement, no breath sounds and no airflow

If appropriate*, consider performing rescue breathing by –
mouth–to–mouth ventilation,
mouth–to–mask or
oro–pharyngeal airway with
bag and mask.

Check for circulation after 2 breaths

Consider securing the airway after assessing circulation

DISTRESSED BREATHING

Respiratory rate raised
Talking impaired and anxious
Accessory muscles used
Late signs (Unconscious, Cyanosis, absent breathing)

Look for and treat   by
Penetrating wound   **an airtight dressing**
Tension pneumothorax   **(needle thoracotomy)**
Flail segment   **'padding in'**

Asthma   **give a bronchodilator**
Heart Attack   **give morphine and GTN**

If RR <10 or >30 per min, consider assisting breathing
Reassess constantly – monitor with SaO$_2$ if available
Keep in the most 'comfortable' position
Urgent evacuation by helicopter if possible

Circulation assessment (with control of haemorrhage)

D – Head / spinal injury – assess neck for formal immobilisation

E – Exposure/extremities

RECORD FINDINGS

* rescuer present at a sudden collapse or lightning strike. After 'drowning' or hypothermia. Rarely appropriate after trauma or after 20 minutes without Basic Life Support

SaO$_2$ = Oxygen saturation (Pulse oximeter)

MRC Medical Subcommittee 2003

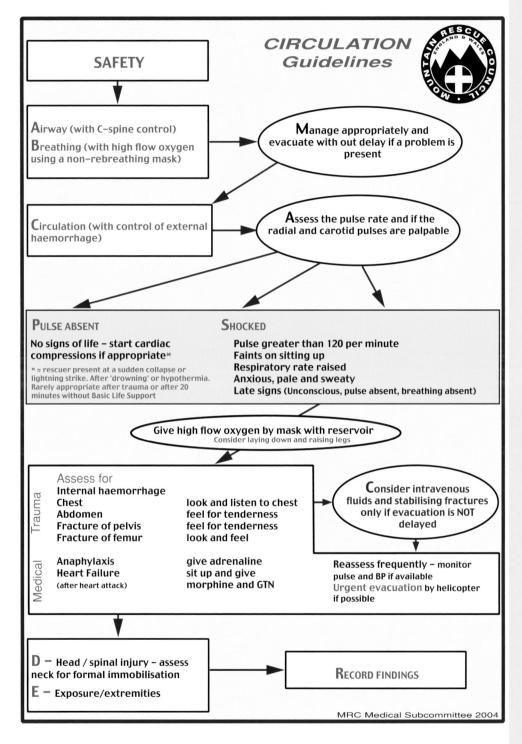

SAFETY

CIRCULATION *Guidelines*

MOUNTAIN RESCUE COUNCIL · ENGLAND & WALES

Airway (with C–spine control)

Breathing (with high flow oxygen using a non–rebreathing mask)

Manage appropriately and evacuate with out delay if a problem is present

Circulation (with control of external haemorrhage)

Assess the pulse rate and if the radial and carotid pulses are palpable

PULSE ABSENT

No signs of life – start cardiac compressions if appropriate✳

✳ = rescuer present at a sudden collapse or lightning strike. After 'drowning' or hypothermia. Rarely appropriate after trauma or after 20 minutes without Basic Life Support

SHOCKED

Pulse greater than 120 per minute
Faints on sitting up
Respiratory rate raised
Anxious, pale and sweaty
Late signs (Unconscious, pulse absent, breathing absent)

Give high flow oxygen by mask with reservoir
Consider laying down and raising legs

Assess for

Internal haemorrhage
Chest   look and listen to chest
Abdomen   feel for tenderness
Fracture of pelvis   feel for tenderness
Fracture of femur   look and feel

Trauma

Anaphylaxis   give adrenaline
Heart Failure   sit up and give
(after heart attack)   morphine and GTN

Medical

Consider intravenous fluids and stabilising fractures only if evacuation is NOT delayed

Reassess frequently – monitor pulse and BP if available
Urgent evacuation by helicopter if possible

D – Head / spinal injury – assess neck for formal immobilisation

E – Exposure/extremities

RECORD FINDINGS

MRC Medical Subcommittee 2004

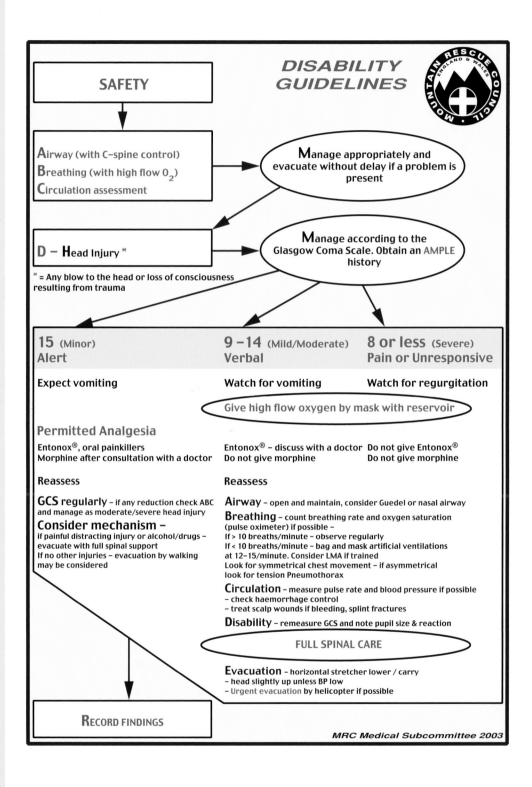

DISABILITY GUIDELINES

SAFETY

Airway (with C–spine control)
Breathing (with high flow O$_2$)
Circulation assessment

→ Manage appropriately and evacuate without delay if a problem is present

D – Head Injury *

→ Manage according to the Glasgow Coma Scale. Obtain an AMPLE history

* = Any blow to the head or loss of consciousness resulting from trauma

15 (Minor) Alert	9 – 14 (Mild/Moderate) Verbal	8 or less (Severe) Pain or Unresponsive
Expect vomiting	Watch for vomiting	Watch for regurgitation

Give high flow oxygen by mask with reservoir

Permitted Analgesia

Entonox®, oral painkillers	Entonox® – discuss with a doctor	Do not give Entonox®
Morphine after consultation with a doctor	Do not give morphine	Do not give morphine

Reassess | **Reassess**

GCS regularly – if any reduction check ABC and manage as moderate/severe head injury

Consider mechanism –
if painful distracting injury or alcohol/drugs – evacuate with full spinal support
If no other injuries – evacuation by walking may be considered

Airway – open and maintain, consider Guedel or nasal airway

Breathing – count breathing rate and oxygen saturation (pulse oximeter) if possible –
If > 10 breaths/minute – observe regularly
If < 10 breaths/minute – bag and mask artificial ventilations at 12–15/minute. Consider LMA if trained
Look for symmetrical chest movement – if asymmetrical look for tension Pneumothorax

Circulation – measure pulse rate and blood pressure if possible
– check haemorrhage control
– treat scalp wounds if bleeding, splint fractures

Disability – remeasure GCS and note pupil size & reaction

FULL SPINAL CARE

Evacuation – horizontal stretcher lower / carry
– head slightly up unless BP low
– Urgent evacuation by helicopter if possible

RECORD FINDINGS

MRC Medical Subcommittee 2003

Paul on Amphitheatre Buttress, Wales. (2004)

Patient Assessment

Objectives

Accurately and confidently assess casualties
Identify and rectify life-threatening abnormalities
Develop an optimal management and evacuation plan
To have a system for managing overwhelming incidents

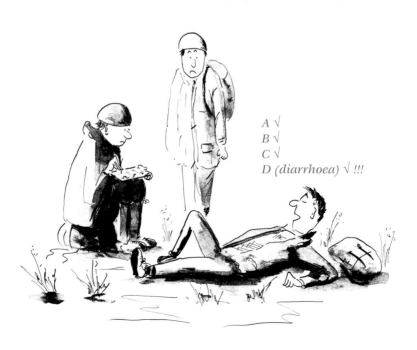

A √
B √
C √
D *(diarrhoea)* √ !!!

Individual Casualty Assessment – the Primary Survey

The aim of casualty assessment is to gain a quick overview of the situation, identify and treat life-threatening injuries, and then (if appropriate) perform a more in-depth assessment of the injuries with treatment aimed at minimising their morbidity. Finally, the casualty is evacuated to hospital for further treatment their injuries. These three discrete phases are called:

Primary survey - the identification and treatment of life-threatening injuries

Secondary survey - a systematic examination to identify all injuries

Definitive care - the treatment provided at the receiving hospital

When approaching a casualty site, it is all too easy to feel overwhelmed by the anxiety of the situation, the distress of the casualty and the perceived pressure from those around to act quickly. It is often said that the first rule in this situation is to check your own pulse! Calm down and think - Safety, safety, safety! This will probably be the last time you think of what is around you and what may be dangerous to yourself and the casualty before you are absorbed into the management of the injured. Only when you have satisfied yourself of scene safety do you proceed to patient assessment. This point cannot be overemphasised. Adding to the casualty list is usually disastrous.

As you proceed to assess the casualty, take a moment to clear your head and collect your thoughts. This will allow you to assess the casualty using a structured approach. A good primary survey will ensure effective identification of the casualty's problems and that treatment is given in a logical and timely fashion. It is vital that rescuers have a systematic approach and stick to it regardless of distractions and interference. Stick to your assessment!

A reliable and systematic approach reduces the chance of failing to identify life or limb threatening problems.

Common mistakes are:

Being distracted by an obvious injury, such as a fractured and deformed forearm.

Focusing on the most painful injury, and missing the spinal injury.

Either under- or over-treating problems during the primary survey. You need to keep a momentum to get to the end.

Ignoring problems that are likely to cause deterioration, such as upper airway swelling after smoke inhalation. Be pro-active!

In the critically ill or injured, a primary survey and the rapid transfer of the casualty to hospital are the goals, as often the situation can only be stabilised in hospital. Minutes can count; the secondary survey can wait. This strategy is commonly referred to as 'load and go' but note that the primary survey should only be cut short in exceptional situations. This will be rare and usually relate to scene safety, for example threat of avalanche or fire.

The primary survey aims to identify and treat life-threatening problems. The priority for assessment and treatment is divided into six sections. These are:

Airway

Breathing

Circulation

Disability

Exposure and Fractures

This approach is based on the concept of oxygen delivery to the tissues. Without adequate oxygenation, the tissues will eventually become irreversibly damaged and the patient will die. The process of oxygenation involves air entering the lungs, where oxygen and carbon dioxide are exchanged between air and blood, and then the blood being pumped around the body to supply the tissues with oxygen. For this to take place, the airway must be open to allow the flow of air, the lungs must be functioning efficiently to permit gas exchange, and the circulation must be sufficient to supply critical areas of the body, such as the brain, heart and kidneys, with oxygen. The priority in the primary survey is a natural extension of these principles. Without a patent airway the lungs will not function properly and likewise without adequate lung function, the circulation cannot hope to deliver oxygenated blood to the tissues.

A primary survey should take no more than five minutes; experienced Doctors and paramedics may take considerable less. Remember in this phase you are only interested in critical problems.

With each section of the primary survey, take a quick but thorough look to identify any life-threatening problems: measure physiological parameters, examine the patient and then act.

Airway with cervical spine control

Quick look:

Is the casualty talking?

Has the casualty noisy breathing or struggling to breathe?

Does the mechanism of injury suggest a potential cervical spine injury?

Are airway problems likely to develop?

If the casualty is speaking normally, then you can assume that the airway is clear. This is the simplest method of assessing whether the airway is open. Noisy breathing, such as snoring, suggests that there is airway obstruction, particularly if the casualty is unconscious. Struggling to breathe, particularly if the casualty is using muscles around the chest and neck to help them, may indicate a problem with the airway. An unconscious casualty is at high risk of airway compromise either currently or later on.

Always consider the possibility of an injury to the cervical spine. Assess the potential for a spinal injury from the history of the accident. A fall from height; high-speed deceleration; trauma when under the influence of alcohol or drugs; or a head injury all have the potential for cervical spine injury. It may appear from the casualty's behaviour (pain-free spontaneous movement of the neck) that there is little evidence of neck injury. However, even in such circumstances, at this stage, failing to think about a neck injury and taking the precaution of in-line immobilization of the neck is indefensible. In-line manual immobilisation of the neck means stabilizing the head in a straight-ahead, neutral position to the rest of the body. It is usual to do this from the top of the casualty though if this is not possible the neck can be stabilized from the front. You are fixing the head by clamping your hands on the mastoid processes (the bony protuberance behind the ears). Clearly, if the rest of the body (the chest) moves relative to your hands, the neck has also moved. The rescuer stabilising the neck is in charge of all movements of the casualty and gives every command when a change of position is needed. (Ensure that everyone is clear when the command to move starts. Be explicit with the instructions! For example, 'one, two, three and move' with the movement starting on 'move'.) It is the job of the rescuer 'in charge' of the neck to also maintain an open airway and constantly reassess that it remains open.

If you suspect an obstructed airway, look in the mouth and remove any visible obstructions using forceps, a suction device or fingers. Blind finger sweeps are ill advised as they can push the obstruction further into the airway and also cause localised trauma. Bleeding and swelling inside the mouth will not be helpful. If a foreign body is causing the obstruction, the choking procedures outline in the next chapter should be carried out.

The most common cause of an obstructed airway in the unconscious casualty is the tongue 'falling back' under gravity. The airway may be opened using either a jaw thrust or a chin lift. A jaw thrust is recommended if there is a suspicion of spinal damage, as this procedure allows the neck to remain immobilised. When a spinal injury is suspected, avoid the head tilt/chin lift procedure, which causes neck extension, if at all possible. Failure to open the airway - noise-free breathing - by these simple measures requires an airway adjunct to be considered. Casualty Carers with appropriate training may insert an airway adjunct at this stage. The oropharyngeal (OPA) or nasopharyngeal (NPA) airways do not protect the airway, but can help maintain it. The casualty needs to be deeply unconscious in order to tolerate the OPA. The main risk with the OPA (and to a lesser extent the NPA) is inducing vomiting from the stimulation of back of the throat.

Consider whether the airway should be protected with an endotracheal tube or a Laryngeal Mask Airway. If the skills, drugs and equipment are available, suitably trained professionals may want to consider and prepare to do this.

Act:

Clear any obstructions.

Open the airway.

Apply in-line manual immobilisation of neck.

Consider whether the airway should be protected.

Breathing with high-flow oxygen

Quick look:

Is there extra respiratory effort?

What is the rate of breathing?

Are both sides of the chest moving together and are there any injuries to the chest?

Adequate breathing depends on the movement of the chest wall and diaphragm being translated into the movement of air into the lungs. One in four of trauma-related deaths are due to a chest injury. To assess the adequacy of breathing you have to do more than measure the number of breaths per minute (the respiratory rate); you need to look and feel round the chest, so don't forget to explain to the casualty what you are doing and check that it is 'OK'.

Most people breathe quietly and without distress. They spend a similar amount of time breathing in (inspiration) and breathing out (expiration). As you approach, observe the casualty for signs of respiratory distress. People who have difficulty breathing often sit up and brace their arms, so that they can use the accessory muscles of the neck and shoulders to help move air in and out of the chest.

Measure the respiratory rate; the normal is 12-15 breaths per minute. Whilst pain and anxiety will naturally increase the respiratory rate, breathing faster than 30 breaths a minute is certainly abnormal, and points to a problem. Note that shock from blood loss also causes a raised respiratory rate. This is discussed further in the following chapter. A breathing rate of less than 10 breaths a minute also indicates a problem, but this is usually related to a dysfunction of the control systems in the brain. Causes include severe head injury and opiate (morphine) overdose.

Check the integrity of the chest wall by looking at its movement and for swollen areas. Puncture wounds, though rare in mountain rescue, should be identified. Asymmetrical chest movement is highly suggestive of a chest injury. The injured side may be splinted and fixed, or may move abnormally compared to the non-injured. A flail chest occurs when 2 or more ribs are broken in 2 or more places. This creates a section of the chest wall which is independent of the rib cage and gives rise to a paradoxical movement, where the segment moves inwards as the patient inhales, and outwards as they exhale.

Gently compress the chest; front to back and then from side to side. Start gently and note any areas of pain. Percussion and listening for breath sounds will help to identify internal injuries such as haemorrhage or abnormal air pocket around the lung (pneumothorax). However using a stethoscope on a windy night in a emergency shelter tent may fail to pick up even gross changes. Observation is usually more reliable.

Conclude by examining the neck for the position of the trachea, wounds, emphysema, laryngeal trauma, vein distension, and oedema (swelling). (Remember the acronym - 'twelve'.) The trachea should be central in the notch above the sternum. Subcutaneous emphysema – this is where the skin feels and sounds like bubble-wrap, because of air in the tissues – is an important sign whether localised at the site of a rib fracture or more generalised on the chest wall and neck. Almost always there is an underlying tension pneumothorax.

If possible measure the oxygen saturation with a pulse oximeter. Normal values are between 97-100%. The devices rely on adequate peripheral circulation, so may not work well if the casualty is cold or shocked. Figures of 96% and below could mean a significant reduction in the amount of oxygen the blood is able to give up to the tissues.

Act:

Start high flow oxygen at 15 litres per minute via a non-rebreathing mask with a reservoir.

Cover penetrating wounds with an air-impermeable dressing ideally taped on 3 sides – the polythene wrapper of an ambulance dressing is good or, alternatively, use a specially designed chest seal. The purpose is to stop air entering the chest cavity when the casualty breathes in and at the same time not allow pressure to build within the cavity thus creating a tension pneumothorax.

Chest wall injuries should be splinted as best as they can without impeding chest expansion. The casualty should be placed in their most comfortable position. After chest trauma, respiratory function is often partially reduced by pain. Flag up that analgesia may be helpful when the primary survey is completed.

Advanced techniques such as needle thoracotomy should be left to those with specific training. Their effectiveness has been questioned.

Circulation with external haemorrhage control
Quick look:
Obvious bleeding?

Pale, sweaty casualty?

Rapid breathing despite normal chest examination?

Shock is an important cause of death in trauma. By shock we mean a failure of the circulation to transport oxygen to the tissues; not a fright or psychological state. In trauma, shock is caused by a lack of blood volume, usually from an injury that has caused bleeding. The bleeding may be obvious – soaking the casualty's clothes or surroundings (external bleeding) or may be concealed within one of the cavities of the body (internal bleeding). The major areas where haemorrhage (the medical term for bleeding) can be concealed are within the chest cavity, within the abdominal cavity, in the pelvis from a fracture or in the thigh from a femoral fracture. The chest cavity can conceal from 1.5 to 3 litres of blood and a fractured femur may cause a blood loss of up to 1.5 litres. There are many large blood vessels around the pelvis, and these are often torn with a pelvic fracture, leading to catastrophic bleeding.

In the early stages of shock, the casualty may appear pale and sweaty due to the release of stress hormones, which shut down nonessential blood vessels, as the body tries to protect vital organs. Rapid breathing, in the absence of a chest problem, may be due to shock.

Measure the pulse rate and estimate the systolic blood pressure by finding a palpable pulse (radial pulse present = > 90mmHg; carotid pulse present = > 70mmHg; none present = < 70mmHg).

In the initial stages of shock, there may be very few physiological signs, particularly in the young and healthy, who can compensate well for a small loss in circulating blood volume. As shock develops, the pulse will start to become rapid. A pulse greater than 120 beats per minute is indicative of a serious circulation problem. Blood pressure will fall only in the later stages of shock, so the pulse is probably a better indicator of shock.

Further assessment should concentrate on the areas of concealed haemorrhage. The chest cavity will have already been assessed during breathing. The abdomen is gently felt where signs of rigidity or tenderness may indicate internal bleeding. Pelvic fractures are tested by gently putting pressure on each side of the pelvis, looking for a 'give'. This should only ever be done once, as repeated examination could disturb a tenuous blood clot and give rise to further bleeding. Finally check both thighs for swelling, pain and shortening as these indicate a fracture of the femoral shaft.

Act:

Treat external haemorrhage with direct compression and elevation.

Lie the casualty down and ensure a high concentration of oxygen is given.

Prepare to splint femoral and suspected pelvic fractures.

Intravenous fluid support is often indicated but this should never delay a rapid evacuation to surgical facilities when internal bleeding is suspected.

Disability

Quick look:

What is the casualty's level of consciousness?

Is there any evidence of head or spinal injury?

The term 'disability' reflects a shift away from life-saving to reducing long-term disability or morbidity from the casualty's injuries. Major disability can be avoided or reduced with good early management.

Measure the conscious level using AVPU and assess the pupils for size and equality. Check reaction to light if the pupils are unequal. AVPU is an acronym describing a simple system to assess the level of consciousness. It is not particularly specific, but is rapidly performed and easy to remember. It is appropriate for the primary survey; when a more detailed assessment is made later the Glasgow Coma Scale should be used.

A – alert

V – responds to voice

P – responds to pain

U – unresponsive

Act:

In appropriate cases, examine the spine by using a log roll technique; any areas of pain or swelling along the axis of the spine should be noted. When doing the log roll, a well-rehearsed team will also package the casualty in a vacuum mattress ready for the evacuation. At this stage, the rescuer providing in-line cervical spine control will be replaced by a rigid cervical collar and axillary support such as head blocks and tape, or a vacuum mattress moulded around the head.

In suitable cases, additional procedures, such as elective intubation and ventilation, may be considered at this stage if the skills, drugs and equipment are available.

Exposure

Quick look:

Is the casualty hypothermic?

Consider hypothermia in appropriate settings such as immersion in water, avalanche and prolonged exposure. Grade the severity of hypothermia into 'severe' or 'mild'.

Act:

Protect the casualty from the environment by insulating from the wind and rain.

In 'severe' hypothermia, take particular care to avoid large movements or procedures that might precipitate ventricular fibrillation.

Consider performing prolonged CPR in suitable cases such as a 'rescue collapse', prolonged immersion or where the casualty has been buried by an avalanche for >35 minutes and has an air pocket.

Fractures

Quick look:

Are the long bones and major joints intact? Do any fractures or dislocations need to be reduced?

Ask the casualty to move each limb in turn, and report any pain or discomfort. Quickly feel down each limb and, if in doubt, check the peripheral pulses.

Act:

If skilled, consider reducing a fracture or dislocation to improve the chances of the viability of the limb.

Keep a Record and obtain a History

Adequate record keeping is normally the last thing anyone thinks about in this situation. However, good notes and observations are absolutely vital when a casualty arrives at a hospital, particularly if they are unconscious. You may not travel with the casualty when they are evacuated and, with out notes, hospital staff face a patient with scant information as to what happened and what has been done. From a safety and legal point of view, all treatment and drugs given must be carefully documented. The records will also show how the casualty's physiological parameters (respiratory rate, pulse, BP, conscious level) have changed over time and help the hospital staff to assess the urgency of their interventions.

A simple history should be obtained from the casualty or his companions. The acronym 'AMPLE' describes the salient points.

A – Allergies

M – Current medication taken by the patient

P – Past illnesses

L – Time last ate and drank (useful if having an operation)

E – Events leading to the current problem

The history contains valuable information that may be important in explaining the current findings.

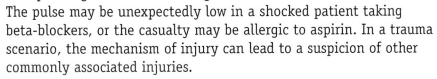

The pulse may be unexpectedly low in a shocked patient taking beta-blockers, or the casualty may be allergic to aspirin. In a trauma scenario, the mechanism of injury can lead to a suspicion of other commonly associated injuries.

The primary survey is now complete. The rescuer should have treated life-threatening problems as best as they can and assessed the urgency of the evacuation. The casualty should be kept warm, reassured, and if time allows, a comprehensive secondary survey carried out. This will be covered in subsequent chapters.

The condition of the casualty is still changing, so it is important to keep monitoring their respiratory rate, pulse, BP and conscious level regularly. Internal haemorrhage may become more evident, so constant vigilance must be maintained. If there are any changes, go back through the 'Safety, A, B, C approach' to reassess and identify possible causes. Some injuries cannot be treated or stabilised without the skills of a surgeon. In such cases, the aim is to optimise A, B, C and minimise the risk of D but not delay the transfer of the casualty to hospital.

Management of Multiple Casualties – Triage

Thankfully, the majority of scenarios encountered in Mountain Rescue will only involve a single casualty. However, there may be situations where a rescue party will be faced with several casualties simultaneously. In this event, it will be extremely likely that the resources of the team will quickly become outstripped by the demand of the injured patients. In effect there is a 'major incident'.

The aim of this section is to help rescuers to deliver the most effective care to the greatest number of casualties possible. The team has to have a systematic approach which can be used to allocate time and resources appropriately to achieve this aim.

Many emergency services, when dealing with a Major Incident (defined at the end of this section), use a series of headings (see box) to enable them to identify important problems in a systematic way. Constraints to treatment and potential *bottlenecks* are recognised and hopefully addressed though, of course, the team is working at or beyond its usual limits and consequently, at times, will be rationing 'care'.

In practice many of the headings are assessed almost simultaneously and different emphasis will be placed on different headings in different situations. They serve as a prompt to try and make sense of the inevitable chaos of a multiple casualty incident.

'Control Spells Calm And Time To Treat'

Command
Safety
Communication
Assessment of the scene
Triage - Assessment of the casualties
Treatment
Transport

Command

The cornerstone of managing any situation is to ensure that someone is in overall charge of what is happening at the scene. This does not have to be the most experienced medical person, as quite often their skills are needed to tend to the casualties. A commander acts to coordinate the efforts of their team, not necessarily provide all the answers. The incident commander should not get involved in the treatment of the casualties as once they are committed to this they lose their overview of the situation. This may sound unusual, but lack of command and control is frequently cited as one of the main flaws when incidents are reviewed.

The commander is the link between the incident on the ground and the outside world; all requests for transport and medical supplies should go through the commander. This avoids confusion and duplication of effort.

An incident commander:

Controls the scene
Keeps hands-off
Is the link between the incident and the outside
Co-ordinates requests for supplies, transport, etc.

Safety

Safety is the next important area to consider. The three elements are the safety of the rescuers, the scene and finally the casualty.

Safety of the rescuers will include areas such as correct equipment (protective clothing, footwear, helmets, belays etc.) as well as protection issues such as surgical gloves when dealing with injured patients.

Scene safety may be particularly important in situations such as avalanche, where there may be secondary avalanche, or in vehicle accidents where there are further risks from other road users or flammable liquid. One person may be designated purely to monitor the scene safety and alert other rescuers to any changes, such as a further rock fall. The commander may even designate a safe area to the rescuers, before the team enter the scene itself, so that everyone knows where to retreat to if the scene safety deteriorates.

Safety of the casualty is the third element to consider. This may involve, for example, securing a casualty to a belay, protecting their eyes from debris when a helicopter approaches or protecting them from the environment with a casualty shelter.

Communication

Alongside command and control, communication problems are one of the biggest *bottlenecks* in any incident. Communication may be considered as horizontal (within the team) or vertical (from the team to outside agencies). Communication serves to pass information, receive confirmation of orders or facts and to allow coordination of effort.

There are many different ways of communicating within the team; the equipment available, the environmental conditions and the geographical spread of the incident will determine what is appropriate. There are no hard and fast rules and teams will have to adapt to the incident. The main points are to ensure that everyone knows what system is in use, and everyone is briefed on emergency signals before they enter the area, for example, a whistle blast to evacuate the area. Any messages passed by runners should be written down to avoid the *Chinese whisper* phenomenon. And, don't forget your phonetic alphabet!

Phonetic Alphabet	
A	alpha
B	bravo
C	charlie
D	delta
E	echo
F	foxtrot
G	golf
H	hotel
I	india
J	juliet
K	kilo
L	lima
M	mike
N	november
O	oscar
P	papa
Q	quebec
R	romeo
S	sierra
T	tango
U	uniform
V	victor
W	whisky
X	x-ray
Y	yankee
Z	zulu

Communication to other emergency services is now done using the CHALET acronym. This has been agreed across the ambulance services, and their control room staff will be trained to expect information to be passed in this way.

CHALET

C - **Casualties** - number and type of injuries/priorities (see triage)
H - **Hazards** to rescuers
A - **Access**
L - **Location** (six figure grid reference if possible)
E - **Equipment** and personnel on scene and required
T - **Type** of incident (aircraft, train, chemical, terrorist, etc.)

Sending an initial CHALET report early on is very useful, as services can start to be mobilised in anticipation of the reported need. Rescuers should update their CHALET reports as information changes or becomes available. Securing an efficient evacuation capability from the scene is crucial when there are many casualties with significant injuries.

(CHALET gives the same information as ETHANE, an acronym used in the past by some services)

PMRT Control rooms. @1980 and 2004

Assessment of the scene

This is partially covered by checking for scene safety, but also encompasses the geographic features of the incident. The commander may designate areas for specific tasks, such as somewhere for the walking wounded or uninjured to congregate, a helicopter landing site, a medical equipment dump or a safe area for the team to retreat to.

Triage

Triage is derived from the French term meaning to sort. The concept of prioritising patients was first documented in the Napoleonic Wars, where Baron Larrey treated the wounded based on their medical priority rather than their rank. The aim of triage is to sort the patients into a priority so that the most can be done for the most, and overstretched resources can be used rationally.

Sorting casualties can be performed rapidly. It is best done by the rescuer with the most medical experience; he/she becomes the Triage Officer and uses a triage sieve. No treatment should be performed whilst conducting triage except opening an airway and arresting major haemorrhage. To do more interventions detracts from the main object of triage; that is sorting the casualties into an order thus allowing the efficient use of the available resources. Casualties should be marked as to their priority; this could be achieved using different coloured light sticks, luggage labels or even writing on the forehead. The marking should be clearly visible so that the Triage Officer can see which casualties he has already assessed and other rescuers, as they arrive, can deal with the highest priority casualties first. Use the Ambulance triage priorities as detailed in the box below.

Triage	
Priority 1	(life-threatening, red)
Priority 2	(Urgent, yellow)
Priority 3	(Non-urgent or delayed, green)
Dead	(white)

The triage sieve

The algorithm on the following page starts by getting non-injured and walking wounded (priority 3) patients to one side. Though these casualties appear to have only minor injuries, it is worth keeping a Casualty Carer with the walking wounded, as they can sometimes deteriorate unexpectedly without the team being aware.

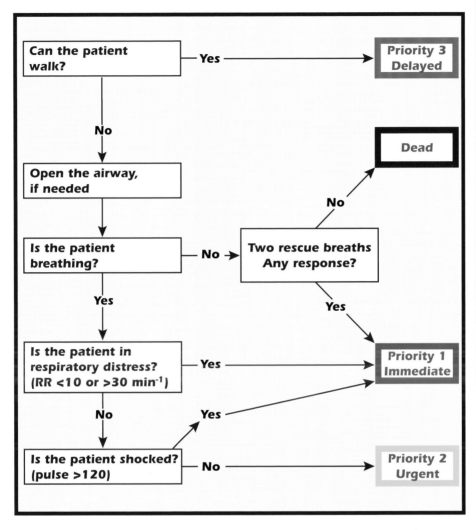

Next, the triage officer follows the familiar sequence of A, B then C to identify those casualties with the most life-threatening conditions. Assess each casualty's airway; if closed, open using a simple airway-opening manoeuvre, such as a jaw thrust or chin lift. If the casualty starts breathing, categorise as priority 1. If the casualty fails to breathe, despite the airway-opening procedure, then they are deemed to be dead. (Two rescue breaths are included in the algorithm – many sieves do not have this step. The breaths are thought to be important in a number of situations particularly crush injury and lightning strike.)

If the casualty is breathing, then the respiratory rate is measured; a respiratory rate of faster than 30 or slower than 10 is classified as priority 1. Those casualties with respiratory rates in between these extremes should have their radial pulse assessed. If the pulse is faster than 120 beats per minute or absent at the radius, the casualty has a serious circulation disorder and should be classified priority 1.

By default, non-walking patients with a respiratory rate between 10 and 30, and a pulse rate less than 120 are a priority 2 classification.

Medically trained responders may find the absence of resuscitation in the algorithm distressing, but cardiopulmonary resuscitation is rarely warranted in traumatic scenarios and, in the absence of early defibrillation, is unlikely to be successful in cardiac events. Team members would be unnecessarily diverted from the main task of doing the most for the most. Rescuers must resist intervening until all the victims have been prioritised. Intervening with one patient, with an obvious distressing injury, may result in time and resources being diverted away from a subtle but nevertheless severe injury in another patient. This patient is often 'the quiet one' in the corner.

Triage is a dynamic process; the situation is constantly changing and the priority given at one instance may change as the casualty's condition deteriorates or improves. For example a casualty with a splenic injury may be able to walk for some time after the accident, but then suddenly collapse having had a large internal bleed. He has changed from priority 3 (delayed) to priority 1 (immediate). Casualties can get better too! A patient with an occluded airway may be a priority 1, but once the airway has been opened and maintained, he/she may have enough oxygen reaching the brain to gain control of the muscles opening the airway. Rescuers should be aware of this changing nature. A formal re-triage may be useful once the initial treatment phase is over particularly if the evacuation phase is going to be prolonged or delayed.

Treatment

Once the casualties have been prioritised for treatment, the incident commander should allocate the available resources to treat the casualties as detailed in the primary survey. Frequent updates on the state of the casualties should be fed to the incident commander to enable decisions regarding further assistance, allocation of resources and evacuation to be made.

Transport

The aim of transport in a multiple casualty incident is to get the right patient to the right place at an appropriate time. Transporting casualties a short distance within the accident site to a designated area may be useful. The seriously ill can be nearer the most experienced medic and resources, such as shelters and oxygen, can be shared. In addition, transport away from the accident site can be from one point; this is likely to be more efficient than having multiple pick-up spots and safer if helicopters are ferrying the casualties away. Casualties can be triaged immediately prior to transportation to make the most of the scarce evacuation resources. Always consider alternative modes of transport, other than ambulances and helicopters. For example, a large number of walking wounded could be transported in a minibus with a Casualty Carer escort.

Yes Tor, Dartmoor. (2003)

Major Incidents

Major incidents are fortunately rare. They can occur in areas where mountain rescue teams are active and increasingly rescue teams are written into the Major Incident Plan. It goes without saying that in remote mountainous locations, MRTs will have a crucial role.

A Major Incident is defined as 'arising when any occurrence presents a serious threat to the health of the community, disruption to the health service, or causes .... such numbers of casualties as to require special arrangements by the health service'. All statutory and NHS bodies will have, and have rehearsed, major incident scenarios. The Plan may appear bureaucratic (Gold, Silver, Bronze command) but in the mayhem and confusion of a Major Incident, the quicker order and efficient practices are put in place the least damage is done. Teams should engage with their Local Authorities and Ambulance Services, and be familiar with the structures that will be put in place. The Plan is likely to use the 'Control Spells Calm And Time To Treat' at the Incident Site, so at least this should be familiar to the rescuer.

Case studies

These cases are fictional but were developed from several real cases. They were commissioned for *Casualty Care in Mountain Rescue* to contribute a sense of real life and to draw attention to the dilemmas that occur in rescue work.

Case 1 - Triage of two casualties

Time and date: 13.00 on the 26th of March

Location: Steep back wall of a corrie, 100 metres above a tarn

Weather: Misty with snow showers

Reported injuries: Head injury but, during the walk-in, sketchy information of a second incident at the same location filtered down

A 24 years old male walker was reported to have slipped from the end of an arete and fallen between 100 and 200 metres to the tarn below. Serious injury was expected. It takes about 50 minutes to walk to the corrie back wall. The team leader sent 12 rescuers, including a team doctor, to walk up. As the cloud cover was just above the tarn basin, helicopter assistance was asked for immediately. Four rescuers, including a second team doctor, were held back to await the helicopter. This usually takes 40 minutes to arrive at the landing site in the valley where it picks up the rescuers. The walking party was carrying resuscitation equipment, oxygen, a casualty bag and stretcher as well as safety equipment; the helicopter party was carrying similar equipment. As the rescue party approached the incident, walkers leaving the corrie basin reported a second incident involving a slip from the same spot. The rescue party reached the incident site before the helicopter rescuers by about five minutes. On approaching they had seen two clusters of people about 15 metres apart. The first casualty encountered was in his fifties, talking and generally responding to a helper. He complained of pain in the right upper leg. A rescuer was designated to the casualty and the rest of the party moved immediately on to the second casualty. This casualty showed no respiratory effort. The airway was opened and two breaths (mouth-to-mouth) were given. The accompanying people gave a history of unconsciousness from the time of their arrival and that breathing had stopped about ten minutes previously. They had also attempted mouth-to-mouth resuscitation. No pulse was detected so cardiac massage was started in addition to bag-and-mask ventilation. Inserting a Guedel airway helped airway maintenance. The second doctor arrived on scene and went to help the first doctor with the resuscitation. Life support techniques failed to establish a cardiac output and after about ten minutes resuscitation was stopped.

During the commotion of the resuscitation the rescuer designated to the first casualty began to request help. Her casualty had become confused and agitated. The skin was cold and sweaty and the pulse 'too rapid to count'. The designated rescuer had examined the first casualty and diagnosed a fractured femur with no other serious injuries. It was felt the deterioration was the result of blood loss. The casualty was laid down from a sitting position. Oxygen and intravenous fluids were started. A further chest, abdominal and pelvic examination did not suggest that blood loss had occurred in these areas though this possibility remained. The pulse quickly improved in both rate and volume. The casualty started talking normally again. The fractured femur was stabilised in a traction splint. Urgent evacuation to the nearest District General Hospital by helicopter was organised and given priority over the recovery of the second casualty.

Comments

Was there effective command and control at the incident and were resources allocated appropriately? Was there effective triage of the casualties before treatment began? Was there effective prioritisation of casualties for transport? What would you change if you were the commander of this incident?

There were two doctors, with relevant experience, and 14 trained rescuers. Was the first casualty 'forgotten'? Each casualty could have been allocated a doctor, a few rescuers and a full kit of equipment. Such a plan might have avoided the dramatic change in the condition of the first casualty. In retrospect, the doctors felt that by trying to save one casualty they had almost lost two. The first doctor was performing triage. He did not stay with the first casualty but rapidly moved on to assess the second and became engrossed in resuscitation. This went beyond what he would have done if still performing triage. The second doctor helped his colleague with some difficult procedures. An important lesson from this case is that a casualty seen during triage has not been properly assessed. Leaving a designated rescuer with the first casualty was, in part, recognising this. In most situations, rescue teams will not have the luxury of one or more doctors; perhaps this will help! The course of action will be more obvious. It still remains difficult to stop resuscitation early. We hope anyone unfortunate enough to have to make these decisions will find comfort in this case.

Case 2 - The bus on the pass!

Time and date: 17.00 in April

Location: A famous pass much feared before disc brakes and oil-cooled engines

Weather: Misty with sleet showers

Reported injuries: Overturned bus; perhaps 40 elderly casualties – no information on injuries

The Ambulance service had received the emergency call, and had sent its nearest ambulance (20 minutes away) with a further three heading towards the incident. A 'Major Incident – stand by' had been declared. Could MR help? A CHALET message was relayed to team leader.

C – Casualties - 40 plus; type of injuries unknown

H – Hazards to rescuers - unknown

A – Access - either up or down the C-class road; unclear if the road was blocked

L – Location - 500 metres from the top on the north side

E – Equipment and personnel on scene - Fire and Police services were also attending but not yet on scene. Air ambulance requested - confirmation of availability awaited

T – Type of incident - Bus crash

The team alerted its neighbouring MR team on the other side of the pass and set off with three team Landrovers and 15 personnel. On arriving, a sole Ambulance had just arrived. The bus was on its side about 5 metres from the road but showed little signs of damage except for lots of broken glass. The engine was off and the bus was in a stable position. Most of the casualties were still within the bus. The road itself was open but blocked by passing cars. One ambulance person was going down to the bus; the other was relieved to see some support arrive! It was agreed that the MR team Doctor, who was Major Incident Medical Management and Support (MIMMS) trained, should take charge of the incident site. The incident site, and the MR duties, are summarised on the next page.

Comments

Fortunately, the injuries were largely minor cuts on the face and hands from glass. Only two casualties required stretcher evacuation; one with a suspected dislocated hip (air ambulance used) and the other with a possible lower back injury (road ambulance) were transferred to hospital. The casualties with minor injuries were treated in the Mountain Rescue base, which was only metres from the hotel where the bus passengers were due to spend the night!

Reference

Driscoll P, Skinner D, Earlam R. (editors) *ABC of Major Trauma* (BMJ Books) 3rd edition (2000). ISBN: 0 7279 1378 6

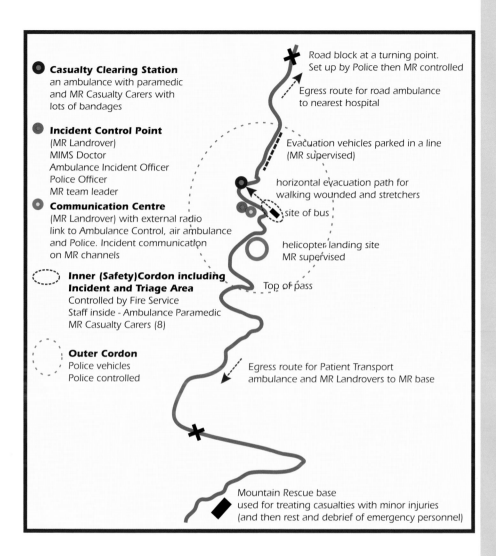

Casualty Clearing Station
an ambulance with paramedic
and MR Casualty Carers with
lots of bandages

Incident Control Point
(MR Landrover)
MIMS Doctor
Ambulance Incident Officer
Police Officer
MR team leader

Communication Centre
(MR Landrover) with external radio
link to Ambulance Control, air ambulance
and Police. Incident communication
on MR channels

**Inner (Safety)Cordon including
Incident and Triage Area**
Controlled by Fire Service
Staff inside - Ambulance Paramedic
MR Casualty Carers (8)

Outer Cordon
Police vehicles
Police controlled

Road block at a turning point.
Set up by Police then MR controlled

Egress route for road ambulance
to nearest hospital

Evacuation vehicles parked in a line
(MR supervised)

horizontal evacuation path for
walking wounded and stretchers

site of bus

helicopter landing site
MR supervised

Top of pass

Egress route for Patient Transport
ambulance and MR Landrovers to MR base

Mountain Rescue base
used for treating casualties with minor injuries
(and then rest and debrief of emergency personnel)

Making a diagnosis

From the first moments of an incident we are starting to formulate a diagnosis. A fell walker is reported as having 'chest pain'. 'Heart attack' has already popped into your mind and will probably stay there until circumstances or an examination of the casualty refute the diagnosis. Adding 'heart attack' to 'chest pain' will change your behaviour, for example the urgency of response, the kit you will carry and the questions you will ask. Why does this happen? Is it helpful?

Much of this textbook is written in a dogmatic and directive style. Managing trauma suits this approach but this section introduces an older form of medicine where 90% of diagnoses are made from the history, with the examination contributing only a small number of additional diagnoses (and tests even fewer). Though a protocol or algorithm approach is accepted, particularly in trauma and emergency medical care, its benefit in terms of survival has been hard to show. Indeed, and rather embarrassingly, advanced skills outside hospital have been shown to be slightly detrimental to survival probably because advanced skills delayed transportation to definitive care. Please bear that in mind!

Diagnosis is defined as 'identification of a disease by investigation of its symptoms and history'. (Shorter Oxford English Dictionary; 1973) It is a term used largely by doctors to help sort individual patients into groups containing patients with similar illnesses or injuries. The knowledge of how that group behaves guides the management of the individual patient. Returning to our fell walker with chest pain, we know that the average person having a heart attack will have a number of symptoms and signs. Our casualty will have some or all of these features and we can surmise that some of the complications will occur. The science of medicine is to recognise the diagnosis and manage the casualty rationally using evidence from similar casualties. Your casualty will receive the best care and be grateful forever etc.....

But do we need to make a diagnosis? Why not treat all 'chest pain' as the worst-case scenario? Here are a few reasons why not:

All treatments can be harmful and some will be dangerous in the wrong circumstances.

The impact the illness has on the patient is influenced by the early treatment - 'it must be serious; I was given oxygen!'

Treating all as if worst-case scenario will be expensive and unnecessary.

Making a diagnosis is not new. Dr. Neville Marsden (Medical Officer, Rossendale Fell Rescue Team and the first MRC medical exam registrar) wrote a book called 'Diagnosis before First Aid' in 1978 explaining why rescuers needed to develop the medical skill of diagnosis. Though the treatments now look dated, the reasons behind his argument stand today.

So how do we make a diagnosis?

Pattern recognition

The casualty's symptoms and signs conform to a previously learned pattern. Physical signs are of particular use in this context especially if the sign is specific to the diagnosis. For example, a 'dinner fork' wrist needs no further examination for the signs of a fracture, just the enquiry whether it is painful. This method requires the clinician to have seen, or at least read about, the condition and that the signs are pretty well confined to a single diagnosis. So the method is not much good to diagnose 'chest pain'. Pattern recognition is also useful when diagnoses cluster together. For example, os calcis (heel) fractures and vertebral fracture; and epileptic seizure and posterior dislocation of the shoulder.

Algorithm

Answer 'yes' or 'no' to a series of questions and you arrive at a diagnosis. Algorithms are often used to lead less experienced clinicians to a diagnosis and direct their treatment. They have to be carefully constructed and each question must have an unambiguous answer. More often than not the questions do not have such a black and white answer; the clinician uses the algorithm to guide the treatment of the casualty. Dogmatic adherence can lead to over-diagnosing serious illness particularly when the questions are poor discriminators. There are a few examples of algorithms in this textbook, for example, grading hypothermia and the triage sieve. Other flow charts, for example the A, B, C and D cards, are not algorithms (no 'yes' or 'no' arrows) but a reminder, prompt, *aide-memoire* or guideline for managing a casualty.

Complete 'history and examination'

A system taught to every medical student - a painstaking, exhausting search for all facts that often becomes so convoluted that the clinician is also left exhausted and confused! A 'top-to-toe' examination (secondary survey) can appear to be in this category, at least in the pre-hospital setting.

Hypothetico-deductive method

Most clinicians use this method most of the time. The earliest clues are used to give a short list of potential diagnoses frequently using the fact that 'common things are common', The potential diagnoses are then tested often by negative questions or the absence of a sign that make a diagnosis on the list very unlikely. In this way the list is shortened. The method works well for symptoms that can be caused by a wide range of diagnoses. For example, 'chest pain' in a 60 year old fell walker leads to a short list of angina; heart attack; indigestion; gall stone pain; chest wall muscular strain and trauma. Is the casualty grey, sweaty, unwell and still in pain? No - remove heart attack and gall stone pain from the list. "Have you fallen or does the pain come on when you move your shoulders?" No - remove chest wall strain and trauma. "Does milk or an antacid help?" Yes - indigestion; no - "Is the pain only on exercise?" Yes - angina sounds possible; let's try to get a few confirmatory symptoms and signs (central, heavy pain going to the jaw, disappears when resting, etc.). In real life, if the potential list contains important and potentially serious diagnoses, even if fairly rare or unlikely, these often stay on the list to the end until a confirmed diagnosis has been reached. In this case, a myocardial infarction is unlikely to be discarded until a blood test and an electrocardiogram have been performed and found to be negative. Likewise, a potential spinal injury after a tumbling fall is, as we shall see later, hard to exclude in the pre-hospital phase, so will often remain on the list. Pattern recognition is creeping in here.

So, next time you see an experienced clinician at work, watch carefully. Outside the primary survey, you may find a correct diagnosis apparently plucked out of the air by use of a combination of the methods outlined above!

References

Marsden N. *Diagnosis before First Aid* (2nd edition) 1985; ISBN 0 443 02837 0

Sackett DL. Evaluation of clinical method in the *Oxford Textbook of Medicine* (3rd edition) 1996; ISBN 0 19 262140 8

Advanced life support versus basic life support in *Pre-hospital initiation of fluid replacement therapy in trauma*. NICE Technology Appraisal 74 (2004). Available at www.nice.org.uk/TA074/guidance

Consent and Ethics

This section has been written for the Casualty Carer who is starting to use invasive ('advanced') techniques. Other rescuers may find some of the ideas useful in managing casualties. You may find a number of the issues difficult, and may need to discuss them with the team doctor or an experienced practitioner. The section is not exhaustive.

Consent

We assume that a casualty wants to be rescued and for his pain to be relieved. But this may not be the case. And as soon as we start to look at invasive techniques, from intramuscular analgesia to needle thoracotomy, consent cannot be assumed and must be established first. To obtain consent the casualty must be given sufficient information, in a way they can understand, in order to make up their own mind. The rescuer should give the casualty:

information on the diagnosis

the options for treatment including likely benefits

the purpose of any treatment

any common and serious side effects of a proposed treatment

a reminder that the casualty can change his mind and can refuse the proposed treatment

This extensive list may seem onerous but it rarely is.

"It looks like your ankle is broken. We should splint it to stop any further damage. Putting on the splint and then transporting you to hospital is going to hurt. We have a number of things we can offer you to make things more comfortable. These include diclofenac tablets, Entonox® and morphine by injection. How bad is the pain – Do you need something for it?"

"It's terrible"

"I think an injection of morphine may be the best. It involves giving you an injection in your leg. The morphine will take about 15 minutes to start working. You may feel sick after the injection but this is usually not a problem; we have an anti-sickness drug if you need it. Is that OK?"

Consent does not need to be written and can be implied; for example, self-administering Entonox® or helping to expose the site for an injection.

In the emergency situation, the casualty may not be able to give consent because he is unconscious. In this case you can go ahead and provide treatment to anyone who needs it using the principle that it is in the casualty's best interest. The treatment provided should be limited to what is immediately necessary to save life. Be aware that many people are making advance directives ('living wills') and, if this becomes known, the information must be respected, as must the right of any competent person to refuse treatment even if this will result in his/her death.

Ethics of using life-prolonging treatments

Modern medicine has proved itself effective at prolonging life. Artificial ventilators, renal (kidney) dialysis, cardiopulmonary resuscitation and defibrillation are examples. These techniques are not without suffering for the patient, therefore there is a balance between when using them will be in the best interest of the patient and when it is not. Life has a natural end; resuscitation attempts in the mortally ill do not enhance the dignity of death, nor would we want to render a patient into a vegetative state, which can last many years. However we all want to prolong life where the patient has a chance. In hospitals this dilemma is acute and commonplace. It has attracted a lot of attention from the public, press, doctors and the Courts. Concerns include over- or under-treatment, and whether the decisions are appropriate. These have led to a set of guiding principles, some of which are listed below.

Patients should be offered those treatments where the possible benefits outweigh any burdens or risks associated with the treatment. The patient's best interest is the first concern. In order that a correct decision is made the practitioner needs to have up-to-date information on the treatments offered particularly the likelihood of benefit.

The benefit and burdens for the patient are not limited to purely medical considerations.

Prolonging life will usually be in the best interests of the patient. In cases of acute critical illness, where the outcome of treatment is unclear, survival of the acute crisis would be regarded as being in the patient's best interest.

Adult patients have the right to decide how much weight to attach to the benefits, burdens, risks and the overall acceptability of any treatment. Where patients lack the capacity to decide for themselves the practitioner can only decide what is in the patient's best interest by seeking the views of those close to the patient.

Although it may be emotionally more difficult to stop a treatment rather than to decide not to start it, this should not be a reason for failing to start a treatment. However, if a treatment becomes 'not in the best interest of the patient' there is no obligation to continue it.

Where time is needed for consultation or a more detailed assessment of the severity of the condition and the likelihood of recovery, treatment that may be of some benefit to the patient should be started. It must be explained that the treatment will be reviewed, and may be withdrawn, if it is proving to be ineffective or too burdensome for the patient.

Fortunately mountain rescuers are rarely faced with dilemmas of this type. However they do occur. Consider CPR in drowning and hypothermia, and defibrillation in a cardiac arrest. The casualty is unknown to us and cannot be involved in the decision-making process. It is unlikely that the information regarding advanced instructions will at hand. Should all casualties have CPR started? Can we make a decision to withhold or stop on the history of the accident and an examination of the casualty? To do so requires:

An accurate history particularly of the time-scale involved.

Up-to-date information on the survival chances – hopefully these are covered adequately in the relevant sections of this book. Ask whether further tests, such as a core temperature or ECG, aid the decision-making process?

Starting, and then stopping, a treatment may be useful because it allows more time for the history to become clearer. Your actions and their effect, the reasoning behind stopping can be discussed with the casualty's companions though ultimately you have to decide in the best interest of the casualty. One of the most important duties of a Doctor is to 'make the care of your patient your first concern'. Rescuers should do the same. This means that you have to make others involved in the rescue aware of what is in the patient's best interest. You may be overruled on, say, safety grounds if you think a helicopter evacuation is appropriate but at the least you have been the patient's advocate when he needed his view expressed.

Reference

General Medical Council. *Withholding and Withdrawing Life-prolonging Treatments: Good Practice in Decision-making* (2002). Available at www.gmc-uk.org

Ring of Steal, Mamores, Scotland. (2005)

Airway

Objectives
To appreciate the paramount importance of an open airway
To recognize an obstructed airway
To manage a casualty with an airway problem
To know about dental and facial problems

Abdominal thrusts in severe obstruction

Introduction

The airway is the part of the body that conducts air to the lungs. Separating the airway from 'breathing' can be hard to understand because the relationship between the two is very close. However it is usual to do this and we have followed this convention.

Anatomy and Physiology

The airway, which is much more than a series of pipes conveying air to the lungs, may conveniently be divided into a) upper and b) lower sections.

The anatomy of the upper airway is shown below; it has three main functions.

Improving the quality of the inspired air

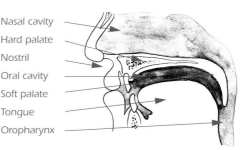

Nasal cavity
Hard palate
Nostril
Oral cavity
Soft palate
Tongue
Oropharynx

Under resting conditions, air is breathed in through the nose. Large particles of foreign material, such as smoke and dust, are filtered from the air and trapped in nasal mucus or on nasal hairs. At the same time the air is warmed and humidified. During expiration some of the moisture content and heat is returned to the nasal lining but the process is incomplete and there is an inevitable loss of both water and heat to the outside. (The loss of both water and heat is much more significant in cold, dry air particularly at altitude.) During exercise, as the rate and depth of breathing increases, air is taken in through the mouth. This bypasses the humidification process in the nose and leads to a greater loss of heat and moisture to the environment.

Recognizing foreign material and mounting an immune response

The upper airway is ringed by lymphoid tissue. The tonsils and adenoids are part of this ring. Lymphoid tissue protects the body against invasion by infective agents, such as viruses and bacteria. When activated the lymphoid tissue swells. The tonsils may become very large and even cause partial respiratory obstruction. Acute infections of the tonsils can cause a one-sided swelling (quinsy), which may cause breathing difficulties.

Directing food and liquid into the oesophagus

The upper airway must separate air from food and liquid. During swallowing the nasal cavity is closed by the soft palate and the trachea is protected by the reflex closure of the epiglottis. Thus no food enters the windpipe or the space behind the nose. The tongue, a large muscular organ, helps in this process as well as being important in speech and taste. Though the front part of the tongue is free in the oropharynx, its back part is connected to the floor of the mouth and the jaw. The tongue's position depends on its muscular tone and gravity. If the tone is lost, usually due to unconsciousness, the tongue can fall backwards blocking the airway. This is particularly likely if the casualty is lying on his back. Moving the jaw forward (jaw thrust) will move the tongue forward and may be sufficient to relieve the obstruction.

The anatomy of the lower airway is shown below, along with a more detailed diagram of the upper section.

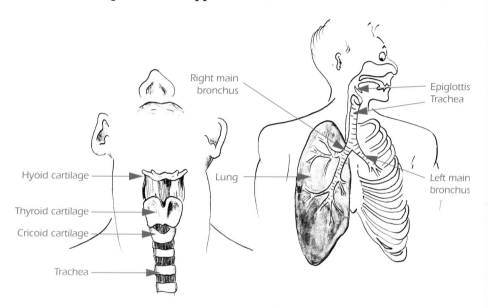

Right main bronchus

Epiglottis
Trachea

Hyoid cartilage

Lung

Left main bronchus

Thyroid cartilage

Cricoid cartilage

Trachea

The lower airway has three main functions:

Supplying air to the alveoli

The lower airway acts as a conduit directing air to the alveoli. The trachea divides into left and right main bronchi at the level of the sternal angle. This level is marked on the skin by the junction of the upper 1/3 and lower 2/3 of the sternum (breastbone) and is felt as a prominent ridge. Whether the casualty is upright or lying on their back, the right main bronchus is more vertical than the left so foreign material, such as vomit, under the action of gravity is more likely to enter the right main bronchus. The airway divides sequentially into smaller and smaller passages termed bronchioles. These in turn lead into sac-like structures called alveoli. The air is now separated from the blood capillaries by the thickness of only two cells. This gap is about two ten thousandths of a millimetre (0.2×10^{-6} metre) and small enough for gas exchange to occur. Gas exchange occurs by a process called diffusion. This depends on the random motion of the gas molecules and the tendency for the concentration of the molecules to become even with time. The total surface area of the alveoli in an adult is approximately $75m^2$. Under normal circumstances, gas exchange is very efficient and the concentration of the gases in the alveoli and the blood capillary becomes equal very quickly. However the tissue is very delicate; trauma and infection commonly upset the process. Moreover any change in blood flow to the lungs, for example when the pulmonary arteries are blocked by an embolus, also reduces the efficiency of gas transfer.

Speech

The movement of air past the vocal cords generates sounds that, after further refinement in the upper airway, create speech.

Clearing and protective functions

The lining of the large air passages secretes mucus, which traps foreign material, such as dust and bacteria. The secretions are wafted upwards towards the pharynx by tiny hair-like structures (cilia). Coughing aids clearing the larger passages and the secretions are normally swallowed. An infection or cigarette smoking temporarily reduces the action of the cilia so bacteria are cleared less well from the lungs and pneumonia can develop.

Pathology - Airway obstruction

The narrowing, or obstruction, of the airway anywhere from the lips to the alveoli can have a great effect on a person's state of wellbeing. There are many causes; a number of the more common ones are listed below.

Obstruction of the airway by the tongue in an unconscious person where the normal muscle tone of the tongue and pharynx is lost. The problem is most pronounced when the casualty is lying on his back.

Obstruction of the larger airways, including the pharynx, larynx, trachea and main bronchi, can follow inhalation of a foreign body (e.g. dentures and peanuts). If a foreign body completely obstructs the airway, death from lack of oxygen occurs in a few minutes.

Bleeding or swelling as a result of trauma to the face and neck can cause airway obstruction. If the victim is unconscious from an associated head injury, then a relatively small amount of bleeding or swelling may prove fatal.

Swelling of the walls of the pharynx and larynx as a result of an allergic (anaphylactic) reaction (bee sting or a drug) or burns (thermal - smoke inhalation or chemical substance.

Distortion of the anatomy, for example when the trachea is displaced from the midline by a tension pneumothorax.

Constriction of the muscles in the walls of the bronchioles, in response to inhalation of an irritant substance (vomit) or allergens (asthma).

Filling of the alveoli and bronchioles with fluid (pulmonary oedema) from heart failure, 'secondary drowning' or high altitude pulmonary oedema can prevent air reaching the alveoli.

'smoke inhalation can cause airway problems'

Assessment

The casualty may report being 'out of breath' and attempting to sit up as this is, usually, the most effective position for breathing. Looking at the casualty may show a facial or neck injury, or tongue swelling. He may be trying to dislodge a foreign body by coughing. The effort of breathing will be increased, with extra muscles in the neck and shoulder regions being used, and the respiratory rate will be raised. The face is often suffused with the effort and the casualty can become agitated and confused from shortage of oxygen. In an unconscious casualty, the extra effort of trying to relieve the obstruction is absent; there are very few signs of the obstruction in these casualties.

In addition to the extra effort of breathing, abnormal noises maybe associated with the breathing. Secretions in the upper airway cause gurgling noises that often vary from one breath to another. Snoring noises may be heard as the back of the tongue intermittently contacts the posterior wall of the pharynx. However if the obstruction is complete there will be no noise. In the first few minutes, the casualty will struggle to dislodge the obstruction but, if unsuccessful, will rapidly become cyanosed and unconscious. The diagnosis may not become apparent until it proves impossible to fill the lungs with air during artificial ventilation.

Narrowing of the upper airway produces a high-pitched noise called stridor. Breathing in and out through pursed lips reproduces the noise. Note the sound occurs in both inspiration and expiration with a short gap in the middle. The length of time in inspiration is about the same as in expiration. In contrast, narrowing of the bronchioles produces wheeze. This is a musical note that is only heard in expiration. The expiration phase of breathing is often much longer than the inspiration phase.

Recording the oxygen saturation by pulse oximetry can be valuable. However improving the reading to normal by using high concentrations of oxygen, as we will see below, should not be taken as a cure of the problem.

Treatment

Airway obstruction is life threatening. It can sometimes be anticipated; prevention is then better than waiting for it to develop. For example, in a facial injury, a gentle 'head up' position of up to 20 degrees from the horizontal can reduce the swelling from injury. (In a casualty with a head and facial injury, do this only if the systolic blood pressure is above 140mmHg.) In anaphylaxis, the allergic swelling of the pharynx can be reduced by the early use of adrenaline (epinephrine).

In the unconscious patient, airway obstruction can take place at any stage. This is especially relevant in the head-injured casualty. There are two main causes: the tongue and regurgitation of stomach contents in to the oropharynx. The next section deals with the first cause.

Obstruction by the tongue

One rescuer needs to take responsibility for the airway to ensure it is always kept open. In casualties involved in trauma, this is normally the rescuer that is applying in-line manual immobilisation of the neck (as demonstrated below) though sometimes two rescuers will be needed if maintaining the airway is difficult. This is demonstrated in the Breathing chapter.

In terms of practical procedures, the techniques of head tilt with chin lift and jaw thrust are simple and frequently effective. They are described in the box on the next page and fully on the Resuscitation Council (UK) web site (http://www.resus.org.uk).

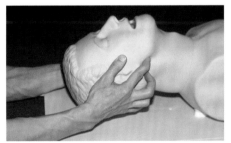

Jaw thurst with manual in-line neck stabilisation

Note that an open airway is paramount; if a cervical spine injury is suspected, try to avoid excessive head tilt but not at the expense of a compromised airway. (The risk that neck extension may worsen a cervical spine injury is unknown; the forces involved in the accident are much greater than those involved in a head tilt and secondary spinal cord injury from hypoxia is certain if hypoxia occurs – an open airway is paramount.)

Basic airway techniques
Head tilt

Place your hand on the casualty's forehead and gently rotate (tilt) the head so the distance between the chin and chest increases. In addition to the head tilt, a chin lift is usually required to open the airway.

Chin lift

Grip the point of the chin between your finger tips and thumb and gently pull the chin upwards. Vary the direction of pull to open the mouth slightly.

Jaw thrust

This technique needs two hands. Grip the jaw between your finger tips and thumb by placing them behind the angle of the jaw and between the mouth and point of the jaw. Gently pull the jaw upwards, varying the direction of pull to open the mouth slightly. Spreading your fingers whilst performing in-line manual immobilisation of the cervical spine can push up on the angle of the jaw and maintain an open airway.

C-clamp (for the advanced)

Usually performed with two hands, this technique allows the airway to be opened and a rigid face mask to be clamped on the casualty's face. Your thumbs go behind the angle of the jaw and your fingers wrap around the face mask (or visa versa - see picture on the next page). You push the jaw upwards and, by counter-pressure, stabilise the mask so creating an airtight seal for artificial ventilation. Useful for bag-valve-mask and mouth-to-mask device ventilation. Experts progress to a single-handed technique!

Beware – none of these techniques are guaranteed to work. Always confirm that the airway is open by observing quiet breathing. This is particularly important with the more complex techniques, where it is easy to obstruct the airway whilst trying to ensure an airtight seal or neck stability. If in doubt, get help and return to the simple techniques.

Many teams will be operating at the advanced life support level and have airway adjuncts available. These may help to provide an open airway in an otherwise difficult case, but manual control of the jaw will still be required.

An oropharyngeal (Guedel) airway should be available in all first aid sacs. The casualty has to be completely unconscious for the airway to be tolerated. Forced insertion could cause further trauma, reflex laryngeal spasm (resulting in stridor) or vomiting. The correct size can be estimated by using the Guedel airway that is the same length as the distance from the casualty's front teeth to the angle of jaw. In an adult, this is usually size 3 or 4. The Guedel is inserted 'upside down' as illustrated below. It is rotated through 180° when about three quarters of the way in and its tip is over the back of the tongue.

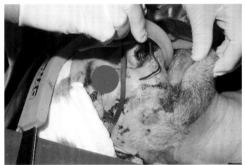

A nasopharyngeal airway is a useful alternative. Compared with a Guedel airway, it can be inserted in a casualty who is less unconscious - perhaps P on the AVPU scale, and may hold the airway open without the need for a jaw lift. Sizing (the casualty's little finger) is unreliable, so it is suggested that

Inserting a Guedel airway

a 6 or 7mm airway is used in an adult. The nasopharyngeal airway should be well lubricated with water-based lubricant, such as K-Y® jelly, and no force should be used. Bleeding from the nose can be a problem. Inserting the airway into the brain through a base of skull

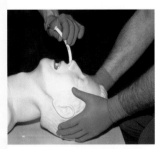

fracture has been reported but is extremely rare. Note, from the following two pictures, the correct angle of insertion along the hard palate and not parallel to the external contour of the nose!

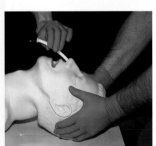

Once the airway is open, artificial ventilation may be required. The techniques used are described in the Breathing chapter.

Incorrect angle

C-clamp with mouth-to-mask device
(Dr. Werner Beikircher)

Choking

Acute airway obstruction by food or a foreign body usually occurs when someone is eating or after vomiting. Incomplete obstruction, where the casualty can talk, cough and breath, should be treated by encouraging the casualty to cough and by using gravity to assist in the removal of the solid object. If the casualty does not progress to show signs of severe obstruction, continue encouraging coughing and monitor carefully.

Severe obstruction, where the casualty cannot talk – nods when asked "Are you choking?", is unable to cough or breathe should be treated with back blows (repeated five times) and then abdominal thrusts (five times) until successful. As soon as the casualty becomes unconscious, perform cardiac compressions as these generate the highest expulsive force of all and maybe successful at dislodging the foreign body.

Regurgitation

Regurgitation of stomach contents into the oropharynx, rather than the active process of vomiting, occurs in the unconscious casualty particularly when on their back. It is frequently missed as the casualty may display only ineffective retching-like movements or a few gurgling noises. The airway becomes blocked and there is a high risk of aspiration into the lungs. This is a very serious problem with a high mortality even with the best treatment. Manage regurgitation immediately by:

> Turning the casualty on their side. Log roll, if possible, if a cervical spine injury is suspected. This can be done much quicker if the casualty is in a vacuum mattress.
>
> Consider a '20° head down' tilt.
>
> Use a wide-bore suction device under direct vision. A laryngoscope is both a good light source and tongue depressor to access the back of the throat.

Unfortunately the problem is likely to recur; consider keeping the casualty on their side or protecting the airway.

Giving oxygen, at 15litres/min using a non-rebreathing mask with a reservoir, will help overcome the damaging of effects of hypoxia and should be administered to all casualties with airway obstruction. However using oxygen cannot replace the basic techniques of opening and clearing an airway. The oxygen might compensate for hypoxia but will do nothing for the rising level of carbon dioxide in the blood. This can be equally harmful to the casualty.

Evacuation

In most situations, a helicopter evacuation, if practical, should be sought. All cases should be reviewed in hospital even if apparently cured. For example, following the removal of a foreign body from the upper airway or inhaling smoke, swelling of the upper airway is possible hours after the incident. Aspiration may also have occurred and lead to a life-threatening pneumonitis (lung inflammation) in the following days.

Extended Management

A surgical airway (tracheostomy, tracheotomy, and cricothyroidotomy) may be needed in rare cases of foreign body obstruction or severe upper airway trauma but the chances of arriving in time must be very remote.

Those with appropriate skills should consider protecting the airway in order to lessen the risk of aspiration from regurgitated stomach contents or blood from a facial injury. The situations where this should be considered include casualties suffering from a severe head injury (GCS of less than or equal to 8; AVPU = U), grade III and IV hypothermia, prolonged CPR and severe facial injury.

The gold standard for protecting the airway is to intubate the casualty with a cuffed endotracheal tube. Alternative devices are available which afford a degree of airway protection; they include the Laryngeal Mask Airway (LMA), which in a study of cardiac arrest patients showed a very low (1.5%) incidence of aspiration. The device used will depend on the experience and training of the operator. It must be noted that, in casualties with traumatic injuries, intubation without anaesthetic/sedative drugs has a very low survival rate ranging from 0.2 to 8%. This maybe because if you can intubate without such drugs the casualty has a severe (head) injury but also intubation itself causes hypertension and a rise in intracranial pressure. This could cause secondary brain damage; anaesthetic/sedative drugs depress this response. In addition to the intubating equipment, you will need monitoring equipment, oxygen and equipment to deal

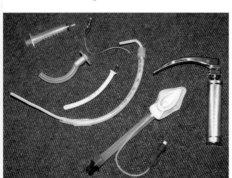

From left to right:

Oropharyngeal (Guedel), nasopharygeal, endotracheal tube with stylet, Laryngeal Mask Airway® and laryngoscope.

with a 'difficult' intubation, such as stylets and bougie, before proceeding. An evacuation plan compatible with artificial ventilation should be assured.

Rapid sequence induction

Rapid sequence induction (RSI) is a name given to a procedure that aims to minimise the risk of aspiration when a patient is anaesthetised with a full stomach. It consists of a number of separate components, which are described below. Though the full procedure for a RSI is unlikely to be used in pre-hospital care, a full stomach is almost certain and, though there is no evidence that RSI is of benefit outside hospital, it is standard practice in those casualties receiving anaesthetic/sedative drugs to aid intubation. The components of RSI are:

Pre-oxygenation - 100% oxygen (with assisted ventilation if tidal volume is low) for at least three minutes.

Cricoid pressure (Sellick's manoeuvre) - identify the cricoid cartilage; with index finger and thumb grasp it and push firmly backwards. An assistant will have to do this; it is important that the larynx is not displaced to the side by too much backward pressure. Cricoid pressure is uncomfortable in a casualty who is awake. Apply it as soon as the induction agent is given and release only when the correctly placed endotracheal cuff has been inflated.

Bolus induction agent followed by a suxamethonium - for the experts. You don't need to read this! Too much and too little of the induction agent can cause serious, perhaps irredeemable, problems.

Intubation with a cuffed endotracheal tube - you are almost committed to intubating the casualty. Have your stylet ready. Cricoid pressure can distort the anatomy making intubation difficult, if not impossible, and there is a reluctance to place the casualty in the optimal intubating ('sniffing the morning air') position because of concern over a cervical spine injury. Whether the LMA is an appropriate alternative remains contentious and, rather worryingly, papers have suggested that the successful placement of a LMA is low when the patient has the LMA inserted in the 'in-line manual neck immobilisation' position compared with the optimal intubating position. In addition, it is unclear how much protection a LMA provides from regurgitation in casualties with traumatic injuries.

Summary

Keeping an open airway is a core skill and can often be achieved by simple measures. Airway problems are common in an unconscious casualty. If the airway is not maintained secondary damage to the brain is likely. It must be emphasized that at the scene of an accident, and during pre-hospital transport, more lives have been saved by simple but meticulous care of the airway using head tilt and chin lift than by intubation.

Dental and Facial injuries

Severe facial injuries are rare in mountain rescue. When seen, the casualty usually has other injuries, particularly to the head, neck and chest. Airway obstruction and shock, from blood loss, are the practical problems seen. Placing facial injuries in the Airway chapter emphasises this.

Anatomy and pathology

A fracture of the maxilla (the bone between the eye and mouth into which the top teeth are inserted) can result in the hard palate and the upper teeth moving backwards, blocking the nasal airway.

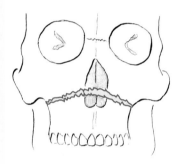

A fracture of the mandible (jaw) can stop the muscles of the tongue keeping the tongue forward. The airway may be lost. (See the case study in the Disability chapter.)

Bleeding from facial fractures can be significant. The airway may be blocked or the blood loss can cause shock.

Teeth and dentures are the commonest 'foreign bodies' to obstruct the airway.

Management

The management of facial injuries is often very technical. Assess by looking at the face and in the oral cavity with a good light source. If the teeth have lost their usual alignment, a fracture is present. The following simple techniques may make a big difference though sometimes the control achieved is less than perfect.

Airway

Open the airway by pulling the angle of the jaw forward (jaw thrust). This will pull the tongue forward and should improve the airway. Alternatively a doctor may insert a stitch through the tongue and pull it forward. Body piercers may have a suitable ring in place! Clear a foreign body from the oropharynx by running a (gloved) finger along the inside of the cheek to the back of the mouth, then hook the finger to pull the foreign body out. Repeat on the other side. (If the finger is inserted in the middle a foreign body may be pushed further back.) A wide bore sucker can be used to suck out a foreign body or blood. A good light and direct vision, using a laryngoscope, are needed. Sucking blindly is not a good idea.

Bleeding

Stopping the bleeding from a fracture of the maxilla is often very difficult. A 'head up' tilt may help. Bleeding from the front of the mouth could be stopped with direct pressure from a gauze swab. Use a big swab - so that it does not get lost! Packing the back of the 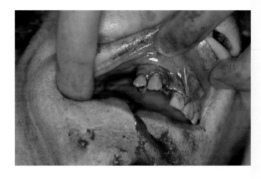 nose may be needed but is impossible unless the casualty is deeply unconscious. It could be done after the airway is secured with a laryngeal mask or an endotracheal tube - techniques beyond most rescuers. Indeed doctors have invented unusual ways round packing the back of the nose using urinary catheters! Packing the front of the nose does not help as the bleeding points are usually too far back and the blood is often diverted into the oropharynx.

A bleeding nasal fracture (and a non-traumatic nosebleed) can be helped by gentle compression of the soft part of the nose. The compression should be held on for 10 minutes with no 'looking to see if it has stopped'.

Foreign bodies

Whole teeth, bits of teeth and dentures should be kept. It is nice to know that all missing bits are accounted for and not further down the airway. If a whole tooth is knocked out it may be possible to replace it. Hold the tooth by the crown (rather than the root) and if it is clean, insert it back in to the socket. Get the casualty to bite gently on a gauze swab to hold it in place. Dental care must be sought as soon as possible. If the tooth is dirty rinse it with water or, ideally, milk. If the tooth cannot be replaced it should be kept moist. Again use milk if available or get the casualty to keep the tooth inside the mouth between the gum and cheek. In most mountain rescue incidents replacing teeth or storing them in the mouth will not be appropriate. The tooth may migrate down the airway when the casualty is jolted during the evacuation - this would be a disaster. Limit your attempts at putting teeth back to the walking casualty with no other injuries.

References

Lockey D, Davies G, Coats T. Survival of trauma patients who have prehospital tracheal intubation without anaesthesia or muscle relaxants: observational study. *BMJ* 2001; 323 141

Guha A. Prehospital care of trauma must be improved in UK. *BMJ* 2001; 323:1070

Christensen EF, Hoyer CCS. Prehospital tracheal intubation in severely injured patients: a Danish observational study. *BMJ* 2003; 327:533-4

Asai T, Marfin AG, Thompson J, Popat M, Shingu K. Ease of insertion of the laryngeal tube during manual in-line neck stabilisation. *Anaesthesia* 2004; 59:1163-6

Sarah on the Devil's Slide, Lundy,. (2005)

Breathing

Objectives
To understand the mechanics of breathing
To accurately assess conditions affecting breathing
To treat the casualty appropriately
To know how to artificially ventilate a casualty

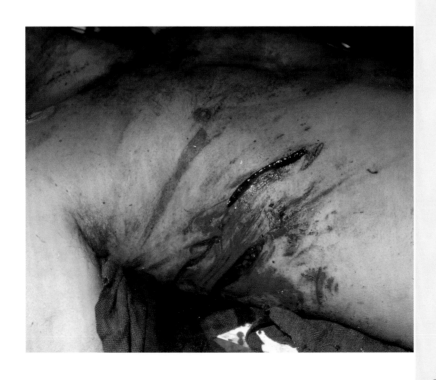

Introduction

Breathing is the process by which air is moved in and out of the lungs and its function is to move oxygen to the alveoli and take away excess carbon dioxide from the body. We need to look at the mechanics of breathing, its control and the underlying process of transporting the oxygen in and carbon dioxide out. As pointed out in the last chapter the airway is an essential element in the effectiveness of breathing. Often in this chapter we will assume that the airway is open but the rescuer will notice that many of the conditions, such as head injury, are discussed in both airway and breathing chapters. In real life, airway and breathing difficulties often occur together.

Anatomy and physiology

The lungs

The lungs have elastic properties. They lie within the thorax (chest cavity) with their outer surface lying in direct contact with the inner lining of the rib cage and diaphragm like an inner tube lying within a tyre. But this analogy stops there, for what keeps the two linings (or pleura) together is not pressure from within the lung, but a negative (sub-atmospheric) pressure in the space (the pleural cavity) between them.

The rib cage and the mechanics of breathing

The mechanism of normal breathing is that the chest cavity expands during inspiration creating a slightly lower pressure in the chest. This results in air being drawn in through the upper and lower airway to reach the alveoli. The reverse process during expiration is a passive process caused by the elastic recoil of the lungs. The expansion of the chest is the same on each side (symmetrical) and is caused by two different actions.

Firstly, the contraction of the muscular diaphragm pulls the dome of the diaphragm into a flatter shape, which has an effect like that of a piston moving down its chamber. This is known as diaphragmatic breathing and is the normal action at rest. Secondly, the intercostal muscles, lying between the ribs, pull the ribs upwards and outwards. This is known as intercostal or chest wall breathing and is seen when the demand on breathing is increased, such as during exercise. When we 'think' about breathing we tend to favour intercostal breathing.

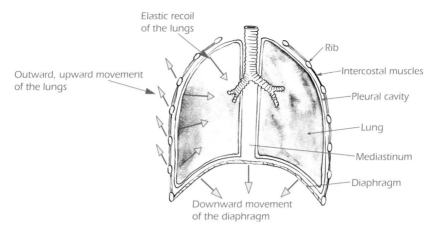

The nerves supplying the intercostal muscles and the diaphragm come from the respiratory centre in the lower part of the brain. The nerves pass down the brain and into the spinal cord. Each intercostal muscle between the ribs has its own supply, which comes off the spinal cord at approximately the level of the corresponding thoracic vertebra. The diaphragm, on the other hand, receives its nerve supply by a different route. From the brain's respiratory centre, the nerve fibres travel in the phrenic nerves; these leave the spinal cord below the third, fourth and fifth cervical vertebrae high up in the neck.

The control of breathing

The trigger for each breath comes from the respiratory centre within the lower part of the brain. It is a reflex process, which has its level of activity set by the amount of carbon dioxide and acid in the blood. The higher the level of carbon dioxide, or acid, the more breathing increases. For example, during exercise, sugars are used to power the muscles in the legs. Carbon dioxide is produced by this process and diffuses into the blood. The circulation moves this blood through the veins and then the arteries until it reaches the respiratory centre, where the raised carbon dioxide level is detected. The respiratory centre responds by increasing the rate and depth of breathing. More carbon dioxide is expelled from the lungs and so the rise in carbon dioxide is halted. This is an example of homoeostasis, a common process to stabilize the internal environment of the body. The control mechanism is a 'negative feedback' loop aimed at maintaining a specific level of carbon dioxide in the blood. The rescuer can be reassured that the above explanation is a very simple one! There are many other sensors and many other triggers, including a low oxygen level that can induce an appropriate increase in breathing.

Oxygen and carbon dioxide transport

The air we breathe contains approximately 20% oxygen and 0.03% of carbon dioxide. Oxygen is normally taken up easily from the alveoli into the blood because it binds tightly to haemoglobin, a protein in the red cells. When oxygen binds to haemoglobin, the resulting compound, oxyhaemoglobin, changes colour from blue to red. The colour change is most obvious when arterial blood is compared with venous blood. The affinity of oxygen for haemoglobin is so strong that normally the haemoglobin is fully converted to oxyhaemoglobin so blood leaving the lungs is fully saturated (97 - 100%) with oxygen. This is the 'oxygen saturation' that we measure by pulse oximetry. In contrast, carbon dioxide, produced in the body as a waste product of cellular metabolism, is carried round the body dissolved in the body fluids. Carbon dioxide reacts with water to produce bicarbonate and hydrogen ions. In the alveoli, where the blood is so close to the air the carbon dioxide easily diffuses out of the blood and is eliminated from the body with the next breath out. The volume of fresh air reaching the alveoli determines the level of carbon dioxide in the blood and this is tightly controlled by homoeostatic mechanisms. This volume (minute volume) is determined by the rate of breathing (breaths per minute) and the depth of breathing (the amount of air moved with each respiration = tidal volume) and is shown in the following equation.

Minute volume = tidal volume x respiratory rate

Normal figures, at rest, are 7 litres per minute for the minute volume, made up of 14 breaths of 500 millilitres each. The relation between minute volume and carbon dioxide levels in the blood is so close that if you double the volume of air that reaches the alveoli each minute, then the amount of carbon dioxide in the blood stream will soon be halved. Likewise, if the ventilation is halved, the carbon dioxide level in the blood will eventually double. If a normal person consciously over-breathes (hyperventilates) for more than a few minutes the blood carbon dioxide concentration falls. The reduction in carbon dioxide in the blood alters nerve conduction; the person experiences tingling in the hands, feet and around the lips. If they continue, consciousness will be lost. This stops the over-breathing and the situation rights itself - an extreme example of 'negative feedback' and homoeostasis at work!

In contrast to the linear relationship between carbon dioxide in the blood and minute volume, the oxygen concentration has a much more complex relationship with minute volume because of the high affinity binding of oxygen to haemoglobin and the effect of a maximum carrying capacity of blood almost regardless of the inspired oxygen concentration. Breathing 100% oxygen, instead of 20%, increases the total oxygen carried in the blood by only 10% (largely dissolved rather than bound). Nevertheless this is useful in some disease states. However, the main advantage of increasing the inspired oxygen in most disease states is to increase the oxygen concentration in the alveoli, as this is normally two thirds of the inspired oxygen concentration. This enables more oxygen uptake from areas of the lung where the alveolar ventilation did not match its blood perfusion.

Pathology

The effectiveness of breathing can be reduced by disruption of the mechanics of breathing or its control mechanisms either in the brain (respiratory centre) or along the nerve pathways. Common problems are listed below.

A pneumothorax (air in the pleural cavity) occurs if there is damage to the surface lining of the lung after blunt trauma (closed pneumothorax) or spontaneously when an air bleb (a thin-walled, air-filled cyst on the surface of the lung) bursts. The latter usually happens during exercise.

In both cases the air leak can occur through tissue acting as a flap valve. Tension can build up in the pleural cavity as every time a breath is taken more air enters and is then trapped. The tension can compress other structures in the chest including the heart, the big blood vessels and the other lung. Although rare, a tension pneumothorax causes a rapid deterioration in the condition of the casualty and often leads to death.

A penetrating wound to the chest causes an open pneumothorax. This is less harmful than a tension pneumothorax but the mechanics of breathing are still greatly disrupted.

The pleural cavity, though usually only a tiny space, can expand to contain a large volume of fluid including blood (haemothorax).

Multiple rib fractures interfere with the mechanics of breathing. If there is an isolated segment of rib cage (flail segment) that moves independently from the remaining chest wall, the

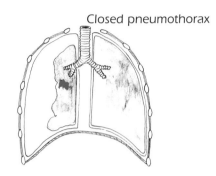
Closed pneumothorax

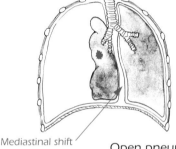
Tension pneumothorax

Mediastinal shift

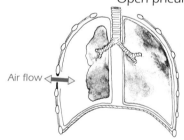
Open pneumothorax

Air flow

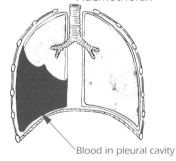
Haemothorax

Blood in pleural cavity

disturbance to breathing is greatest. Switching to diaphragmatic breathing does not improve the mechanics as the flail segment moves in the opposite direction to the rest of the rib cage with some of the minute volume being shunted within the lungs and not contacting fresh air. Worse than this, the lung tissue has been 'bruised' (pulmonary contusion) with oedema and blood filling the alveoli and preventing gas exchange; this is the principal cause of hypoxia.

2nd rib

sternal notch

sternal angle

2 simple fractured ribs

O = needle decompression site

lung bruising (pulmonary contusion)

Flail segment

Downward movement of the diaphragm is prevented in a casualty who has excessive pressure across the abdomen. This happens when a casualty is hanging from a poorly fitting climbing harness or when the stretcher straps are too tight.

Damage to the spinal cord low in the neck region (below the fifth cervical vertebra) may cause paralysis of the intercostal muscles; the casualty must rely on diaphragmatic breathing. This is usually sufficient provided there is no airway obstruction or splintage of the diaphragm. If a spinal cord injury occurs higher in the neck the nerve supply to the diaphragm will also be lost and the casualty will only survive if breathing is done for them. The old medical saying 'C4 keeps you alive' expresses this.

The respiratory centre may fail. The commonest cause is severe damage to the brain. Other causes are drugs that suppress the centre such as the opiates, morphine and buprenorphine. This side effect is common after an intravenous injection but rare after intramuscular use. The respiratory drive often recovers quickly if breathing is maintained artificially for a short period as the drug is redistributed in the body. Alternatively, an injection of naloxone can be given but this also reverses the analgesic effect of the opiate. A cause of temporary respiratory paralysis is electrocution from a lightning strike. The cessation of respiration always demands immediate and effective artificial breathing. In electrocution, if this is started and continued, full recovery can occur even if the respiratory paralysis lasts a long time.

Assessment

The assessment of breathing starts only after airway obstruction has been considered and corrected. As with the airway, continuing to assess the casualty throughout the whole of the rescue is critical, as things readily change over the few hours that the casualty is in the care of the rescuer. Simple observation is the key. Feeling for tenderness and distortion of the rib cage should follow. Comparing one side with the other is good practice and allows much information to be obtained before the ubiquitous stethoscope is brought into play!

In a conscious casualty signs of distress and respiratory effort will be evident. They will complain of 'difficulty breathing'. The respiratory rate should be measured and the type of breathing noted. Cyanosis, the blue colour of blood with low oxygen content, may be detected. Is the breathing diaphragmatic because of pain from rib fractures? Are there any areas of the chest moving in the 'wrong direction' giving a seesaw effect (flail segment) or differently on one side compared with the other? The injured or diseased side is likely to be the one that does not move. You do need to get down to skin if you are going to properly assess the chest - explain to the casualty what you need to do and obtain consent. Removing a bra is required only exceptionally and should not be done unless essential.

An uncomplicated closed pneumothorax may be hard to detect; the degree of difficulty in breathing will be modest. However if a tension pneumothorax has developed more signs will be present. In major trauma, the incidence of a tension pneumothorax has been quoted as 5.4%, rising to 64% in ventilated casualties. In the conscious casualty, chest pain and respiratory distress will be marked. A raised pulse rate and decreased breath sounds on the affected side are common findings. The casualty's oxygen saturation is likely to be reduced though supplementary oxygen will, to some degree, mask the fall in the initial stages. Deviation of the trachea away from the affected side and shock are late signs. (The trachea is normally central in the notch at the top of the sternum.) In the ventilated, unconscious casualty, a tension pneumothorax presents with a sudden fall in oxygen saturation. The sign that clinches the diagnosis is subcutaneous emphysema, a crackling sensation under the skin caused by air trying to escape from the high pressure in the pleural cavity. Pneumothoraces after injury can be complicated by large amounts of blood in the pleural cavity. This can be very difficult to detect and is one of the classic sites of concealed internal haemorrhage. If shock is present and an area of the rib cage is painful a haemothorax should be considered.

In an unconscious casualty separating airway and breathing problems can be very difficult as both often coexist. The airway may be inadequate and the respiratory drive may be reduced. Careful examination of the chest and listening for breath sounds must be carried out. Occasionally a type of breathing where the rate and depth increases and then decreases in a rhythmical pattern (Cheyne-Stokes breathing) is seen. It is associated with severe brain injury or circulatory failure. The rate and depth may reduce so much that the casualty appears to have stopped breathing altogether; it is always a serious sign.

Has the stethoscope any role in mountain rescue?

Rescuers are reminded that the stethoscope was developed long before the chest x-ray and has become a status symbol for doctors. How can you tell who is a doctor nowadays without a stethoscope dangled around their neck! Examining the chest for breath sounds, the gentle sound of air flowing in and out of the chest, can help confirm what has been deduced from looking at and feeling the chest. For example, in all but the smallest pneumothorax no breath sounds will be heard on the affected side and no breath sounds will be heard over a large haemothorax. Added crackles and wheezes may be heard; this confirms a diagnosis of heart failure or asthma but you would not make the diagnosis without a suitable history and other signs because a multitude of other reasons can cause these added sounds. In the noisy environment of mountain rescue, breath sounds are hard to hear. Experience suggests that the role of the stethoscope is very limited until the casualty is being ventilated.

In contrast to the stethoscope, oxygen saturation measurements, obtained by pulse oximetry, have been used on the fells for many years. Despite the limitations outlined in the Monitoring chapter, the use of pulse oximetry has been of practical benefit though, as with all monitors, it does not replace the observant rescuer. A guide to the meaning of the values obtained is given in the box on the next page along with some interesting figures for when you are next at altitude!

Condition	SaO$_2$ (%)	Comments
Normal	97 - 100	
Acute mild hypoxia	93 - 96	Oxygen sensors detect the fall and both the depth and rate of breathing increase.
Acute moderate hypoxia	85 - 93	Anxiety and confusion develop from brain hypoxia. Secondary injury to brain and spinal cord occurs.
Acute severe hypoxia	< 85	Loss of consciousness and circulatory collapse imminent.
Well acclimatised at 3660m	84.5	Acclimatisation is the process that allows people to cope with the hypoxaemia of altitude; without this process they would be unconscious in minutes
Well acclimatised at 6140m	65.6	And still able to climb upwards!
Chronic hypoxia (from lung or heart disease)	85 - 96	Tolerated by adaptations to the oxygen release process at the tissue level. Breathing rate normalises as the oxygen sensors become desensitised. Exercise capacity very limited

Treatment

Recognition of a breathing problem is the first goal in treatment. In the conscious casualty it is likely that the casualty will complain of difficulty getting his breath; often the problem is assessing the cause and severity of the symptom. However in the unconscious, it is the rescuer that has to actively search for breathing problems. Treatment of any breathing problem always follows treatment of the airway.

General treatment

Oxygen

Moving oxygen to the alveoli is one of the core tasks of breathing. Increasing the concentration at the mouth, by using extra oxygen, would seem to be of value. It is! This is particularly true if there are other injuries. In mountain rescue, the types of patient with chronic hypoxia that could be made worse by oxygen will not be seen, so

high concentrations can be used on all casualties. The equipment used should be a non-rebreathing mask with a reservoir attached to an oxygen cylinder capable of supplying 15 litres per minute. This is now standard teaching and should be adopted, at
least initially, in all cases. In certain conditions this may be unnecessary, or even detrimental, but when time allows the oxygen flow rate can be adjusted. Please refer to the section on myocardial infarction for a more detailed discussion. Despite the introduction of lighter and higher-pressure oxygen cylinders, there will still be cases where the oxygen has to be rationed to last through the evacuation. Titrating the flow rate to the casualty's oxygen saturation is appealing and deserves more attention.

'Adapting' breathing equipment to suit must not be tried; there are many considerations, such as 'dead space' and the breathing pattern of the casualty, that are critical to the actual oxygen concentration reaching the alveoli. Serious problems with carbon dioxide retention can be easier to induce by 'adaptations'.

Artificial breathing

The minute volume of the casualty may be too small, causing unconsciousness from brain hypoxia and carbon dioxide retention. Artificial breathing (assisted ventilation) is needed. This can be achieved using the exhaled air from the rescuer (mouth-to-mouth; mouth-to-face shield; mouth-to-mask device) or by using a bag-valve-mask. (Some teams and many helicopters even have portable ventilators.)

Mouth-to-mouth ventilation remains the standard technique; it requires no equipment and, though it delivers a lower concentration of oxygen than in the air (14%), its use should not be abandoned. The risk of infection passing from the casualty to the rescuer is extremely small; there is no documented case of HIV transmission by mouth-to-mouth ventilation.

In organised rescue, aids to facilitate artificial breathing are likely to be available and are considered to have ventilatory advantages (in terms of tidal volume being within the recommended range) over mouth-to-mouth ventilation. ICAR recommend a mouth-to-mask device is used; particularly one with an axillary oxygen port so that the casualty's inspired oxygen concentration can potentially be increased. Unfortunately no model with an oxygen reservoir is available. Mouth-to-face shield ventilation cannot be recommended.

courtesy of Dr Werner Beikircher

Bag-valve-mask ventilation with a reservoir bag has the potential to provide the casualty with the highest inspired oxygen concentration (95% with an oxygen flow rate of 12 litres/min). There is concern that the tidal volumes given may be excessive particularly in a casualty with an unprotected airway but this can be overcome by using small bag sizes (500 - 700ml) rather than the current standard adult bag. However the technique is complex and frequently requires two rescuers; one to provide the C-clamp and one to squeeze the bag.

Whatever artificial ventilation technique is used, studies have shown a high incidence of stomach inflation often because the tidal volumes given are excessive. Stomach inflation can cause the stomach contents to regurgitate and then aspirate into the lungs with the next inflation. This is a serious problem; a suction device and light source should be instantly available and the rescuer should try to maintain an ability to turn the casualty on their side or tilt them 20° 'head down' should regurgitation occur.

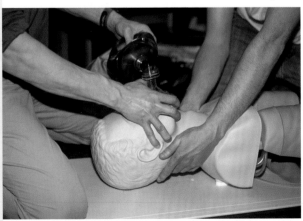
Bag-valve-mask ventilation using C-clamp technique with a second rescuer immobilising the neck.

Artificial ventilation makes a tension pneumothorax declare itself. Subcutaneous emphysema can become gross and the pressure needed to inflate the lungs too great for the bag and mask. Decompressing the tension pneumothorax is dealt with later in this chapter.

Much has been written recently on the risks of overventilation both in terms of stomach inflation and poorer outcomes, possibly from the resultant low blood carbon dioxide concentration. The recommended minute volume is now a tidal volume of 500ml (6-7ml/kg body weight) with 10 breaths per minute. A breath should be delivered smoothly over one second and the chest should still be seen to rise and fall. Despite this, in practical terms, under ventilation, due to an air leak around the mask or a partially obstructed airway remains the commonest problem.

All ventilation techniques require regular training and practice (at least six monthly) if skills are to be maintained.

Extended management

Protecting the airway from regurgitation and providing a breathing system with few leaks and a high-inspired oxygen concentration is standard practice during prolonged artificial ventilation. Both endotracheal intubation and Laryngeal Mask Airway insertion are skills that should be considered for health care professionals and a few Casualty Carers. Inserting a LMA may be the most appropriate to help protect the airway and ease the effort of maintaining an open airway for those of us that rarely have to intubate a patient. Once learnt, the technique is reliable and probably an easier method than endotracheal intubation, particularly as muscle relaxation is unlikely to be used. However, there is very little published pre-hospital research to confirm this impression and the risk of aspiration in trauma cases is unknown. Hyperventilation is likely to occur in a protected airway so a 500 - 700ml bag should be used and, if possible, the end-tidal carbon dioxide concentration measured. Supplementary oxygen is recommended to reverse the inefficiency of the ventilation.

Laryngeal mask

Analgesia

Many breathing problems are very painful and benefit from analgesia. However of the drugs (Entonox®, morphine and diclofenac) available, care has to be taken to balance the improvement in breathing with any side effects caused by the drug. Entonox® worsens a tension pneumothorax as the nitrous oxide diffuses rapidly into the pleural cavity. (See Drugs chapter) How often this happens in reality is unclear; Entonox® is a valuable drug particularly when the casualty is being transferred onto the stretcher. The analgesic effect should rapidly reverse when the Entonox® is stopped but the damage caused by the expanded pleural cavity may not. So Entonox® should be avoided in any chest injury where the ribs appear damaged. Morphine causes a reduction in the rate and depth of breaths by acting on the respiratory centre in the brain. The effect can be severe if the casualty is breathing 'as hard as they can' to maintain homoeostasis. This occurs in a complicated chest injury. However in a simple rib fracture, morphine is entirely safe and very appropriate. Good assessment skills and a cautious approach, perhaps starting with 5 mg intramuscularly in an adult, are needed to avoid giving morphine to the wrong casualty. Oral diclofenac is an alternative to morphine without the risk of respiratory depression but it may not have enough analgesic action and is slow to work.

Intercostal local anaesthetic infiltration and nerve blocks do not feature in recent pre-hospital papers. Though effective, have the complication rates barred their use?

Specific treatment

Rib fractures

Analgesia and support, usually by padding the casualty on the injured side, is sufficient for simple rib fractures. The casualty should be assessed in hospital to exclude any complicating factors but a chest x-ray is not always needed. A flail segment is a much more serious injury. Oxygen and careful padding to reduce the paradoxical movement of the flail segment are needed. Adequate pain relief to allow chest expansion is more important than aggressively 'padding in' the segment. The latter is so painful that it works against any advantage from reducing the seesaw movements and, as we have seen, most of the hypoxia is due to pulmonary contusion anyway. As there is a chance that the casualty will become exhausted, evacuation by helicopter is appropriate.

For experienced Doctors faced with a casualty *in extremis*, there is a place for anaesthesia and artificial ventilation but bear in mind that any tension pneumothorax will worsen and treatment is likely to be required to decompress the pleural cavity.

Pneumothorax

A casualty usually tolerates an uncomplicated pneumothorax; no specific interventions are needed. A tension pneumothorax however is a life-threatening emergency; casualties have died on the fells from this condition. In a non-ventilated casualty, the condition may stabilise but frequently deteriorates over time until a respiratory arrest occurs. In the ventilated, the deterioration is sudden and often dramatic.

The treatment aims to relieve the high pressure in the pleural cavity by inserting a large bore needle (such as a 14-gauge cannula) into the cavity. This procedure, called needle thoracostomy or decompression, is indicated in non-ventilated casualties when there are signs of significant respiratory or circulatory distress, such as an oxygen saturation of <92% on oxygen, systolic BP <90mmHg or respiratory rate <10. Rescuers may feel that, with appropriate instruction, this is a technique within their scope. Certainly, Doctors should consider it as a skill that they can bring to mountain rescue.

The site to perform needle decompression is usually the second intercostal space in line with the middle of the clavicle. (The second rib abuts on to the sternum at the sternal angle – see page 83) As with all chest wall procedures, try to avoid the intercostal artery by going in perpendicular to the skin just above the rib defining the lower margin of the space. The standard 14-gauge cannula is only 4.5cm long and may fail to penetrate the pleural cavity in up to a third of casualties. A 7cm trocar may be more appropriate or consider inserting the needle in the 4th or 5th intercostal space in the mid-axillary line where the pleura is nearer the surface. Attaching a syringe partially filled with sterile water or saline may help confirm that the pleural cavity has been penetrated as air can be drawn into the syringe barrel. Needle decompression can cause complications such as haemorrhage and pneumothorax but, perhaps more importantly, it cannot be used to exclude a tension pneumothorax because of the moderate failure rate of the technique. A tube thoracostomy (chest drain) by blunt dissection may be a more appropriate technique. This is particularly true in the ventilated casualty where the role of 'speculative' needle decompression has been questioned.

A successful decompression is usually an indication for a tube thoracostomy. Whether this needs to be done at the incident site or can be delayed until after the evacuation will depend on the casualty's condition, the evacuation time and the equipment and expertise available. A ventilated casualty is likely to need a tube thoracostomy performed within minutes of decompression.

The breathing difficulty caused by a penetrating wound to the chest (open pneumothorax) is reduced if an airtight dressing is applied over the wound. The rescuer should notice an improvement almost immediately. If the dressing starts bulging a tension pneumothorax has developed. Lifting one edge of the dressing should allow for the exit of air under tension while preventing the inward suction of air.

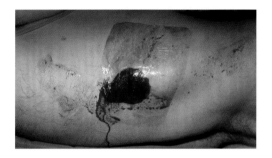

Evacuation

Any casualty with a significant chest injury may become exhausted so rapid evacuation should be planned. The speed of evacuation and low altitudes flown by helicopters make them an appropriate choice. It is unlikely that the reduced atmospheric pressure of altitude will be critical to outcome in the UK.

Blencathra, Lake District. (2003)

Case study - Chest injury

This case is fictional but was developed from several real cases. It was commissioned for *Casualty Care in Mountain Rescue* to contribute a sense of real life and to draw attention to the dilemmas that occur in rescue work.

Time and date: 21.00 on 11th of June

Location: Track up steep valley side above village

Weather: Dry and sunny

Cause of incident: Fall from horse whilst riding along a rough track

Reported injuries: "Back injuries"

An incident on a beautiful evening just above the local watering hole! The initial call had gone to the ambulance service. They had been unable to get their vehicle to the scene. The casualty, a 46-year-old lady, had fallen from a horse whilst trotting and was clearly distressed with pain. The casualty was able to give a history; she remembered falling and hitting her right side on the ground. She then hit her head on a stone but didn't think she had lost consciousness. Her companion confirmed the history. Her riding helmet had been removed. Examination quickly confirmed that she was finding breathing difficult. She was taking short shallow breaths at an increased rate of 40 breaths a minute. She was using her left hand to support the painful area of the chest. She was not cyanosed; her pulse rate was 120. Further gentle examination showed the area of tenderness extended from below the armpit to the spine between the shoulder blades. There was a little swelling but no subcutaneous emphysema. The breath sounds were equal on both sides of the chest and the trachea was central above the sternum. There were no other apparent injuries.

A diagnosis of fractured ribs was made. Pain relief was required so it was elected to give 7.5 mg of Cyclimorph® by the intramuscular route. Whilst waiting for this to have an effect, her blood pressure (160/96) and oxygen saturation (98%) were measured. In view of the history of a fall and tenderness spreading round to the spine along combined with a painful injury, the potential for a spinal injury had to be considered. A cervical collar was fitted and she was carefully 'log rolled' onto a vacuum mattress. As the morphine took effect her pain and respiratory rate reduced. The oxygen saturation remained 98%. Moving the casualty to the ambulance was tolerable with frequent reassurance.

Comments

The chest needs to be examined and this cannot be done through three layers of fleece! Rescuers can be a bit bashful at looking and feeling around the rib cage particularly when the casualty is female. The early telltale signs of a more serious chest injury will be missed if these inhibitions are not overcome. Explanation and considering the casualty's modesty go a long way to developing the correct approach. Baring all to the fell side would be a mistake; it is extremely rare that a bra needs to be removed. The casualty should feel confident to consenting to the examination. The early signs of a complex or serious injury, for example subcutaneous emphysema, may be found over a small area at first but are, never the less, very important. It can almost be guaranteed that serious breathing difficulties will develop over the next minutes or hours.

Analgesia for chest injuries has become complicated by over zealous generalisations. Certainly, both Entonox® and morphine can cause a worsening of respiratory function in chest injuries, but this is rare and particularly in an uncomplicated injury, such as simple rib fractures. Both have been safely used in chest injuries but Entonox® should be last on the list as a tension pneumothorax would be a tragic and terrifying experience. Oxygen delivery into the blood is often improved by giving the right amount of pain relief even in the more serious chest injuries.

References

Eaton CJ. *Essentials of Immediate Medical Care* 2nd edition 1999. ISBN 0443 05345 6

Auerbach PS. *Wilderness Medicine* 3rd edition 1995; ISBN 0 8016 7044 6

Paal P, Ellerton JA, Sumann G, Demetz F, Mair P, Brugger H. Basic Life Support ventilation in mountain rescue. Official recommendations of the International Commission for Mountain Emergency Medicine (ICAR MEDCOM) 2006 *in press*

Leigh-Smith S, Harris T. Tension pneumothorax - time for a re-think? *Emerg Med J* 2005; 22:8-16

L'Ciaval, Alta Badia, Dolomites. (2005)

Circulation

Objectives
Appreciate the basic anatomy and physiology
Understand the principles and types of shock
Find a pulse and count its rate
Assess, classify and manage a patient with shock
(appropriate to your skill level)

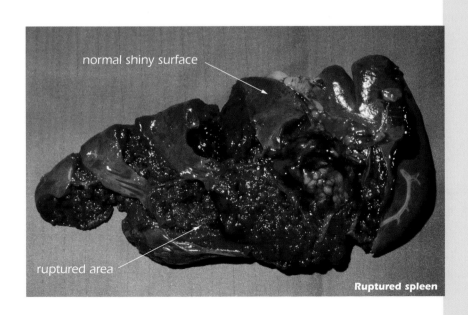

normal shiny surface

ruptured area

Ruptured spleen

Introduction

The term 'circulation' is designed to focus the rescuer on the process of getting oxygenated blood from the lungs, through the heart, to the rest of the body and thereby supplying oxygen to the tissues. In simple words, it is about having enough blood and an effective pump, the heart, to move the oxygen around. But it is not that simple; not only do we have to consider the removal of waste products through the lungs and kidneys but also how the failure of the circulation leads to shock and multiple organ failure. Apart from the very simple measures in the first edition of *Casualty Care in Mountain Rescue* this section has changed the most. Though the complexities of what we are dealing with have become clearer, definitive answers are still a way off.

About 30% of those dying of trauma will die within several minutes of their accident and the cause will be a direct consequence of a devastating primary injury. Examples would include massive crush injury, major head injury or high cervical spinal cord transection. The vast majority of these deaths will be unavoidable; a small number may be preventable by, for example, wearing a helmet.

About 50% of trauma deaths occur within 60 to 90 minutes of the injury. In these cases the severity of the primary injury is not fatal but secondary injury develops and leads to death. Here we have the opportunity to intervene and evidence shows that about a third could survive if they are correctly managed. This is the 'Golden Hour'. The factors contributing to death are airway, breathing and circulation failure. The time to definitive care (particularly to hospitals that have the equipment and skills to control bleeding) is also an important factor and one that could be significantly altered by using a helicopter.

The remaining 20% of trauma deaths occur 10 to 14 days after the event and are often due to infections, kidney and multi-organ failure, and other complications of severe injury. Progress is being made to reduce death in this phase. An important factor is getting the management right in the early stages and, particularly, correcting an inadequate circulation. Shock is the major cause of 'preventable death'.

Against this background, we have to consider the studies that have been carried out on mountain accidents. The vast majority of 'our' casualties suffer from blunt trauma (as opposed to penetrating trauma from knives and bullets) with the most seriously injured having 'polytrauma' - blunt trauma to multiple organ systems. In all casualties (both the survivors and fatalities), bleeding to death is an uncommon cause of death though personal experience and Stephen Hearn's Scottish mountain rescue casualty study suggest that exsanguination may contribute to deaths occurring during the evacuation of the casualty. The analysis of mountain accidents to date suggests that there is more to be gained by correctly managing the injured spine. These considerations will have a bearing on whether it is effective to train team members in the more advanced skills of cannulation and intravenous fluid administration.

Shock is the word used to describe the complex state of the body when the circulation is failing. Inadequate perfusion of the tissues leads to a lack of oxygen in the tissue, consequently normal cellular metabolism falters and a cascade of changes in the cells and their surroundings are started that ultimately leads to cell death. Shock is not a disease in its own right but a consequence of a circulatory disturbance and it is the severity and duration of the disturbance that dictates the outcome for the individual. Much of the clinical course is determined early in the pathological process.

Anatomy and physiology

The circulatory system can be divided into three essential components. Each component can fail in its own right or each can partially contribute to the failure of the circulation as a whole. The three components are the heart (pump), the blood (fluid) and the blood vessels (container)

The heart is a complex pump composed of specialized muscle fibres that make up the myocardium. As with all muscle, the myocardium needs a blood supply and this is provided by the coronary arteries. With the aid of one-way valves blood is squeezed in one direction. The heart is really two pumps in-line with the lungs connected in between. The right side of the heart receives venous blood from the body and pumps it to the lungs where it is oxygenated. The blood then returns to the left side of the heart. Here it is squeezed again, propelling it at higher pressure through the aorta and then the other arteries to the rest of the body. The body's tissues extract oxygen and, by way of the veins, return the oxygen-depleted blood to the right side of the heart to complete the circuit.

The heart from the front

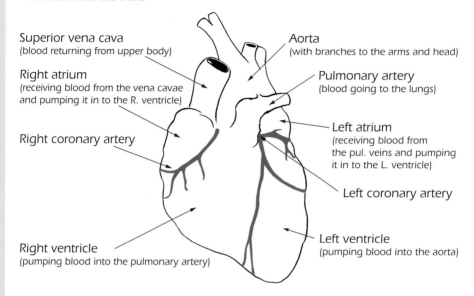

Superior vena cava
(blood returning from upper body)

Aorta
(with branches to the arms and head)

Right atrium
(receiving blood from the vena cavae
and pumping it in to the R. ventricle)

Pulmonary artery
(blood going to the lungs)

Right coronary artery

Left atrium
(receiving blood from
the pul. veins and pumping
it in to the L. ventricle)

Left coronary artery

Left ventricle
(pumping blood into the aorta)

Right ventricle
(pumping blood into the pulmonary artery)

The amount of fluid pumped with each heartbeat is called the stroke volume (SV) and the amount pumped per minute is known as the cardiac output (CO). A simple equation can be written:

CO = SV x heart rate (HR)

At rest, the average SV is 70 ml and the HR is 70 beats per minute. Therefore the CO is approximately 5 litres per minute. The cardiac output is balanced to the metabolic needs of the body. At times of exercise, when the oxygen consumption of the body increases, both the SV and the HR increase. The CO can reach 25 litres per minute. The HR should be the same as the radial or carotid pulse rate except when the heart is going so fast either it does not fill with enough blood to give a pulse or you can't count fast enough.

The blood consists of 60% plasma (predominantly water) and 40% cells. The cells have a number of important functions and are divided into types depending on their function. The red blood cells carry oxygen, the white blood cells fight infection and the platelets help plug any holes! It is the red blood cells that are critical from our perspective as they avidly take up oxygen in the lungs and release it to the tissues. Red cells contain a special protein for this task called haemoglobin. For further details see the sections on oxygen and carbon dioxide transport in the Breathing chapter, and pulse oximetry in the Monitoring chapter.

The blood vessels are the containers through which blood is pumped and are divided up into arteries, veins and capillaries depending on the direction of flow (arteries away from the heart) and their function. Capillaries allow oxygen to diffuse into the tissues. The system must not leak, otherwise blood volume will be lost and oxygen delivery will fail. Unlike a normal pipe, the size of a blood vessel is variable - the wall of a blood vessel contain muscle fibres that can contract or relax - so the resistance to blood flow can be altered. This can be on a regional scale diverting blood away from less important organs, such as the skin, to more important organs, like the brain and heart, in times of stress. The muscle fibres in the blood vessel walls are controlled by signals from both nerves (largely sympathetic nerves) and hormones released from endocrine glands. Adrenaline (epinephrine), released into the blood from the adrenal glands, is the best known of these. Normally the blood vessels are slightly constricted under the influence of the sympathetic nerves. If a tissue uses up more oxygen than usual, the blood vessels feeding the tissue dilate causing the blood flow to increase. This effect, along with the ability of the sympathetic system to divert blood to vital tissues in times of stress, guarantees an efficient use of the available oxygen. If all the vessels became maximally dilated, the volume of the blood vessels would far exceed the blood volume. The pressure in the container would fall and the circulation of blood through the arteries and veins would cease and flow would be determined by gravity alone. The normal, partially constricted state of the arteries must be maintained by most of the blood vessels in order to maintain an adequate blood pressure (BP).

The BP under which the circulation will work effectively depends on many factors. Important ones include gravity, the thickness (viscosity) of the blood and whether there is any narrowing in the internal diameter of the blood vessels.

Pathology

Shock is a state when, due to a derangement of the circulatory system, there is inadequate perfusion of the tissues leading to 'too little' oxygen being delivered for normal cellular metabolism.

Compensation

If the injury or insult to the body allows, the body compensates for shock by increasing both stroke volume and heart rate. This is achieved largely by activating the sympathetic nervous system and can be very effective especially in children and those who are physically fit. These individuals can have significant injuries yet their ability to compensate is so great that to the unwary rescuer they may appear 'well'. However, a point is reached when the casualty can no longer compensate; at this stage they deteriorate catastrophically.

End-organ perfusion

This is a useful concept in both the early stages of shock and its consequences - multi-organ failure. End-organ perfusion looks at how an organ is functioning on its current oxygen supply. As shock develops, the brain rapidly reflects the reduced oxygen supply by reducing its higher mental functions. This is reflected in a reduced level of consciousness.

Causes of shock

These are heart failure, blood loss or an increase in capacity of the blood vessels.

Heart failure

Damage to the heart will affect its ability to work efficiently as a pump. A reduced stroke volume or heart rate will reduce cardiac output and, if severe enough, reduce oxygen delivery to the tissues resulting in shock. Of course, the heart itself is a muscle with its own metabolic need and oxygen demand. When the circulation begins to fail the heart also suffers and may become too weak to effectively pump blood. Pump failure occurs for three main reasons:

The heart muscle may be injured either by a direct blow to the chest wall over the sternum or, more commonly, when its own blood supply is stopped (myocardial infarction). The heart becomes too weak to squeeze enough blood through the one-way valves.

The rhythm of the heart may be too slow (bradycardia) or too quick (tachycardia). This can result from heart damage, drugs or hypothermia. The

Outline of the heart and carotid arteries

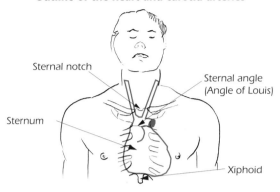

rhythm may also become irregular and uncoordinated as a response to a number of insults. The efficiency of pumping may be slightly affected (e.g. atrial fibrillation) or totally disrupted (e.g. ventricular fibrillation).

The stroke volume of the heart may be too small. If the heart does not receive sufficient venous blood from the body it does not fill adequately between beats and cardiac output is not maintained. Outside pressure on the heart (cardiac tamponade) preventing it from filling with blood between beats is rare but occurs in the presence of a tension pneumothorax or when there is blood in the sac around the heart.

Blood loss (Hypovolaemic or haemorrhagic shock)

When a casualty has been injured, blood loss is by far the most common cause of shock. The bleeding can be external, and therefore obvious, or internal and more easily missed (thus the name - concealed haemorrhage). The blood volume can also be reduced in casualties with burns, diarrhoea and vomiting, diabetic ketoacidosis or dehydration.

Increased blood vessel capacity

If the normal constriction (vasomotor tone) of the blood vessels is lost, the available blood has to fill a much greater space resulting in a fall in blood pressure, which may cause insufficient oxygen to be delivered to a tissue. This happens when a casualty has:

A simple faint where, due to a psychological stress (e.g. the sight of blood), prolonged immobility (the soldier on parade) or sudden movements (standing up suddenly), the blood vessels are unable to compensate for the effect of gravity. Pooling of blood in the veins of the legs occurs; the venous return to the heart falls and with it the cardiac output. The brain does not receive enough oxygen so consciousness is lost. Fortunately the casualty usually falls over, eliminating the effect of gravity! The blood returns to the heart and the casualty regains consciousness quickly.

Neurogenic shock when a spinal cord injury stops the sympathetic nerves from controlling the diameter of the blood vessels. At times of stress the sympathetic nervous system increases the heart rate and also the vasomotor tone. This diverts blood to where it is most urgently required. There is no better description of this response than 'the fight or flight response'. To balance the actions of this system the body has a system capable of the opposite actions, the parasympathetic nervous system, which tries to slow the heart. It is the dynamic equilibrium between these two control systems that keeps the body finely tuned to its environment and circumstances. The sympathetic nerves run in the spinal cord and can be damaged in spinal injuries; indeed the whole system can be lost in a cervical spine injury. In contrast, the parasympathetic system is outside the spinal cord and is not damaged. Therefore, in a high spinal injury, there is a potential for unopposed parasympathetic activity to occur. This results in a slowing of the heart rate and the loss of vasomotor tone. In neurogenic shock the patient has a low blood pressure, a slow pulse and a warm skin. This rare form of shock differs from hypovolaemic shock where a fall in blood pressure can be offset by an increase in the heart rate.

Anaphylactic shock when a patient develops a dramatic and severe allergic reaction. Triggers include bee stings and drugs. Please refer to the section on anaphylaxis in the Medical chapter for more detail.

Septic shock may be encountered when a patient develops a blood borne infection. Some cases of meningococcal infection present like this.

Assessment

Shock may be obvious but, at other times, it is insidious and concealed. In the early stages, shock is hard to detect as the body compensates. Many organs in the body can manage with less oxygen, at least for a time before they fail. There is no simple test or observation that shows that shock is present. Rescuers must think of the history and examine the casualty for the constellation of symptoms and signs that develop in shock. The average adult blood losses from common fractures are shown below.

Though rare in mountain rescue, undetected, underestimated and under-treated shock is the prime cause of preventable deaths in the injured casualty. Team members must think of the effects of trauma as dynamic (i.e. evolving with time) and reassess the casualty regularly.

Average adult blood lost	
in the first 4 hours after injury	
Upper arm	500 - 1000ml
Lower leg	500 - 1000ml
Shaft of femur	1000 - 2000ml
Rib fracture - haemothorax	150 - 2000ml
Pelvis	500 - 3000ml
If the fracture is compound, the amount is doubled.	
Scalp laceration	250 - 1000ml
Ruptured spleen or liver	1000 - 4000ml

Symptoms and signs of shock

The early symptoms and signs of shock reflect the pathophysiology described above. In summary, they are: a raised pulse; pale skin; thirst; raised respiratory rate; general weakness; anxiousness then confusion or aggression followed by drowsiness and coma and reduced blood pressure. In most cases the appearance of the symptoms and signs relate to the amount of blood loss as shown in the box below. However, please note that no one sign is infallible; in one study, 35% of patients with trauma and a systolic BP of <100mmHg had a pulse rate of <100/min. Nevertheless, the best parameters to measure are the pulse rate, respiratory rate, the Glasgow Coma Scale, and systolic blood pressure and combine them with an appropriate history. The cold environment affects the capillary refill time and pulse oximetry often fails to pick up a reliable signal, so these parameters should not be used.

Class of haemorrhagic shock (adult)						
	% loss	Vol.(ml)	Pulse	RR	Mental state	BP	Example
I	<15	750	<100	<16	alert	normal	lower leg fracture
II	15-30	8-1500	1-120	16-20	anxious	normal	femoral shaft
III	30-40	15-2000	>120	>20	confused	reduced	fractured pelvis
IV	>40	>2000	>140	>20	drowsy/coma	very low	ruptured spleen

Finding a pulse

Finding a pulse and counting its rate is fundamental to first aid and medicine. The counting bit is easy; finding the pulse in the first place is the hard bit!

Counting the pulse

Count the number of beats in 15 seconds and then multiply by 4 giving the pulse rate per minute; above 140, it is hard to keep up but it is fair to say the casualty is pretty ill. The 'normal' pulse rate is about 60 to 70 at rest and, in the absence of pain, it quickly returns to this range after exercise. A slow pulse (bradycardia) is a rate of less than 60 per minute. A fit athlete and a person on beta-blockers can have this with no consequence; however, heart block or a severe head injury can also cause a slow pulse and indicate a serious problem. A fast pulse rate (tachycardia) is more common and is defined as a rate of greater than 100 per minute. Exercise, anxiety and pain cause a tachycardia; more worrying causes are shock and abnormal heart rhythms (arrhythmia). Now find your pulse!

Where to feel a pulse

Finding a pulse, particularly in the emergency situation, is hard - indeed the BLS guidelines have dropped it because the procedure is time consuming and inaccurate in up to 50% of cases. Having said that, in the majority of casualties - those showing signs of life - finding a pulse and counting its rate is helpful and a standard part of the primary survey. Knowing the anatomy and practice is essential. *(In an exam feeling for a pulse in the wrong place is a bad, almost fatal, mistake - editor.)*

Radial pulse

Though sometimes absent, the radial pulse can usually be felt if the systolic blood pressure is greater than 80mmHg. Start by looking at the palm of the hand. At the base of the thumb, where the skin changes from palm-type to forearm type, gently place your index, middle and ring fingers on the lateral (outside) aspect of the casualty's forearm. Rock your fingers round to the front surface of the forearm and press a little harder. *Hey presto,* you will feel a pulse. Other tips are to extend the casualty's wrist backwards by about 30 degrees (but not too far as the pulse gets harder to feel again), and check that you are feeling between the tendons going to the back of the thumb and the large tendon running from the forearm to the wrist. (Try flexing the wrist against resistance to make this tendon stand out.)

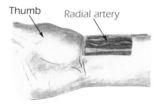
Thumb   Radial artery

Carotid pulse

Feeling the carotid pulse can be uncomfortable and frightening to the casualty. Explain what you are doing and be gentle - light pressure is all that is needed; firm pressure can cause a severe bradycardia and collapse. With the head and neck in the neutral position, find the thyroid notch (Adam's apple) in the mid line. Roll your fingers gently down the sides of the thyroid cartilage and towards the posterior (back) edge, the pulse is felt about 2 cm from the mid line. Further laterally a muscle running from the sternum to the mastoid (behind the ear) gets in the way; so don't come in from the side - always start in the middle.

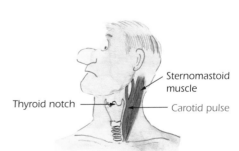
Sternomastoid muscle
Thyroid notch
Carotid pulse

Capillary Refill Time

The capillary refill time (CRT) is often taught as a method for detecting shock. The patient's skin (usually a nail) is compressed for five seconds with sufficient pressure to cause blanching. After release of the compression, the time taken for the area to return to the same colour as the surrounding skin is measured. The upper limit of normal is two seconds. Unfortunately, this figure has no scientific basis; in a cold environment and in the presence of poor ambient lighting the CRT is often prolonged when shock is not present. A CRT of two seconds or less will indicate good peripheral perfusion, but a prolonged CRT should be interpreted cautiously in the mountain rescue environment. Look at other circulatory parameters, such as pulse rate, conscious level and blood pressure in preference.

Measuring blood pressure

As shock develops, the peripheral pulses become weaker in character and more difficult to feel. The pulse may only be detectable and counted centrally, i.e. the femoral pulse in the groin or the carotid pulse in the neck. Measuring blood pressure can be a difficult and time-consuming procedure in mountain rescue; it is recommended that a systolic BP be measured manually by the technique described here. For further details on measuring blood pressure please refer to the relevant section in the Monitoring chapter.

Alternatively, determining which pulses are palpable can be used to estimate the systolic BP. The following 'rules' are practical and well accepted measurements though whether accurate or not is unclear.

Measuring a manual systolic BP
Use the most convenient uninjured arm. Blow up the BP cuff until the brachial pulse disappears. Slowly let the pressure down and note the pressure when the brachial or radial pulse just appears. This is the systolic BP.

Brachial pulse

Radial pulse

Deflate the cuff completely between readings.

Palpable radial pulse = systolic blood pressure >80 mm Hg
Palpable femoral pulse = systolic blood pressure >70 mm Hg
Palpable carotid pulse = systolic blood pressure >60 mm Hg

In view of the body's compensation, it may be felt that measuring BP is an unnecessary luxury. Certainly delaying an evacuation even by a few minutes to measure BP in a shocked casualty is not appropriate unless advanced techniques of management are readily available and the casualty's pulse and consciousness level indicates deterioration.

Concealed haemorrhage

The cause of shock after trauma is invariably due to bleeding. The site of blood loss may be obvious, i.e. gross external bleeding from a large open wound or an arterial injury, but this is usually not the case. It is vital that all the body compartments, into which large volumes of blood could be lost, are systematically assessed as part of the assessment of the circulation.

The chest will have been examined as part of the breathing assessment and a large haemothorax hopefully excluded. Heart failure caused by tension pneumothorax or cardiac tamponade may be apparent. The abdomen is one of the most common sites for concealed haemorrhage. The liver or spleen is frequently damaged. Gently press over all areas of the abdomen to see if there is any tenderness. If the patient complains of pain take this very seriously. Bleeding behind the abdomen (the retroperitoneum) is very difficult to diagnose. It is often associated with fractures of the lumbar spine or pelvis. Signs of these fractures will be present. Fractures of the femur, in an adult, can result in the loss of 1000 ml of blood (20% of the circulating volume). This should be tolerable in the fit individual but if associated with additional blood loss elsewhere may 'tip them over the edge'. Quickly assess the upper legs for a fractured femur.

Treatment

When shock is recognized or the potential for it to develop has been identified, urgent steps should be taken to control external haemorrhage by direct pressure (if applicable) and get the casualty to definitive care. The best initial treatment is the application of the general principles of resuscitation, regardless of the cause of the shock. That is ensuring an open airway, optimising the mechanics of breathing and giving oxygen at 15 litres/min using a non-rebreathing mask with a reservoir. Once these components have been optimised then other treatments can be introduced. Remember the definition of shock is 'inadequate tissue perfusion leading to a failure of oxygen delivery'. If each of the components of the oxygen delivery system is improved the effect of shock can be reduced. The rescuer is unlikely to be able to offer definitive care on the mountain side - even the RAF helicopters lack an operating theatre!

Lie the casualty down and elevate the legs if possible. Control external haemorrhage by direct pressure, elevation and dressings. (Refer to 'Managing a soft tissue injury' in the Extremities chapter for details.) Internal haemorrhage needs to be anticipated and appropriate evacuation plans made. Minimise blood loss from a fracture by splinting. It is particularly useful to apply a traction splint to a fractured femur and to stabilise a fractured pelvis with the application of a vacuum mattress.

Elevation alone will often stop bleeding

In anaphylactic shock give the potent vasoconstrictor adrenaline (epinephrine) by subcutaneous or intramuscular injection.

MAST (Medical Anti-Shock Trousers)

These garments are wrapped round the legs and lower torso and then inflated to a pressure of 60-100 mm Hg in an attempt to squeeze fluid into the upper body and control blood loss in the lower body. Studies have shown no advantage to the casualty, indeed the use of MAST may increase mortality. In cases of a fractured pelvis causing shock, the pelvic and abdominal compression may have a role to play but simpler devices are available to perform this role. The use of MAST should be abandoned.

Evacuation

All cases of shock have a high priority for a rapid evacuation. This is also reflected in the triage sieve when multiple casualties are being assessed. Shock is often reversible and early effective surgical treatment to stop bleeding improves the casualty's outlook. Emergency operations and radiological techniques to control blood loss are literally life-saving. In other situations, fluids or drugs can be effective. Time is of the essence so helicopter evacuation should be the norm; anticipating this at an early stage of a rescue from the history is quite acceptable.

Summary

Have an index of suspicion based upon the mechanism of the injury. Be pro-active and ask yourself:

Is this patient shocked? Is there any obvious external haemorrhage? Is there the possibility of concealed haemorrhage? Assess the level of consciousness and the state of the peripheral circulation - is the radial pulse present? Apply A, B, C and control external haemorrhage. Be suspicious for internal bleeding. Evacuate the casualty as speedily as his condition and your suspicions dictate.

Extended management

Cannulation

Cannulation is an advanced technique that enables direct access to the circulation. Drugs and fluids can be placed in the blood and transported round the body almost instantly. Compared with a drug taken by mouth or given intramuscularly, the delay in action is frequently reduced though is not always instant as the drug still has to diffuse to its site of action. Usually this involves crossing a barrier, such as the blood-brain barrier, which takes a finite time depending on properties of the drug such as its fat solubility. The table below is for morphine.

Comparision of routes of administration			
	time to max effect	duration	typical adult dose
Oral	2hr	6hr	20-30mg
For a single dose, five times the dose given parentally is needed.			
Intramuscular	1.5hr	4hr	10-15mg
Relatively smooth drug concentration. Effective analgesia in 20min.			
Intravenous	20min	4hr	5-8mg
High concentration if given as bolus. Effective analgesia in 5min.			

Cannulation is not easy particularly in those casualties that need it most as the veins are constricted. It is frustrating and time consuming to the operator, and painful to the recipient! No more than two attempts should be made. In almost all pre-hospital care situations, cannulation should not delay evacuation as it has been shown that the time to transfer to definitive care is an important factor in outcome. Whether this is true for mountain rescue is unknown - it may be that the time critical injuries, such as internal bleeding, are rare in our situation, so time to insert a cannula and achieve adequate analgesia is acceptable. However we don't know and the best course of action would be to follow the majority particularly when we have the option of a rapid helicopter evacuation (though here other considerations will be raised when we look at the role of helicopters). Cannulation in a helicopter, with the inevitable noise and vibration, is possible but even harder than on the ground; it is easy to fail and this needs to be considered if the casualty is likely to deteriorate and drugs need to be given during the flight.

Anatomy

The best place to cannulate is the back of the hand or the lateral border of the wrist - watch out for the radial artery - though the commonest site for success is one of the veins crossing the antecubital fossa. However this site has a number of structures that need to be avoided as indicated on the following diagram.

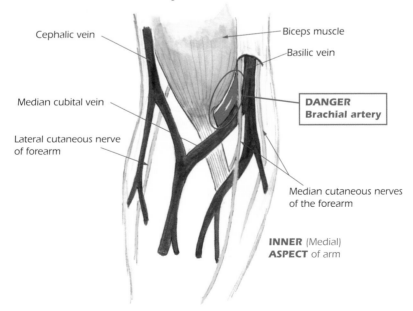

The anatomy of the antecubital fossa

Cephalic vein

Biceps muscle

Basilic vein

Median cubital vein

**DANGER
Brachial artery**

Lateral cutaneous nerve
of forearm

Median cutaneous nerves
of the forearm

INNER (Medial)
ASPECT of arm

Short notes on procedure - practical training is needed, not book reading!

Reassurance and explanation are crucial. You are about to assault the casualty and you need consent.

Use the uninjured side only, or failing that insert the cannula above (proximal) to the injury.

Wear gloves; clean the skin; use a tourniquet; insert the cannula; secure with tape - preferably use a sterile purpose-made dressing; remove the tourniquet; safely dispose of the introducer in a 'sharps box' and, finally, flush the cannula with sterile water on 0.9% saline as thrombus can block it after a few minutes.

The size (and number) of cannula has always been seen as a rite of passage in hospital. Two big brown ones (14-gauge) were the sign of a serious resuscitation. This may still be so, and benefit the patient just about to go to theatre. However, outside hospital the balance has shifted and a smaller, easier to place, cannula is going to be sufficient. After all a 21-gauge cannula is big enough to infuse 250 ml of fluid in 5 minutes. In addition hospitals are full of devices that can expand your small cannula to drainpipe dimensions.

Walking along with a bag of fluid makes a great picture but is it necessary? The cannula can easily be tugged out; the fluid gets cold and the speed of evacuation is slowed. Switching off and laying the bag on the casualty is OK for short transfers, perhaps during winching, but air tends to get in the wrong place or blood coagulates in the cannula or infusion tubing. Why not have an air-free system and infuse bags of 250 ml as a bolus, or more slowly using the casualty's weight? Any giving set without a ball valve can be used and the system is contained within the casualty bag. No good for the photos but much more practical!

Intravenous fluids

Replacing the fluid lost, or filling up the vascular container if its tone has been lost, is appealing as it directly overcomes the pathology. Unfortunately it is not as simple as this. First of all, on the fell side, the replacement fluid is not going to be blood; saline does not carry oxygen. There are dangers of increasing the blood pressure thereby causing newly formed clots to be pushed off the leaking blood vessel, hence reactivating bleeding. The problems of practicality, infection and training also need to be considered. Giving cold fluid to a cold casualty with an already irritable heart may precipitate heart irregularity or fibrillation. In addition, the clotting of blood is reduced by dilution and the induced hypothermia. Having looked at the negative side, there is a positive side! A saline infusion can increase the effectiveness of the circulation and reverse brain dysfunction. The case report in the chapter on Patient Assessment demonstrated this. Finding the right balance is difficult.

Which fluid should be given?

Isotonic (0.9%) saline (also called normal saline) is the fluid of choice. Hypertonic hyperoncotic saline/dextran may have a role, particularly in head injured casualties. For further details see the relevant section in the 'For rescuers' chapter.

How much fluid?

There are a number of strategies for pre-hospital fluid resuscitation as outlined below.

Strategies for intravenous fluid resuscitation	
	target BP (mmHg)
Immediate or 'Forced volume' resuscitation	100-120
large volumes of isotonic fluid via several large cannulae or hypertonic fluids and catecholamines Example: Severe head injury	
'Permissive' hypotensive resuscitation	80-100
250ml of isotonic saline boluses when the radial pulse is not palpable. Hypertonic saline? Example: Blunt polytrauma	
'Delayed' resuscitation	60-80
minimal or no fluids until definitive surgery to control bleeding is carried out Example: Penetrating torso wound	

The present advice seems to be for reducing the quantities of intravenous fluids given in the pre-hospital stage. For example, a recent consensus view (see Revell, Porter and Greaves) was that fluid should not be given to casualties with trauma if a radial pulse could be felt; at least until haemorrhage control had been achieved. If the radial pulse was absent, boluses of 250 ml of fluid should be used carefully until the radial pulse returns, at which stage the infusion is stopped and the situation monitored. (In penetrating torso trauma, such as gunshot, the presence of the carotid pulse should be considered adequate.) Whether such an approach is correct in mountain rescue is unknown. Many of our casualties will be dehydrated from their exertions before the accident and the time scales are frequently so much longer than urban roadside casualties that it has to be questioned whether this degree of hypotension is harmful. Most mountain rescue casualties will have blunt polytrauma, often with head injury, from tumbling falls rather than penetrating trauma or arterial damage. In response to these concerns, ICAR Medcom is developing practical recommendations to balance these factors with the simple notion that 'permissive' hypotensive resuscitation should be applied to all casualties. This is *work in progress* as we go to print; check the ICAR website (www.ikar-cisa.org) for up-to-date information.

Case study - Intravenous fluids

This case is fictional but was developed from several real cases. It was commissioned for Casualty Care in Mountain Rescue to contribute a sense of real life and to draw attention to the dilemmas that occur in rescue work.

Time and date   15.00 Spring

Location   Major climbing crag five miles from the nearest road

Weather   Dry and sunny

Cause of incident 15 metre 'lead climber' fall

Reported injuries Multiple

Because of the isolated location, seriousness of the incident and the reported injuries, the team asked for helicopter assistance immediately. The helicopter airlifted team members to the incident site. The casualty had been lowered to a large terrace and had been secured to the crag by his partner. When the rescuers arrived, the casualty was talking. He complained of pain in front of the left shoulder. The casualty's partner confirmed the cause of the incident and the distance fallen. He estimated that the casualty had been unconscious for about 10 minutes immediately after the accident. The rescue team performed a rapid assessment of the casualty, aware that the helicopter was standing by to carry out an evacuation. The airway was open and breathing appeared adequate, though a little painful and shallow. Tenderness over the left clavicle was noted. The radial pulse was easily felt; it had a rate of 106 beats a minute. Tenderness over the pelvis was found. The casualty was fully alert though tenderness at the back of the head and around the neck was also noted. The systolic blood pressure was 99 mm Hg. The rescue team concluded that a number of injuries were present:

A head and possible neck injury

A fractured clavicle

A possible fractured pelvis with internal bleeding causing shock

Oxygen by face mask and a rigid cervical collar were applied. Intravenous fluids were started. Evacuation by helicopter on a stretcher direct from the incident site was performed. When the casualty arrived at the District General Hospital 1.5 litres of colloid and 1 litre of saline had been given.

Comments

Lead climber falls resulting in injury are often serious. The rescue team often fear difficult access, even the possibility of re-climbing part of the route, and confined working spaces. Fortunately these problems are rare in England and Wales. However the casualties often have multiple injuries as a result of the helter-skelter effect of the fall. Many areas are bruised or worse; assessing the severity of each injury is very hard on the fell. In this case there was sufficient concern about internal haemorrhage from a possible fractured pelvis for 2.5 litres of fluid to be given to the casualty over 45 minutes. With the pressure of the helicopter and the evacuation it is unlikely that further assessment other than a pulse reading could be taken during this time. In retrospect too much fluid was given as the casualty developed pulmonary oedema (an excessive amount of fluid in the lungs), which reduced the efficiency of respiration.

This could have been dangerous. Separating out 'too much' from 'too little' fluid can be very difficult even in hospital. Often special measurements of urine output or venous pressure have to be made. None of these are available to the rescuer. It may be impossible to generalize and/or advise a figure, such as a systolic pressure of 70 mm Hg or a pulse of less than 120 per minute, which is acceptable during the pre-hospital phase. The situations and uncertainties are so great. This area has been thrown into disarray with the finding that aggressive pre-hospital fluid replacement in penetrating torso injuries may be detrimental.

However, what is well known is that rapid transfer of a casualty with internal bleeding to a surgeon with the skill to stop the bleeding is the most important factor. If setting up intravenous fluids delays evacuation, it should be discouraged. This casualty would have benefited more from the appropriate rapid evacuation organised by the team rather than any amount of intravenous fluid. In reality the casualty came to no harm from the over enthusiastic fluid replacement. He had a fractured clavicle and mild concussion though the next may have a fractured pelvis and a ruptured spleen!

Postscript (2006)

A strategy of 'permissive' hypotensive rather than 'forced' resuscitation would have been appropriate in this scenario as the head injury was not severe (GCS less than or equal to 8). The time saved could have been spent applying a vacuum mattress (tumbling fall). Inserting a cannula would have been adequate so that a 250ml bolus of intravenous fluid could have been given during the evacuation should the casualty deteriorate.

Drei Zinnen, Dolomites, (2005)

References

Eaton CJ. *Essentials of Immediate Medical Care* 2nd edition 1999; ISBN 0443 05345

Driscoll P, Skinner D, Earlam R. *ABC of Major Trauma*. (3rd Edition) 2000; ISBN 0 7279 1378 6

Maconochie I. Capillary refill time in the field - it's enough to make you blush. *Pre-hospital Immediate Care* 1998; 2: 95-6.

Moore FA, McKinley BA, Moore EE. The next generation in shock resuscitation. *The Lancet* 2004; 363:1988-96

Crawford I. The prehospital use of pneumatic anti-shock garments. BestBETs. Accessed at http://www.bestbets.org

Hearns S. The Scottish mountain rescue casualty study. *Emerg Med J* 2003; 20:281-4

Hohlrieder M, Eschertzhuber S, Schubert H, Zinnecker R, Mair P. Severity and Pattern of Injury in Survivors of Alpine Fall Accidents. *HAMB* 2004; 5:349-355

Thomas I, Dixon J. Bradycardia in acute haemorrhage. *BMJ* 2004; 328:451-3

Deakin CD, Low JL. Accuracy of the advanced trauma life support guidelines for predicting systolic blood pressure using carotid, femoral, and radial pulses: observational study. *BMJ* 2000; 321:673-674

Revell M, Porter K, Greaves I. Fluid resuscitation in prehospital trauma care: a consensus view. *Emerg Med J* 2002; 19: 494-498

Pepe PE. Shock in polytrauma. *BMJ* 2003; 327:119-20

Pre-hospital initiation of fluid replacement therapy in trauma. NICE technological appraisal 74 (2004). Accessed at www.nice.org.uk/TA074guidance

Sumann G, Zen-Ruffinen G, Ellerton J, Paal P, Dahlberg T, Zafren K, Brugger H. Traumatic shock: pre-hospital management in mountain rescue - practical recommendation and short review of the literature. Recommendation of the International Commission for Mountain Emergency Medicine (ICAR MEDCOM) 2006 *(in press)*

Ski tour, ICAR Medcom, Liechenstein (2004)

Disability

Objectives
To understand the basic anatomy
To be able to discuss the common types of injury
To understand primary and secondary injuries
Discuss ways to minimise secondary injury
To assess the Glasgow Coma Scale of the casualty
To demonstrate immobilisation of the spine
To manage an eye injury

Head Injury

The management of patients who have sustained an injury to the head remains one of the most taxing situations in pre-hospital care and particularly so in a hostile, isolated situation. The diagnosis of a 'minor head injury' is one that can only be made with hindsight. All head injuries where the casualty has a reduced level of consciousness at the time of call-out initiation must be managed with the worst possible scenario in mind. Whilst it can be safely assumed that a major accident will result in a major brain injury, the opposite is certainly not true and even a relatively minor incident, such as a fall from a stile, can produce a serious head injury. Head injuries are common in mountain rescue and, as early treatment has a major effect on outcome, both in terms of survival and quality of life, this imposes a responsibility on all team members to be well versed in the management of head injuries.

Anatomy and Physiology

The brain is housed within a rigid container, the skull. Under most circumstances this affords excellent protection from the minor knocks and blows of day-to-day life. The brain is held within the skull by a number of suspensory ligaments that provide some cushioning effect. Three membranes, called the meninges, surround the brain. The meninges resemble polythene bags wrapping and protecting the brain and also carrying blood vessels to its surface. There is an extensive supply of blood to the brain with arteries within the brain and over its surface. Cerebrospinal fluid (CSF), a watery, slightly yellow fluid, circulates around the brain and in cavities (ventricles) within it. The CSF plays a part in protecting the brain and supplies nutrition and removes waste products. Its total volume is 150 ml. The brain itself is divided into three major areas as shown on the next page. The midbrain/brain stem is the most basic part and contains the centres that control, among other things, respiration and heart rate. It is important to note that this part lies close to the main outlet from the base of the skull through which the spinal cord passes. The cerebellum is the area controlling movement and coordination. It is thus most highly developed in the gibbon, probably the most agile and athletic of animals. The cerebrum, the largest area in man, is responsible for all higher activity including memory, emotion and intellect. As the most highly developed area it is also the most susceptible to the effects of injury. The areas involved in vision, voluntary movement, sensation and speech have specific locations and damage to these areas will cause disability in the corresponding function.

The brain from the side

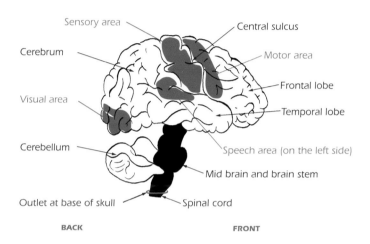

The skull varies in thickness and has weaker areas at the sides and near openings in the skull, for example around the eyes. Overlying the skull is a dense layer of periosteum; over this is the scalp. This is relatively loosely attached to the underlying structures and can therefore be torn away quite easily. The scalp has a very generous blood supply and wounds will bleed profusely. The arteries supplying the scalp arise from the surrounding face and neck.

Cross section through the scalp and skull

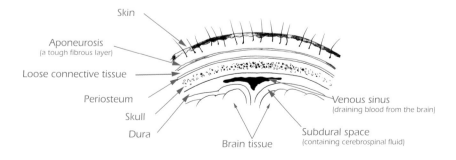

Brain tissue is the most sensitive and specialised of all tissue. Its constant activity requires a very high level of oxygen and glucose. This in turn means that a very generous blood supply is needed. Brain cells cope very badly without oxygen and glucose. Only a few minutes of impaired supply will lead to permanent damage. Brain tissue has virtually no power to heal or regenerate and thus the effects of damage are much more profound than is the case with structures such as bone and liver where repair and new growth are possible. Brain tissue is also of different densities and forces applied are likely to cause shearing between the layers of differing density with tearing of nerves and blood vessels.

Prevention

Evidence shows that helmets will always lessen, and often prevent, a person having a significant brain injury while engaging in a number of activities (bicycling, skiing, snow boarding). For skiers and snow boarders, the relative risk reduction is between 29% and 56%. In everyday terms, if you wear a helmet you stand at least a one in three chance of reducing the seriousness of head injury. (The evidence for climbers is suggestive but the numbers involved have not been large enough to produce a good paper.) Concern that wearing a helmet may increase the chance of a significant neck injury, by transmitting greater forces to the neck, have largely been discounted though not entirely.

Pathology

Almost all head injuries away from military conflict are the result of a blunt blow to the head. This will often be caused by a fall, but falling objects are also a common occurrence. Penetrating injuries from impact with sharp implements can occur in a mountaineering situation but are very uncommon.

The scalp, the skull and the brain may each be involved in a head injury. Frequently all of these will be damaged but this will not always be the case. The scalp may suffer extensive injury without involvement of underlying structures and severe brain injury may be present with little or no evidence of trauma to the scalp or skull.

Scalp Wounds

The most striking feature of a wound to the scalp is profuse bleeding. In large wounds the bleeding may be sufficient to produce shock. The bleeding is coming from the edges of the wound and is therefore controlled by pressure on the edges of the wound. Sustained pressure over several minutes will control the  bleeding in most cases. Bandaging of the head will rarely control bleeding but will conceal it. Bandaging should only be applied when the bleeding has stopped. Assessing the extent of scalp wounds in casualties with a generous crop of hair can be difficult and the wounds may be more extensive than first imagined. However even gentle probing can reactivate bleeding so it is best to leave a more thorough inspection until the casualty is in a well-lit Accident and Emergency Department.

Unless safety dictates otherwise, helmets should always be removed to look for scalp wounds. The procedure for removing a helmet is described later. A helmet can contain a large quantity of concealed haemorrhage. Once the bleeding is controlled and dressings have been applied, a helmet could be replaced, though often the stretcher head guard will be more appropriate. (With a helmet on, it is difficult to ensure that the neck remains in a neutral position.)

In a situation where extensive wounds are present and evacuation is likely to be prolonged, temporary suture of the wound should be seriously considered before the process of packaging and extrication begins.

"Apply pressure to the edge of the wound"
(Gloves please)

If possible, leave all foreign bodies in place
whether impaled in the head, chest, abdomen or limb

Suturing

In mountain rescue, suturing is a quick way of reducing bleeding by opposing the edges of a laceration. Its use is limited to wounds where pressure dressings cannot stop the bleeding. On convex surfaces, such as the skull, direct pressure can widen the wound and so encourage bleeding. A few sutures can have a dramatic effect. The technique is easy once taught. Clean the skin with normal saline or povidone-iodine solution; take a hand needle and go straight through the skin and scalp aponeurosis starting at 90 degrees to the surface and about 1cm from the laceration; go across the base of the wound and then out through the aponeurosis and skin on the other side, again ideally 1cm from the laceration; tie an overhand knot and pull the edges of the laceration together before locking off the knot with a second overhand knot. Cut the thread 3cm from the knot and start again. Of course, local anaesthesia reduces the pain of inserting the needle but with a cooperative casualty, explanation and a confident approach, the rapid insertion of a couple of sutures can be achieved without its use.

Skull Fracture

In most instances skull fractures are, in themselves, of no consequence. They consist of a hairline crack in the skull that requires no specific treatment. Without X-rays they cannot be detected. Their importance is as an indication that the head has been hit with significant violence.

A skull fracture with an overlying scalp wound is a compound fracture. Like compound fractures elsewhere, they run the risk of introducing infection into the bone or worse still into the cranial cavity. Specific forms of compound fracture connect the cranial cavity with the nose and ear. These are often indicated by the loss of cerebrospinal fluid and/or blood from the nose or ear though often the latter is from local tissue damage. In these pictures, a basal skull fracture has caused 'racoon eyes' and bleeding from the ear canal.

Comminuted compound fractures, with displaced fragments of bone in the brain tissue, represent a quite different situation. These injuries usually follow a severe blow to the skull and require early surgical treatment to minimise their effects. In the field control of bleeding and appropriate wound dressing is the best that can be achieved.

Brain Injury

Injury to the brain is described as primary - the damage occurs at the time of impact - or secondary - the damage develops after the initial impact usually within first few hours after the accident. Tertiary injury is also described. This refers to later complications, such as infection, and is outside the scope of pre-hospital care.

Primary brain damage

The pathology involved in primary brain injury includes:

Disruption of nerve activity

There is no visible brain damage (even under the microscope). This is a diffuse effect and its severity varies with the severity of the blow. Higher brain activity is particularly affected.

Shearing of brain tissue

This type of injury is associated with accidents that transmit acceleration or deceleration forces on to the brain. The layers of different density within the brain are torn apart leading to disruption of nerve connections and often the tearing of small blood vessels within the brain tissue. Even in cases where the injury is severe enough to be fatal there may be little to see with naked eye examination of the brain. The damage is most evident at the site of impact on the head. Remember however the contra-coup effect when the brain impacts against the opposite side of the skull and sustains damage. Nothing can be done to treat these primary injuries outside hospital.

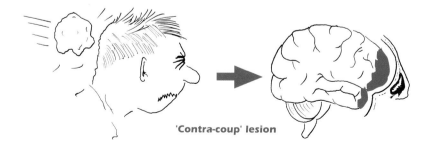

'Contra-coup' lesion

Secondary brain damage

The processes that cause secondary brain injury are hypoxia; hypotension; swelling of the brain (oedema); bleeding within the skull and venous stasis.

Damaged brain tissue is even more sensitive to lower oxygen supplies than normal brain tissue. Even short periods of hypoxia (partial oxygen starvation) may turn a recoverable brain injury into a fatality or a long-term vegetative state. A compromised airway, an associated chest injury, a low systolic blood pressure, or anything leading to a diminished oxygen supply has the potential for disaster in a head injury.

Shock, usually from bleeding elsewhere, leads to a reduced cerebral blood flow and will have the same effect of reducing the oxygen supply to the brain.

Swelling of the brain (cerebral oedema) occurs as a result of fluid accumulation in response to brain injury. Because the skull is a rigid container this swelling has a serious effect. The increased intracranial pressure (ICP) will in itself interfere with the blood supply, which in turn causes more tissue damage, and thus a vicious circle is set in motion. The speed with which cerebral oedema develops varies considerably; in most situations it only becomes a problem after the patient has reached hospital.

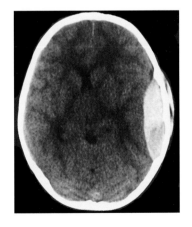

Bleeding within the skull can be within the brain itself (intracerebral) or in the potential spaces around the brain (subdural and extradural) as shown in this CT slice. (The blood is the white bulge under a skull fracture.) The bleeding arises from blood vessels within the brain substance or those in close relation to the skull. In the latter situation a skull fracture is almost always present. It is impossible to be certain which type of bleeding has occurred without a CT scan. For the purposes of pre-hospital care, it is unimportant since the effects are the same. Since CT scanning became available the incidence of small intracranial bleeds has been found to be much more common than previously thought. Bleeding has exactly the same effect as cerebral oedema in raising the ICP. There are two important differences. Firstly, it may develop much more rapidly, certainly beginning within the first two hours after injury. Secondly, urgent surgery is often required and may lead to full recovery.

If the venous return from the brain is impeded, the venous pressure increases and with it the ICP. This may happen in two ways. An incorrectly sized, or applied, cervical collar can constrict the neck veins and raise ICP. Transporting a casualty in a head-down position can have the same effect.

Unlike primary brain injury everything can and must be done to prevent, recognise and treat secondary injuries.

Intracranial pressure

In many cases, a raised ICP is the common pathway to secondary brain damage. It can easily become self-perpetuating. The first effects of a rising ICP are diffuse and act particularly on higher brain function. Compression of the cerebrum occurs; changes in the conscious level follow. Initially these are subtle and may easily go undetected unless actively sought. The changes will progress to an eventual loss of consciousness. As consciousness is lost, the raised ICP begins to push the brain stem through the outlet of the skull. In effect the brain stem is being forced through the narrow opening. The control centres within the brain stem begin to malfunction leading to changes in breathing and the heart rate. Respiration becomes slow and laboured and the heart slows. Blood pressure rises. When these signs are noted the picture is bleak and death is imminent unless drastic measures can be taken. Note that these effects are the opposite of those seen in shock. If a patient with a head injury is shocked, look elsewhere for another injury. Local effects of increased pressure may also appear. For example, a pupil may dilate. It is a late sign of raised ICP and often difficult to interpret as there are other reasons for the pupil to dilate.

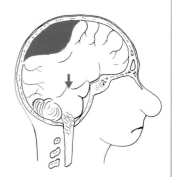

Management

Two matters dominate the management of head injuries. The first is optimising the physiological parameters of the primary survey, and particularly maintaining an open airway, and the second is assessing and recording the conscious level. In the unconscious head injury, the first three stages of care have been described as

AIRWAY   AIRWAY   AIRWAY

It is impossible to overemphasise the importance of maintaining a good oxygen supply to the brain. The airway must be kept open at all times; one rescuer must take responsibility to ensure this is so. It should be their sole task and they should not simultaneously be recording the conscious level, making radio calls or having a cup of coffee. At the most, they should be maintaining in-line manual immobilisation of the neck though even this may need to be delegated to a second rescuer if the airway is difficult to maintain. There is a high incidence of vomiting and regurgitation at all stages of a head injury. It will often occur without any warning and will represent a serious threat to the airway. Be prepared for vomiting and have a plan of action ready. Remember the possibility of cervical spine injury but do not let this stop you giving the best airway treatment. Give oxygen as soon as it is available at 15 litres/min by a non-rebreathing mask with a reservoir. ('Rationing' the flow rate to ensure there will be enough oxygen for the casualty during the evacuation can be considered after the primary survey is completed.)

Significant bleeding should be stopped. Do not forget that if the patient is shocked another cause apart from the head must be sought. We have seen in the Circulation chapter that, if at all possible, a normal blood pressure should maintained at all times.

It is important to record the history of the accident. Obtain the best account you can from either the casualty or witnesses and record this, as yours may be the only available story when the casualty reaches definitive care. If a helmet has been worn, look for damage and also send it with the casualty to hospital. It may provide valuable information about the anatomical site of injury. (Ideally you should arrange for the helmet to be sent to the British Mountaineering Council Technical Committee after this.)

You will need to perform a clinical examination of the casualty. Examine the head for wounds. The care of scalp wounds has previously been described. Look for scalp bruising, detected as a 'boggy' swelling; this is sometimes associated with bruising or bleeding on the inside of the skull.

Bleeding from the nose is almost always due to local nasal damage but bleeding from one or both ears is very suggestive of a skull fracture. Thin watery fluid leaking from the nose or ears may be cerebrospinal fluid indicating a skull fracture. Neither the nose nor the ears should be packed to prevent leakage. Bruising immediately behind the ear (Battle's sign) is very suggestive of a skull fracture. Bruising around both eyes (Racoon Eyes) usually indicates a skull fracture. Bleeding into the conjunctiva (white of the eye) where the outer limit cannot be seen might also point to a skull fracture.

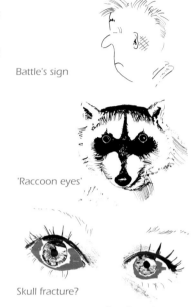

Battle's sign

'Raccoon eyes'

Skull fracture?

Local eye trauma

Assessment of conscious level

The ability to do this is the most important skill after airway management. Early and effective treatment of complications, particularly intracranial bleeding, is totally dependent on the detection of changes in the conscious level of a patient. The need for this has not been diminished to any extent by the development of techniques such as CT scanning. The introduction of the Glasgow Coma Scale (GCS) represented a massive step forward in head injury care. Although at first sight the scale appears complex, with a little practice and familiarity its use becomes straightforward. It is the 'gold standard' in head injury assessment, is recognised internationally, is used by all the emergency services and is employed at all the decision-making stages in patient care. This includes the audit of outcomes.

Glasgow Coma Scale

Three parameters: eye opening, verbal response and motor response are assessed. The best response in each category is used to obtain the total score. The maximum score is 15; this represents a fully conscious individual. The lower the score the more severe the injury until the lowest score of 3 is reached. Coma is defined as a GCS of less than or equal to 8.

Eye opening –		Comments
spontaneous	4	Eyes open without any stimulation
to voice	3	Eyes open in response to a request including shouting
to pain	2	Eyes open in response to a standard pain stimulus
none	1	
Verbal response –		
orientated	5	Knows who he is and where he is
confused	4	Unable to answer above but can produce sentences or phrases
inappropriate words	3	Speaks or shouts words (often swears), usually when disturbed
incomprehensible	2	Groans – no intelligible words
none	1	Repeated stimulation produces no attempt to speak
Motor response –		
obeys commands	6	Holds up two fingers if compatible with other injuries
localises pain	5	Casualty reaches to site of the pain stimulus to remove it
withdraws from pain	4	A painful stimulus to the nail bed produces a rapid movement (elbow flexion) to withdraw the finger from the painful source
flexion response	3	A painful stimulus anywhere produces a slow bending of the elbow and wrist, so the arm is held against the chest
extension response	2	A painful stimulus anywhere produces a stiff extension of the limbs with internal rotation of the shoulder and elbow
none	1	

Some time must be spent becoming adept in using the GCS. The questions you will use to determine awareness must be well rehearsed, sensible and able to be used over and over again. The technique to elicit a response to pain must be consistent. Pressure on a fingernail bed or the sternum is the usual means employed. Once confidence with the GCS is acquired transmission of patient information using a number is both simple and less open to misinterpretation. A number of assessments should be made, with the frequency being determined by not only the severity of the injury but also the circumstances of evacuation and the ease of access to the patient. However in an unconscious casualty or where the observations are fluctuating an attempt should be made to record the findings every 30 minutes.

Amnesia (loss of memory) surrounding the accident should be considered. It is divided into two types using the time of the accident as the divider. Amnesia before the accident (retrograde amnesia) is of little value in assessing the severity of head injury. However post-traumatic amnesia (PTA), loss of memory following the injury, is of considerable importance. Its duration is a good indicator of the expected duration of after effects following a head injury. Patients do not usually return from unconsciousness directly. There are usually 'islands' of consciousness and amnesia. PTA has ended only when continuous memory for events has returned. To determine whether this has happened it is useful to ask the patient to recall the last conversation you held with them.

Alcohol complicates the assessment of a head injury, though the combination is rare in mountain accidents. However, in normal Friday night situations, it often contributes to the reduced level of consciousness and makes the assessment much more difficult. The golden rule is never to blame alcohol for any impaired conscious level, in any casualty who has, or may have, a head injury. It is better to over treat intoxication than under treat a head injury.

Seizures are uncommon immediately following a head injury. If an attack does occur, it may well seriously compromise the damaged brain tissue by interfering with oxygen supply and by raising ICP. Intravenous or rectal diazepam may be required to stop the attack and ideally should be given within two minutes of the onset of a seizure.

Antibiotics should be given if there is a compound skull fracture and hospital treatment will be delayed by more than 6 hours from the time of the accident. The intravenous route is preferred, as oral medication should be avoided in a casualty with a GCS of less than 15.

Giving pain relief to a casualty with a head injury has always been contentious. Traditional teaching advised that no analgesia should ever be given in the presence of a head injury. This view is no longer held. A patient with a head injury and a major limb fracture is more likely to suffer untoward effects from the severe pain than from the analgesia. Morphine and Entonox® can be administered provided that the airway and respiration are normal. Very careful documentation and assessment must be continued. Small doses of morphine, at intervals of 15 minutes, are more appropriate than a single large dose.

Practitioners with the required skills, equipment and drugs should, in appropriate circumstances, consider anaesthetising ('sedating') and protecting the airway to ensure that a casualty with a GCS of less than or equal to 8 receives the best oxygenation and least risk of aspiration during the evacuation phase.

Minor and Mild Head Injury

90% of head injuries attending an Accident and Emergency department are classed as having a minor (GCS 15) or mild head injury (GCS 13 or 14). Originally a 'minor head injury' covered a GCS 13, 14 and 15 but when CT, and more recently, MRI scans became widely available it became apparent that a significant number of casualties with a GCS of 13 and 14 did have demonstrable brain injury. So the term 'minor' is now restricted to casualties with a GCS of 15. Mild head injury is not a harmless injury; some of the casualties continue to have symptoms a year later. There is debate over what role psychology has in the clinical picture – some casualties are pursuing litigation claims – and what is the best management. From a mountain rescue perspective, manage a mild head injury with oxygen, cervical spine immobilisation but maintain a positive approach. This may be important; rehabilitation starting straight away may be the key to helping these casualties overcome their ordeal.

Summary

Broadly speaking your head-injured casualties will fall into four groups.

Unconscious and have been from the time of the accident. The casualty will require intensive management and urgent evacuation. They are likely to have a major primary injury.

Unconscious following the accident but now regained consciousness. These casualties are at risk of developing secondary injury. Careful monitoring and evacuate as soon as possible.

Conscious following accident but now deteriorating. The casualty is developing a secondary brain injury. The casualty is potentially fully recoverable. Rapid assessment and treatment of hypoxia, hypotension and venous stasis is needed followed by an urgent evacuation.

Conscious throughout. The least worrying group but must nevertheless be treated with circumspection.

Case studies

These cases are fictional but were developed from several real cases. They were commissioned for *Casualty Care in Mountain Rescue* to contribute a sense of real life and to draw attention to the dilemmas that occur in rescue work.

Case 1 - Head and facial injury

Time and date: 15.00 in early February

Location: Steep corrie back wall, 200 metres above tarn

Weather: Snow showers

Reported injuries: Long fall (? 100 metres)

A witness initiated the rescue. He called on a mobile phone - 'he has not got up'. The team were on exercise climbing a snow gully in the next corrie with enough safety and first aid equipment to go straight to the incident. The team arrived at the incident twenty minutes after the fall; the usual time would have been over an hour, perhaps even 2 hours.

The casualty was on a small buttress (marked by the red dot). The snow was hard and icy. There was a real danger of the casualty or the rescuers falling a further 200 metres. Securing the casualty and the team member assessing him took priority. The casualty was lying on his back; he was moving his four limbs in a seemingly non-purposeful way. As the rescue party approached the casualty could be heard snorting and snoring. On arrival, it was  apparent that the airway was partially blocked; this was overcome by a gentle chin lift. The cause for the partial blockage was a fracture on each side of the jaw. Any relaxation of the chin lift resulted in the immediate return of the snorting noise as the tongue fell back against the back of the throat. A second rescuer was tasked to perform manual immobilisation of the neck. There was good chest movement when the airway was supported. A pulse was easily felt in the neck; blood loss from a scalp wound had stopped. The casualty had not responded to the approach of the rescue team or to commands. He responded to 'firm touch' by thrashing his limbs and head around; the only intervention tolerated was the gentle chin lift and neck support. (AVPU = P) What next? A helicopter was requested but direct winching from the incident site was unlikely to be possible because of the cloud base. Putting on a cervical collar was attempted. This proved difficult as either the airway became obstructed or the casualty thrashed around alarmingly. Attempts were abandoned and the manual immobilisation maintained. Oxygen therapy via a face mask was tolerated but an oral airway certainly was not. The chin lift was maintained. A secondary survey was carried out. The injuries seemed confined to the head and face. The Glasgow Coma Scale was assessed as 6 - no eye opening, no verbal response and withdrawal to pain. The left pupil was dilated and did not respond to light; there was no obvious direct damage to the eye. The right pupil reacted normally. These are classic signs of brain distortion from an extradural haematoma. The casualty was placed in a vacuum mattress on his side with his neck supported as well as it could be in a neutral position and then placed on a stretcher. Despite this approximation to the lateral position, the airway still required manual support. The stretcher and the attendant rescuer were roped down the 200 metres slope, where the helicopter landed. The casualty was in hospital about 2 hours after he had fallen.

Comments

Modern technology saves lives. Mobile phones, radios and helicopters reduce the time it takes to get a casualty to hospital by hours. Surgical removal of an extradural haematoma often needs to be done promptly before further deterioration occurs. However flying direct to a neurosurgical hospital is not to be encouraged. Despite the urgency of the situation, other injuries need to be excluded by careful assessment and x-rays. For example has a chest or abdominal injury been ruled out satisfactorily? If flying the casualty to the neurosurgical team is going to take 15 minutes more than a nearer hospital, it is wisest to go for the nearest District Hospital. All of these hospitals have the necessary scanners to make the diagnosis, and with modern communications obtaining the advice and guidance from the more distant neurosurgical centre is straightforward.

This casualty demonstrates how compromises sometimes have to be made. Consider 'airway first' and 'head injury - is there a cervical spine injury?' Stabilise the neck until it is formally assessed. The second point is often emphasised, and rightly so. But it is often simplified too. Head injury = Cervical collar. Cervical collars can have disadvantages. In this case airway control was lost. Collars are uncomfortable and can lead to an irritable patient becoming more restless and as a result moving his neck more. Recent work has shown that rigid collars can sometimes increase the pressure around the brain. Could this be enough to alter the outcome of the head injury? A careful assessment has to be made. In this case, there was no swelling or distortion of the neck and the casualty was moving all his limbs. Even so there remained a possibility of a serious cervical spine injury. The airway had priority but the neck was not ignored. The airway attendant made sure that no unnecessary movement occurred. The compromise wasn't appreciated by the receiving hospital! The thick-skinned airway attendant, having been publicly 'dressed down', didn't enjoy seeing the collar applied with the help of four nurses and then the airway compromise being overcome by an anaesthetic and endotracheal tube. He was sorely tempted to use his crampon front points in an unkind way but resisted, preferring a coffee back at the helicopter! The casualty had his extradural haematoma surgically drained and he made a full recovery.

(2006) Should the casualty have been intubated? Certainly this would have been considered at the roadside. However, at the incident site with no prospect of transferring the casualty into a helicopter, the Doctor deferred the option. Would it have been harder to move over the terrain ventilating the casualty but (presumably) not having to manually support the airway? By luck, on this occasion, aspiration did not occur and the neck was uninjured. Perhaps the evacuation phase, shortened by approximately 15 minutes, made some difference.

Case 2 - Scalp laceration

Time and date: 12.00 in early June

Location: On the 'granny trod'

Weather: Warm and sunny

Reported injuries: Fall hitting head

The 'granny trod' is one of those walks between two convenient parking spots. It is derided as a flat walk – 'one for the oldies' – though the path itself is rough. The views are spectacular and you can get the steamer to take you back to the car.

The casualty is 84 years old and has stumbled and hit his head on a pointed stone. "No" he was not 'knocked-out' but the wound on the back of his head has bled a lot and if he gets up, he feels dizzy and the wound starts bleeding again.

A small group of team members are sent to the incident site. They find the gentleman sitting by the path with a very bloody tee shirt held to the back of his head. The pointed stone is a metre away and shows signs of impact; it is covered in lots of blood! The casualty confirms that he did not lose consciousness. A primary survey is performed at which stage an irregular pulse is noted. *"Oh yes, I have an irregular pulse and take warfarin".*

It is impossible to tell if the wound has stopped bleeding or complete a compression bandage with the tee shirt *in situ*. The tee shirt is carefully removed to reveal a gash of about seven centimetres just below the bony protuberance at the back of the head. It starts bleeding almost straight away but applying a non-adherent dressing, then two large ambulance dressings and finally a compression bandage with a large crepe bandage quickly stop this. The casualty asks: 'Now what?' Yes, he is dizzy on standing and yes, it has reactivated the bleeding, so a stretcher evacuation is agreed between the casualty and the team. This is duly carried out and, fortunately with little dissent, the casualty went to the Accident and Emergency department for suturing.

Comment

The casualty was surprised to have a two-unit blood transfusion and an overnight stay in hospital; the external blood loss had been significant. Had the appropriate skills been available at the incident site, an intravenous cannula and possibly a bolus of intravenous fluid could have been justified. However, the casualty's general condition did not suggest shock and raising his blood pressure might have just reactivated the bleeding. It was a surprise to the team that the automatic blood pressure monitor would not work despite a good radial pulse. This is often the case when the pulse is irregular. You have to revert to a manual method. The team were pleased that they had recognised atrial fibrillation and the importance of warfarin in prolonging the bleeding. They were also relieved that the casualty had consented to go to hospital, as they were rightly concerned that such a blow to the head in a casualty on warfarin can lead to a delayed haemorrhage within the skull and secondary brain injury. A period of hospital observation was certainly appropriate. By the end of the rescue, the team had learnt that life is full of surprises; the casualty had climbed 40 of the Alpine 4000m peaks, still enjoyed a gentle walk, had never used the rescue services before but had always donated some money to mountain rescue 'just in case'!

References

Driscoll P, Skinner D, Earlam R. *ABC of Major Trauma*. 3rd Edition 2000. ISBN 0 7279 1378 6

Teasdale GM, Murray G, Anderson E et al. Risks of traumatic intracranial haematoma in children and adults: implications for managing head injuries. *BMJ* 1990; 300:363-7

Porter KM et al. Are we able to comply with the NICE head injury guidelines? *Emerg Med J* 2005; 22:861-2

Hagel BE, Pless IB, Goulet C, Platt R, Robitaille Y. Effectiveness of helmets in skiers and snow boarders: case-control and case crossover study. *BMJ* 2005; 330:281-3

Wasserberg J. Treating head injuries. *BMJ* 2002; 325:454-5

Batchelor JS, Jenkins DW, Dunning J. Minor head injuries in adults: a review of current guidelines. *Trauma* 2003; 5:191-8

Spinal Injury

Spinal injuries, either suspected or confirmed, occur in 7% of mountain rescue casualties. Early recognition and appropriate treatment are important to avoid aggravating severe injuries. A delayed diagnosis of a cervical spine injury has been associated with 10-fold increase in permanent neurological damage. In addition, incorrect techniques do increase the disability suffered by the casualty and can even cause death. It is generally known that a head injury with a reduced GCS makes a neck injury likely – in some studies one third of those with a head injury also had a neck injury. However, in the last few years, a number of poorly managed cases have occurred, amongst the high standard of care given to the vast majority, in casualties without a head injury but a significant neck injury. Fortunately the casualties have suffered no serious consequences. Of particular concern is the lack of appreciation that in a casualty with a tumbling fall and a distracting injury, spinal injury has not been considered sufficiently, and spinal immobilisation not performed even when there has been ample time for it to be done.

Suspect a spinal injury in accidents involving a free fall from a height, tumble falls and falls from a height directly onto the feet. A number of cases have been reported from sledging accidents. Any casualty found unconscious or semiconscious, any casualty with an injury to the face or head could have a spinal injury. A casualty complaining of pain on or near the spine or complaining of sensation changes in the limbs following injury is l ikely to have a spinal injury.

"Suspect a spinal injury in accidents involving a free fall …"

Anatomy

There are 33 bony vertebrae in the spinal column. Each vertebral bone has a load-bearing portion in the front called the body. Behind the body of the vertebra there is a bony arch that surrounds the spinal cord. The bones are separated from each other by an intervertebral disc and linked together by stabilising ligaments. The disc performs the function of a shock absorber and allows flexibility of the spine. The vertebral column provides the basic support for our upright posture and forms part of the cage around the chest. It also protects the delicate spinal cord in the same way that the skull protects the brain.

A longitudinal section of the spine

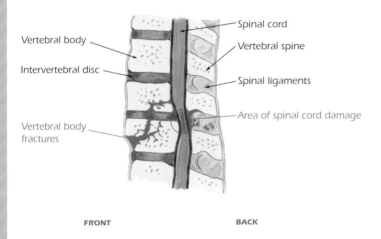

Spinal cord

Vertebral body

Vertebral spine

Intervertebral disc

Spinal ligaments

Area of spinal cord damage

Vertebral body fractures

FRONT   BACK

The spinal cord is an extension of brain tissue and carries nervous system information about sensation and movement between the brain and the limbs. Injuries to the bones of the spine can damage the delicate spinal cord. Cord injuries in the upper part of the cervical spine can cause death by respiratory arrest. Lower down the neck and in the thoracic and lumbar regions the function of the limbs can be lost.

Whatever the mechanism of injury, 14% of spinal injuries will have spinal cord damage. Of the cases with spinal cord injury, 40% are in the neck, 10 % in the thoracic region, 35% at the junction between the thoracic and lumbar spine and 3% are in the lumbar region. The neck and thoracolumbar junction injuries are therefore the areas most at risk from spinal cord injury.

Pathology

Spinal injuries consist of a bony and a spinal cord component. The bony injury consists of a fracture or dislocation of either the vertebral bodies or the bony arch. External forces can compress, bend (flex or extend) or twist the spine. A direct blow to the spine can also occur. The fracture is stable when the fragments of bone are held together and are thus unlikely to move again. In this situation, further damage to the spinal cord is rare. In contrast, when the bone fragments are not held together (unstable injuries) further movement can damage the spinal cord. It is not possible to tell if the injury is stable or unstable on the mountain and therefore any casualty with neck or back pain should receive full spinal injury care until they are adequately assessed in hospital.

Damage to the spinal cord is divided into a primary injury, occurring at the time of the accident, and a secondary injury when further damage occurs sometime later as the result of another insult. We have already seen this way of thinking when head injuries were discussed.

The cord can be completely divided as a primary injury. The result is a complete loss of movement in the muscles supplied by the injured area of the spinal cord and all the muscles further caudally (towards the tail). There will be a loss of all sensation too. Loss of the sympathetic nervous system will also occur resulting in changes in heart rate, blood pressure, bladder emptying and bowel function. Partial primary injuries, with the type of nerve damage seen in the brain, are more common than a complete transection. The loss of function in the motor, sensory and autonomic nervous systems can be patchy, complex and confusing. Muscle weakness and dysaesthesia (pins and needles or burning sensations) caudal to the site of spinal cord damage will usually be present. In general the higher the damage to the spinal cord, the greater is the risk of disability and death. Upper limb symptoms and signs are possible only if the damage involves the cervical spine.

Secondary injury may be mechanical when further displacement of an unstable fracture increases the spinal cord damage. This occurs if the patient is not handled with appropriate care. Non-mechanical secondary injury may occur as the result of lack of oxygen or blood to the nervous tissue. As seen with brain injury, hypoxia,

Typical histories and resultant spinal injuries

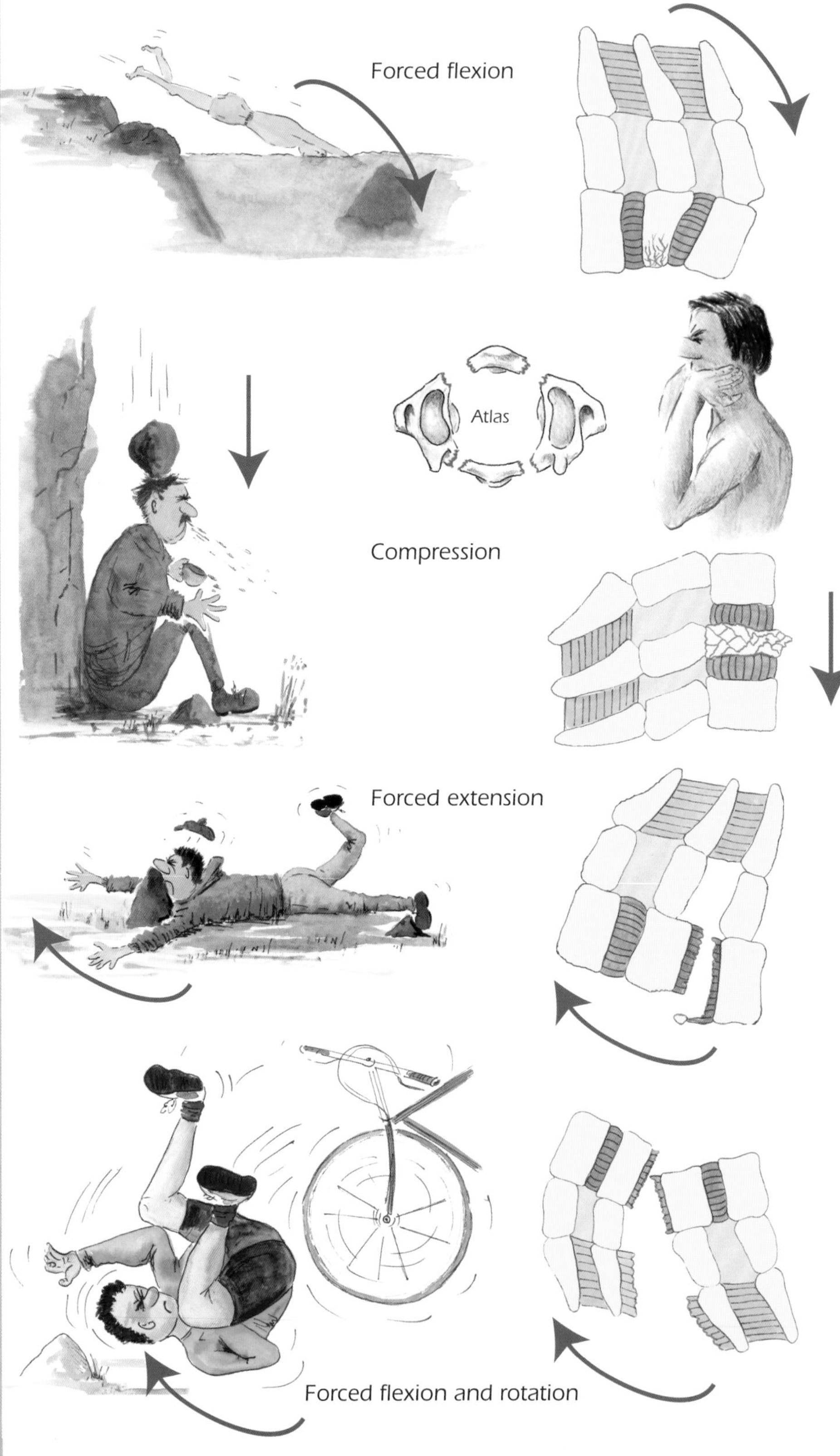

Forced flexion

Atlas

Compression

Forced extension

Forced flexion and rotation

hypotension, oedema, bleeding into a confined space and venous stasis can all contribute to further damage. These may have been preventable. By placing the spine in the neutral position the volume of the spinal canal is maximised, so hopefully secondary injury is reduced.

Assessment

It is important to recognise the potential for spinal injury based upon the mechanisms of the injury. A high index of suspicion must be maintained. An accurate history of the mechanism of the injury is invaluable. Examples of the common forces and possible events leading to injury are illustrated opposite. Flexion and rotation to the cervical spine is the most likely to produce an unstable injury with cord damage. Whilst we concentrate on the neck, the same forces result in similar injuries in the lower parts of the spine. Of particular note is the casualty who lands on his feet and then cannot walk because of a fracture of the os calcis (heel bone); the axial (compression) force can cause a covert spinal injury anywhere in the spinal column. A vacuum mattress should be taken to any casualty with such a history!

The symptoms of spinal injury may be dramatic with complete loss of muscle power in the legs and, possibly, in the arms as well. Sensation might also be absent. However more usually a spinal injury presents with a mix of pain at a point along the spine with reduced power in the legs (and possibly arms). Sensation may be reduced or altered to an abnormal sensation usually in the form of a burning or shooting pain. Beware the unconscious casualty who may have an unrecognised spinal injury and beware a casualty with a painful distracting injury elsewhere for this may mask neck pain. The simple screening test of asking the casualty to move his fingers and toes is too insensitive to diagnose a spinal injury. At times, the symptoms can seem bizarre and unusual but always treat them as serious and protect the spine until an examination can be carried out in hospital.

The aim of spinal injury treatment is to prevent secondary mechanical injury and to minimise other factors such as hypoxia and hypotension that might add to the disability. The full spine, from the pelvis to the head, must be immobilised.

Special consideration in spinal injury

Airway

Care of the airway and manual in-line immobilisation of the cervical spine are the first priorities in initial management of patients with spinal injury. To open the airway use a jaw thrust or chin lift manoeuvre. Avoid using a head tilt. Use suction with care to avoid causing a profound bradycardia (slow pulse) and even cardiac arrest. Remember that the airway must be open and clear at all times. If the casualty vomits they should be turned to the side maintaining full spinal care in order to clear and drain material from the airway.

Breathing

In cervical spine injury the nerve supply to the muscles of respiration can be affected. Sometimes the muscles between the ribs are paralysed and only the diaphragm is working. Normal chest expansion may not be evident but the abdomen may rise and fall markedly with respiration. Observe the pattern and respiratory rate to assess ventilation and, if available, use a pulse oximeter to measure the oxygen saturation. Give all patients with significant injuries oxygen at 15 litres/minute via a non-rebreathing mask with a reservoir.

Circulation

Some patients with spinal cord injuries will develop neurogenic shock. Look for a slow pulse (< 60 per minute) and signs of shock. The shock will be made much worse if the casualty is moved into a 'head up' position. Avoid this even when the casualty is ensconced in a vacuum mattress. Remember that the casualty may also have 'true' blood loss from other injuries. Advanced methods of treatment can benefit these casualties.

Disability

Continue to record conscious level. These patients often have several injuries and a change in conscious level may indicate deterioration due to hypoxia, poor respiratory effort, blood loss or head injury.

Pressure area care

Skin with poor sensation or limbs that are paralysed are at risk from pressure sores. The casualty should lie on a surface that is free from hard or sharp objects. Be especially aware of climbing harnesses and attached gear. A vacuum mattress contours the shape of the body and avoids areas of high pressure. It is therefore the gold standard for spinal injury care.

Temperature control

Casualties with spinal cord injury may have damage to the part of the nervous system that controls heat regulation. They cannot shiver and may lose heat from dilation of blood vessels in the limbs. In the mountain environment there is a risk that hypothermia will develop more rapidly than you would normally expect. Casualties should receive early protection from the elements.

Pain relief

Spinal injuries are painful and analgesia should be given early. Entonox®, morphine and nonsteroidal anti-inflammatory drugs can be given as long as care is taken to minimise respiratory depression and vomiting.

Moving the patient

The casualty should be moved as little as possible and then only in a controlled manner. Consider the objective dangers in the mountain environment. A swift but controlled movement to a place of relative safety may be required in extreme circumstances. At no time should a casualty with suspected spinal injury be stood or sat upright. There should be manual in-line stabilising of the cervical spine from the moment an injury is considered. A rigid neck collar must be applied in almost all cases before discontinuing the manual in-line stabilisation. (A section on 'clearing' the neck follows.)

A thoracolumbar splint, such as a Kendrick Extrication Device® (KED®), can be used for short periods (<30 minutes) particularly to aid the extrication of the casualty from a confined space. ICAR have recommended that should such extrication involve lifting vertically – for example, from a narrow vertical crevasse – an additional lifting seat is used as the main weight bearing attachment as demonstrated in the pictures below. Thanks to Dr Greg Zenruffinen for the pictures.

Long or spinal boards have a very limited place in mountain rescue. The degree of immobilisation, the casualty's comfort and sacral interface pressure are all inferior to a vacuum mattress. Sacral interface pressure is a risk factor for the development of pressure sores; these are a major preventable cause of morbidity in spinal injury. And anyway, consider the risk to the rescuer of carrying one on a windy ridge!

The patient is best transferred onto a vacuum mattress as soon as practical and the casualty transported on his back if possible. At all times a team member is appointed solely to monitor the airway and casualty's condition. Portable hand suction should be readily available.

Cervical collars

These are applied to the neck in all known or suspected cervical spine injuries and unconscious patients as a precaution against causing further injury. The collar must be of an appropriate size for the casualty. The manufacturer's instructions should be followed in respect to sizing and application. Collars basically come as either the semirigid variety, commonly referred to as a 'hard' collar, or a flimsy 'soft' collar. 'Soft' collars have no place in *Casualty Care* and should be thrown out. The application of a cervical collar requires at least two people. The first maintains the head and neck in a neutral position using gentle in-line manual immobilisation whilst the second applies the collar without moving the neck.

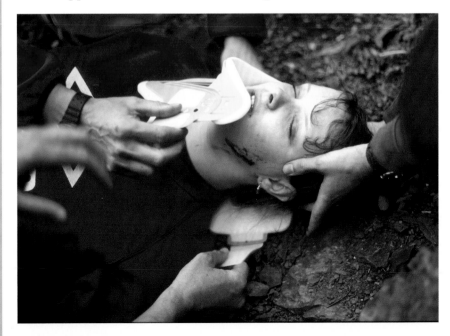

Once in place it should not assumed that the neck is completely immobilised; additional external stability is required to prevent head rotation. This can be achieved by packing the vacuum mattress around the head and neck prior to deflation. (On a long board, head blocks and tape are used as shown in the picture on page 68.)

Collars themselves can cause complications. Collars that are too tight or small can initiate skin pressure ulcers and can raise the pressure within the brain by obstructing venous blood flow in the neck. Too large a collar may allow too much cervical spine movement with the risk of secondary mechanical damage. Collars that are too tall may force the neck into an excessive amount of extension as well as not allowing the patient to open their mouth, a problem that may become catastrophic if they vomit.

The log roll and application of spinal splints

At least four people are required to perform a safe log roll and immobilise the spine. Six people are ideal. This keeps the casualty in a neutral position and avoids bending or twisting the spine. Limb injuries should be splinted before a log roll is performed. 'Rescuer 1' maintains in-line immobilisation of the head and neck (even when a collar is in place), at least one person (rescuer 2) is responsible for the chest and abdomen and at least one person (rescuer 3) is responsible for the pelvis and legs. The fourth person will manoeuvre the vacuum mattress or spinal splint into position and is the best person to feel down the spine. The log roll method needs the casualty's arms to be straight and next to the body. The legs need to be placed in a straight line with the body and ideally the ankles tied together with a figure of eight bandage.

Alignment of the head and neck is maintained by rescuer 1 while rescuer 2 reaches across and grasps the casualty's shoulder and wrist. Rescuer 3 reaches across to grasp the hip and the lower legs. On the instruction of rescuer 1, the casualty is rolled cautiously as one unit towards rescuer 2 and 3. Rescuer 4 then feels down the spine for areas of tenderness, swelling or deformity. Looking at the areas identified can usually be done without removing clothing - heavy scissors should be handy! Only the minimum amount of movement is used to enable the spinal splint to be positioned under the casualty.

If the casualty has limb or chest injuries, it is usual to roll him onto the uninjured side supporting the injured and previously splinted limbs. The casualty is rolled back onto the splint at the command of the person in control of the head (rescuer 1). Finally the casualty is secured on the splint and a check made of the casualty's condition and pain.

The vacuum mattress

Ideally the vacuum mattress should be used on all unconscious casualties and all those with suspected spinal injury. It gives better splintage, stability and pressure area care than the standard mountain rescue stretcher. Its disadvantages are its bulk and vulnerability to puncture. A rigid stretcher is still required for evacuation. The following practical points have been identified when deploying the vacuum mattress.

> Unroll mattress and press out flat. Partial inflation or deflation at this stage help to distribute the filling evenly and assures appropriate splintage and pressure distribution.
>
> See that the casualty has no sharp objects on his person or in his pockets, e.g. climbing gear.
>
> Gently form the mattress around the casualty and maintain the shape with the straps provided as the mattress is fully deflated.

Evacuation

The casualty should be transferred on a rigid mountain rescue stretcher. The rescue team should aim to provide a controlled and smooth evacuation. In an isolated spinal injury a gentle evacuation is more important than speed. In the presence of life threatening injuries a more rapid evacuation must be performed. If a crag has to be descended a horizontal, rather than vertical, stretcher lower should be planned if at all possible. This avoids axial loading of the spine. Evacuation by helicopter generally provides a smooth journey with smaller acceleration and deceleration forces so is usually preferred to a carry out and then land ambulance journey. The casualty should be transferred to a local Accident and Emergency department equipped to receive patients with major injuries. Initial transfer to a specialist spinal injury unit is not appropriate. A written record should always accompany the casualty to hospital.

Removing a helmet

For years we have encountered injured climbers with a helmet on. Initially the cervical spine is stabilised with the helmet on but it is usual to remove it when the danger from falling rocks has been minimised. A casualty lying on a flat stretcher with a helmet on has his neck flexed as the occiput (back of the skull) is lifted up; this is not a good position. Compare the angle of the neck to the rest of the spine with the helmet on and off as shown below.

To remove a helmet, a 'two person' approach is usual with one rescuer stabilising the head and neck and the second undoing the chin strap and removing the helmet. This presents few difficulties as the first rescuer can still stabilise the head and neck effectively by placing their hands on the bony protuberance just behind the ears from the standard position - kneeling at the casualty's head end. Though the helmet prevents the forearms from securing the skull above the ears the rescuer's hand position can easily revert to the normal position when the helmet has been removed. The neck is placed in the neutral position and a cervical collar applied. Rarely the helmet has to be removed immediately to get better access to the airway or to stop blood loss from the scalp. In these circumstances a single rescuer may need to do their best with one hand supporting the occiput as the other hand removes the helmet.

Until now we have been spared the 'full-face' helmet that has been the nightmare of those rescuing injured motorcyclists. But now such helmets are appearing for mountain bikers. Different hand positions need to be adopted and a careful rocking motion of the helmet is needed. At the same time flexion of the neck (the worst movement) has to be minimised! The procedure is:

Undo the chin strap

One rescuer (the most experienced and one giving the commands) supports the neck from the front by placing thumb and index finger of one hand on the angle of the jaw. The other hand cradles the back of the neck and is slowly slid onto the skull as the second rescuer removes the helmet as shown in the pictures below.

Remove the helmet

How this is done will depend on how tight the helmet is. If it is slack, it may be possible to remove the helmet in an axial (in-line) direction perhaps with careful lateral expansion of the rim of the helmet as shown below. Be careful not to apply excessive axial traction to the neck. If the helmet is too tight for this manoeuvre, the helmet may need to be tipped forward and backwards in a vertical plane as it is extracted.

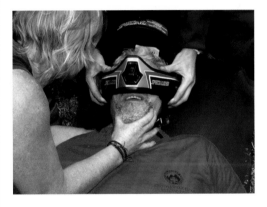 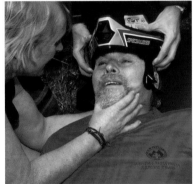

Secure the neck

With the helmet removed, the second rescuer assumes the normal hand position for stabilising the neck in the neutral position. The first rescuer applies the rigid cervical collar. Adjustable collars are space saving. The casualty is moved onto the vacuum

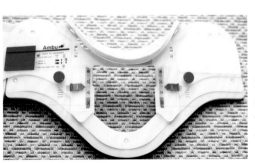 mattress and additional external support applied to the head to supplement the collar.

"When do I apply a collar and immobilise the spine?"

" My Accident and Emergency department (or ambulance crew) will only take trauma casualties with a rigid collar and on a long spinal board with neck blocks on".

Looking after the spine after injury is a relatively new area. Neck collars used to be soft and comfortable. They were no more than 'neck warmers'. Standard practices became established on opinions and particularly fear rather than good evidence of benefit. Missing an unstable fracture of the spine, particularly of the neck, has serious medical and financial implications, and remains one of the greatest tragedies. It must be avoided if at all possible. There was only one way to go – anyone with a history of twisting or forced movement of the spine needed full spinal immobilisation. This became easy with the widespread adoption of rigid collars and the long spinal board by the Ambulance Service.

But at what cost?

Spinal immobilisation is at the best uncomfortable, often frightening, can cause pressure sores, reduce the tidal volume of breathing and increase intracranial pressure. It can delay transporting casualties to hospital as usually an ambulance can only take one 'boarded' casualty at a time. Is it possible to be selective picking out those casualties with a spinal fracture so avoiding unnecessary immobilisation? American studies show it is possible, using a protocol, to make sure that 99% of cervical fractures are immobilised. The protocol would look like this:

Implement spinal immobilisation in the following:

Spinal pain or tenderness with a history of trauma.
Severe head or facial trauma.
Numbness or weakness in any extremity after trauma.
If altered mental state whether from alcohol, drugs or head injury and –
    no history available.
    or found in the setting of trauma (i.e. at the bottom of the stairs).
    or near drowning with a history or probability of diving.
Distracting injury, such as a fracture elsewhere, in the casualty with a mechanism of injury that may have injured the spine.

Implementing such a protocol may allow a few casualties to escape from unnecessary spinal immobilisation but the predictive value remains very low. For example in one study, for each person with a spinal fracture, 85 were immobilised unnecessarily. This is acceptable given the tragic consequences of not immobilising an unstable spinal fracture. Fortunately mountain rescue is ahead of the game. Long spinal boards are too unwieldy for the fell. The vacuum mattress with a rigid cervical collar has become standard and is much more acceptable to the casualty and at the same time reduces problems induced by the long board. Comfort, security and insulation are added benefits that allow rescuers to be very conservative immobilising every casualty with a tumbling fall. The question remains as to when the cervical collar can be omitted – carefully applying the protocol above would seem reasonable.

Summary

Suspect a spinal injury in anybody who has localised pain along the spine. The unconscious casualty and those with a painful distracting injury are at risk of having a spinal injury going unrecognised. Give full spinal care to prevent secondary injury in all casualties with a potential spinal injury.

Case studies

These cases are fictional but were developed from several real cases. They were commissioned for *Casualty Care in Mountain Rescue* to contribute a sense of real life and to draw attention to the dilemmas that occur in rescue work.

Case 1 – Fractured spine with numbness and weakness in legs

Time and date: 19.40, midsummer

Location: Bottom of steep crag, 70 m from the road

Weather: Dry and mild

Cause of incident: Fall whilst rock climbing, landing on broken rocks

Reported injuries: Leg injuries

The incident was at a roadside crag. The team met at the crag. The casualty had not been moved since his fall and it was apparent that he had fallen/tumbled 20 metres. He was draped over a large boulder with his head below his legs and face down. This made spinal examination unusually easy! The casualty was fully conscious and could recall his fall. He said he had pain in his back. When asked by the team, he said he couldn't feel one of his legs. An examination of the casualty showed no apparent head, neck, chest or abdominal injury. The lower lumber spine was tender with swelling in the 'small of the back'. Loss of sensation in the left lower leg was confirmed and he could not move that foot when asked to do so.

The diagnosis was a fractured lumber spine with nerve damage. Equipment on site included Entonox®, and a Bell® stretcher. A KED® was rapidly brought from the roadside and this was applied to the casualty by wrapping it round him before moving him. Once the KED® was securely fastened the casualty was log rolled through 180 degrees and placed on the Bell stretcher. This procedure required 5 rescuers but went smoothly, with the legs being kept in a neutral position. Self-administered Entonox® was used. A check on the numbness and weakness of the left leg showed no change following the transfer. A gentle carry out to the roadside took only a few minutes; the casualty was then transferred about 45 kilometres in the ambulance to the local District General Hospital.

Comments

We had to think how best to apply the KED®; it is worth practising splintage in unorthodox positions. It is sensible to delay any movement of the casualty until the spine has been immobilised. Sometimes there is concern about other injuries, particularly affecting the airway or chest, which might need early movement of the casualty to the normal face up position. In these cases, care and clear instruction on how the casualty is going to be moved is essential. The KED® does not prevent leg movement; this needs controlling to reduce pelvic rotation. In 1992 vacuum mattresses were not widely available but would it have been preferred if the incident repeated itself? The vacuum mattress is not designed for extrication, unlike the KED®. It would be difficult, if not impossible, to apply the vacuum mattress in the position in which the casualty was found. However, it has been shown that spinal boards, and the KED®, can cause pressure sores in as little as 45 minutes. The ideal management would have been to transfer the casualty from the KED® to a vacuum mattress using an orthopaedic (scoop) stretcher from the ambulance at the roadside. In this way the time in the KED® would have been limited to less than 30 minutes and the casualty would have been in the more comfortable and potentially safer vacuum mattress during the 40 minute journey to hospital. It is certainly important to record the time the spinal board or KED® is applied and if it left on during the transfer of the casualty to hospital that the hospital staff are aware of this.

Case 2 – Occult Spinal injury

Time and date: 15.00, early Spring

Location: Mountain ridge about 40 minutes walk from the nearest road

Weather: Intermittent light cloud cover at the casualty site but only a moderate wind

Cause of incident: Fall whilst crossing an old patch of snow

Reported injuries: Tumbling fall of 20 metres.

There was no injury report – no one could get to the casualty though she was shouting and apparently responding to the calls from the other members of her party. The accident had occurred over 30 minutes ago; no working mobile phone in the party!

The team set off on foot with resuscitation and monitoring equipment, oxygen, Entonox®, a vacuum mattress and a rigid rescue stretcher. A helicopter had been asked to assist – it would arrive at the scene at about the same time as the team.

To reach the casualty a bit of snowy scrambling was required and some simple safety work at the scene to secure the casualty and rescuer.

The casualty had not moved from her position after the fall. She was alert and talking normally but complained of pain on breathing. Her respiratory rate was 24 per minute with a painful area on the front of the chest just below the clavicle (collar bone). The radial pulse was counted at 100 beats per minute and the oxygen saturation was 97% in air. And that's as far as the assessment went! The helicopter arrived, the winch man descended with a rigid mountain rescue stretcher and, with the single mountain rescuer, got the casualty into the stretcher and was off to the nearest hospital, which was 15 minutes away, with in-flight oxygen therapy.

Comment

You will have guessed that this lady had an occult cervical spine fracture; you are right! The seventh cervical vertebrate had been crushed. There were no permanent neurological sequelae and she made a full recovery from this injury and her fractured ribs. The rescuers involved were very quiet when told of the diagnoses and I am sure learnt that distracting injuries really do mask a spinal injury. Why was this casualty's care compromised? This is an important question as such poor care has occurred on a number of occasions including ones where clearly no spinal support was used.

Occasionally a 'load and go' rescue is justified but was there an A, B or C problem in this case? Perhaps there was a potential B problem but with an oxygen saturation of 97% in air an hour after the accident it seems unlikely that it could be life threatening.

Was the opportunity to use the helicopter limited to one attempt by the weather, fuel load or another factor? Hard to say but the time to get manpower and apply the vacuum mattress would have been no more than 15 minutes.

Were the rescuers too eager to do the rescue 'alone' as a consequence of their heightened state of arousal – the 'red mist' or 'adrenaline rush' – that we all suffer from? Was the situation too scary? Working in teams and doing risk assessments are hard skills to put into practice when you are in such a state.

Had the casualty been unconscious, would the spinal care have been more thorough? Possibly; the importance of mechanism of injury and distracting injury in the alert casualty is relatively new and may have been forgotten on the day.

Let's learn from this case study and reduce the risks that have been taken in the past.

References

Joint Royal Colleges Ambulance Liaison Committee. *Clinical Practice Guidelines* 2004. Available at www.nelh.nhs.uk/emergency

Morris CG, McCoy W, Lavery GG. Spinal immobilisation for unconscious patients with multiple injuries. *BMJ* 2004; 329:495-9

Wardrope J, Locker T. Risk assessment for spinal injury after trauma. *BMJ* 2004; 328:721-3

Luscombe MD, Williams JL. Comparison of a long spinal board and vacuum mattress for spinal immobilisation. *Emerg Med J* 2003; 20:476-478

D'Costa H, George G et al. Pitfalls in the clinical diagnosis of vertebral fractures: a case series in which posterior midline tenderness was absent. *Emerg Med J* 2005; 22:330-2

Murrills J. Management of spinal injuries in mountain rescue. Accessed in the members' area of the MRC website (www.mountain.rescue.org.uk)

A poor way to lift a casualty
with a possible spinal injury

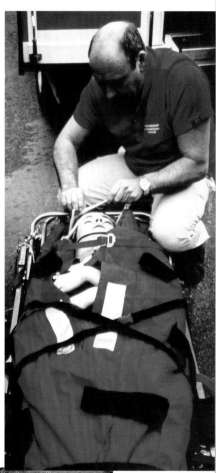

Good packaging ready
for an evacuation

Teamwork is crucial in spinal injury

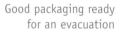

Emergency Care of Eye Injuries

The emergency management of traumatic eye injuries can be crucial to saving the eye and its sight. Trauma to the eye and its surrounding tissues can cause rapid lid swelling. This can make it impossible to open the eye again for days. A prompt eye examination before the eye closes can supply valuable information, which otherwise may be delayed for a few days. However the assessment and stabilisation of potentially life-threatening injuries must obviously take priority over any eye injury.

Eye injuries can be deceptive. Mild trauma can cause marked bleeding under the thin "skin" (conjunctiva) covering the eye to produce a bright red swollen eye and gross lid bruising. This looks dramatic but there may not be any underlying eye injury. On the other hand sight-threatening injuries may look trivial on cursory inspection. For example sharp foreign bodies may penetrate through a small lid puncture wound and lodge within the optic nerve. Serious eye injuries are usually not particularly painful. A high index of suspicion is required to detect an occult injury. The history of the incident helps. How severe was the blow to the eye, was a foreign body potentially involved, and are there associated facial injuries? An estimate of the vision in each eye individually is an important sign. Can the casualty count fingers at 1 metre away, or at 10cm, detect hand movements, or only see light?

A history of previous eye surgery makes the eye more likely to rupture from a moderate blow. If the person was wearing glasses these should be inspected for damage to the frames and lenses. Sending the pieces with the patient can be useful in x-ray detection of retained foreign bodies. Contact lenses should be removed only if this can be achieved without exerting significant pressure on the eye, and after a ruptured globe has been excluded. If possible the contact lens should be removed before marked lid swelling occurs. If not, extra care is needed to prevent the eye surface from drying and the medical staff should be informed of the contact len's presence.

Ruptured eye injuries

Severe blows to the eye can rupture the eyeball. The vision is usually very poor. A large laceration of the cornea or anterior sclera (white wall of the eye) is usually readily visible on close inspection. A subconjunctival haemorrhage, blood in front of the iris (coloured part of the eye), a distorted irregular pupil and protruding ocular contents may be present. This tissue often appears as brownish debris or translucent "jelly" on the eye. If in doubt do not try to wipe it away, as you may remove more than you bargained for!

If a ruptured eye injury is suspected it is essential that no pressure is exerted on the eye. Complete expulsion of the eye contents can occur. The eyelids must not be forcibly opened, and the patient should not squeeze their eye closed. Do not cover the eye with a dressing or tape the eyelids closed. Protect the eye with a rigid eye shield during evacuation. (Cut up a bit of plastic from a cervical collar?) Relieving pain and preventing vomiting greatly lessens the risk of further ocular damage.

Foreign bodies

Windblown foreign bodies often become lodged on the cornea or under the upper eyelid. This results in sharp pain, watering and redness of the eye. A clean cotton-wool bud can sometimes dislodge the offending foreign body. However there is no need for its urgent removal outside hospital.

Foreign bodies ricocheting into the eye with force e.g. during rock hammering, or during falls can potentially lead to loss of the eye. Sharp slivers can penetrate through the wall of the globe or pass through the eyelids to enter the posterior part of the eye or even the brain. The speed, length and trajectory of the foreign body are important considerations. Any object that appears to pierce the eye or orbit should not be removed as further irreversible damage may occur from severe bleeding and extrusion of eye contents. Protruding objects should be protected from accidental movement. A plastic eye shield or any substitute rigid protective cover can be taped to the face. If this is not suitable gentle wrapping with soft bandages can help. Care must be taken to avoid any pressure on the eye.

Orbital fractures

A blunt blow directly to the eye can lead to bony fractures of the eye socket. Usually the floor of the eye socket is involved; the bony orbital rim remains intact. The patient experiences eye pain worsened by eye movements, possibly numbness on the cheek and upper gums from the associated nerve damage and bleeding from the nose. The eye may appear displaced in the socket and its movements tend to be restricted with double vision in some directions of gaze. An occult eye injury is often present. Air can escape from the sinuses through the fracture into the soft tissues surrounding the eye. This causes a crackling sensation in the skin (surgical emphysema) on palpation. It is important that the patient does not blow their nose as this increases the emphysema, potentially spreading infection and risking further tissue damage.

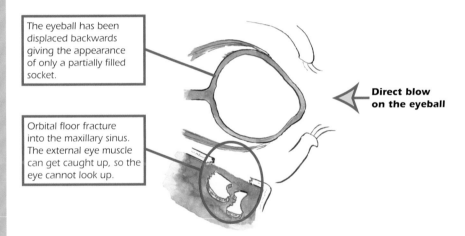

The eyeball has been displaced backwards giving the appearance of only a partially filled socket.

Orbital floor fracture into the maxillary sinus. The external eye muscle can get caught up, so the eye cannot look up.

Direct blow on the eyeball

Lid lacerations

If an eyelid is cut, it is important to prevent further tissue damage and protect the underlying eye from drying out. Putting a moist non-adherent dressing over the eye can prevent drying during the evacuation. The dressing must be kept damp; a dried dressing against the eye can cause severe surface damage and risk blinding the casualty. A penetrating eye injury must be excluded first.

Chemical injuries

Battery explosions are one potential cause of chemical eye injuries. Emergency treatment can make the difference between permanent blindness and useful visual recovery. The eye may initially retain good vision and not be particularly red or painful. A lacklustre appearance and distorted light reflection from the cornea (clear window of the eye) are early warning signs of a significant injury. Any suspicion of a chemical injury requires copious irrigation with fluid as soon as possible. This is begun at the same time as the eye examination. At least a litre of saline or water to each eye should be used. Ideally an intravenous fluid giving set is used, fully opened, to direct the fluid into the eye and wash the inner surfaces of the eyelids. If there is no obvious penetrating eye injury the eyelids can safely be held forcibly open. Irrigation of a closed eye is ineffective! There is no need for specialised solutions. Any source of water can be used in an emergency. A sample of the stream water used can be sent with the patient for infection screening. If a contact lens is present it needs to be removed as soon as possible, as it will prevent adequate irrigation and act as a reservoir for the chemical. Do not pad the eye closed. Urgent ophthalmic consultation must be obtained.

Other considerations

The eyes of an unconscious patient may not be fully closed. Taping them shut or applying eye ointment to prevent the cornea drying is a straightforward measure that can prevent potentially blinding complications.

Direct eye injuries can produce dilated non-reacting pupils. This can cause confusion when there is an accompanying head injury.

Evacuation

The assessment of a potential eye injury must not delay the transfer of a potential seriously injured person to hospital. If necessary the eye examination can be performed *en route* when the patient is stable. There are no problems transporting an eye-injured casualty by air. Hypoxia should be avoided as it increases the risk of a severe intra-ocular haemorrhage, and expulsion of ocular contents in penetrating eye injuries. Care must be taken to avoid the oxygen mask pressing on the eye. The gas flow should not be allowed to dry the cornea. A moist dressing can help prevent this. The casualty should be positioned with their head up, or if not on their uninjured side, if their general condition allows.

Summary

The acute management of eye and orbital trauma aims to prevent further damage during transfer. The essentials are to prevent any pressure on the eye, which can lead to irreversible damage. This takes priority over a detailed eye examination. Local protection with a rigid eye cover and general measures such as an upright position, prevention of vomiting and hypoxia can be sight saving. Simple care to avoid an exposed cornea from drying may have profound benefits to the person's visual rehabilitation.

Colin and Jenny on Thoule, Cogne, Italy. (2005)

Katy at a frozen Stickle tarn, Langdale. (2004)

Extremities

Objectives

To stop a wound bleeding and reduce the risk of infection
To recognise the common fractures and dislocations
To manage these with appropriate pain relief and splinting
To know when an injury requires urgent evacuation

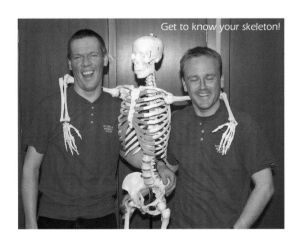

Get to know your skeleton!

Introduction

This chapter will cover more casualties than the rest of the book put together! Lower leg injuries are the 'bread-and-butter' of mountain rescue. Rescuers should grasp the basics and then develop an interest in the subtle differences between one fractured tibia and the next. There is a lot that can be done to reduce the disability from an injury to the arm or leg as the level of skill of the rescuer increases. We can all improve our management of these mundane injuries.

Managing a soft tissue injury

Abrasions, cuts and lacerations

These are all soft tissue injuries that occur when a casualty falls. The aims of treatment are to stop bleeding and reduce the risk of infection. These aims are achieved by following the suggestions below.

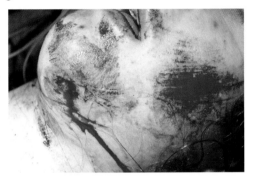

Elevate the injured part and, if bleeding, apply pressure over the wound. In the first instance this can be done with a gloved hand and then with a sterile dressing that is both absorbent and non-adherent (i.e. Melolin®) to the skin. Maintain a moderate pressure on the wound for 10 minutes. Taking the dressing off to look is a certain way of restarting the bleeding. Don't do this. Apply fresh dressings (i.e. ambulance dressing) on top of the old ones if the blood seeps through. Only if you think your ability to apply direct pressure has been reduced is it worth removing some of the older dressings. When the 10 minutes is up, it may be worth removing the outer layers of the dressing and inspecting the wound. This risks reactivating the bleeding but allows the wound to be washed with an antiseptic, such as povidone-iodine (Betadine®). This reduces the chance of infection. Use a water-based compound; an alcohol-based one stings! You may feel that the risk of restarting the bleeding is too great - that's fine, add a Betadine® soaked dressing over the lower one. Now bandage the dressing in place using a crepe bandage so that a moderate pressure can be kept on the wound. Check that the bandage is not too tight and acting as a tourniquet on the limb. Immobilise the wound, using a splint if necessary, and maintain the elevation if practical. Rarely stitching (suturing) a wound, particularly on the scalp, may be needed to stop the bleeding. (For further details, see page 124.) In the extreme case of entrapment, perhaps from a rock fall, a tourniquet may be the only way of controlling ongoing bleeding where direct pressure cannot be applied. Consider the risk to the life of the casualty; the tourniquet will certainly threaten the life of the limb!

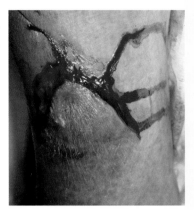

Bruises and haematoma

A bruise is a soft tissue injury where the small blood vessels in and just under the skin break causing tissue discolouration. The skin is not broken. A haematoma is the result of a similar injury to a deeper blood vessel. It becomes important when it occurs in a muscle, such as the quadriceps (thigh muscle), where the blood loss can be significant. In contrast to a fracture of the femur, there will be no leg

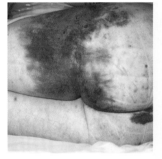

shortening and the casualty may be able to limp. If the injury is too painful for the casualty to walk, give appropriate analgesia and bandage the whole of the thigh with a moderately firm crepe bandage. Check you have not formed a tourniquet and evacuate the casualty on a stretcher. Exercise can reactivate the bleeding in the muscle and may need to be avoided for at least a number of days. Soft tissue injury can be extensive as shown below.

Fractures and Dislocations

Anatomy

Bones form an internal framework upon which muscles can act; this allows limbs to move. They also support and protect soft structures such as the brain and, within the marrow, provide the sole blood-forming tissue of the body. Knowledge of the correct medical name for a bone is not necessary though familiarity with the major bones does aid communication. Bones are not inert hard structures made of calcium. In life, they are active tissues with a significant blood supply. Damage to a bone inevitably leads to some degree of blood loss, the larger the bone the greater, and more important, the blood loss. When a bone is broken there is always considerable damage to the surrounding soft tissues. This causes further blood loss and accounts for most of the swelling associated with a fracture. A fracture of the femur in an adult can lead to the loss of 1000 mls of blood i.e. one fifth of the total blood volume; fractures are an important cause of shock!

Fractures are divided into closed fractures, where the skin has not been broken, and open (compound) fractures, where there is direct communication between the fracture site and the outside. The risk of infection is much greater in an open fracture. An infection, at best, delays the healing of the fracture; at worst, it can cause part of the bone to die leaving a gap in the skeleton.

Fractures can be simple or complicated. Displacement of the bone ends or soft tissue damage to the skin, nerves or blood vessels makes the fracture complicated. This may threaten the survival of the limb.

The history of the event leading to the injury, including the direction of the impact, the way the force was transmitted and the amount of energy involved may suggest a fracture is likely. Though some fractures (a fractured wrist) can be caused by relatively trivial violence, other fractures (a fractured femur) require a major force. It is worthwhile considering the mechanism of injury to try to predict the type of fractures that may be present. This is particularly so for axial forces such as landing on your feet from a height. The force is transmitted from the os calcis (heel bone) right up the spine to the base of the skull. Any of these bones can be fractured - indeed the painful heel may distract from more important fractures above.

Signs and symptoms of a fracture

Pain is the commonest
symptom. It originates
not only from the
fracture site but also the
damaged soft tissues. The
nature and severity of
the pain varies from
injury to injury and

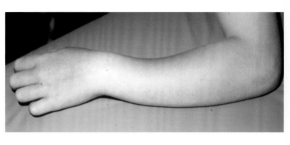

person to person. Apparently similar fractures can be an 'ache' to
one person yet intolerable to another. Children are poor at localising
the site of pain; this makes the examination more important. Some
degree of discomfort will be experienced all the time. This element is
particularly marked in dislocations and displaced fractures where the
soft tissue is being stretched. The casualty will experience an
increase in pain with any movement of the injured part. Pain can be
provoked by gentle pressure at the site of the fracture though a soft
tissue injury without fracture can be equally tender. A fracture is
more likely if gentle axial compression causes an increase in pain.

Deformity occurs when a bone
or joint is displaced from its
normal position. This may be
visible on examination as
angulation of the bone or
shortening of the limb.
However, it can be difficult to
detect and may be disguised to

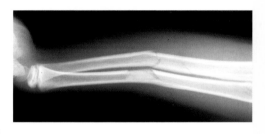

some degree by surrounding soft tissue swelling.

Swelling is usually present over a fracture. It can be massive and, as
commented above, contain a large quantity of blood.

Loss of function is often difficult to assess. People will say - "I don't
think my ankle is broken because I can move my toes" - yet will be
unable to weight-bear. In a fracture around the ankle, the likely loss
of function is the inability to weight bear. Abnormal mobility may
occasionally occur. If seen it should not be repeated for fear of
worsening the injury.

Crepitus is the 'crunching' sensation when the irregular bone ends
rub against each other. Like abnormal mobility it is very useful when

diagnosing a fracture but once recognised the limb should be left in the normal anatomical position and appropriately splinted. Both crepitus and abnormal mobility should be noted if present but not be actively sought. Demonstrating either may do more harm to the tissues.

Symptoms and signs of a dislocation

Dislocations occur at joints. The pain is often intense and unremitting. Moving the affected joint is often impossible and deformity is usually obvious. As with fractures, there is always a soft tissue injury. Usually the ligaments surrounding the joint are torn. Long-term problems result from this - a dislocated joint is more likely to dislocate again often with a lesser force. Fractures and dislocations often occur together so a radiogram (x-ray) should be taken at an early stage.

Managing a fracture

A fracture is the commonest injury seen in mountain rescue. You may be surprised to see only three pages written in this book about how to manage a fracture. The reason is that the principles behind the treatment are simple and we do not want to recommend specific equipment to a team. Teams will have ingrained preferences as to which splints they will use - the section on immobilising a fracture illustrates some of the options.

There are two components to managing a fracture - pain relief and preventing complications. Splinting the fracture is the key to reducing both the pain and the complications. The rescuer should always consider life-saving before limb-saving; do not become distracted by the distress of a fracture until the primary survey has been completed. A fracture may impact on the primary survey - for example a fractured femur will cause shock - the aims of treatment at that stage are very different from the aims of the treatment we are now discussing.

Fractures are painful when moved. Stand back and think about how you are going to proceed before you start messing about. If you suspect a fracture you need to see the skin. Clothing and boots will need removing. A good pair of scissors are invaluable. (See page 398!) Can pain relief be given first?

Pain relief

There are three methods available for reducing pain. These are reassurance, analgesia with drugs (Entonox®, morphine, diclofenac) and reduction/immobilisation of the fracture by splinting. Details on the individual drugs are included in the Drugs chapter. Rescuers need to develop a skill in giving the right amount of analgesia at the right time. Think about the time it takes for the pain relief to become effective. Contrast the rapid onset of action of

Entonox® with the delay of 15 - 20 minutes for an oral drug like diclofenac. Are there episodes where the pain will be more intense? For example, when the fracture is initially splinted, when the casualty is moved to the stretcher and when the evacuation path becomes rough. How long will the rescue take? We all know an injury is less painful when we are safe, warm and relaxed. Plan, with the casualty, giving suitable pain relief for the whole rescue. Explain the options, the reasons for using a particular type and the problems with the analgesics available. Don't forget that you have more experience than the casualty; recommend certain options like morphine for a lower leg fracture when the evacuation is going to be a few hours over the moors.

Preventing complications

As we have seen in the chapter on head and spinal injury preventing secondary damage is important. In fractures, infection and ischaemia (loss of blood supply) cause secondary damage.

Infection

All open fractures are contaminated with bacteria either from the skin or the soil. The wound should be washed with Betadine® and a sterile, non-adherent dressing applied. If grossly contaminated with soil, etc. copious amounts of clean water should be used to wash the worst off first before the Betadine® is applied. (If spare, a bag of saline for intravenous use would be appropriate). Giving antibiotics as soon as possible reduces the chance of the contamination developing into an infection of the fracture site. Most studies have been done in hospital using intravenous antibiotics. This would be the preferred treatment but risks a serious anaphylactic reaction.

Managing this on the mountain side would be frightening and potentially dangerous. A compromise is to give an oral antibiotic (cefuroxime - details in the Drugs chapter). Note the evidence for doing this is weak but it would seem appropriate when the hospital is two hours away and absorption of the antibiotic from the stomach is likely.

Ischaemia

If a fracture distorts a blood vessel, the tissues further down the limb may become short of blood. Reducing the fracture (or dislocation) often improves the blood flow. Details are given in the section on individual fractures. The skin over a fracture may also become ischaemic (waxy white or blue) from the soft tissue swelling. Avoiding pressure on the skin and elevating the fracture site help to reduce the chance that the skin will die.

Immobilising a fracture

Splinting a fracture reduces the movement of the sharp bone ends. This reduces the pain and the risk of complications. How a fracture is splinted depends on the site and the availability of special equipment. The team will have its preferred methods. The common types of splint used are described below along with some of their advantages and disadvantages:

Skis, ladders, ice axes etc!

Collar and cuff, broad arm sling and fracture straps

Malleable neoprene splints and Kramer wire splints - versatile, cheap and expendable but need padding and it may be difficult to monitor the limb once applied. (See page 170.)

Inflatable splints - easy to apply, cushioning and comfortable but punctures and limb deformity render them useless. The inflating pressure must be right; should the pressure used be recorded? The fracture area cannot be inspected without deflating and removing the splint. Compressing the skin over a fracture may further compromise its already fragile blood supply and lead to skin necrosis. Converting a simple fracture into a compound fracture is poor management and potentially devastating so inflatable splints are no longer recommended.

Box splints - easy to apply, adjust and monitor but bulky to carry and the immobilisation can be poor.

Vacuum splints - flexible and excellent immobilisation though expensive to buy. Punctures and forgetting the pump are hazards!

Traction splints - these are indispensable for fractures of the shaft of the femur where the degree of pain and the amount of blood lost are reduced. There are three basic types: double strut – like the original Thomas splint; a telescopic modern version, such as the Donway®, is practical and robust; a mono-strut – such as the Sagar®, which can splint bilateral femoral fractures; and a foldable strut – such as the Kendrick traction device®, which appears rather flimsy but is light and folds away.

Fracture mid-shaft femur

Thomas

Sagar®

Kendrick

The rescuer needs to think of a few general points before the splint is applied.

Expose the skin all the way round and 10 cm above and below the fracture site.

Stop external bleeding and apply dressings to wounds.

Think how a splint is going to immobilise the joint above and below the fracture. Is the splint big enough and can you get adequate access to apply it?

Is it necessary to reduce deformity and can this be achieved?

Then apply the splint of your choice ensuring that the limb is supported over as much of its surface area as possible (extra padding) and that there are no pressure points particularly on areas of ischaemic skin. The circulation distal to the fracture should be checked (and recorded). Ask the casualty what degree of pain remains and discuss whether further analgesia is appropriate.

Forearm splinting

Lightly wrap the forearm in a soft wool bandage,

ensuring that the bandage will cover the splint.

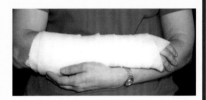

Measure the length of a conforming splint and

carefully mould it to the arm without putting pressure on the fracture.

Secure the splint with a crepe bandage,

securing the ends with tape and then check the distal circulation.

Secure to the body if necessary and check that the arm is comfortable.

When does the limb need checking? This is a difficult question as once the casualty is ensconced in a casualty bag (with its enclosed heat) and the evacuation started, the whole momentum of the rescue seems at risk if progress is halted for a limb inspection. A definite reason to stop and look at the limb is if the casualty's pain increases. Don't wait for the casualty to complain - ask him frequently. It may be that the initial pain relief is wearing off or the splint has lost its function, moved or is rubbing on the skin. More worryingly the dressings or splint may now be acting as a tourniquet and be reducing the blood supply to the distal limb; this needs rectifying immediately. Sometimes the casualty will describe the pain as intense, dull, persistent and distal to the original fracture pain but the rescuer cannot rely on these distinctions. The limb should be carefully inspected to exclude a tourniquet effect. This may require the splint to be partially removed, circumferential bandaging cut and dressings disturbed. The degree of inspection needed has to be gauged on the individual case but the general rule is that you need to be happy that a tourniquet effect has been definitely excluded by seeing down to skin. A circumferential bandage, that is a bandage wrapped round a limb, is notorious for restricting blood flow as the fracture site swells. Cutting or slackening the bandage will result in the casualty feeling the blood return and then a reduction in pain. Careful handling of the limb should avoid unstable fractures from becoming displaced again. However a fracture of the shaft of the femur is an exception. In this case, it would be unwise to reduce all the traction, as deformity will recur. Compare the legs to judge whether the fracture has been distracted (pulled apart) too much and check that the peripheral pulses are still palpable. Consider slightly reducing the traction if it looks as if you have overdone it or add further support to the leg if the leg length looks OK. Once you are satisfied that a tourniquet effect has been excluded, further pain relief can be given and the evacuation recommenced.

Recording what you have done is very important. The hospital will need to know. Precisely what position was the limb in? How did you reduce the deformity and how did the circulation improve? Where is the fracture and how unstable is it? Can it be x-rayed before the splint is removed? Remember that some mountain rescue splints are so specialised that the staff in the Accident and Emergency department may have no idea how to remove them. A pair of scissors is not the best way of removing a vacuum splint!

Injuries about the shoulder

The incidence of shoulder injury in Alpine skiing has been reported to be almost 1 in 2000 days of skiing. (Mountain biking must have similar incidence!) The most common shoulder injuries were rotator cuff strains (24.2%), shoulder dislocations or subluxations (21.6%), acromioclavicular separations (19.6%), and clavicle (collar bone) fractures (10.9%).

Rotator cuff strains and tears

The rotator cuff is comprised of four muscles that surround the head of the humerus and stabilize the shoulder joint. A quick look at any anatomical drawing will show that without muscles the shoulder joint would never be a stable base for arm movement. Injuries to the rotator cuff can occur during a fall but are more commonly seen following minor injury to a shoulder already showing signs of cuff degeneration. This is common in the 5th and 6th decades or when forceful overhead manoeuvres of the shoulder have been done. The casualty complains of pain that is often poorly localized in the shoulder area. The pain is worse on shoulder movement and frequently has prevented sleeping in the past. There may be local tenderness but swelling and deformity will not be present.

Treatment

The acute treatment comprises of analgesia and support for the arm. It would be unusual if the casualty could not walk from the fell. Rotator cuff injuries tend to be chronic and specialist management is often needed for the active.

Acromioclavicular injuries

Acromioclavicular injuries are usually caused by a fall directly onto the shoulder. The clavicle is forced downwards with the shoulder until it impacts the first rib. If the shoulder continues to move, the ligaments holding the clavicle to the shoulder are damaged, as the clavicle is unable to be depressed further. The ligaments (acromioclavicular and coracoclavicular) can be: partially torn resulting in a tender swelling at the outer end of the clavicle; torn enough for the outer end of the clavicle to become prominent - shoulder movements are painful; or completely torn - the clavicle is markedly raised and the arm depressed, and movements are very painful, as shown in the diagram on the next page.

Acromio-clavicular disruption

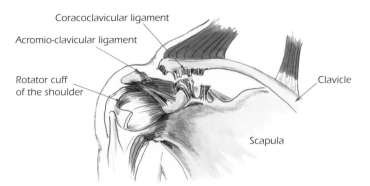

Coracoclavicular ligament

Acromio-clavicular ligament

Rotator cuff of the shoulder

Clavicle

Scapula

Fracture of the Clavicle

A fracture of the clavicle is extremely common and occurs in all age groups. The mechanism of the injury can vary from a fall onto an outstretched hand, with transmission of force up the arm, to a fall directly onto the outer aspect of the shoulder. Most fractures of the clavicle occur between the middle and outer third of the bone, some 5 cm medial to the site of acromioclavicular injuries. Deformity can vary from none to gross, though the latter is rare. Typically, the casualty holds the arm supporting its weight. Look at the clavicle; it shows local swelling and is tender to touch.

Treatment (acromioclavicular injuries and fractured clavicle)

Give adequate analgesia for the degree of pain.

Support the weight of the whole arm across the body (as in the pictures on page 170) and minimize upper arm movement. Possible methods vary from a simple broad arm sling or Velcro straps holding the upper arm into the chest wall and the lower arm across the body. Wrapping the arm inside clothing such as a snug fitting, zipped fleece is helpful.

If this is the only injury and morphine has not been given, it may be feasible to walk the casualty off with some assistance. Often a stretcher evacuation will be more comfortable. The casualty should go to an Accident and Emergency department in the next 24 hours for further management.

Shoulder dislocation

A shoulder dislocation is a common injury. The force needed can vary from a heavy fall onto a raised arm to an awkward manoeuvre in someone with a history of previous dislocation. Though there are three varieties of shoulder dislocation, only the commonest (>95%) anterior dislocation is described. The casualty is often in acute distress and will be both clutching and supporting the injured arm. Any movement of the shoulder is extremely painful and vehemently resisted. The profile of the shoulder, as seen from the front, is abnormal. The normal round contour from the top of the shoulder down onto the deltoid muscles is lost and the point of the shoulder is almost square as shown below. In addition it is possible to feel a depression just below the upper bony prominence of the shoulder, a depression that cannot be felt on the uninjured side.

Right anterior shoulder dislocation (as seen from the front)

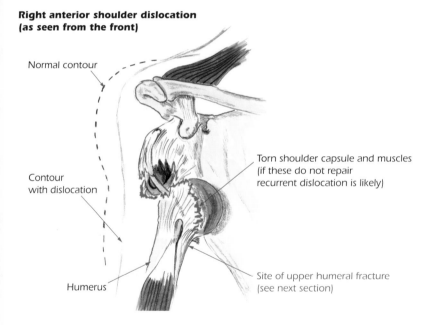

Normal contour

Contour with dislocation

Humerus

Torn shoulder capsule and muscles (if these do not repair recurrent dislocation is likely)

Site of upper humeral fracture (see next section)

Treatment

Reducing a dislocated shoulder can be extremely difficult and requires extra skills and competency. Though the methods used are becoming easier and safer, it is unlikely that a rescuer will have a chance to gain the necessary experience. (A description of shoulder reduction is included in the advanced section of the 'For rescuers' chapter.) The shoulder needs to be supported in the position of most comfort. Padding and Velcro straps can be used to minimize movement. Morphine is likely to be required. Many casualties with this injury are so debilitated that they need to be carried. A few stoic individuals with a recurrent dislocation may be able to walk off with adequate support, assistance and analgesia but this is rare.

Fractures of the upper humerus

Fractures of the upper humerus occur either in a high-energy fall or by direct impact. They are more common in the elderly when only relatively minor falls can break the humerus just below the shoulder joint. The casualty complains of a deep dull and debilitating pain just below the shoulder joint. The appearance of the casualty is very much like that of a casualty with a shoulder dislocation with the arm held in a position of comfort and supported by the other arm. However, the contour of the shoulder is normal and the maximum tenderness is below the shoulder joint though it is often difficult to be certain of this.

Treatment

Support the arm in the position of comfort with a broad arm sling or Velcro straps. Give analgesia appropriate to the degree of pain, and evacuate by stretcher or walking with assistance. This depends upon the degree of distress and stoicism of the casualty; most should be able to walk off with assistance and analgesia.

Injuries about the elbow

Fractures of the lower humerus (supracondylar fracture)

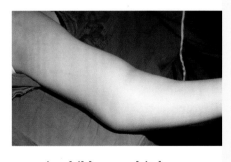

A fracture just above (supra) the bony points of the humerus (the condyles) can occur in a high velocity fall, as the casualty puts out a hand in a 'fending off' gesture. The injury is particularly common in children and it has a bad reputation, as complications are common and serious. The bony fragments from the fracture often damage the important structures (large nerves and the brachial artery) that cross in front of the elbow joint. The injury is extremely painful; deformity around the elbow and extensive soft tissue swelling frequently occur. The radial pulse must be assessed as well as nerve function (loss of sensation) in the hand.

Left supra condylar fracture with brachial artery damage

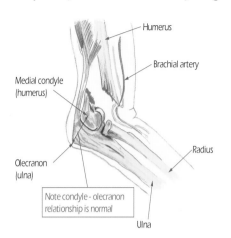

- Humerus
- Brachial artery
- Medial condyle (humerus)
- Radius
- Olecranon (ulna)
- Note condyle - olecranon relationship is normal
- Ulna

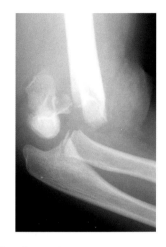

Treatment

The critical factor in the management of a supracondylar fracture is the presence or absence of damage to the blood supply. If the blood supply is damaged then this injury is a surgical emergency and needs to be in hospital as soon as possible. Evacuation by helicopter would be appropriate. If the blood supply is OK (a good pulse easily felt at the wrist), then a more sedate evacuation is possible. Support the arm in the position of comfort and immobilise it there. Check the radial pulse on a regular basis and give adequate analgesia.

Elbow dislocation

Like a supracondylar fracture, the commonest mechanism for causing an elbow dislocation is a fall from a height. There will be marked deformity of the elbow, typically with a prominent step down the back of the arm. The normal relationship between the condyles of the humerus and the olecranon (point of the elbow) is lost;

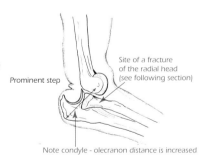

Site of a fracture of the radial head (see following section)

Prominent step

Note condyle - olecranon distance is increased

compare with the normal side – the distance on the injured side is increased. Soft tissue swelling is not usually pronounced but pressure on the blood vessels may cause the loss of the radial pulse.

Treatment

Like a shoulder dislocation, these can be difficult to reduce (get back in place) unless seen by those with experience of such injuries. It is safest to immobilise the elbow in the position found and prevent any excessive movement. Analgesia will be needed. Check for the presence of a pulse at the wrist on a regular basis. If this is absent then consider the injury as a surgical emergency and arrange speedy evacuation.

Fracture of the olecranon

This injury always results from a direct blow to the point of the elbow. It does not have the risk of serious complications unlike the two previous injuries though the fracture is frequently compound. A broad arm sling gives satisfactory support.

Fracture of the head of the radius

The radial head is commonly broken at the elbow when the arm has been put out defensively to break a fall. The radius is compressed and often 'gives' at a weak point within the elbow joint. Movement of the elbow is reasonably normal though typically the casualty is unable to fully straighten the elbow. The commonest sign is pain in the elbow when the hand is turned over. In addition, local tenderness may be present just below the outer aspect of the elbow joint.

Treatment

A radial head fracture is painful but not debilitating. The arm should be supported in a sling, oral analgesia given and the casualty walked off with assistance.

Injuries about the wrist and hand

Wrist fractures

A fractured wrist is typically caused by a fall onto an outstretched hand when the body weight causes the hand and wrist to be forced backwards. They are one of the commonest fractures and can occur at any age. The degree of pain is

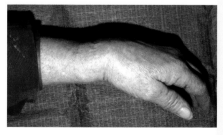

highly variable. Likewise the degree of deformity can vary. Some fractures will not be displaced and only suspected from the mechanism of injury accompanied by swelling just above the wrist joint. Others will show the classic 'dinner fork' deformity of a Colle's fracture. When deformity is present, it is important to assess the blood and nerve supply (sensation in the fingers) beyond the fracture site.

Left fractured distal radius (Colle's Fracture)

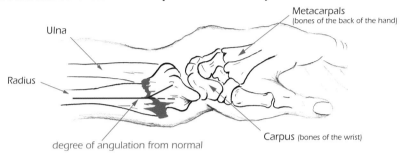

Ulna

Metacarpals (bones of the back of the hand)

Radius

Carpus (bones of the wrist)

degree of angulation from normal

Treatment

The arm needs to be supported in a position of comfort. A supportive splint, preventing movement of the fracture, needs to be applied as illustrated on page 170. The fracture is usually stable as the bones impact into each other; reduction should wait until the casualty is in hospital. Elevation in a sling helps reduce the pain and swelling at the fracture site. The amount of pain relief needed will vary but could include tablets (i.e. paracetamol or diclofenac), Entonox® or intramuscular morphine. Most casualties will manage to walk off with assistance. A greater degree of urgency is required if the blood or nerve supply is compromised or the fracture is compound. In these cases, a helicopter evacuation may be indicated.

Finger and thumb injuries

These injuries are usually due to falls but may be caused by crush injuries to the hand. The digits have a very good blood supply so swelling is prominent. Deformity will be due to either a fracture of one of the finger bones or to a small joint dislocation. Injuries to the thumb where it joins the palm frequently result from a fall onto a grasped ski stick. The thumb is bent back too far and the medial collateral ligament ruptures (Skier's thumb) causing pain, swelling and an inability to pinch thumb and index together. Though unlikely to result in a call-out, the injury is quite disabling and should be fully assessed in hospital within 48 hours. (Keeping your thumb in the palm of your mitts or glove particularly when you are on a dry ski slope helps prevent the injury.) A dislocation or fracture dislocation can occur at the base of the thumb where it meets the wrist. This is a painful injury that removes the ability to grip with the hand.

Fractures of the thumb

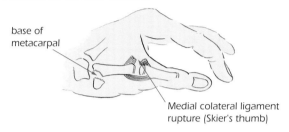

base of metacarpal

Medial colateral ligament rupture (Skier's thumb)

Treatment

Unless grossly deviated (i.e. bent at 90°), deformity is best left alone and finger splinted in the position it is found. Elevation in a sling and pain relief should be given. Distinguishing between some fractures and a dislocation can be difficult hence the advice not to try to reduce a dislocation. The blood supply to the fingers is so rich that ischaemic damage to the digit from an uncorrected deformity is extremely rare. The casualty will usually be able to walk off with assistance.

Sport climbers frequently pick up finger injuries - either acute injuries from falls or chronic overuse injuries from training and climbing. Specific treatment is often needed from an orthopaedic surgeon specialising in hand injuries and training programmes should be modified to avoid the worst finger grips. A selected list of references is included at the end of the chapter.

Aiguilles Rouges d'Arolla, Switzerland. (1990)

Fractures of the pelvis

A major force is needed to fracture the pelvis. It must be assumed that other injuries have occurred particularly to the abdominal organs and/or the spine.

The pelvis is a ring of bone and cannot be broken in a single place when the force acts directly. Try it with a polo mint! (If the force acts via the femur, a single fracture can occur.) The bladder and urethra (exit pipe from the bladder) as well as a number of major blood vessels are closely applied to the inside of the pelvis and are easily damaged when a fracture occurs. Extensive internal bleeding, shock and death are commonly seen with severe pelvic injuries. The casualty will have suffered a fall from a height or been subject to a blunt crush injury. He or she will complain of pain around the pelvis, which will make movement impossible. Gentle side-to-side and front-to-back compression of the pelvis will elicit pain. The force applied should be no more than gentle pressure to confirm the site of the pain and only done once, so as to minimise the chance of reactivating internal bleeding. If the blood vessels have been damaged, shock will develop as the blood loss becomes significant. Be vigilant for the developing signs of shock.

Disruption of the pelvis with gross movement of the left side

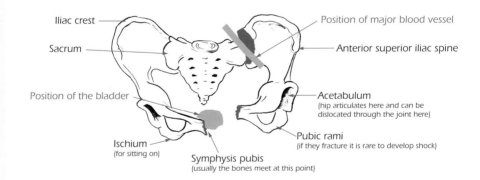

Iliac crest — Position of major blood vessel

Sacrum — Anterior superior iliac spine

Position of the bladder — Acetabulum
(hip articulates here and can be dislocated through the joint here)

Ischium
(for sitting on)

Pubic rami
(if they fracture it is rare to develop shock)

Symphysis pubis
(usually the bones meet at this point)

Treatment

The casualty must have a full primary survey looking for any associated injuries. Particular attention needs to be directed at the circulation and feeling for abdominal tenderness. Oxygen should be given at 15 litres/min via a non-rebreathing mask with reservoir.

Casualty movement must be limited to a minimum; the spine will need examining by the log roll technique. The vacuum mattress is very good for this type of injury. Wrapped around the pelvis, it splints the pelvic bones to some degree. It also usefully splints the spine, as there is often doubt as to whether a spinal injury is also present. Strong analgesia, usually with morphine, will be required. This is the type of injury for which intravenous fluid may be beneficial; try to get a person with the suitable skills to the casualty as soon as possible. The casualty should be evacuated urgently as shock is a constant threat. If feasible, helicopter evacuation would be appropriate. Anything delaying the start of an evacuation should be avoided. This is not the casualty to 'stay and play', rather a 'scoop and run' in a vacuum mattress!

Improvised and specific pelvic splints have been developed; these are discussed in *Further thoughts* in the 'For rescuers' chapter.

Injuries about the hip and upper leg

Fractures of the neck of the femur

The term 'hip fracture' is commonly used; a fracture of the neck of the femur is the correct description. It is rare in people aged 65 years old or less. Osteoporosis, largely an age-related process, is an important risk factor. As people of all ages take up walking, fractures of the femoral neck are likely to be seen by mountain rescue teams. The history is usually of a relatively trivial fall onto the side. The casualty complains of pain in the groin and is unable to stand on the leg. The leg is a few centimetres shorter than the other one and is externally rotated (i.e. the foot is rolled outwards). Moving the leg causes severe pain. Typically the blood and nerve supply to the limb is not disturbed; the peripheral pulses are present and the casualty can feel the skin being touched. Shock is not normally present. If the leg is not shortened or rotated but the other symptoms are present, a fracture of the acetabulum (the pelvic socket of the hip joint) is most likely.

Fortunately this fracture behaves like a fractured neck of femur rather than of the pelvis.

'a few centimetres shorter ... and externally rotated'

Hip dislocation

A dislocation of the hip joint is a serious injury. It requires a high degree of violence and is associated with a lot of soft tissue damage. Disruption of the blood and nerve supply (loss of pulses, cold skin, pins & needles or areas of numb skin) to the leg can occur. The casualty is unable to straighten the hip and they adopt a posture like that of a model posing - the hip and the knee are slightly bent and the leg is internally rotated (i.e. the knee is turned inwards) and often resting on the front of the other leg.

Treatment (hip 'fracture' and dislocation)

The hip should be immobilised and pain relief given. Padding between the legs and strapping them together is the easiest way to immobilise the leg. A vacuum mattress can be very useful in these circumstances and morphine is often appropriate. A traction splint should not be used. The casualty will require a stretcher evacuation. Helicopter assistance would be appropriate for any casualty with a dislocated hip and for many casualties with a fractured neck of femur if the evacuation route were long or difficult.

Fractures of the shaft of the femur

The femur is a strong bone and requires a considerable force to break it; a significant fall is needed. There is always extensive soft tissue injury (muscle tearing & bleeding). The blood loss is often sufficient to cause shock. The fall often results in other serious injuries and

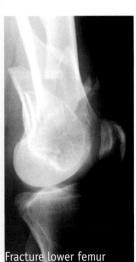

Fracture lower femur

these must be looked for. A casualty with *only* a fractured shaft of the femur has a life-threatening injury. If the fracture is associated with other injuries, the casualty is in a serious state - he may die during the evacuation. The ends of the bone are displaced by spasm of the thigh muscles. This worsens the discomfort and deforms the leg. The casualty (if conscious) will complain of pain, the leg between the hip and knee will be shortened and there will be considerable swelling. Occasionally blood vessels are damaged; check the pulses in the foot.

Treatment

The diagnosis should be made at an early stage during the 'C' of the primary survey. The casualty needs to be resuscitated. Ensure the airway is open, assess the breathing, start oxygen and treat for shock. Further blood loss needs to be limited by good splintage; a traction splint is the best way of doing this. It is worth its weight in gold. Not only will it lessen the ongoing blood loss but also provide considerable pain relief by reducing the muscle spasm. Think about the pain of cramp and how comforting it is to have the muscles stretched. Morphine will still be required. A femoral nerve block is an excellent alternative - perhaps your doctor could do this! It is described on page 389. Intravenous fluids are likely to be helpful though, once the leg is splinted, don't delay starting the evacuation. As soon as a fractured shaft of the femur is suspected, plans for a rapid evacuation should be drawn up. A sense of urgency must be maintained throughout the incident. Keep a close eye on the casualty - deterioration during the evacuation is common.

Injuries about the knee

Fractures and dislocations of the patella (knee cap)

Fractures of the patella are usually due to a direct blow to the front of the knee. The casualty will complain of pain on the patella. Trying to walk will increase the pain. Swelling will be present.

Dislocations of the patella occur after falls or stumbles when the knee is bent, the force needed may be quite small particularly if the casualty has had previous patella dislocations. The casualty will complain of quite severe pain around the knee and will be unable to straighten the leg. Examination will show deformity; the front of the knee is flat and the patella can be felt on the outer side of the knee. If you compare with the other knee when it is bent to the same degree, the dislocation is usually obvious. Many patella dislocations reduce spontaneously; the knee will be swollen and bearing weight will still be difficult.

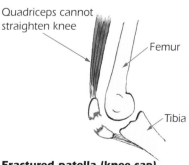

Quadriceps cannot straighten knee

Femur

Tibia

Fractured patella (knee cap)

Treatment

A fractured patella or one that has been dislocated but is now
reduced should have a long leg splint applied and the casualty given
appropriate pain relief. A dislocated patella is much more
comfortable if it is reduced. This is relatively easy and should be
attempted. Analgesia should be given; Entonox® is ideal. Reduce the
patella by straightening the knee and at the same time gently
pushing the patella forward and inwards to its normal position. It
will be obvious when the patella pops back. The casualty's pain will
almost disappear and you may well get a big hug! Immobilise in a
splint and evacuate by stretcher. All cases should be seen in an
Accident and Emergency department before the leg splint is removed.

Ligament injuries around the knee

Injuries to the ligaments of the knee are common. The mechanism
usually consists of a stumble or fall when the knee is bent. Think of
skiing! The signs and symptoms are very variable. The knee may be
swollen though in most cases the swelling takes an hour or two to
develop. The degree of pain and ability to walk varies considerably.
If the forces involved are significant, the knee can dislocate. The
anatomy is grossly abnormal and there is often damage to the blood
vessels and nerves behind the knee.

Treatment

Pain relief needs to be given and the knee splinted with a long leg
splint. Morphine is not normally required unless the injury is severe.
If the knee is dislocated and the arterial supply to the lower leg is
damaged, consider a single attempt at reducing the dislocation by
applying longitudinal traction to the leg. Reduction may not be
possible but, if successful, it can be crucial in limiting the morbidity
from the injury. Repeated attempts or excessive force should not be
used. If the blood vessels have been damaged considerable blood loss
can occur so check for signs of shock.

By their nature, most knee injuries are evacuated by stretcher; be
warned that these injuries tend to get worse over time and a
decision to walk the casualty off with assistance may need to be
reviewed. A dislocated knee, whether reduced or not, should be
evacuated urgently. Blood vessel damage is a particularly poor sign
and has resulted in leg amputation in 15-50% of casualties.

Injuries about the lower leg

Fractures of the tibia and fibula

These fractures are very common. Most are the result of a twisting fall onto the leg though some are due to a direct impact on the shin. The fracture site will depend on the mechanism and the casualty's footwear. The more 'supportive' the footwear the higher the fracture; the casualty with the fracture illustrated here had a plastic winter boot on! The injury is very painful and the casualty will not be able to stand or bear weight on the affected leg. Local swelling and deformity is usually evident. Because there is very little tissue between the front of the tibia and the skin surface the injury is often a compound fracture. Infection of the fracture is a serious complication.

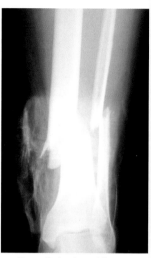

'Top of the boot' fracture

Fractures near the knee (tibial plateau) can damage the blood supply to the lower leg as shown below.

Right tibial plateau fracture with popliteal artery damage

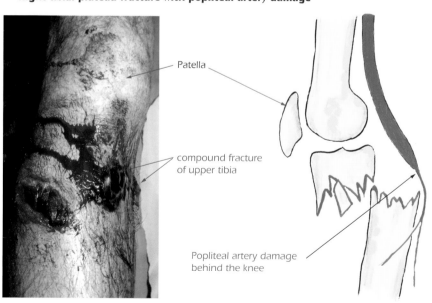

Patella

compound fracture of upper tibia

Popliteal artery damage behind the knee

Treatment

Entonox® and often morphine are indicated. To splint the fracture, use a long-leg splint so that knee movement is prevented. The fracture may need to be manipulated to restore the blood supply to the foot or to reduce the deformity so a splint can be applied. The rescuer must be confident in their actions. The aim is to quickly disengage the fracture site by distracting the bone ends and simultaneously straightening the limb back into the normal position. This must be done swiftly. Halfhearted and repetitive attempts at manipulation are to be avoided.

Reducing a deformed, compound fractured tibia

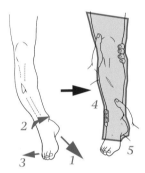

1 - Apply axial traction
2 - Correct rotation
3 - Restore to 'straight' line
4 - Apply splint
5 - Check pulses

Evacuation by stretcher is acceptable for an uncomplicated fracture. However, if the blood supply to the foot is poor or the fracture is compound then a helicopter evacuation should be contemplated unless the evacuation route is short.

Types of long bone fracture

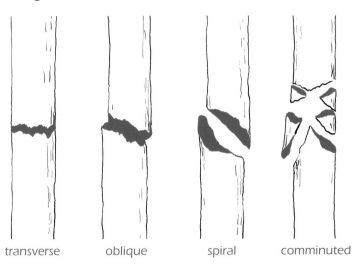

transverse   oblique   spiral   comminuted

Injuries about the ankle

Ankle injuries are the commonest injury in Mountain Rescue. All types of injury will be seen including:

Simple sprains

Rupture of the lateral ligaments of the ankle

Rupture of the Achilles tendon

Fracture of the lateral malleolus

Fractures of both medial and lateral malleolus

Dislocation of the talus

Fracture of the fifth metatarsal

And many more.

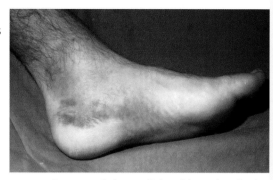

Fracture of the medial and lateral malleolus

The casualty trips, falls or stumbles. It is usually an isolated injury. The casualty complains of pain around the ankle that is worse on walking. Swelling over the lateral, and sometimes the medial, malleolus is common. Is the ankle badly sprained or broken; it can be difficult to tell. It doesn't matter! Clearly if the ankle is deformed there is a fracture. Carefully feeling the area of tenderness might suggest the damage is confined to a ligament. However if the casualty cannot weight-bear a radiogram (x-ray) will be needed to exclude a fracture. There is a common misconception that if the casualty is able to wiggle their toes then the ankle cannot be broken; this is untrue.

Inversion injury of the ankle leading to a fracture of the medial and lateral malleolus

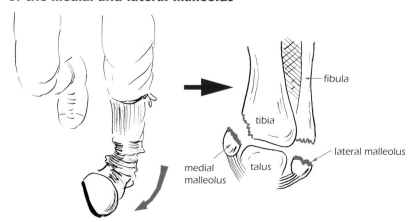

Treatment of the injured ankle

If the injury is very painful, or if the casualty has great difficulty in walking, then treat the ankle as broken. Adequate pain-relief needs to be given, the boot removed and the ankle splinted. There is no common sense in leaving the boot on once the decision has been made to treat the injury as a fracture. Any deformity should be corrected by first applying axial distraction, then correcting rotation and finally alignment. (See fractured tibia above.)

When preparing to splint the ankle think about the skin over the malleoli. The skin may already be stretched and ischaemic (white) from a poor blood supply. Applying direct pressure here may cause a pressure sore. This effectively converts the injury into a compound fracture. Gauze or felt should be handy to pad the sides. After applying a splint, the pulse on the top of the foot should be checked.

Dislocations of the talus regularly occur and are relatively easy to reduce. Usually the talus ends up behind the tibia with the skin in front of the tibia stretched white. The heel 'protrudes' too far backwards as shown in the picture below. With good pain relief (morphine and Entonox®), the heel can be pulled down with axial traction and then forwards usually with a satisfying clunk and an instant improvement in the casualty's pain level and foot circulation. There is a case study on page 391.

Evacuation

The majority of casualties can be safely evacuated by stretcher but where the foot remains dislocated or the skin looks ischaemic helicopter assistance would be appropriate, as urgent reduction is needed. Only in situations where the casualty will have to assist in the evacuation would it be wise to leave the boot on.

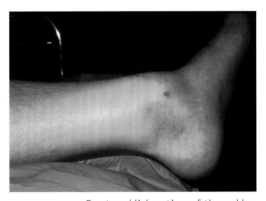

Fracture/dislocation of the ankle

On the following page some examples of ankle injuries are illustrated.

Left ankle injury
Bilateral malleolus fracture with lateral shift of the talus

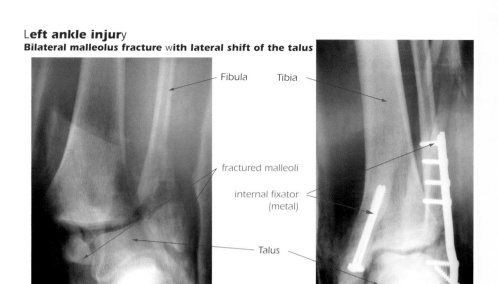

Fibula
Tibia
fractured malleoli
internal fixator (metal)
Talus

Right ankle lateral ligament injury

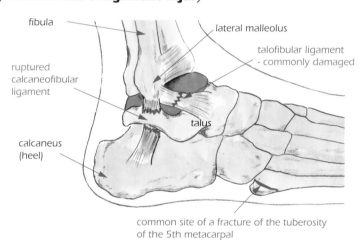

fibula
lateral malleolus
talofibular ligament - commonly damaged
ruptured calcaneofibular ligament
talus
calcaneus (heel)

common site of a fracture of the tuberosity of the 5th metacarpal

Achille's tendon tears

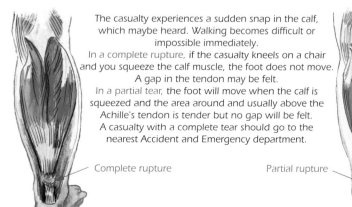

The casualty experiences a sudden snap in the calf, which maybe heard. Walking becomes difficult or impossible immediately.
In a complete rupture, if the casualty kneels on a chair and you squeeze the calf muscle, the foot does not move. A gap in the tendon may be felt.
In a partial tear, the foot will move when the calf is squeezed and the area around and usually above the Achille's tendon is tender but no gap will be felt.
A casualty with a complete tear should go to the nearest Accident and Emergency department.

Complete rupture
Partial rupture

Injuries to the foot

Foot injuries are relatively rare. Most casualties do not have open toed sandals! There is little value in a comprehensive list of injuries to the various parts of the foot and toes. Treat what you find. If the casualty is in severe pain and unable to walk then pain relief should be given, a splint applied and the casualty carried off. When the evacuation will be long and difficult, it may be possible to splint the foot adequately to allow progress to be made on foot with assistance. Be prepared to change your plan if progress is poor.

References

Lee C, Porter KM. Prehospital management of lower limb fractures. *Emerg Med J* 2005; 22:660-3

Cole AT. Fingertip injuries in rock climbers. *Br. J. Sports Med.* 1990; 24:14

Bollen SR. Soft tissue injury in extreme rock climbers. *Br. J. Sports Med.* 1988; 22:145-7

Vallotton J, Dubas F. *A colour atlas of mountain medicine* 1991; ISBN 0 7234 0965 X page 176-182

Harries, Williams, Stanish and Micheli. *Oxford Textbook of Sports Medicine* 1994; ISBN 0 19 262009 6

Terry Relph, Kandersteg, Switzerland (2003)

Environmental Problems

Objectives
To understand the effects of heat and cold on the casualty
To correctly assess and manage hypothermia
To be aware of other environmental problems

Hypothermia

Hypothermia is defined as a core body temperature of less than 35°C and occurs when heat loss exceeds heat generation. In almost all cases, it is precipitated by an increased heat loss through convection (wind and water currents) and conduction (water, ice, metal). Hypothermia can occur at modest environmental temperatures; for example, a victim immersed in 20°C water or exposed to an air temperature of 5°C in a 30km/hr wind and driving rain will (eventually) become hypothermic. The true incidence of hypothermia in mountain rescue is unknown. In England and Wales, it is recorded in 9% of casualties, but it is generally accepted that milder forms go unrecorded or unrecognized in many more, perhaps up to 25% of all casualties. This may be more important than has been recognised in the past. Severe hypothermia israre and fortunately the number of fatalities in a year rarely exceeds five.

Basic physiology and pathology

We try to maintain our body temperature at 37°C. Heat generation must be balanced with heat loss to achieve this. This balancing is done in special areas of the brain. A lowering of skin or core temperature is sensed and the body responds by reducing heat loss and increasing heat generation. These responses can be divided into involuntary and voluntary, and are summarised in the box below.

Responses to the cold	Reduce heat loss	Increase heat generation
Involuntary	Skin vasoconstriction	Shivering (heat production increased by a factor of 3-5 times)
Voluntary - behavioural	Seeking shelter and putting on clothing	Exercise and food intake (heat production increased by a factor of 10-15 times)

The involuntary responses are the perhaps the most visible - the cold white skin and shivering. Though shivering increases heat production five times, the involuntary responses are not generally effective at preventing hypothermia - just delaying its onset. Shivering raises the heart rate, respiratory rate, energy metabolism and hence oxygen consumption of the person. At rest, the oxygen consumption increases by 360% for a 0.6°C reduction in core temperature. In contrast to the involuntary responses, the voluntary responses are much more effective. Exercising can increase heat production by a factor of 10 to 15, and modern clothing can conserve much of this. So much so that even extreme temperatures, wind and altitude can be survived. However, in terms of maximal and steady state oxygen consumption, the individual has to be fit and, like an athlete, fed and hydrated with carbohydrates and liquid to maintain the level of exertion. This brings us back to an old concept of *'exhaustion hypothermia'*; fitness - particularly endurance - and food intake are as important as clothing and the environment in the onset of hypothermia, at least on land. Likewise, injury or illness, preventing voluntary muscle activity, may precipitate the onset of hypothermia. In the water, things are different. The conduction of heat is so much greater in water that, unless special clothes (wet or dry suit) are used to insulate the person, heat generation cannot match the heat loss. In addition, 'swim failure' also limits the ability to generate heat. The onset of hypothermia is much more predictable and can be estimated fairly accurately from just the water temperature and the victim's clothing.

Symptoms and signs

Even before the core temperature reaches 35°C there is the loss of manual dexterity and muscle strength. The victim may stumble or find doing up zips and placing climbing equipment difficult. They may feel cold or just lethargic and become the quiet, slow member at the back of the party. At this stage, additional clothing and food along with goal-orientated muscle activity can reverse the decline in core temperature. Avoid alcohol, as it inhibits shivering and impairs judgement, and drinks with high levels of caffeine as they encourage dehydration. Involuntary shivering is triggered as the core temperature falls below 35°C (approximate) and more vigorous attempts have to be made to reverse the heat loss; a period of shelter, refuelling and additional insulation is required urgently. Goal-orientated activity must take into account the reduced dexterity - walking down a path may be all that is possible. With exhaustion, the core temperature will start to fall more quickly. Shivering ceases, as the muscles and nerve pathways become unable to sustain their actions. The functions of the body, particularly those of the brain and heart, slowly shut down as the core temperature reduces. The casualty is likely to be dehydrated as a result of their exertion and a cold-induced diuresis. The sequence of developing a particular symptom or sign, and the core temperature at which it develops, varies from person to person, so a simple diagram, like the one shown below, is only a reminder of important changes in body function.

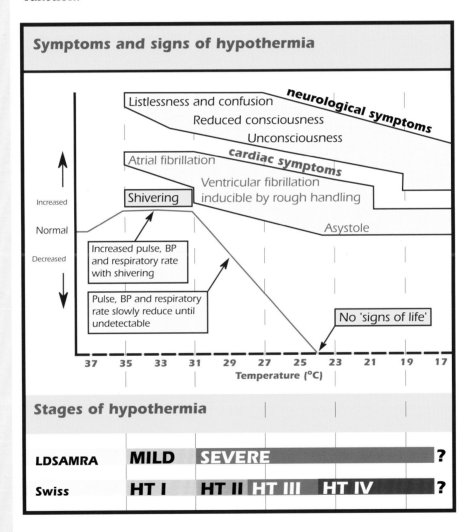

Predicting the casualty's core temperature from his symptoms and signs is impossible, especially when symptoms like burrowing and paradoxical undressing (inexplicable removal of clothes when the casualty is confused) occur. The consequence of this is that our assessment of hypothermia, and its management, has to be based on clinical parameters rather than the core temperature.

The heart becomes irritable as the core temperature reduces. An irregular pulse (atrial fibrillation) is common when the core temperature is less than 32°C. More worryingly, ventricular fibrillation (VF) becomes common when the core falls below 28°C but is inducible by 'rough handling' at a higher core temperature, perhaps up to 31°C. 'Rough handling' includes large movements of the limbs, rapid changes in body position, voluntary exertion, cardiac massage and invasive procedures such as intubation and the insertion of airway adjuncts. (The risk of invasive procedures inducing VF may be less than originally suggested.)

A curious, and almost pathognomonic, sign of hypothermia is the J wave on the ECG. It is beloved by examiners testing medical students and therefore of no clinical relevance!

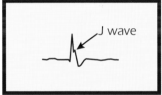

The end point of hypothermia, death, is only loosely related to core temperature. Without rewarming, survival is highly unlikely at the modest core temperature of 26°C. However with treatment - rewarming - survival from a much lower temperature is possible. Many factors, such as the rate of cooling, the way the heart stopped, whether asphyxia occurred at a 'warm' body temperature, and which rewarming technique was used determine which casualty can or cannot be resuscitated. Surviving lower and lower core temperatures has been documented as the methods of rewarming have improved. This shows what is possible, and reminds us that the old adage *'not dead, until warm and dead'* remains true though does not resolve the ethical and financial conflicts that arise when managing hypothermia.

Assessment

Assess your personal and the casualty's safety. Carry out a primary survey. If no other injuries are apparent, the primary survey is modified in severe hypothermia. The changes are in red type and the reasons are explained later in the section on no 'signs of life'.

A - ensure the airway is open.

B - assess breathing and ensure adequate ventilation; start oxygen. (The use of a mouth-to-mask device with an oxygen port is attractive as the air/oxygen mix is going to be partially warmed.)

C - record whether a pulse is palpable and its rate. Take 60 seconds to assess the carotid pulse. Do not start cardiac massage at this stage.

D - assess consciousness (AVPU).

E – Exposure - stage the hypothermia using either of the two systems detailed below.

In severe hypothermia, monitoring equipment can detect heart activity (ECG) and breathing (end-tidal carbon dioxide concentration) when, due to the slowness of the change, clinical assessment cannot. Until a monitor is available it is better to assume that there is a cardiac output but it is too small for you to detect. Routine measurement of the core temperature is not necessary; it does not change the management of the casualty. An accurate measurement of the core requires either an oesophageal or rectal temperature. The former needs an unconscious patient without their protective swallowing reflexes and the later will often require moving the casualty too much to gain access. Also, sticking a thermometer or probe into the rectum is not good enough in these constipating times. The probe has to be against the bowel wall not...! (I will allow you to complete.) In an intubated casualty, an oesophageal probe in the lower third of the oesophagus can be considered. This measures the true core temperature directly and is not subject to error but requires expensive equipment that only the busiest mountain rescue teams could justify. The alternative is an epitympanic thermometer; these are used extensively in the European Alps but rarely elsewhere. The reading can be too low when: the environmental temperature is very low; or during a circulatory arrest or when the auditory canal is blocked by snow or debris. An accurate core temperature may be of interest but its only real value would be if it encouraged a hospital to get its invasive active rewarming facility ready in advance of the patient's arrival.

Staging hypothermia

Two different scales are detailed in the box below. Why? The simple LDSAMRA 'mild - severe' scale is safe and adequate for the initial assessment and for rescuers without additional equipment (particularly an ECG). However the Swiss Society of Mountain Medicine staging gives more precise information and helps inform the rescuer on the further management of the unconscious casualty as well as indicating which hospital facilities are most likely to be needed. An appropriate destination hospital can then be chosen. The Swiss staging also has the virtue of being used in other mountainous areas of the world.

Staging hypothermia	
LDSAMRA	
MILD	Shivering and alert.
SEVERE	Shivering stopped and/or reduced consciousness.
Swiss Society of Mountain Medicine	
HT I	Alert and shivering.
HT II	Reduced consciousness without shivering.
HT III	Unconsciousness but breathing.
HT IV	No 'signs of life'.

Management

Two management algorithms are presented on the following pages. The first is modified from one developed for team members in 1995 by the Lake District Mountain Rescue Team doctors. It reflects the type of rescue of that time - poor helicopter coverage and few specialist hospitals with rewarming facilities.

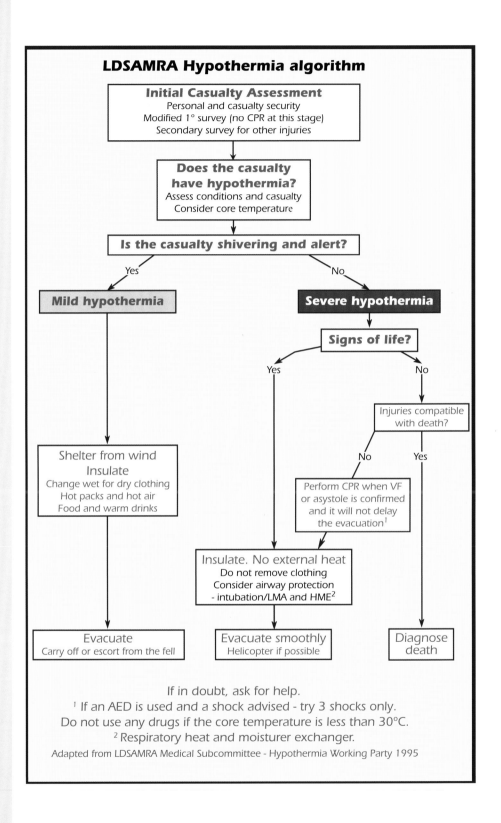

LDSAMRA Hypothermia algorithm

Initial Casualty Assessment
Personal and casualty security
Modified 1° survey (no CPR at this stage)
Secondary survey for other injuries

Does the casualty have hypothermia?
Assess conditions and casualty
Consider core temperature

Is the casualty shivering and alert?

Yes → **Mild hypothermia**

No → **Severe hypothermia**

Signs of life?

Yes / No

Injuries compatible with death?

No / Yes

Perform CPR when VF or asystole is confirmed and it will not delay the evacuation[1]

Mild hypothermia:
Shelter from wind
Insulate
Change wet for dry clothing
Hot packs and hot air
Food and warm drinks

Insulate. No external heat
Do not remove clothing
Consider airway protection
- intubation/LMA and HME[2]

Evacuate
Carry off or escort from the fell

Evacuate smoothly
Helicopter if possible

Diagnose death

If in doubt, ask for help.
[1] If an AED is used and a shock advised - try 3 shocks only.
Do not use any drugs if the core temperature is less than 30°C.
[2] Respiratory heat and moisturer exchanger.
Adapted from LDSAMRA Medical Subcommittee - Hypothermia Working Party 1995

The second (overleaf) is from ICAR; it is designed around the European Alps and assumes skilled medical input at the incident site, expensive monitoring equipment and a short evacuation by helicopter. Both are presented with the aim not to confuse but to suggest that you should adapt one or both algorithms to fit your rescue.

Regardless of which algorithm you use, the immediate goals in the management of hypothermia are:

Preventing physiological deterioration by inducing VF.

Preventing a further reduction in the core temperature.

Getting the severely hypothermic, unstable casualty to the right facility as soon as possible.

Separating which casualties with no 'signs of life' should be resuscitated, and which can be diagnosed as dead.

Unfortunately the best strategies to use have not been researched adequately and much of our management is based on personal experience rather than clinical trials. For example, many manoeuvres have been described as capable of inducing VF but the likelihood that they will in an individual casualty is unknown. Perhaps the casualty would have developed to VF anyway. Nevertheless, try avoiding rough handling in any casualty who is vulnerable to VF. That is any one in stages 'severe' (LDSAMRA) or HTII or worse (Swiss). Do not allow the casualty to make active movements; and do not perform large passive movements on the casualty. This often means cutting off wet clothing rather than undressing the casualty. Tracheal intubation, and other pharyngeal procedures, may precipitate VF but the risk has probably been over estimated (see Larach). An unconscious casualty should have the airway and lungs protected and ventilation assured as soon as the relevant skills are available.

In an unresponsive patient with severe hypothermia in whom you would normally start CPR, cardiac compressions may also precipitate VF and, potentially, convert a slow, clinically undetected rhythm to VF. Starting CPR is then a commitment to continue until rewarming is achieved. In exposure hypothermia, the importance of CPR in the pre-hospital stage is poorly understood with case reports showing

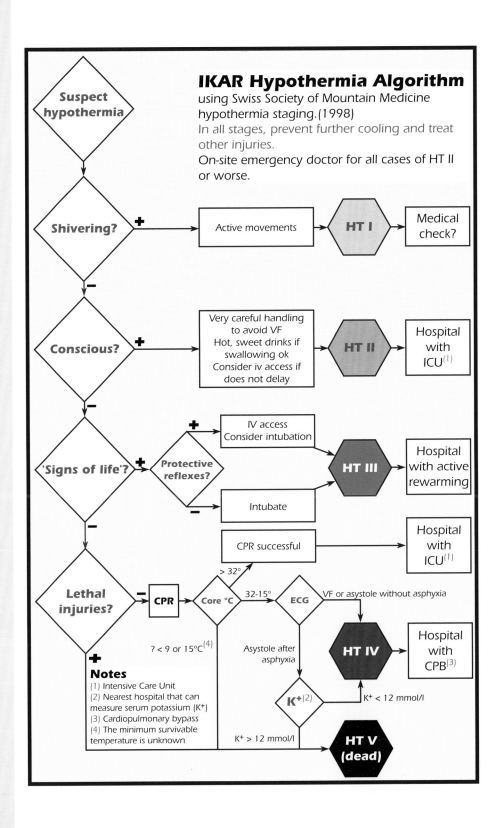

IKAR Hypothermia Algorithm

using Swiss Society of Mountain Medicine hypothermia staging.(1998)

In all stages, prevent further cooling and treat other injuries.

On-site emergency doctor for all cases of HT II or worse.

Suspect hypothermia

Shivering? +
→ Active movements → **HT I** → Medical check?

−

Conscious? +
→ Very careful handling to avoid VF
Hot, sweet drinks if swallowing ok
Consider iv access if does not delay
→ **HT II** → Hospital with ICU[1]

−

'Signs of life'? +
Protective reflexes? +
→ IV access Consider intubation
−
→ Intubate
→ **HT III** → Hospital with active rewarming

−

CPR successful → Hospital with ICU[1]

Lethal injuries? −
CPR → **Core °C**
> 32° ↗
32-15° → **ECG**
VF or asystole without asphyxia

Asystole after asphyxia
→ **HT IV** → Hospital with CPB[3]

K+ < 12 mmol/l

? < 9 or 15°C[4]

K+[2]
K+ > 12 mmol/l → **HT V (dead)**

+

Notes
(1) Intensive Care Unit
(2) Nearest hospital that can measure serum potassium (K+)
(3) Cardiopulmonary bypass
(4) The minimum survivable temperature is unknown

not performing or even intermittent CPR does not preclude survival. (In submersion cases, early CPR has been shown to be of survival benefit in children.) A strong argument has been made for not starting until an ECG has shown VF or asystole. (See the Alaskan guidelines.) An AED without an ECG screen will not give this information, as both asystole and a very slow, clinically-undetected rhythm will return a 'no shock' instruction. It could also be argued that CPR itself will increase the time it takes to get to hospital, at least until you are in a vehicle or helicopter. Others, such as the Resuscitation Council and American Heart Association, argue that, in the absence of 'signs of life', the resuscitation should be largely the same as for the normothermic casualty, and that CPR should be started immediately. The proponents of this view are frequently operating in less isolated situations, with rapid transfer times to hospital, and with full equipment. No comparison between these two views has been carried out and, as yet, there is no definitive answer. Each case should be assessed individually with all the relevant factors being considered.

In the UK, we are likely to be operating somewhere between the extremes. Consider whether your rescue is nearer the remoteness of rescue in Alaska or a rescue in the European Alps with a rapid evacuation to a fully equipped hospital, and adapt your management appropriately. In the first edition of *Casualty Care in Mountain Rescue,* the phrase used to describe starting CPR in hypothermia was 'unless it can be continued until the casualty reaches hospital'. The change in emphasis has led to a new phrase being introduced into the algorithm - 'perform CPR when VF or asystole is confirmed and it will not delay the evacuation'. However, in the case of a rescue-related collapse (where signs of life were present but suddenly disappear during the rescue and evacuation phase), it can be assumed that asystole or VF has started, and CPR should be started immediately if practical.

If VF is precipitated, it is generally accepted that defibrillation is ineffective though some studies of casualties report the occasional one where it is (see Segesser). It is recommended that only three shocks are performed until the casualty is rewarmed.

Preventing a further reduction in core temperature.

The chance of survival from hypothermia is directly related to the core temperature, so it makes sense to try to stabilise the core temperature by insulating the casualty from further heat loss if this can be achieved without detrimental effects. The purpose is not to rewarm the casualty but to stabilise or reduce the rate of fall of the core temperature. This aspect of management is just as important in 'mild' (or HTI and II) as in the more severe cases. Many studies, across the whole range of traumatic injuries and surgical procedures, have shown that mild hypothermia on admission to hospital is an independent risk factor for death and poor outcomes, such as wound infections. Hypothermia causes coagulopathy (abnormal blood clotting) and an increased risk of infection; these are thought to cause the increased mortality and morbidity. Rigorous attempts must be made to avoid even mild hypothermia in all casualties.

Methods include:

Reducing conduction losses by insulating the casualty from the ground and changing wet clothes for dry if this can be done without large movements of the limbs.

Reducing convection currents by sheltering the casualty from the wind, and putting on extra layers of dry clothing, covering the head with a hat as well using a modern casualty bag.

Using hot packs on the torso, particularly in the axillae and groins. Do not place them directly on the skin as burns can result.

Using warm/humidified air or oxygen. Less than 10% of the casualty's heat loss is from the respiratory tract. Most of the heat is used to saturate the (relatively dry) inhaled air with water before it reaches the alveoli. The 'breathing out' process does not recover all the water, hence condensation on glass etc. in the cold. The percentage heat lost through breathing increases with altitude as the air becomes cooler and dryer, and the respiratory minute volume increases; an effect that will not be significant in the UK. Airway warming (as opposed to insulating) has a limited potential to rewarm the body though, of course, the heat is going directly to the right place and it will help other rewarming techniques. For rescue work, there are a number of ways to improve the quality of inspired air or oxygen. The simplest methods include breathing in and out through a respiratory heat and moisture exchanger (HME) or even just a scarf, and keeping stored oxygen cylinders warm and putting them in insulated sleeves when they are taken out. Portable equipment is available to heat and humidify oxygen. Examples can be seen on the Alaskan guidelines website. The 'Little Dragon' is used extensively in the UK. There are many potential problems with such equipment, such as over-heating the gases (potentially causing airway burns), increasing the resistance to breathing and adding irritants. International standards have been set for this type of equipment. Where does this leave the rescuer? In mild hypothermia, a casualty who is fully aware of the limitations of equipment may benefit from its application though preventing heat loss from conduction and convection will be materially more important. In such casualties providing a warm drink may be just as effective and certainly provides necessary calories for the casualty to restart active movements. In severe hypothermia, the respiratory rate is low and oxygen is preferred to air. In addition, the casualty cannot safely use the equipment so accepted international safeguards need to be rigorously followed. The portable equipment used in the Alps and North America is too expensive and bulky to be justified in the UK and, currently (2005), the Little Dragon does not meet these standards. A respiratory heat and moisture exchanger would be a simple and effective way to reduce heat loss in those casualties with hypothermia stage III and IV where ventilatory support is being used. Oxygen delivery systems using a closed circuit and CO_2 absorber are becoming available, and these may overcome the technical issues outlined above.

Getting the severely hypothermic, unstable casualty to the right facility as soon as possible

In the severely hypothermic casualty with circulatory failure (asystole or VF), the best form of rewarming is by cardiopulmonary bypass (CPB). In suitable patients, survival rates (with little or no neurological sequelae) are approximately 50% even for asystole and when up to three hours of CPR has been carried out before CPB is established. To survive, asphyxia must not precede cardiac arrest even in the hypothermic, so the mechanism of hypothermia needs to be considered. Is this why rescue-related collapse has a very good prognosis as asphyxia is reversed immediately? Factors that are associated with a good outcome reflect this - rescue-related collapse; cold air and immersion compared to submersion; no pre-existing illnesses and no significant trauma. On arrival at hospital finding a blood pH >6.5, blood pCO2 <9.7 kPa, serum potassium <10 mmol/l, and core temperature >12°C should encourage aggressive rewarming even in the apparently lifeless. These findings should be known to an admitting hospital but a reminder may be needed. Certainly the evidence is strong enough that the preferred destination hospital should have these facilities and a longer evacuation phase, with continuing CPR, to such a hospital is in the casualty's interest. Rescuers should know where CPB services are available. Warn the destination hospital that these may be needed as soon as it is anticipated.

Separating which casualties with no 'signs of life' should be resuscitated, and which can be diagnosed as dead.

You find an unresponsive cold casualty with no detectable breathing, no palpable pulse, fixed dilated pupils and flaccid limbs - in short, no 'signs of life'. What do you do?

A common definition of death in a cold casualty is 'failure to revive on rewarming to 35ºC' - 'Not dead until warm and dead!' As rewarming is impractical on the fell, should all casualties with no 'signs of life' be thought to be revivable? Clearly this is an extreme view, as some casualties will be dead; their case history has not been taken into account. We should not underestimate the stress and negative experience that advanced, invasive medicine can impose on rescuers, as well as the companions and family of the casualty. The section on ethics addresses some of these issues. Over the last ten years, attempts have been made to improve the selection of casualties that might benefit from aggressive rewarming. Asphyxia preceding the cardiac arrest is known to be a very bad omen. In submersion and avalanche rescue, asphyxia can be assumed by taking into account the time under water or whether an air pocket was present. But for the hypothermic casualty in air, we have no way to know whether the cardiac arrest preceded asphyxia. Did the tongue obstruct the airway early in the unconscious phase? We cannot know. As we have seen the ECG does not help - even asystole has a 50/50 survival rate in severe hypothermia if aggressive rewarming is given, and, as our management improves, casualties survive lower and lower core temperatures. The table on the following page shows a selection of criteria used to refrain from resuscitating, in effect diagnosing death, at the incident scene.

Only the Alaskan guidelines take into account the evacuation time - the time from rescue to a destination hospital with rewarming facilities. Three hours is the time used - one that we could anticipate in the UK in bad weather when helicopter assistance is unavailable. And here we have to complicate things further depending on whether an ECG has confirmed asystole or VF in the casualty. The second table on the following page is based on the Alaskan guidelines and, perhaps, can serve as a summary to managing the severely hypothermic casualty with no 'signs of life'.

Author	Do not resuscitate:
Lloyd **(1986)**	'if the body is frozen solid so that it is impossible to alter the person's position, the mouth or nose are blocked by ice, the eyes are frozen, or the patient's rectal temperature is less than ambient air temperature.'
Wilderness Medical Society	'obvious lethal injuries are present; chest wall depression is impossible'.
State of Alaska Cold Injuries Guideline (2005)	'if the patient has been submerged in cold water for more than 1 hour; has a core temperature of less than 10°C; has obvious fatal injuries, e.g. decapitation; is frozen, e.g. ice formation in the airway; has a chest wall that is so stiff that compressions are impossible; rescuers are exhausted or in danger ...'.

Scenario	Actions
A severely hypothermic casualty shows no 'signs of life' and is eligible for resuscitation (see above). *definitive care is a hospital with rewarming facilities.	
No ECG; evacuation to definitive care* < 3 hours	Ventilate the casualty and evacuate to definitive care as soon as possible. If an ECG becomes available and shows VF or asystole, start CPR.
No ECG; evacuation to definitive care* > 3 hours	Perform CPR for 30 minutes at the incident scene whilst trying to rewarm the casualty. If the CPR is ineffective, stop after 30 minutes. Arrange an appropriate evacuation.
ECG shows asystole or VF; evacuation to definitive care* < 3 hours	Perform CPR as soon as practical and evacuate to definitive care as soon as possible. In VF, try 3 shocks if an AED is available.
ECG shows asystole; evacuation to definitive care* > 3 hours	Perform CPR for 30 minutes at the incident scene whilst trying to rewarm the casualty. If the CPR is ineffective, stop after 30 minutes. Arrange an appropriate evacuation.
ECG shows VF; evacuation to definitive care* > 3 hours	Perform CPR; try 3 shocks only if an AED is available. Evacuate to definitive care whilst trying to rewarm the casualty. If the core temperature becomes >30°C, try defibrillating again.

Case Studies - Hypothermia

These cases are fictional but were developed from several real cases. They were commissioned for *Casualty Care in Mountain Rescue* to contribute a sense of real life and to draw attention to the dilemmas that occur in rescue work.

Case 1

Time and date: 18.40 on the 3rd of April

Location: Open fell at an altitude of 700 metres

Weather: High winds, heavy rain/snow and cloud down to 650 metres

Cause of incident: Experienced fell runner overdue

Reported injuries: None

The team was requested to search a possible escape route for a missing fell runner. In foul weather, the team's search dog located the casualty almost immediately about 700 metres from the end of a 3 kilometre Land Rover track. The casualty showed no 'signs of life'. The party insulated the casualty using a tent and their spare clothing. Eight minutes later, further team members arrived with a casualty bag, oxygen, a portable ECG and a doctor. The doctor confirmed no palpable pulse, absence of breathing despite an open airway and unresponsiveness. The limbs were stiff and the jaw immovable. There were no other injuries.

The working diagnosis was severe hypothermia. A helicopter had been requested when the casualty was found but it was having difficulty getting over the intervening hills. The crew had asked if they could turn back 'if life didn't depend on it'. The casualty had been missing for 5 hours; when had she become unconscious? Evacuation would involve a stretcher carry to the valley floor before a helicopter evacuation could be attempted. How should the team manage the evacuation? Should it be speedy or should the casualty be pronounced dead?

Comments

An acceptable approach, on the information given so far, is a smooth but rapid evacuation to the Land Rover (20 minutes). At that point, the ongoing evacuation plan would have become clear and the situation reviewed. It would have been incorrect to diagnose death at the incident site. Helicopter transfer to the nearest hospital (20 minutes) could potentially save a life. It would be inappropriate to start CPR at the incident site, as it could not be continued during the stretcher phase of the evacuation. The time factors and potential lack of asphyxia are within published case reports, so there is hope.

In this case, the ECG showed no heartbeat (asystole) and the core temperature recorded in the oesophagus was 14°C. These readings were done carefully to ensure their accuracy. If they are accepted as real then the chance that an adult could recover is very small. The poor chance of survival was relayed to the helicopter and it returned to its base. A smooth evacuation to the Land Rover took 30 minutes. In the quiet atmosphere of the Land Rover, the ECG and core temperature measurements were repeated and a diagnosis of death made at that stage. The core temperature had fallen to 12.5°C despite copious insulation. The long period of uncertainty was uncomfortable for the team and the waiting relatives. However it was better than a precipitate diagnosis. The adage "not dead until warm and dead" is a good one and in most circumstances should be applied.

Postscript (2005):

How would the case be managed using the ICAR algorithm? Could the helicopter have made it? It is very rare for them to 'back off'. Without a helicopter, the evacuation to a hospital with cardiopulmonary facilities would have taken over three hours excluding the potential to stop at the nearest hospital (90 minutes) to measure the serum potassium. Perhaps the core temperature of 14°C remains the critical factor that supports the original management.

Case 2

Time and date:	February
Location:	High mountain range
Weather:	Fine, cold and clear in the morning deteriorating to blizzard conditions in the afternoon; clearing again overnight
Cause of incident:	no comment
Reported injuries:	'Girls unable to walk down'

A very generous layer of snow had fallen and winter conditions prevailed. A 30-year-old man with relatively little experience chose this afternoon to take two female friends, one aged 30 and one 22, onto the hills for a walk to experience winter conditions. As events unfolded there was no doubt this at least was achieved! As they ascended, and the afternoon progressed, the weather deteriorated, darkness fell and in near blizzard conditions they became lost and disorientated. After several hours they wisely went to ground in snow holes and remained there until daylight. Although the next morning was fine and clear neither of the ladies was able to get out of the snow holes and mobilize, so the male companion set off for help and raised the alarm.

It was fortuitous that a rescue team, who were out on a winter exercise, came upon the two casualties in the snow holes. It was apparent that both were hypothermic and indeed the younger of the two appeared not to be breathing, her face was covered in ice crystals and the initial fear was that she might be dead. However a careful examination found that she was alive; her breathing was shallow and intermittent but no pulse could be felt and she was unconscious. (Severe hypothermia or HTIII) The older lady was very cold and distressed but was fully conscious. (Severe hypothermia or HTII)

Both casualties were very rapidly, but gently, ensconced in casualty bags and evacuated by helicopter to hospital. The older lady was found to have a core temperature of 32°C. She responded very rapidly to passive rewarming in the Intensive Care Unit. Very extensive bruising on her lower limbs was noted, presumably from repeated falls in the darkness on the previous night. When the younger lady arrived in hospital she had become restless and very confused. Her pulse was irregular, probably due to atrial fibrillation. Her core temperature, measured in both the rectum and oesophagus, was 20°C. She was actively rewarmed in the Intensive Care Unit using a number of techniques (external forced warmed air; internal rewarming with warm intravenous fluids and, after she was sedated and intubated, warm inspired oxygen. Her temperature steadily improved and fortunately the heart rhythm problems resolved without specific treatment. Indeed apart from some temporary fluid and electrolyte imbalance, the only significant complication was a severe psychiatric disturbance in the first few days of her recovery.

Comments

It is interesting to note some of the factors that almost certainly contributed to the marked core temperature difference between the two casualties who had been exposed to identical conditions. The older lady, whilst not obese, nevertheless had a good covering of subcutaneous fat. She was also wearing a full layer of fibre pile clothing including fibre pile mitts, balaclava and socks. Over this she was wearing an adequate windproof and to a certain extent waterproof layer. The younger lady was decidedly thin with a very poor layer of subcutaneous fat. She was not wearing any form of fibre pile clothing but was wearing simple tracksuit type clothing with an outer layer of a very thin feather ski jacket. All her clothing was saturated and holding significant quantities of water.

This was a very 'low tech.' rescue. Careful handling, and possibly luck, maintained a cardiac output in the younger lady. A rescue-related collapse was a distinct possibility; should the lady have been managed more pro-actively with airway protection etc? The helicopter transfer time was 15 minutes - a more pro-active approach would have delayed transportation by at least this length of time, and would it have provoked VF? The skill level required was not available at the incident site, so it is only a hypothetical question. Rapid evacuation with careful clinical monitoring was the correct choice.

Case 3 - Resuscitation from 13.7°C - a case taken from the Lancet (see references)

Time and date: 1999

Location: Norway

Cause of incident: Fall under icy waterfall, continually flooded by icy water

Reported injuries: Hypothermia

A letter in the Lancet describes a casualty falling, in an inaccessible position, under icy water; 40 minutes later she stopped struggling. A further 40 minutes later she was extracted from the water and BLS started. She was 'clinically dead'. A helicopter arrived one and a half hours after the fall. Advanced life support (intubation and ventilation) was added to the CPR and continued during the winch into the helicopter. The helicopter flight to the hospital took 1 hour. On arriving at hospital, the heart was asystolic. Rapid rewarming by cardiopulmonary bypass was performed and despite complications the casualty made a good physical and mental recovery. The authors say

Epitympanic thermometer – the probe, the probe in position and connected to the monitor

'victims of very deep accidental hypothermia with circulatory arrest should be seen as potentially resuscitable with the prospect of full recovery'. The rapid cooling may have been a factor in the excellent outcome or are hospitals getting better at managing such cases?

Case 4 - a case taken from Resuscitation (see references)

Time and date: 21st Century

Location: Austria

Cause of incident: A night in a snow bank

Reported injuries: Hypothermia

A man was found semiconscious after spending a night in a snow bank. The ambient temperature had been minus 20°C. Assessment at the incident site showed that he had hypothermia stage III (Airway clear, breathing, palpable pulse of 50 beats per minute and GCS of 5) with a core temperature of 21°C, and his extremities were frozen solid. The medical team took a 'scoop and run' approach. During the evacuation by helicopter, the casualty vomited (and aspirated), lost his palpable pulse and became unconscious - a classic rescue-related collapse. CPR was started immediately. The hospital had been warned of the imminent arrival of the casualty; two cardiac surgeons were in the admission room and having inserted an extracorporeal membrane oxygenation device, the casualty was internally rewarmed to 29°C within 20 minutes of admission. At this stage, asystole converted to VF and a single defibrillation resulted in a normal heart beat. The casualty then progressed well and even the previously frozen forearms showed signs of perfusion. Amputations of the hands were required for severe frostbite at day 11 despite intensive treatment and surgery.

Again this case demonstrates a remarkable survival story, despite the limited intervention in the pre-hospital phase. The authors were slightly critical of this yet acknowledged intervention in a snow bank at minus 20°C would be difficult and would have delayed the evacuation. Of course, if the case had not had a successful outcome it would probably not have been published. The paper from Southern Finland has

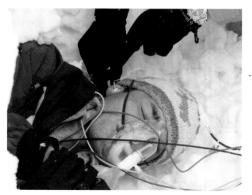

confirmed that survival is not unusual in these circumstances. We now need similar papers looking into what aspects, apart from rapid transfer to hospital, are critical in the pre-hospital phase.

References

Durrer B, Brugger H, Syme D. The medical on site treatment of hypothermia in *Consensus guidelines on mountain emergency medicine and risk reduction* edited by Fidel Elsensohn 2001 ISBN 88 884 29 00 X Guideline number 14 and accessible on the ICAR website (www.ikar-cisa.org)

State of Alaska. *Cold Injuries Guidelines* (2003, updated 2005); accessible at http://www.chems.alaska.gov

Keatinge W. Cold, drowning, and seasonal mortality. *Oxford textbook of medicine* 3rd edition 1996 ISBN 0 19 262140 8; chapter: 8.5.5(c)

Lazar H. The treatment of hypothermia. *NEJM* (1997); 337: 1545-1547

Larach M. Accidental hypothermia. *Lancet* (1995); 345: 493-8

Ainslie P, Reilly T. Physiology of accidental hypothermia in the mountains: a forgotten story. *Br J Sports Med* (2003); 37: 548-550.

Walpoth B, Walpoth-Aslan B, Mattle H, Radanov B, Schroth G, Schaeffler L, Fischer A, Segesser L, Althaus U. Outcome of survivors of accidental deep hypothermia and circulatory arrest treated with extracorporeal blood warming. *NEJM* (1997); 337: 1500-5.

See also correspondence on the above article in *NEJM* (1998); 338:various

Silvast T, Pettila V. Outcome from severe hypothermia in Southern Finland - a 10 year review. *Resuscitation* (2003); 59: 285-290

Gilbert M, Busund R, Skagseth A, Nilsen P, Solbø J. Resuscitation from accidental hypothermia of 13.7°C with circulatory arrest. *Lancet* (2000); 355: 375-6

Moser B, Voelckel W, Gardetto A, Sumann G, Wenzela V. One night in a snowbank: A case report of severe hypothermia and cardiac arrest. *Resuscitation* (2005); 65: 365–368

Weinberg A. The role of inhalation rewarming in the early management of hypothermia. *Resuscitation* (1998); 36: 101–104

Lloyd E. Airway warming in the treatment of accidental hypothermia: a review. *Journal of wilderness medicine* (1990); 1; 65-78

Harper C, McNicholas T, Gowrie-Mohan S. Maintaining perioperative normothermia. *BMJ* (2003); 326: 721-2

Wang H, Callaway C, Peltzman A, Tisherman S. Admission hypothermia and outcome after major trauma. *Critical Care Medicine* (2005); 33: 1296-1301

Safar P, Ochanek P. Therapeutic hypothermia after cardiac arrest. *NEJM* (2002); 346: 612-3

Narayan R. Hypothermia for traumatic brain injury - a good idea proved ineffective. *NEJM* (2001); 344: 602-3

Beveridge M. Hypothermia doth not staunch haemorrhage. Rapid response *BMJ* (1999); accessed at http://bmj.com/cgi/letters/319/7224/1561

Frostbite

Frostbite is a localised cold injury where the tissues freeze and ice crystals form between the cells. It can only occur in subzero temperatures. Most of the tissue destruction comes from secondary blood vessel occlusion from intraluminal thrombus and endothelial damage. Predisposing factors are poor insulation; restrictive clothing; hypothermia and exhaustion, particularly at altitude; and nicotine. The injury can be superficial (epidermis and superficial layers of the dermis) or deep (involving deeper layers of the dermis and the structures underneath), and can lead to amputation. It should be entirely preventable with modern well fitting clothing. Boots fit to climb to the top of Everest are available in outdoor shops today, but this does not guard from 'the extra pair of socks for the cold' causing restriction and then frostbite! It is worth noting that the insulating materials used in a modern glove are so good that the main heat loss has become radiation. As this is proportional to the surface area of the glove, making the cross sections of the fingers smaller makes the gloves warmer and finally allows outdoor tasks to be done without degloving.

Recognising frostbite

The onset of frostbite is recognised by pain followed by a loss of sensation in the affected part. The fingers feel 'wooden in the glove'. They look pale, sometimes purplish, and feel cold. In more severe causes the area is firm to the touch. Some people feel little or no pain at the onset of frostbite making it harder to recognise in the early stages.

Managing frostbite

As frostbite is unlikely, by itself, to lead to a call to the rescue services in the UK this section has been written for the ordinary mountaineer - perhaps even a mountain rescuer on his holidays!

What do you do if frostbite occurs whilst on the move?

First decide whether you can stop and find a temporary safe shelter from the wind. If you cannot - turn back.

If shelter can be found, remove the casualty's boots or gloves and warm the extremity in a companion's axilla (armpit) or groin. Give aspirin 300mg to reduce the production and propagation of intraluminal thrombi. After ten minutes, replace the boots and outer mitts, changing, if possible, wet for dry. If the extremity has fully recovered within the ten minutes, superficial frostbite with a good prognosis has been treated. However, there is a high probability of recurrence but, with better preventive measures, continuing is acceptable.

If the extremity has not fully recovered after ten minutes of warming, the frostbite is much more serious. This is particularly so if there has been no return in sensation; the frozen extremity is in peril. The casualty should go to the nearest warm shelter, such as a hut or base camp, without further attempts to thaw out the affected part. Bear in mind that from this shelter the casualty will not be able to walk if you are treating the lower limb. Once there, remove boots and rings, give aspirin (if not already given) and treat any hypothermia. Warm the extremity as rapidly as possible. The best method is to immerse it in warm water (37 - 42°C) until it is warm and colour returns. This typically takes 20-40 minutes but may be an hour with a foot. A suitable disinfectant can be added to the water if available. The water temperature will need topping up as the extremity warms and strong pain relief may be needed. Even if the affected part has thawed during the walk to the shelter it is often wise to employ the rapid rewarming technique, if at all possible, to ensure as much tissue as possible survives.

Having rewarmed the extremity, dry, elevate and apply non-adherent dressings and loose bandages. Blisters develop rapidly at the site of tissue damage though, as in burns, these usually carry a good prognosis. Like burns, it is hard to be accurate as to the degree of irreversible loss at this early stage. All extremities require further specialist medical assessment and so need evacuating as soon as possible. The casualty must not walk on an affected limb - transport is mandatory. Watch out for infection - wash with an antiseptic and redress daily if possible, and be ready with an antibiotic should infection appear. Continue 300mg of aspirin every day during the evacuation period. Never rub - Never use direct heat - Never allow re-freezing or walking - or you are courting a major amputation.

Hospital management of frostbite

Some local hospitals will be expert in managing frostbite; others may not! The combination of a digital camera and the Internet allows you to get expert help from the UK almost immediately via the British Mountaineering Council Medical Advisors or from holders of the Diploma in Mountain Medicine listed at:

http://www.medex.org.uk/dimm_(mountain_medicine_diploma).htm.

For example, Adam, after climbing Aconcagua (6960m, Argentina) suffered frostbite of his toes. A local hospital suggested amputation and grafting. However, he conveyed his condition by digital photographs to the UK. They advised him to defer surgery and, through his insurance company, he was repatriated with his toes intact. He has made an excellent recovery with local conservative management as his photographs demonstrate.

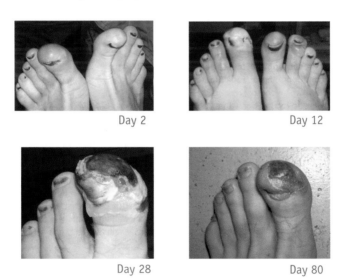

Day 2   Day 12

Day 28   Day 80

Frostnip

This is simply a very minor early manifestation of frostbite. Contact with a good heat conductor, such as a metal stretcher, is the usual cause. The skin becomes white but rapidly returns to normal when the contact is broken and gloves applied.

Immersion foot (Trench foot)

Trench foot is a cold (but non-freezing) injury that results from prolonged exposure to wet and cold conditions over a number of days. It has not been recorded in mountaineering activities; indeed, it is rare outside scenes of military conflict. The foot is extremely sensitive with what is often described as a burning sensation. The skin becomes white or mottled grey-blue. On warming, the skin becomes red, friable and swollen, and the foot remains very sensitive. Dry dressings, elevation and prolonged avoidance of cold, wet conditions are required.

Reference

Syme D. On site treatment of frostbite for mountaineers. Guideline number 15 in *Consensus guidelines on mountain emergency medicine and risk reduction* edited by Fidel Elsensohn 2001 ISBN 88 884 29 00 X and accessible on the ICAR website (www.ikar-cisa.org)

Clarke C. *UIAA Mountain Medicine Centre* Information Sheet 10 (Frostbite). Accessed at http://www.thebmc.co.uk/world/mm/mm10.htm

Serious heat on honeymoon, Black Cullin, Skye! (1981)

Heat-related illness

Heat-related illnesses are a spectrum of conditions precipitated by exposure to 'too much' heat. It includes heat syncope, heat exhaustion and heat stroke as well as sunburn. The classical description of heat stroke occurring in the elderly and frail as the ambient temperatures approaches 37°C is not relevant to this book. However, exercise-induced heat stroke certainly is as it occurs at modest ambient temperatures - the lowest quoted temperature being 21°C in Norway - and is a common cause of death in fun runs.

Physiology and pathology

The metabolism of the body produces heat as a by-product. The heat generated by muscular activity is many times that of the background rate, so the body core temperature rises with exercise to a new steady level - perhaps up to 38°C at high levels of activity. If the tissues get too hot, the enzyme systems vital to the cells fail and a number of detrimental processes occur that lead to death.

The body has a number of ways to increase the loss of heat to the outside. In a hot environment, thermal receptors, both in the skin and brain, induce vasodilatation of the blood vessels in the skin, and sweating. Up to an environmental temperature of 32°C, vasodilatation alone is effective if the casualty is resting. With exercise, or a higher temperature, sweating is needed to prevent the core temperature rising higher and higher. Sweating (the evaporation of water from the skin) depends on having water and, in the heat-unacclimatised person, salt to produce the sweat, and ambient conditions that allow evaporation.
(As the relative humidity approaches 100%, evaporation falls to zero.) Dehydration is developing as the person sweats. Once dehydration is established the person sweats less and is therefore less able to dissipate the unwanted heat with the consequence that the body temperature increases.

Prevention

This section gives some useful pointers to those of us who take part in races to raise the profile of mountain rescue. There is no definite case of heat shock reported in a mountain rescuer responding to a call-out, though it has been described in similar circumstances.

Heat acclimatization improves a person's ability to cope when exercising in warm temperatures. To achieve acclimatization, athletes are advised to train, with an increasing degree of exposure to heat, for at least seven days until the environment corresponds to that expected during the event. Of course, the problem in the UK is that hot days, particularly in the Spring, can be unseasonable! Start the event well hydrated, exercise within your capabilities and stop if headache, dizziness or lack of coordination occurs. Febrile ('having a temperature') and dehydrating illnesses, such as gastroenteritis, increase the risk of heat stroke; so don't start if you have not completely recovered.

Symptoms and signs

Sunburn

This is caused by excessive exposure to ultraviolet light causing the skin to burn. Fair-skinned people are more at risk. In the UK, altitude has only a small effect though snow cover can catch the unaware mountaineer. After exposure, the skin becomes red; swelling and blisters may appear later. Treatment involves cooling the skin, covering up with clothes, simple analgesia such as paracetamol and, if severe, non-adherent dressings.

Heat syncope

This is a simple faint precipitated by a person stopping exercise in a warm environment. The blood flow to the skin is substantial, and when the muscle pump in the legs (returning blood to the heart) stops, the cardiac output fails and the person faints. A period of lying down and some water by mouth should rapidly resolve the problem.

Heat Exhaustion and Heat Stroke

There is disagreement as to whether these conditions are the mild and severe ends of a spectrum of heat-related illness or whether heat exhaustion has a different pathological cause from heat stroke. It is not clear if you progress from heat exhaustion to heat stroke.

Heat exhaustion

The symptoms of heat exhaustion are headache, fatigue and nausea. Muscle cramps are common. The casualty usually has a fast heart rate and the blood pressure often drops when the casualty stands from a sitting position (postural hypotension). Dizziness may result. In more severe cases, thirst may occur. The body temperature may be normal but never exceeds 40°C. The condition is the result of dehydration from sweating - over two litres of water can be sweated out in an hour - and salt depletion in the heat-unacclimatised person. There is no tissue damage or medical complications.

The condition is easy to treat on the fell by reducing exertion, finding shade, fanning and tepid sponging. It is important to replace the lost water and salt. Drinking two litres of water and eating a bag of crisps is a good start though the total body deficit is much larger. When exercise restarts the condition is likely to recur. Most casualties will need to be escorted from the fell for a night's rest and rehydration!

Heat stroke

Heat stroke is a much more serious condition with a mortality rate ranging from 25 to 50%. It is defined clinically as a core body temperature of greater than 40°C and a neurological abnormality such as confusion, convulsions or coma. Two types are recognised:

The classical form, resulting from exposure to temperatures close to 37°C, characteristically has a hot, dry skin and is seen in the elderly and frail.

An exercise-induced (exertional) form occurs during exercise at lower temperatures in young, fit, usually male persons. It is increasingly recognised as a cause of death in fun runs etc., though less so in marathons, where the cause of death is predominantly heart disease. The skin does not have to be hot and dry; indeed it may be cold and sweaty. This delays the diagnosis unless a core temperature is routinely measured in anyone with a collapse or neurological symptom. Carrying a tympanic (infra-red) thermometer would be ideal for those marshalling a running event.

The initial symptoms are irritability, impaired judgement and headache. A high pulse rate and a low blood pressure are common. Seizures, coma and circulatory collapse develop rapidly as the core temperature rises and culminates in death. Many other features that resemble septic shock, such as kidney failure, clotting abnormalities and brain dysfunction, occur both during the onset and treatment of the condition.

Treatment

Treatment is urgent at whatever stage the casualty has reached. The thermoregulatory mechanisms have failed and the core temperature is only going to increase with further tissue damage. Follow a primary survey approach:

Is it safe to approach the casualty?

A - ensure the airway is open.

B - assess the breathing and start oxygen at 15 litres/minute using a non-rebreathing mask with a reservoir.

C - assess the circulation.

D - assess the conscious level.

E - measure the core body temperature.

Start cooling the casualty immediately; this will not wait. There is controversy over the best means. Immersion in cool water, tepid sponging and fanning, and atomised water sprays have been used. Arrange an urgent evacuation to hospital using a helicopter, if available, keeping a careful eye on the condition of the casualty. Sudden deterioration is common.

If skilled, an intravenous infusion of one or two litres of saline may be considered; it may help the circulation and will cool the core directly. No drug has been shown to help in heat stroke.

References

Bouchama A, Knochel J. Heat stroke. *NEJM* 2002; 346:1978-1989

Sutton J. Physiological and clinical consequences of exercise in heat and humidity. *Oxford textbook of sports medicine* 1994 ISBN 0 19 262009 6

Glazer J. Management of heat stroke and heat exhaustion. *American Family Physician* 2005; 71:2133-2140

Burns

Burns are not common in mountain rescue. Nevertheless, when man and cooking materials are in proximity, accidents do happen. A friend of mine was climbing in the Caucasus; at advanced base camp (5500m), the petrol stove exploded followed instantaneously by the tent, and fortunately only his eyebrows. A couple of days in a snow hole gave him time to cool down!

A burn can be produced by direct heat (flame, hot metal, scalds) or radiant heat from the sun, electricity or a chemical. Remember, most deaths in house fires are due to airway and breathing problems rather than the skin injury.

Physiology and pathology

It is important to understand what has happened when someone is burnt. Think of the local and the systemic (general) effect of the burn.

Local effect

The severity of the local effect will depend on a number of factors listed in the following table.

Factors affecting the local severity of the burn
The agent (electrical, chemical) causing the burn or the temperature of the burning substance - the hotter, the greater the tissue damage.
The time exposed to the burning agent.
The condition of the skin and the site of the damage.
The age of the casualty - the skin is relatively thin at both ends of the age spectrum.
Concurrent medical problems, such as Diabetes, that reduce the ability of the tissues to fight infection.

Think of a burn as having three zones.

There may be a central area where the burn has completely destroyed the tissue; this is a zone of irreversible tissue loss. Around this zone, there is an area of severe inflammation. Here, tissue perfusion becomes reduced as fluid and protein accumulate outside the blood vessels and leaks to the surface. This area is called the stasis zone and is potentially salvageable. Outside the stasis zone is an area of hyperaemia (redness) where the tissue perfusion is increased. The tissue here inevitably recovers unless severe infection sets in. The initial management of a burn is to minimise the area of the central zone, and tip the balance towards healing in the stasis zone.

Systemic effect

The burn releases inflammatory substances into the circulation. These act on the rest of the body causing further fluid loss from the circulation, bronchoconstriction, reduced heart contractility, and vasoconstriction of normal skin and gut. The severity of the systemic effect, particularly the response of the circulation and respiration, depends on the percentage of the total body surface area damaged. With the exception of electrical burns (see lightning for details), systemic effects become important once the burn reaches 30% of the total body surface area.

Symptoms and signs

The history, or the situation surrounding the casualty, will indicate that a burn has occurred. It is important to establish the causative agent for future management. Scalds usually cause superficial burns. These are intensely painful, as the nerve endings in the skin are exposed and not destroyed. The severe inflammatory reaction causes fluid to pour out of burnt area and large blisters frequently develop at the site of the burn. Scalds often look much worse than they turn out to be.

In contrast, flame and hot fat burns are often deeper and remove all the layers of the skin (full thickness). In flame burns, the area may be contaminated with burnt clothing. Blisters are less often seen and the pain may not be as intense.

Inhaling noxious substances, such as smoke, can burn the airway. The casualty may be coughing, have a hoarse voice, or respiratory distress. Look for burns around, or inside, the mouth and nose; singed nasal hairs and particles of smoke and carbon in the mouth and nose suggest that an inhalation burn has occurred. The inflammatory response can cause the walls of the upper airway to swell and, if severe, the airway to block. This can occur with alarming speed and requires specialist management to secure an airway. Any symptoms or signs of an inhalation burn should be treated seriously and the urgent evacuation of the casualty arranged. Noxious air may also cause bronchoconstriction and carbon monoxide, produced by the fire, can add to the casualty's problems.

Chemical burns tend to be deep, as the corrosive element continues to cause tissue destruction until it is completely removed. In general, alkalis, such as cement, tend to cause more damage than acids.

The fluid loss from the burn and, more importantly, the systemic effects mentioned above cause the casualty to develop hypovolaemic shock in the hours following the burn. If shock is present in the first hour, other causes, such as a heart problem and internal bleeding, should be considered.

Management

Primary survey

An assessment of safety should be made first. Is the electrical source turned off? Are the chemicals and fire controlled? Is the air safe?

A - Airway and, if appropriate, cervical spine control.

If the casualty has been injured in a fire, particularly in a confined space, then the possibility of airway damage or inhalation injury is the first consideration. If symptoms or signs are present, or there is simply a strong suspicion, then the priority is to give oxygen at 15 litres/minute by a non-rebreathing mask with a reservoir and arrange a rapid evacuation. Pulse oximetry may help in monitoring but should not be relied on as carbon monoxide poisoning would give a falsely high (reassuring) 'oxygen saturation'. A helicopter would be appropriate if journey times were reduced.

B - Breathing and high flow oxygen.

Start oxygen if the burn area (see below) looks to be greater than 10% of the total body surface area or there is a possibility of carbon monoxide poisoning.

C - Circulation and external haemorrhage control.

Record and chart the pulse rate.

D - AVPU assessment.

Quickly move on to the treatment of the burn.

Reassurance is important. The casualty is often anxious and distressed; an early positive approach is most helpful along with explaining what you are doing.

Stop the burning process - remove the heat source, remove clothing unless adherent to the skin - and then cool the burn if within 20 minutes of the injury. Immerse or irrigate in clean water for up to 20 minutes. The water should not be cold; ideally 15°C, and certainly not iced. You can rapidly induce hypothermia! Intravenous fluids could be used on the burn if clean water is not readily available. All chemical burns should be thoroughly washed with large amounts of water.

Assess the extent of the burn quickly though this is likely to be inaccurate as, in the first few hours, skin redness (that should be excluded) is hard to separate from superficial burns. The easiest way to assess the burn area is to refer to the hand and closed fingers of the casualty. This represents 1% of the total body surface. If the burnt area is less than 10% then the risk of serious fluid depletion is very small. If more than 10% of the total body surface area is involved then fluid replacement should be considered as well as oxygen and an urgent evacuation.

1%

The casualty is likely to be in pain, though cooling often reduces the severity; if needed, morphine can be given.

The burns can then be covered to reduce bacterial colonisation. Polyvinyl chloride film (cling film) is ideal. It is pliable, non-adherent and transparent for inspection. Lay the film on the burn rather than wrapping the burn. This is especially important on limbs, as the cling film can act as a tourniquet, and compromise tissue perfusion, as the limb continues to swell. Polythene bags are good for hands and feet. If cling film is unavailable, sterile non-adherent dressings (e.g. Melolin®) can be lightly placed on the burn and secured by loose bandaging (bearing in mind the potential for creating a tourniquet). Finally ensure that hypothermia does not develop after all the cooling and water. Elevate the affected part, if possible, and do not allow walking on a burnt lower limb. All casualties with burns, except the most minor, should be advised to seek further medical assessment as other issues beyond the scope of Casualty Care, such as tetanus prophylaxis, need considering.

Extended Management

Burns covering more than 15% of the total body surface area warrant formal resuscitation. The fluid losses need to be replaced to maintain homoeostasis. Getting significantly behind is detrimental. A commonly used formula, the Parkland formula, gives a guide to the amount of fluid needed. The total fluid requirement in first 24 hours from the time of the burn = 4 ml x (total burn surface area (%)) x body weight (kg). 50% of the total fluid is given in the first 8 hours. A worked example is:

> If the total burn surface area is 30% in a 70 kg casualty, the total estimated fluid requirement is 4 x 30 x 70 = 8400 ml in the first 24 hours of which 4200 ml is required in the first 8 hours from the burn.
>
> You arrive 2 hours after the injury leaving 6 hours to infuse the fluid at 700 ml an hour. If the evacuation is going to take 3 hours - no, you can't have a helicopter because of the weather - 2 litres of Hartmann's solution (or Normal Saline) would be an estimated volume to infuse during the evacuation if this was practical.

References

Hettiaratchy S, Papini R, Dziewulski P. ABC of burns. *BMJ* 2004; various articles accessible at http://bmj.bmjjournals.com/

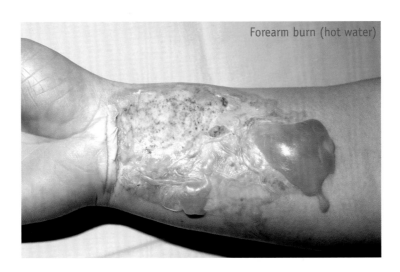
Forearm burn (hot water)

Bites and Stings

Animal bites

Although animal bites are a common feature of Accident and Emergency work in this country, they very rarely present to mountain rescuers. Immediate treatment is important because of the special features of these wounds. All animal bites are potentially infected and the extent of tissue damage is usually greater than first appears. Dog bites are the most likely wound to be encountered (not, of course, from SARDA dogs!). Most bites will affect the extremities. Considerable tissue crushing can occur and at least 30% of such wounds will be seriously infected and bites potentially could transmit tetanus, rabies (dog or bat bites) hepatitis B, and/or HIV (human bites).

Management

After controlling haemorrhage, immediate copious irrigation with normal saline or, if not available, drinking water, has been shown to reduce the chance of infection by five fold. Povidone-iodine aqueous solution (for example, Betadine®) would be an alternative in all but the largest wounds. A non-adherent dressing should then be applied. No attempt should be made to close the wound. Splints may be necessary in the event of extensive injury. All injuries of this nature should be seen at an Accident and Emergency department as soon as feasible. Prophylactic ('before infection starts') antibiotics are often given to human and cat bites as the rate of becoming infected is >50% without.

Snake bites

The advice here is only intended for the management of bites from the European Adder (Vipera berus). If you are unfortunate enough to come across bites from more exotic snakes the principles of management are the same but the risks are greater and transfer to hospital must be urgent. Adders bite more than 100 people each year in Britain with a significant number of these occurring in moorland and relatively remote areas. Severe effects are unusual and no deaths have been recorded since 1975 but children are more at risk of developing a serious reaction than adults. Most bites are on the hand or fingers (often from picking up the snake!) though occasionally on the toes or feet. The symptoms and signs vary but in at least two thirds of those bitten venom is not injected to a significant degree. In these casualties the wound is a small puncture to the skin. With the injection of venom, local pain and swelling develops in minutes though sometimes this is delayed for up to 30 minutes. The swelling may rapidly advance to involve the whole limb and bruising may appear. The venom can, in rare cases, cause a systemic anaphylactoid reaction. In these cases, general symptoms occur as early as five minutes after the bite. The most frequent symptoms are vomiting, diarrhoea, abdominal pain, shock and loss of consciousness. These symptoms and signs can be difficult to distinguish from those arising from the acute anxiety that a snakebite induces. If in doubt, assume that the symptoms are due to effects of the venom. In rare cases persistent severe shock with a very low blood pressure may develop, in addition to urticaria (hives), bronchospasm (resembling asthma) and angio-oedema (swelling of tongue or face).

Prevention

Wear adequate protective clothing: long baggy trousers, long boots or gaiters, and thick socks. If you see a snake, move carefully away from it. Don't try to kill or get a closer look at a snake as nearly all bites in humans result from a snake defending itself when it feels threatened. Look carefully where you are going to sit and avoid putting hands into areas where snakes may be hiding such as long grass, under rocks or in old buildings. Be aware of snakes even when climbing and don't handle recently killed snakes.

Management

Follow the primary survey approach managing systemic symptoms as described under the section on anaphylaxis (page 230).

Cover the bite with a sterile dressing. There is no place for a 'traditional' attack on the wound with a knife or using any of the commercial suction devices. The casualty should be rested and transferred to hospital with as little active movement as possible. Therefore, a stretcher evacuation will be required for most casualties.

The bitten extremity should be immobilized with a splint and, if possible, elevated. Paracetamol may be required for pain. Antivenom is available in the UK; the destination hospital should be warned as early as possible that antivenom may be needed so as to give them time to acquire it. Antivenom is indicated for casualties with signs of systemic envenomation or a rapidly spreading local swelling. (For example, if the swelling has spread beyond the wrist or ankle after a bite on a digit within the first four hours.)

For most exotic snakebites, there is some evidence that applying a bandage to the bitten area, with the same pressure as would be used for a sprained ankle, helps to contain the venom. Details are shown in the references quoted. It goes without saying that venturing outside the UK usually increases your exposure. For example, our viper's near relative, the horned viper, is much more dangerous and frequently leads to a mountain rescue in Croatia.

Stings

Stings from bees, wasps and ants usually cause little problem except in those persons sensitised to that particular sting.

In a non-sensitised person, a single sting will cause local pain and a wheal at the site of the sting. A wheal is a raised area of tissue reaction that is often whitish and surrounded by an area of redness. Itchiness is variable. It is common for the local reaction to spread to a diameter of 15cm or more and persist for 24 hours. Multiple stings in an non-sensitised person, perhaps from disturbing a nest, can cause vomiting, diarrhoea, breathlessness, collapse and, even, myocardial infarction but this is rare. These symptoms are the result of the histamine release. The lethal dose is around 'hundreds of stings' though as few as 30 have been fatal and as many as 2243 survived!

A sensitised person is one who has developed an allergic reaction to the proteins in the bee or wasp venom. Approximately one in 200 persons are sensitised and risk a fatal anaphylactic - a general allergic - reaction to a single sting. The severity of reaction can be mild, moderate or severe as described in the section on anaphylaxis. The more severe the reaction, the more rapid the onset; most fatalities occur within an hour of the sting.

Management

In a non-sensitised person, cooling the area of the sting with ice packs or cold water is usually sufficient to relieve the symptoms. Stings left in the wound should be scraped off rather than removed with forceps as the squeezing action can release more venom into the wound. Homely remedies, such as baking powder for bee and vinegar for wasp stings, are probably of little benefit, as are commercial 'sting sticks'. Oral antihistamines, such as chlorphenamine, may help when the local reaction is marked and, rarely, oral steroids can be used to hasten resolution of the swelling. When a person has had multiple stings, and has symptoms of histamine excess, those with the necessary skills should consider an antihistamine by injection and intravenous fluids.

The management of anaphylaxis is covered in the following section.

References

Anonymous. Managing bites from humans and other mammals. *Drug and Therapeutics Bulletin*. 2004; 42: 67-71

Agazzi G, Svajda D, Morgan A, Ferrandis S, Boyd J. Snakebite injuries in mountainous terrain: prevention and on-site treatment. In press 2005; available on the ICAR website (www.ikar-cisa.org)

Warrell D. Treatment of bites by adders and exotic venomous snakes. *BMJ* (2005); 331: 1244-7

Auebach PS. *Wilderness Medicine: management of wilderness and environmental emergencies (Third edition)* 1995. ISBN 0 8016 7044 6: page 744-748

Home of the horned viper
ICAR Medcom meeting, Paklenica, Croatia. (2005)

Anaphylaxis

It is hard to know where to put this section; it could go in the medical, drugs or environmental section. While it is relevant to all these subjects, I will put it here, as stings are probably the commonest trigger in mountain rescue.

Anaphylaxis is a clinical syndrome that has more than one triggering mechanism, and hence a number of different terms that can be applied. These include 'severe allergic' and 'anaphylactoid' reaction, such as occurs after snakebite. Though the differences are important for future preventative actions, the acute management is the same. Therefore I will use just one term - anaphylaxis - for the syndrome.

Physiology and pathology

Anaphylaxis results from activation of mast cells and basophils (a type of white blood cell). It can be triggered by a large number of factors; the common ones are bee and wasp stings (25%), peanut and shellfish ingestion (25%), and drugs (50%), particularly antibiotics and NSAIDs (aspirin, diclofenac and ibuprofen).

The activated mast cells and basophils release mediators, such as histamine, both locally and into the circulation. These cause the clinical features of anaphylaxis; the cardinal features being urticaria, angio-oedema, bronchospasm and hypotension. These features and their associated symptoms and signs are described in the box on the next page. One feature may dominate but usually a few are present. Skin rash is the most consistent. Severe reactions tend to start within minutes of the trigger and evolve rapidly. The condition is life threatening in a number of ways:

Swelling of the upper airway, particularly of the laryngeal cords, can obstruct the upper airway.

Bronchospasm can cause severe hypoxia leading to a cardiac arrest.

Shock can lead to a cardiac arrest when insufficient blood returns to the heart.

Cardinal feature	Symptoms and signs
Urticaria	A skin rash. Raised and itchy; it's like nettle sting over a larger area. The edges are pinkish whereas the central areas tend to be paler. It can spread very quickly.
Angio-oedema	Subcutaneous swelling of tissues. Typically this occurs on the face particularly on the lips and in the upper airway (tongue, uvula, laryngeal cords). The swelling does not itch but can obstruct the airway causing stridor and respiratory distress. (See differential diagnosis of a raised respiratory rate in the Asthma section).
Bronchospasm	Asthma. Wheeze, raised respiratory rate; see Asthma.
Hypotension	Shock. High pulse rate, anxious, pale; see Circulation.

Management

Get the casualty to sit or lie down depending on which is most comfortable. (If there are breathing difficulties sitting will be preferred.) Perform a primary survey, that is: Safety, A, B, C and D. A recent history of a common trigger, such as a wasp sting, and a past history of similar reactions/allergies help make the diagnosis. Any abnormal finding in the primary survey signifies severe anaphylaxis and should lead on to the anaphylaxis algorithm produced overleaf. This is based on the UK Resuscitation Council's algorithm.

Severe anaphylaxis

Intramuscular adrenaline (epinephrine) should be given as soon as a severe reaction is diagnosed as it is associated with an improved outcome. Each step of the algorithm should be carried out; each is of benefit by modifying part of the underlying pathological processes. Monitor the casualty carefully measuring pulse, respiratory rate and, if possible, oxygen saturation and ECG. Cardiac arrest regularly occurs during anaphylaxis so be prepared.

Glucagon can be tried in refractory anaphylaxis – see Rususcitation Council guidelines.

Mild and moderate anaphylaxis

The diagnosis will be based on exposure to a precipitating trigger and urticaria or angio-oedema without respiratory difficulty or shock. The most appropriate treatment is an antihistamine, such as chlorphenamine, by mouth in a mild attack, perhaps intramuscularly in a moderate attack. It is sometimes difficult to separate a mild attack with (understandable) anxiety from a severe attack. Panic attacks cause hyperventilation and can be associated with a red rash usually of the neck and chest but it is flat (impalpable) unlike urticaria. Hypotension, reduced oxygen saturation and the pattern of breathing (see asthma section) should help. If in doubt give adrenaline, as it is very safe in fit people.

Self-treatment with auto-injectors

Patients with previous severe attacks may carry adrenaline auto-injectors. These give either 300 mcg or 150 mcg of adrenaline, and are usually adequate to treat a reaction. If no improvement has occurred in 5 minutes, administer the standard (500 mcg or 250 mcg) dose of adrenaline as indicated on the algorithm.

Evacuation

The casualty will need to be evacuated to hospital; a helicopter would be appropriate for a casualty suffering a severe reaction as long as monitoring can be continued.

References

Project team of the Resuscitation Council (UK). Update on the emergency medical treatment of anaphylaxis reactions for first medical responders and for community nurses. *Resuscitation* 2001:48:241-3 (revised May 2005: available at www.resus.org.uk/pages/reaction/htm)

Sheikh A, Walker S. Anaphylaxis. *BMJ* 2005; 331:330

McLean-Tooke A, Bethune C, Fay A, Spickett G. Adrenaline in the treatment of anaphylaxis: what is the evidence? *BMJ* 2003; 327:1332-5

Anaphylaxis
(with respiratory difficulty or shock, especially if skin changes present)

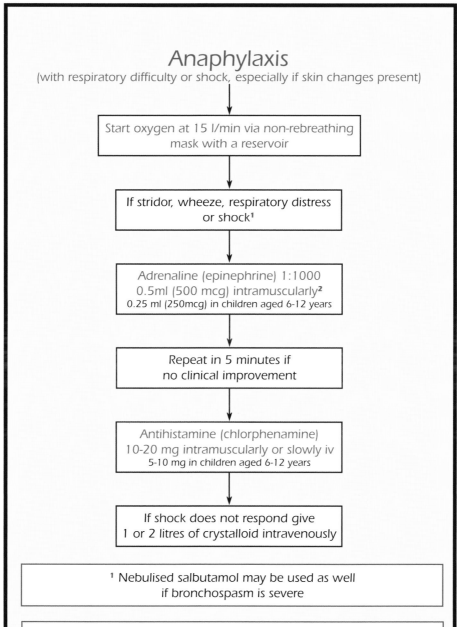

Start oxygen at 15 l/min via non-rebreathing mask with a reservoir

If stridor, wheeze, respiratory distress or shock[1]

Adrenaline (epinephrine) 1:1000
0.5ml (500 mcg) intramuscularly[2]
0.25 ml (250mcg) in children aged 6-12 years

Repeat in 5 minutes if no clinical improvement

Antihistamine (chlorphenamine)
10-20 mg intramuscularly or slowly iv
5-10 mg in children aged 6-12 years

If shock does not respond give 1 or 2 litres of crystalloid intravenously

[1] Nebulised salbutamol may be used as well if bronchospasm is severe

[2] If profound shock (unconscious and not breathing) start BLS/AED protocols and attach an AED.
Give 1mg of adrenaline intravenously as per AED protocol

For all severe reactions or patients with wheeze
give hydrocortisone 100-500mg intramuscularly or slowly iv

Lightning injury

Lightning is a rare but recorded problem with a 30% case-fatality rate. The insult consists of a brief exposure to Direct Current (DC) electricity at a voltage of many millions of volts. Lightning takes the path of least resistance to the centre of the Earth and, as a solid is a better conductor than air, people attract lightning so can be subject to a direct strike. Likewise, summits and ridges are particularly dangerous places and the rescuer must consider the risk of being in such a place during a storm. In addition to a direct strike, side-flashes occur when the current jumps from the primary contact with the Earth to another prominent object. The current passes along the ground away from the direct strike so injury can occur when the casualty is close to the direct strike and struck by the so-called 'ground current'. The human body has a relatively high resistance to electrical conduction so most of the current passes around and across the surface, especially if it is wet. This is the 'flash-over' effect. This reduces the likelihood of damage to the internal structures. However, as the moisture against the skin turns to steam, boots and clothes tend to 'explode' off the casualty and may result in superficial burns (see page 237)

Unfortunately some of the current does pass into the body and, as might be expected, a dramatic effect on the body's electrical circuitry occurs; there may be both a cardiac and respiratory arrest from the direct effect of the current upon the heart and brain. Both events may resolve spontaneously but the consequences of oxygen starvation to the vital organs are directly related to the duration of the arrest. The most common pattern is for a transient cardiac arrest with spontaneous recovery of the heart rhythm but a prolonged respiratory arrest. Indeed, lack of breathing is the most likely cause of death after a lightning strike. In such circumstances, artificial breathing, even for prolonged periods, may be all that is needed. A casualty who does not suffer a cardiac or respiratory arrest has an excellent outlook; if supported and protected, spontaneous recovery occurs.

Many casualties suffer some degree of paralysis of the lower limbs. This is caused by disruption of the electrical activity in nerves and muscles. Normally full recovery occurs though an additional spinal injury should be considered if the force of the strike has thrown the casualty.

As well as burns from the 'flash-over' effect, burns occur at the entry and exit points of the DC electricity. These wounds vary in the amount of tissue damage; usually they are of a full-thickness type and so relatively painless.

Significant damage can occur to the internal structures between the entry and exit points. Often the damage is not evident immediately but presents days or months after the strike. Examples include spinal cord dysfunction (sensory and motor problems in the limbs), rhabdomyolysis (damaged skeletal muscle), kidney failure (from the release of muscle proteins into the circulation) and cataracts to name a few!

Alternating current (AC) from electrical cables is more deadly than direct current of the same voltage. The victim may be fixed to the source by their muscle spasm so ensure that the electrical supply has been switched off before attempting to remove the casualty from the power line.

Prevention

Be aware of the weather forecast when planning events, and consider whether a safer venue is available. It is said that there is a risk of being struck if the interval between the lightning and the thunder is less than 30 seconds, and the risk persists for 30 minutes after the last strike seen. In such circumstances, areas to avoid and precautions to take are listed in the box on the next page.

Precautions during a lightning storm

Avoid:

    Ridges and summits.
    Sheltering in small caves, under overhangs, in stream beds or small
    open barns in flat areas.
    Single trees and forest clearings.
    Power lines and ski lifts.
    Via Ferrata metal work as soon as safe to do so.

Do not carry anything (skis, poles etc.) above shoulder height but keep your helmet on! Store all metal objects ideally in a dry area of your rucksack.

Try to:

    Shelter in a hut away from open doors and windows.   SAFE AREA
    Stay in the safe triangle at the base of a wall or cliff –   wall
    the height of the wall minus the first metre.

If your hair stands on end, immediately crouch down with legs together to minimize the area in contact with the ground. Sitting or standing on a dry rucksack or rope may reduce the effects of a ground current further.

Management

Consider the safety of the incident site. Lightning does strike the same place twice. Is moving the casualty to a safer area feasible? Helicopter safety should also be discussed.

Triage

If a group of people are affected, the priority of the rescuer is, unlike other situations, to leave anyone showing signs of life and concentrate on those with no breathing. Almost all people with any signs of life will recover without intervention.

Perform a primary survey on the casualty:

A - Airway. Consider the potential for a cervical spine injury.

B - Breathing. A prolonged respiratory arrest is relatively common. Artificial breathing will be required and oxygen at 15 l/min should be started. Airway adjuncts can added as appropriate.

C - Circulation. Cardiac arrest is often transient but an AED may be required to treat a secondary cardiac arrhythmia.

D - Disability. Unconsciousness and paralysis often resolve but secondary spinal injury is common; a vacuum mattress should be used if available.

Consider the possibility of secondary injury when performing a secondary survey. These occur from the casualty being thrown by the strike or from the strong muscle contractions induced by the lightning. Cover burns with a sterile non-adherent dressing.

Internal injuries often present late; all casualties need to be transported to hospital for an assessment.

Further management

If time permits, and an appropriately qualified person is present, an intravenous infusion of saline may be appropriate to ensure that dehydration does not compound the effects of rhabdomyolysis on the kidney.

Case Study - Lightning

This case is fictional but was developed from several real cases. It was commissioned for *Casualty Care in Mountain Rescue* to contribute a sense of real life and to draw attention to the dilemmas that occur in rescue work.

Time and date: 18:45 on the 15th of January

Location: Close to a pointed summit

Weather: Heavy showers

Reported injuries: Lightning strike

Four people were injured by a lightning strike; they called for assistance using a mobile phone. At the time of the strike they were separated from each other by about 10 metres, with the highest casualty still standing on the summit. At the time of the incident the party recalled one or two flashes. The first flash was described as a ball of light passing close to their heads. The blast threw the second highest casualty 3 to 5 metres. Fortunately this did not cause any injury. However, the third casualty was standing legs apart. The electrical current had passed up one leg and down the other. He fell to the ground and could not move his legs for 10 to 15 minutes. He had deep but small burns on both big toes but had recovered sufficiently to walk to the helicopter when it arrived about 30 minutes later. The lowest casualty suffered from transient deafness and tinnitus

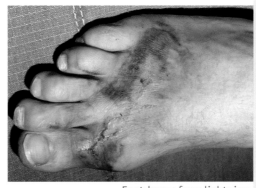

Foot burns from lightning

(ringing in the ears) from the blast and then became light-headed. An irregular heartbeat observed by the rescue team on the ECG monitor may have accounted for the light-headedness. Normal heart rhythm had returned, without treatment, by the time the casualty had been flown to the hospital. He had superficial burns to his feet. The electrical current had blown his synthetic boot apart and melted part of his nylon socks. Unfortunately the highest casualty had been the lightning conductor. When the rescue team arrived 30 minutes after the strike, the casualty had not received any BLS. It had taken some time for his colleagues to recover sufficiently to assess him and telephone prompting by the emergency services was not practised at the time. The team performed BLS for a short period until an ECG confirmed asystole. The team doctor called a halt to further attempts at resuscitation.

Comments:

A call-out to a lightning strike often involves a number of casualties; if triage is needed remember that priority should be directed at the 'apparently dead' as those with signs of life tend to recover unaided. Having said that, survivors all need to be assessed in hospital as late complications occur. The third casualty in this incident had significant muscle damage and had a period of reduced kidney function. Fortunately he recovered completely.

References

Zafren K, Durrer B, Herry J, Brugger H. Lightning injuries: prevention and on-site treatment in mountains and remote areas. *Resuscitation* 2005; 65:369-372 and accessible on the ICAR website (www.ikar-cisa.org)

Patterdale MRT rescue boat on Ullswater

Drowning

Drowning is death by asphyxia caused by submersion in water; near drowning is survival from asphyxia caused in the same way. About 700 people die as a result of drowning accidents in the UK every year, with many more near drowning episodes. Mountain rescue gets involved more often than commonly appreciated, for example drowning accounts for 9% of deaths in the Lake District (LDSAMRA statistics 1996-2001). Exhaustion, hypothermia and alcohol consumption often complicates immersion accidents.

Note: **Submersion** = head under the water and **immersion** = head above water.

Physiology

Sudden contact with cold water causes an inspiratory gasp even in clothed people and this overcomes any diving response. If submerged, the maximum breath-holding time is reduced to 10 seconds. The breathing rate is considerably increased; this can lead to confusion from the resulting low carbon dioxide concentration in the blood. The circulatory system has to cope with a sudden constriction of the blood vessels supplying the skin, an increase in heart rate and increase in demand for blood to supply the muscles. This combination can leave the heart in an irritable state, possibly leading to ventricular fibrillation or induce acute ischaemia, particularly in people with coronary artery disease.

After these initial changes, immersion in cold water starts to cool the body. General (Core) hypothermia needs significant time to develop – perhaps one hour if the water temperature is 5°C or two hours at a water temperature of 10°C. However the limbs cool much more quickly and to such an extent that coordinated muscle action is prevented by increased muscle tone and a reduction in nerve conduction. Swimming or holding on to an object becomes impossible; this is called 'swim failure'. The person will submerge unless he has a life jacket on. The time to 'swim failure' is very variable and depends on a number of factors such as the amount of body fat, whether the person keeps still and their clothing, and whether they are used (habituated) to cold water. However approximate times for half of a group of swimmers to reach 'swim failure' are 90 minutes at a water temperature of 10°C, and 10 minutes in icy water.

A life jacket will keep the casualty's head above the water and allow time for hypothermia and unconsciousness to develop. Waves splashing over the face will then result in aspiration.

Pathology

In 85% of drowning and near-drowning accidents fluid is aspirated into the lungs. The volume of water involved is small and can be as little as 50 ml. In these cases, aspiration causes a respiratory arrest – the breathing stops. Hypoxia sets in and the casualty becomes unconscious. The circulation fails some time later; perhaps up to 40 minutes later.

In the remaining 15%, aspiration does not occur but problems arise from asphyxia caused by spasm of the vocal cords (laryngospasm) or a cardiac arrhythmia (ventricular fibrillation) as described above.

Aspiration of water into the lungs often causes severe lung damage such as pulmonary oedema or Adult Respiratory Distress Syndrome ('secondary drowning'). These problems usually develop quickly after an apparently successful resuscitation though can be delayed up to 4 hours. Infection and blood clotting problems can follow near drowning.

Management

Safety should be at the forefront of the rescuer's mind. Cold water will have its effects on the rescuer in a similar way to the casualty unless specialist clothing (wet suit/dry suit) is used. Ice breaks - don't follow the casualty!

Managing the casualty in the water is very difficult, perhaps even impossible. The casualty needs to be on the shore or in a boat before resuscitation starts. Try to keep the casualty horizontal at all stages; his cardiovascular responses to being upright are greatly impaired, and a vertical rescue is associated with sudden collapse and death. See the section on Suspension Induced Shock syndrome. Remember that the casualty may have other injuries - the classic combination is near drowning and a fractured cervical spine from diving into a shallow pool (see page 140).

Managing a casualty rescued from water	
Safety first	**Swim failure** occurs quickly even in expert swimmers. **Assess consciousness and survival factors** such as immersion or submersion, time in the water, water temperature and age of casualty.
Get the casualty out of the water horizontally	
Primary survey	Airway (with cervical spine control) Open the airway. Breathing (with O_2) Start oxygen at 15 l/min via non-rebreathing mask with a reservoir and use appropriate equipment to aid breathing and protect the lungs from aspiration. Circulation (with external haemorrhage control) Start cardiac compressions as appropriate. Use an AED or ECG monitor to assess the cardiac rhythm and employ ALS techniques as appropriate. Disability Consider spinal injury and manage appropriately. Exposure Insulate from further heat loss to prevent any hypothermia from getting worse.
Assess whether the casualty might have severe hypothermia and might benefit from prolonged CPR. Measure the core temperature (if practical). **Be vigilant** for vomiting	
Evacuate the casualty urgently in cases of circulatory or respiratory collapse. **All casualties need to go to hospital for further assessment**	

Do a primary survey carrying out the 'ABCD' of resuscitation and intervene as appropriate. The box on the next page summarises the management.

Bear in mind that cardiopulmonary resuscitation has been successful even after prolonged submersion (62 minutes) without brain damage. Note the word 'submersion'- that is completely under the water. It is thought that resuscitation may be successful because the heart continues to beat for some time after unconsciousness intervenes and the victim may even inhale cold water, which cools the core and hence protects the brain as they become submerged. Indeed it is not unusual for the casualty to be unconscious with a respiratory arrest but a palpable pulse when removed from the water. Contrast this with a cardiac arrest complicating a myocardial infarct where the first event is the heart stopping and resuscitation needs to be started much more quickly if it going to be successful. Resuscitation following drowning is more likely to be successful if the pulse is palpable (70% expected survival); a life jacket has prevented submersion; the water is cold; and the casualty is under five years of age.

Do not do any specific drainage techniques before starting resuscitation; be aware that vomiting is likely at some stage of the resuscitation. Be ready to turn the casualty on his side using a log roll. If skilled, protect the airway with a Laryngeal Mask Airway® or endotracheal tube.

All casualties will need to be insulated to avoid further heat loss and be assessed in hospital even if they appear to have fully recovered from the unconscious state because of the risk of delayed lung damage.

When to start or stop resuscitation?

Black and white answers cannot be given that could be applied to every case of an unconscious casualty removed from water. Judge the facts as they appear at the time in order that the right decision is made. It is just as wrong to attempt resuscitation in a hopeless case as it is not to start it in another. Resuscitation prevents a more measured and dignified evacuation, and for the relatives or friends the opportunity to get in close and start the grieving process. So what is a hopeless case? Here are a few comments that might help.

If the pulse is present or an ECG shows cardiac activity, artificial respiration (mouth-to-mouth, mouth-to-mask, oral airway with bag and mask attached to high flow oxygen, LMA® with bag with oxygen) should be started. The chance of survival is high.

If the pulse is absent but the chest wall is pliable and the time since submersion is less than an hour, artificial ventilation and cardiac compression should be started as soon as practical and continued until the casualty is in hospital. This is not 'passing the buck' – the hospital can rewarm the casualty effectively or do other tests to be sure of the diagnosis of death. Particularly with children who have fallen through ice resuscitation attempts lasting many hours can result in survival hence once started don't stop resuscitation until the casualty has been rewarmed.

Think of immersion (head above the water so can breathe) as different from submersion (dived or immediately under the surface of the water). If the casualty has been immersed in cold water and is found to be lifeless; start CPR. If there is no response after 30 minutes and the immersion time has been less than 45 minutes, it is unlikely that the casualty is significantly hypothermic; asphyxia is the cause of lifelessness. Resuscitation could be stopped ideally having confirmed asystole and a core temperature of > 35ºC. The longer the time of immersion in the water, the more chance that hypothermia could cause the state of the lifelessness. Rather counter to intuition, these casualties, as with the avalanche victim with an air pocket, may benefit from prolonged CPR and aggressive rewarming.

A common scenario is that a bystander started resuscitation when the casualty was pulled from the water but has since stopped because of exhaustion or failure to revive. Paralleling the case study on cardiac arrest (page 272), asystole on an ECG and a core temperature of > 35ºC would allow death to be diagnosed. If the time since loss of consciousness is still under 1 hour should the rescuer restart resuscitation? In most cases, evacuation rather than resuscitation will probably seem most appropriate unless the initial attempts had been very short lived, the casualty is a child or the water is close to freezing. The situation may be complicated further by a passing doctor confirming death. What does the rescuer do then? That depends on so many factors it would be an essay on its own. Suffice to say the rescuer needs to record the doctor's name, address and record clearly that death has been diagnosed. A colleague from ICAR Medcom has reported an avalanche victim who was diagnosed 'dead' by a doctor but a second doctor, 30 minutes after the initial resuscitation was abandoned with the casualty in asystole, thought it worth prolonged CPR. The casualty was, of course severely hypothermic and recovered with rewarming! Hopefully the third edition of this text will have the reference to this case and firmer guidance on these matters. However, it is fair to say that in both drowning and hypothermia our ideas that CPR needs to start early and continued continuously until the casualty is rewarmed are beginning questioned.

Case study - 'Local PC rescues "drowned" man'

This case is fictional but was developed from several real cases. It was commissioned for *Casualty Care in Mountain Rescue* to contribute a sense of real life and to draw attention to the dilemmas that occur in rescue work.

Time and date: 22.00, summer

Location: A popular lake with a campsite on its shore. About 15 minutes walk from a minor road

Weather: 1st warm day of the summer

Reported injuries: Boating accident; mountain rescue called as part of the lake's emergency plan

A 56 year-old man had been 'messing about' in a rowing boat. He had had quite a lot of alcohol to drink and had decided to swim from the boat to the shore - a distance of 75 metres. His friends noticed he started struggling after about 7 minutes of swimming but was almost to the shore when he went under the surface and did not bob up again. They called for help immediately by mobile phone and the Police Constable arrived ten minutes later. He stripped off and waded to the site where the casualty had last been seen. He thought he felt a body on the lake bed and, despite the water being about 1.5 metres deep, he managed to get hold of the casualty and pull him to the shore. The total time of submersion was 20 minutes. The rescue team and an ambulance technician took over the management of the casualty. The casualty was lifeless so BLS was started. Oxygen, ventilation aids and cardiac monitoring were added as the equipment and expertise arrived. The AED did not advise a shock, so the ALS protocol was initiated; adrenaline was given and a cardiac rhythm was noted about 15 minutes after the start of BLS. The casualty's blood pressure was soon normal though no respiratory effort returned. He was transferred to an Intensive Care Unit and required ventilation for three days during which time many lung complications occurred. However slowly brain function returned and after a long period of rehabilitation the casualty returned home; he had no recall of the accident and his ability to develop a short-term memory did not return causing ongoing management problems.

Comment

Well done; textbook resuscitation! A classic case of 'swim failure' fortunately just within a safe area though the PC was certainly brave wading to his neck in the cold water. The rescue was multi-agency; with seamless care and protocol adherence. If a heart rhythm had not returned within 30 minutes of starting BLS, stopping CPR would have been entirely appropriate, particularly if the core temperature had been measured and found to be above 35°C. The water was cold and probably protected, to some degree, the casualty's brain from the asphyxia. However, as might have been expected, this protection was not complete.

References

Harries M. ABC of resuscitation: Near drowning. *BMJ* 2003; 327: 1336-1338

Various. See rapid responses to above article at www.bmj.bmjjorunals.co.uk

Tipton M. Cold water immersion: sudden death and prolonged survival. *The Lancet* 2003; 362: S12 at www.thelancet.com

Tipton M, Golden F. Immersion in cold water: effects on performance and safety in *Oxford textbook of sports medicine* edited by Mark Harries et al. 1994 ISBN 0 19 262009 6

Tipton M, Eglin C, Gennser M, Golden F. Immersion deaths and deterioration in swimming performance in cold water. *Lancet* 1999; 354: 626-29

Milne S, Cohen A. Secondary drowning in a patient with epilepsy. *BMJ* 2006; 332:775-6

Avalanche

A lot of work, backed by research, has been published about avalanche survival and the medical aspects of rescuing casualties trapped from within. Though rare in the UK, in the more snowy areas of the world avalanches are a major problem causing, on average, 140 deaths a year. Avalanches are the second commonest cause of death in the rescuer! As many UK rescuers travel to these regions a more detailed synopsis of the medical aspects has been included. Also an understanding of the pathophysiology may be relevant to other situations where asphyxia occurs, such as mud slides and prolonged immersion. Readers are directed to standard mountaineering texts for an understanding of avalanche anatomy, assessment and avoidance. In addition, ICAR Medcom has produced a training DVD covering avalanche medicine and survival equipment that deals with the subject in far greater depth.

Transceiver training, Diploma in Mountain Medicine, Glencoe. (2004)

Physiology and pathology

When caught in an avalanche, the casualty has three principal threats to his life:

Trauma from colliding with fixed objects or from the forces within the avalanche (20%)

Asphyxia from being buried and unable to breathe (65%)

Hypothermia from the greatly increased heat conduction (15%)

Not surprisingly, the risk of death is much higher in those casualties who are completely buried (51%) than those whose head and chest are free (4%). In those completely buried, the risk factors for asphyxia are the time buried and whether an air pocket is present. Data from the Swiss Institute for Snow and Avalanche Research in Davos, Switzerland has been used to produce a survival curve for those casualties completely buried. The curve and its interpretation into various stages is described on the next page.

Management

The shape of the survival curve indicates two time goals for a successful recovery. Uninjured companions should try to locate and extricate their colleagues within the first 15 minutes by all possible means, since 90% of victims who were extricated within this time span survive.

Organised rescue teams have about 90 minutes to save the victims with a closed air pocket. In this "latent phase", which extends to about 2 hours after burial, the rescue team has a real chance of finding a buried person alive using electronic transceivers, dogs and probing. Though hope (and digging) should not be abandoned at 2 hours, the chance of survival is now small.

Assess the safety of the accident site fully before committing rescuers; this can frequently be done by air as a helicopter is often used to rapidly deploy rescuers to the incident area. The hazards from a secondary avalanche, poor weather, darkness and the topography of the accident site are significant.

Locate the casualty as quickly as possible, dig diagonally down to the casualty from the downhill side. Rapidly clear the snow from the area round the face, noting the presence of an air pocket and whether the air passages are clear of obstruction. The medical

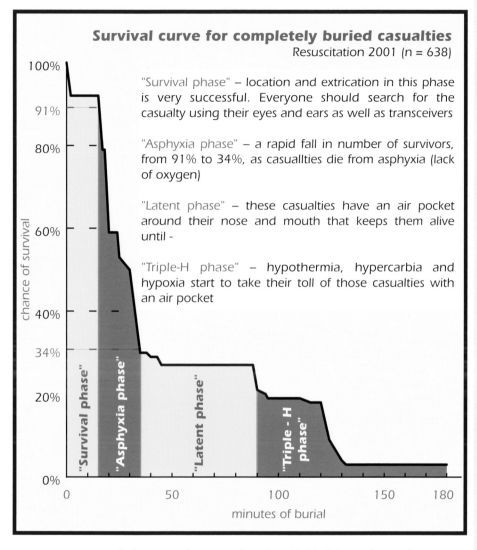

Survival curve for completely buried casualties
Resuscitation 2001 (n = 638)

"Survival phase" – location and extrication in this phase is very successful. Everyone should search for the casualty using their eyes and ears as well as transceivers

"Asphyxia phase" – a rapid fall in number of survivors, from 91% to 34%, as casuallties die from asphyxia (lack of oxygen)

"Latent phase" – these casualties have an air pocket around their nose and mouth that keeps them alive until -

"Triple-H phase" – hypothermia, hypercarbia and hypoxia start to take their toll of those casualties with an air pocket

chance of survival

"Survival phase"   "Asphyxia phase"   "Latent phase"   "Triple - H phase"

minutes of burial

management of the casualty can then be divided into those that have been buried for < 35 minutes and those buried for > 35 minutes. If the casualty has been buried for < 35 minutes, his condition is the result of asphyxia and trauma. Rapidly extricate and assess the casualty using a 'Safety, A, B, C approach', managing the problems found as you proceed. If the casualty shows no signs of life and does not respond to CPR carried out for 20 minutes, the casualty may be pronounced dead at the scene. (Ideally a core temperature of > 35°C and asystole on an ECG should be recorded.)

If the casualty has been buried for > 35 minutes, hypothermia is likely to be a significant factor in their condition. To avoid inducing a cardiac arrhythmia, the casualty should be treated as gently as possible with minimal manipulation of the limbs. Dig as big a hole as needed. Start oxygen and ECG monitoring as soon as practical and insulate the casualty as well as you can. During extrication and the transportation phase the casualty can collapse, so be prepared to start CPR. If the casualty shows no signs of life but had an air pocket with clear air passages, manage the casualty with prolonged CPR and urgent evacuation as described in the management of stage IV hypothermia. If, during extrication, an air pocket is not found and, on assessing the airway, the air passages are obstructed with snow and debris, the casualty is likely to have been asphyxiated and CPR should be abandoned. A copy of the ICAR Medcom algorithm for the on-site management of avalanche victims is produced on the next page.

Comment

It may seem counter to your gut feelings that a longer burial time may, in the presence of an air pocket and clear air passages, result in prolonged attempts to resuscitate the casualty compared with a short burial. What we are attempting to do here is separate those casualties with irreversible asphyxia from those with potentially reversible severe hypothermia using simple on-site parameters. A similar train of thought can be applied to immersion (but not submersion) victims. Of course, the rescuer is at liberty (and should not be criticised) for sidestepping the issue by continuing CPR and arranging a rapid evacuation to hospital if this can be done safely.

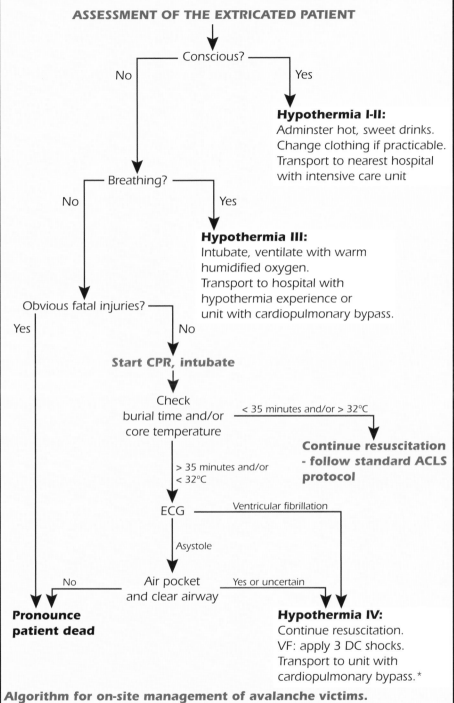

ASSESSMENT OF THE EXTRICATED PATIENT

Conscious?

No — Yes

Hypothermia I-II:
Adminster hot, sweet drinks.
Change clothing if practicable.
Transport to nearest hospital
with intensive care unit

Breathing?

No — Yes

Hypothermia III:
Intubate, ventilate with warm
humidified oxygen.
Transport to hospital with
hypothermia experience or
unit with cardiopulmonary bypass.

Obvious fatal injuries?

Yes — No

Start CPR, intubate

Check
burial time and/or
core temperature

< 35 minutes and/or > 32°C

**Continue resuscitation
- follow standard ACLS
protocol**

> 35 minutes and/or
< 32°C

ECG — Ventricular fibrillation

Asystole

No

Air pocket
and clear airway

Yes or uncertain

**Pronounce
patient dead**

Hypothermia IV:
Continue resuscitation.
VF: apply 3 DC shocks.
Transport to unit with
cardiopulmonary bypass. *

Algorithm for on-site management of avalanche victims.
Staging of hypothermia according to Swiss Society of Mountain Medicine
guidelines.
* Transport to the nearest hospital for serum potassium (K+) measurement if
hospitalisation in a specialist unit with cardiopulmonary bypass is not logistically
possible.
Based on: Brugger H, Durrer B, Adler-Kastner L, Falk, M, Tschirky F. Field
management of avalanche victims. Resuscitation 2001; 51:7-15

Case Study – Search in avalanche debris

This case is fictional but was developed from several real cases. It was commissioned for *Casualty Care in Mountain Rescue* to contribute a sense of real life and to draw attention to the dilemmas that occur in rescue work.

Time and date: Early evening in February

Location: Steep, north-sided valley

Weather: Cold and clear, starting to freeze hard after a heavy snow fall

Cause of incident: Unknown

Reported injuries: Shouts coming from the fells

A farmer heard shouts for help over a period of 15 minutes. They appeared to originate from an area of fell with an altitude of between 300 and 450 metres. It was decided that the area should be searched. The time between the shouts being heard and the call-out was two hours. An extensive slab avalanche was found with the head wall being about 20 metres long and three metres high. The debris had swept down the valley side for about 150 metres. A casualty was visible on the surface of the avalanche debris approximately three quarters of the way down the fan. He was lying flat on the surface of the snow and did not respond when shouted to. Due to the risk of further avalanches, it was decided that one rescuer should traverse the avalanche debris to assess him. The rest of the team stood in a safer area. On arrival at the scene, the casualty was apparently dead and inspection showed he had severe lower leg and pelvic injuries. Priority was then given to searching for another casualty, as it was unknown whether he had a companion. The team evacuated the casualty later when it was judged to be safe to do so. No other casualties were found.

Comments

Avalanches do occur in the U.K. They arise in inherently dangerous conditions. It is essential that team members with appropriate winter skills assess the safety of the approach route and incident site. Avalanches can occur low in the valley and cross the path of a low-level walk. Avalanche search and rescue conjures up lines of rescuers probing the debris. From the medical point of view, this scenario is unlikely to provide an opportunity for treating a casualty.

References

Brugger H, Durrer B, Adler-Kastner L, Falk, M, Tschirky F. Field management of avalanche victims. *Resuscitation* 2001; 51: 7-15

ICAR Medcom recommendation 13. On site treatment of avalanche victims in *Consensus guidelines on mountain emergency medicine and risk reduction* (2001). Accessed at www.ikar-cisa.org

DVD *Time is life: Medical training in avalanche rescue.* 2006; available from ICAR Medcom and info@newportmusic.it Cost = 20 Euros (2006)

Going to Altitude

One mountain medicine topic that cannot be included in this book is altitude medicine and illness. It would be rather pretentious when we have no mountains above 1500m! However altitude medicine is very important to anyone travelling to areas above 2500m. The effects of 'going high' on pre-existing medical conditions and contraceptive use should not be underestimated, and should be researched in good time to allow changes to be made. In addition to the BMC website, I have found the following references useful:

Pollard AJ, Murdoch DR. *The High Altitude Medicine Handbook* 2003; ISBN 1 85775 849 8

Barry PW, Pollard AJ. Altitude illness. *BMJ* 2003; 326:915-919

Maggiorini M, Buhler B, Walter M, Oelz O. Prevalence of acute mountain sickness in the Swiss Alps. *BMJ* 1990; 301:853-5

Schoene RB. Dexamethasone: By Safe Means, by Fair Means. *HAMB* 2005; 6:273-275

Cogo A, Fischer R, Schoene R. Respiratory Diseases and High Altitude *HAMB* 2004; 5:435-444

Leal C. Going high with Type 1 Diabetes. *HAMB* 2005; 6:14-21

Jean D, Leal C, Kriemler S, Meijer H, Moore L. Medical Recommendations for Women Going to Altitude. A Medical Commission UIAA Consensus Paper. *HAMB 2005; 6:22-31*

Matterhorn from the Plan (1990)

Jeff and Ann-marie on VF Ettore Bovero - Col Rosa, Dolomites. (2005)

Medical problems

Objectives
To recognise and manage a myocardial infarction
To treat acute asthma, seizures and diabetic problems
To appreciate the psychological aspects of rescue work

Ischaemic Heart Disease (Coronary Artery Disease)

Narrowing or blockage of the coronary arteries is called Ischaemic Heart Disease (IHD). Studies have shown that it occurs in almost everybody over the age of 40. As the coronary arteries supply blood to the heart muscle, enabling it to pump, significant IHD has serious consequences. It is the cause of 30% of male deaths and 22% of female deaths. From the mountain rescue perspective, about half of 'our' deaths are from IHD. Diabetes, high blood pressure and, most importantly, smoking increase the chance and severity of IHD. Patients can be asymptomatic or suffer from angina, myocardial infarction (MI), sudden death or heart failure. The clinical presentation depends on how the blood supply is altered. For example, if the blood supply to a section of the heart muscle is suddenly cut off the heart muscle dies. The usual cause is a thrombus (clot) developing within the coronary artery as shown in figure 1. The clinical picture is of an acute MI or 'heart attack'. Alternatively, the coronary artery may be partially occluded. This is the result of cholesterol building up in the walls of the artery. The partial obstruction to blood flow leads to a reduction in the maximum flow (and oxygen delivery) to the heart muscle. During exercise the heart muscle's oxygen need outstrips its supply. As a result, noxious substances are released locally causing pain. The clinical picture is called angina. Classically, the exercise needed to produce the pain is similar day in and day out and is relieved by rest. However, things are often not as clear-cut as this and it can be very difficult to tell the difference between angina, MI or even indigestion! In practical terms, any casualty with chest pain should be treated as having a suspected myocardial infarct.

Figure 1

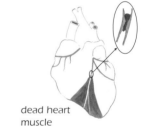

dead heart muscle

Angina

Patients with angina complain of a pain or ache in the centre of the chest. It may radiate to the jaw or the left arm. On resting, the pain disappears. It would be rare for it to continue for more than 15 minutes. Occasionally shortness of breath or dizziness may be the main symptom. As described above, it is provoked by exercise particularly when the weather is cold or windy, or after meals where blood is diverted to the gut to aid digestion. The provocation can range from getting dressed, to walking 100 metres or, in the author's case, climbing uphill at 4000 metres! Many hill walkers will have angina and, as long as they work within their limits, are probably benefitting from their hobby. Patients aware of the diagnosis are often on treatment. One of the commonest is sublingual glyceral trinitrate (GTN), either as tablets or spray. This drug dilates the coronary arteries so allowing more blood and oxygen to be delivered to the heart muscle. GTN works within seconds to relieve the pain completely. A headache is common after its use. The patient may be on many other drugs too. These are 'preventers' and are taken regularly in an attempt to increase exercise tolerance or reduce the chance of MI. They include beta-blockers, aspirin and 'statins'. Beta-blockers 'block' the heart from beating too fast. If the casualty develops shock (from whatever cause), the high pulse rate that is usually found does not develop, and therefore the diagnosis may be delayed. Aspirin, by reducing the chance of thrombus formation, reduces the chance of MI. 'Statins' reduce the blood cholesterol and the chance of MI though it may not be through the simple notion of dissolving the cholesterol from the thickened arterial walls.

Management

A patient will usually self-manage an attack. He will have stopped the exertion and, if necessary, used GTN. The episode should resolve spontaneously and most walkers will evacuate themselves by turning back. If the attack does not resolve or is more severe than normal, then help from the rescue services may be initiated. In practical terms, the team should manage the incident as if the casualty has suffered from an MI (see below). The team may find the casualty pain-free with a normal pulse and blood pressure. In this case, pain relief and GTN will not be required. A stretcher evacuation without a helicopter may be appropriate in a few situations but often a prolonged attack of angina (greater than 15 minutes) has been a small MI. It is prudent to attach an ECG or the pads of an automatic external defibrillator (AED) and to use a helicopter if its use will reduce the time to hospital.

Myocardial Infarction

The casualty can be any age from the 20s upwards though most will be 50 or older. A previous history of angina or heart attack may be present along with the risk factors diabetes and high blood pressure. The clinical presentation varies tremendously though most casualties will describe a pain or heaviness in the chest. The common features are listed below. An individual casualty may have just one of these features but more often three or four are present. Occasionally a patient may experience a 'silent MI' when they do not suffer any pain and typically complain simply of lethargy, nausea and, perhaps, shortness of breath.

Common features of myocardial infarction

Sudden onset of central chest pain; it is often described as 'heavy', 'crushing' or 'gripping', and frequently radiates into the throat, jaw or left arm. It is not unusual for the pain to be at its worst in the epigastrium (below the rib cage). Less commonly it may be greatest in the upper back. The severity of pain varies from slight (like persistent indigestion) to severe and unbearable.

Shortness of breath may be present.

Nausea and vomiting are common.

On examination, the most obvious feature is that the casualty really looks very ill. The skin is pale, cold and clammy. The respiratory rate is raised in response to pain or, more worryingly, from heart failure. The pulse can be fast or slow, regular or irregular. A low blood pressure is also a worrying sign. In even the most minor MI a cardiac arrest can occur at any time.

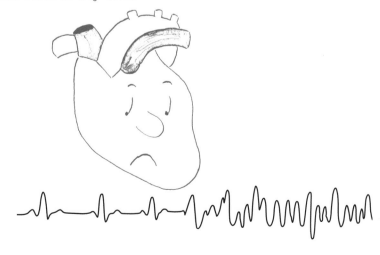

Differential diagnosis

Not all chest pain is from the heart. What other causes of chest pain need to be considered? The table below describes some of alternative diagnoses.

Diagnosis	Symptoms	Comments
Indigestion Stomach acid burning the lining of the stomach or oesophagus	A burning pain behind the sternum that rarely radiates to the left arm. Usually relieved by food/milk and antacids.	Patients and doctors often confuse the two! Aspirin may aggravate but unlikely to do harm.
Biliary Colic Pain from the gall bladder as it contracts around a gall stone	Food brings on the pain. It is most marked on the right below the rib cage and goes through to the back. Tenderness may be found.	Pain relief with morphine and an antiemetic is frequently needed.
Aortic dissection The wall of the aorta tears. It can rupture (usually leading to death) or block an artery causing a stroke	A searing pain in the chest often with collapse.	Very hard to diagnose but the acute management is the same as an MI.
Pulmonary embolus A thrombus usually from the veins in the legs or pelvis breaks free and passes through the circulation to the lungs where it occludes the pulmonary blood flow	A small pulmonary embolus (PE) presents with pleurisy and coughing up blood. A large PE causes collapse, central chest pain and severe hypoxia.	The patient may prefer to lie down rather than sit up. Higher concentrations of oxygen may be needed.
Pleurisy or pneumothorax Local chest wall inflammation occurring in response to infection or bleeding from a spontaneous air leak	A localised pain on one side of the body. Worse with a deep breath. The rubbing may be heard with a stethoscope.	Unless a spontaneous tension pneumothorax (very rare) develops the casualty usually displays only mild distress.
Musculoskeletal chest pain A sprain or strain of the ribs and the associated muscles	Localised pain worse on twisting and moving. Respiratory rate and pulse usually normal.	Does not feel life-threatening!

Management

Follow a primary survey approach.

Check safety.

In an unresponsive casualty, start Basic Life Support (BLS) immediately and use an AED as soon as possible. (See below)

In the responsive casualty, ensure that the casualty is sitting down in a position of comfort. Reassure the casualty that help, particularly pain relief, is at hand.

A - check the airway is open.

B - assess the breathing and start oxygen by face mask. Though there is no evidence that oxygen is of benefit to a casualty with an uncomplicated MI, it is standard practice. There is no need to use high flow rates; 4-6 l/minute through a non-rebreathing mask with a reservoir should be adequate and will avoid excessive oxygenation. Pulse oximetry may be of benefit to titrate the oxygen flow during a long evacuation.

C - assess the pulse rate and blood pressure.

Start monitoring the heart rhythm via the self-adhesive defibrillator pads or an ECG. If the casualty has not tried GTN and the systolic BP is >90 mmHg, 400mcg of GTN can be given under the tongue (sublingual) to see if the pain responds.

Give pain relief if the pain has not completely gone within a few minutes of the GTN. 10-15mg of morphine and an anti-vomiting drug will be required. There are a number of options available - these are discussed in the section 'Analgesia in MI'. Entonox® should not be used as an alternative.

As soon as vomiting is controlled, give 300mg of aspirin orally unless there is a definite contraindication such as anaphylaxis. Use a chewable or soluble form of aspirin to speed its absorption. Some casualties will already be taking aspirin regularly. Do you give the casualty more? Yes, give 300mg if the dose is 75 or 150mg daily; no, if the casualty is already taking 300mg daily. If the dose is unknown, give 300mg of aspirin.

The risk of deterioration and cardiac arrest is ever present. Rescuers need to plan, mentally and physically, for such an event. Can the casualty be laid down? This is often needed as the morphine and GTN take effect. Is the defibrillator immediately available? Continuously observe the conscious state of the casualty; regularly ask about pain relief and, if necessary, give more analgesia. Measure the pulse and, if possible, blood pressure and oxygen saturation at least every 15-30 minutes.

Evacuation

Arrange an urgent evacuation to hospital without delay. A major advance in the reduction in the death rate after an acute myocardial infarction has been thrombolysis. 'Clot busting' drugs dissolve the thrombus blocking the coronary artery allowing blood to reach the damaged section of heart muscle again. The sooner these drugs are given the better. A delay of an hour is extremely significant to the casualty's long-term prognosis. A helicopter is appropriate if the time to hospital is shortened by 15 minutes or more.

Analgesia in MI

This section is not intended for when you are on scene! You and your team should have decided what to do long before the incident.

In the 20th century, mountain rescuers were faced with casualties in isolated settings with little medical or paramedical support. The standard pre-hospital treatment of an MI was intramuscular Cyclimorph®, and General Practitioners managed many patients at home. Thrombolysis, along with recognition that the intramuscular route was slow and erratic, changed all that. Hospitalisation and intravenous analgesia has become the norm. Mountain rescue's standard teaching of intramuscular Cyclimorph® is looking outdated particularly as the problem of muscle haematoma after thrombolysis is well recorded. Mountain rescue has also changed. The introduction of NHS Paramedics, with their ability to give intravenous morphine, and closer working with ambulance and air ambulance services mean that a skilled practitioner reaches the casualty site more frequently than in the past. In addition a small number of mountain rescuers have acquired cannulation skills. What is the range of options available now?

1) Intravenous morphine, administered by an NHS paramedic, doctor or suitably qualified mountain rescuer.

Practitioners using this approach will want naloxone (to reverse the effect of morphine) immediately available, and may want to use a different combination of drugs. Most would use 10-15mg of morphine (diluted with water for injection given at a rate of 1 or 2mg a minute) and 10mg of metoclopramide (given at a rate of 2mg a minute). Cyclizine (25mg) can cause detrimental changes to the circulation, and though this has not been shown to be clinically important, many practitioners prefer to avoid its use. This gives rise to practical issues of carrying a small quantity of a large number of different injectable drugs and using multiple syringes in a hostile environment. These challenges can be overcome.

2) Intramuscular morphine administered by an MRC Casualty Care rescuer.

Either morphine with Buccastem® (the preferred option), morphine with metoclopramide or Cyclimorph® is entirely appropriate in the classical mountain rescue where medical/paramedical help is unavailable at the incident site. It would be indefensible to stop this practice.

Cardiac arrest, the Chain of Survival and defibrillators

A cardiac arrest occurs when the heart stops pumping blood. The commonest cause (85%), resulting in the sudden and unexpected collapse of the patient, is fibrillation of the main heart muscle - the ventricle. Fibrillation occurs when small areas of the heart muscle contract with no overall coordination. As a result, blood is not pumped out of the heart; no pulse is palpable and the casualty rapidly becomes unconscious. Without resuscitation death follows quickly. Even with resuscitation, the chance of surviving an out-of-hospital cardiac arrest is only 2-5%. Ventricular fibrillation (VF) is important as it can be very successfully treated by defibrillation.

The most frequent trigger to VF is Ischaemic Heart Disease where the heart muscle becomes electrically irritable and sets off the uncoordinated electrical activity. An example of the type of heart tracing seen is shown on the opposite page. The risk is greatest immediately after a myocardial infarct. The heart cannot maintain VF for long. For each minute that elapses, 20% of fibrillating hearts become asystolic with no electrical or muscular activity. Basic Life Support (BLS), by improving cardiac blood supply, reduces the conversion rate to 7-10% per minute. Successful resuscitation from asystole is extremely unlikely.

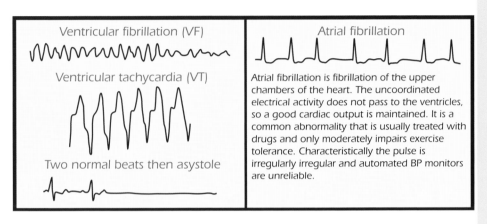

Ventricular fibrillation (VF)

Ventricular tachycardia (VT)

Two normal beats then asystole

Atrial fibrillation

Atrial fibrillation is fibrillation of the upper chambers of the heart. The uncoordinated electrical activity does not pass to the ventricles, so a good cardiac output is maintained. It is a common abnormality that is usually treated with drugs and only moderately impairs exercise tolerance. Characteristically the pulse is irregularly irregular and automated BP monitors are unreliable.

The Chain of Survival

How can we influence these events?

The sooner the heart is defibrillated the better the chance of a return in cardiac output and the lower the chance of residual brain damage. Asystole does not respond to an electrical shock at all. The Chain of Survival describes a strategy to increase the chance of survival from a cardiac arrest, and has fuelled the investment in public access defibrillators. The chain is a strong image pulling you

Early access to emergency services — Early BLS — Early defibrillation — Early transfer to advanced care

back from death. However, reality is that the first two links are stretching and breaking over about five to ten minutes - a time scale that is hard to work within. BLS delays death; it gives time for the defibrillator to arrive and be applied. It is extremely unlikely that a cardiac output will be established after 30 minutes of BLS except in specific situations such as drowning and hypothermia.

Unresponsive?
(Sudden cardiac arrest)

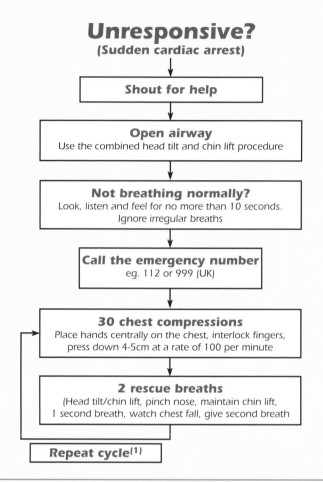

Shout for help

Open airway
Use the combined head tilt and chin lift procedure

Not breathing normally?
Look, listen and feel for no more than 10 seconds.
Ignore irregular breaths

Call the emergency number
eg. 112 or 999 (UK)

30 chest compressions
Place hands centrally on the chest, interlock fingers,
press down 4-5cm at a rate of 100 per minute

2 rescue breaths
(Head tilt/chin lift, pinch nose, maintain chin lift,
1 second breath, watch chest fall, give second breath

Repeat cycle[1]

**For a cardiac arrest in other situations refer to the
appropriate section in this book**

**Use an AED as soon as possible.
Add oxygen and ventilation aids as appropriate.**

[1] Resuscitation should be continued until qualified help arrives,
the casualty shows signs of life, you become exhausted or 20 minutes
of resuscitation has been unsucessful (except in severe hypothermia).

Note that each successive step is based on the assumption that the
one before has not been successful.
If the casualty shows signs of life, the airway must be kept open, oxygen
given and the casualty placed in the recovery position, as vomiting is likely.

Basic Life Support

Basic Life Support (BLS) is life support using no aids. It consists of opening an airway, support for the breathing (mouth-to-mouth ventilation) and support for the circulation (cardiac compression). Cardiopulmonary resuscitation (CPR) is a term that can be used when all three elements are performed regardless of whether aids are used. As explained above the purpose of BLS is to delay the heart going into asystole giving time for a defibrillator to reach the casualty. An algorithm adapted for mountain rescue is reproduced overleaf.

The algorithm encompasses the guidelines published in 2005 by the International Liaison Committee on Resuscitation (ILCOR) and adopted by the European Resuscitation Council (ERC) and the Resuscitation Council (UK). A few comments may help you understand the changes and the implications for your management of a casualty:

Previous guidelines remain effective and safe. It may not be possible to change equipment to comply with the guidelines. For example, an AED programmed protocol may be fixed and want to deliver a cycle of three shocks instead of the one in the new guidelines. Defibrillating early, whether one or (if necessary) three times, is vastly more important to the casualty than the change in the algorithm. An 'old' AED is not obsolete or dangerous.

The BLS algorithm has become more specific to the circumstance of a sudden cardiac arrest (SCA). (That is the heart goes wrong first.) This is entirely appropriate as this is the case in 82.4% of pre-hospital arrests. Research shows that in the first five minutes of an arrest there is enough oxygen in the blood if only it can be pumped round. Ventilation is less important. Early chest compression reduces the conversion of VF to asystole, and, therefore, increases the chances that defibrillation will be appropriate and successful at restoring a beating heart. Delays to starting cardiac compressions have been removed. For example, assessing breathing has been simplified to whether it is normal or not. The irregular breaths as you die are to be ignored and the time taken to do two rescue breaths before chest compressions has been removed. These changes may not be appropriate in other, non-SCA, circumstances where asphyxia has preceded the cardiac arrest. For example, drug overdoses, drowning, lightning and arrests in children and after trauma. In such cases, a primary survey approach may be more appropriate. So we have to reverse the trend to a single resuscitation algorithm for all casualties - use the BLS algorithm for the sudden cardiac arrest (the majority of cases); use a primary survey approach for the rest. This is acknowledged in the ERC guidelines when special cases, such as drowning and hypothermia, are discussed.

Advanced Life Support

As an organised rescue service, we would rarely do BLS without aids. Elements of Advanced Life Support (ALS) are likely to be used. These include airway adjuncts such as the oropharyngeal and nasopharyngeal airway, and a mouth-to-mask device with supplementary oxygen to aid ventilation. (Mountain rescue colleagues in South Tirrol have shown the pocket-valve mask to be superior to both mouth-to-mouth and face-shield ventilation in  terms of the tidal volumes delivered.) More advanced adjuncts such as the Laryngeal Mask Airway and endotracheal tube with bag/valve ventilation in addition to intravenous epinephrine (adrenaline) are appropriate for those trained in their use. Of course, using any of these aids should not delay the use of a defibrillator – the most important element of the management of a cardiac arrest.

Defibrillators

Defibrillators were introduced into mountain rescue in the early 1990s. They have become progressively lighter, cheaper and easier to use. The public have been encouraged to expect all ambulances to be equipped with defibrillators and widely reported schemes of 'public access' to defibrillators have led to an expectation that first responders will carry one. Against this background questions about the reality and cost effectiveness of defibrillators have often been overshadowed.

A defibrillator is used only when the heart is in ventricular fibrillation or in pulseless ventricular tachycardia (see page 263).

The defibrillator discharges a large electrical shock to the heart of the casualty and makes all the heart muscle refractory to electrical currents for a brief time. When electrical activity restarts it is often more coordinated, and so provides a cardiac output. The pulse would return and the casualty would 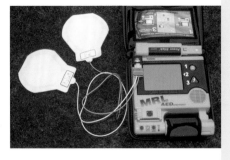 become conscious again. As explained above, the earlier the defibrillator is used the better the chance of a successful resuscitation.

Defibrillators can be automatic, semiautomatic or manual. This refers to the degree of conformation required by the operator before the apparatus delivers a shock. The defibrillator can be external (used through the skin) or internal (implanted like a pacemaker). An automatic external defibrillator (AED) does not need the operator to analyse the ECG trace; the heart trace alone is used to determine whether a shock is needed. This is the commonest type used outside hospital. Sometimes it is referred to as a public access defibrillator (PAD) when it is located in a public place and intended for public use. A modern AED is very sophisticated and almost foolproof. There is a box and the self-adhesive pads; two or three buttons and usually voice prompts! The technical manual needs to be studied so that the operator is familiar with how to use the AED and its storage and maintenance requirements. From a practical point of view, do the self-adhesive pads need to be connected to a switched-on machine before being applied to the casualty? And does the AED continuously analyse the ECG? (It is best if the answers are 'no' and 'yes' respectively.) There are a number of excellent AED models available and it is well worth the time studying their operation in detail. Don't forget the maintenance schedule. The pads and battery have to be 'in date'. The pads are particularly expensive but they do deteriorate with time, so don't cut corners. It is difficult to train with an AED beyond 'apply pads' for obvious reasons! 'Training' AEDs are available; try your local Ambulance Trust, the AED company's sales representative or neighbouring teams.

Safety factors when using an AED

An AED delivers a large electrical shock and, therefore, is inherently dangerous. Objects in the path of the electric current can heat up or ignite. Chest wall burns are a real problem after defibrillation when there has been moisture between the pads. If the current passes through the normal heart of a rescuer on the way to the Earth, cardiac arrest can occur with catastrophic results.

When applying the pads:

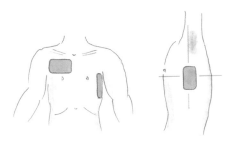

> Open or cut clothing so that the whole of the front of the chest is bare.
> Remove metal objects, such as chains, from the front of the chest.
> Remove any medication patches from the front of the chest.
> Ensure that the chest is dry; consider shaving thick body hair from the area covered by the pads to improve adhesion.
> Place one AED pad to the right of the sternum, below the clavicle, and the other centred on the intersection of the mid-axillary line and a horizontal line 2cm below the nipple. This position should be clear of any breast tissue. It is important that this electrode is placed sufficiently laterally. In order to improve efficiency, place the mid-axillary pad with its long axis vertical as shown.

Do not use cell phones or mobile radios within 2 metres of the AED when it is analysing the ECG.

And when shocking:

> Ensure the chest is dry and there is no clothing between the pads.
> Switch off the oxygen or remove the mask temporarily.
> Warn people to stand clear and visually check that no one is touching the casualty or the stretcher, and that pools of water do not connect you to the casualty. Always remember to disconnect the AED before commencing evacuation of the casualty on a stretcher.

An AED protocol adapted for mountain rescue is produced on the next page.

Limitations

Occasionally VF does not respond to an electrical shock. If nine shocks do not work and a shock is still advised, change the AED pads and their position and try another 3 shocks. ALS drugs may help but are usually unavailable. Most hearts will have converted to asystole by this time despite CPR.

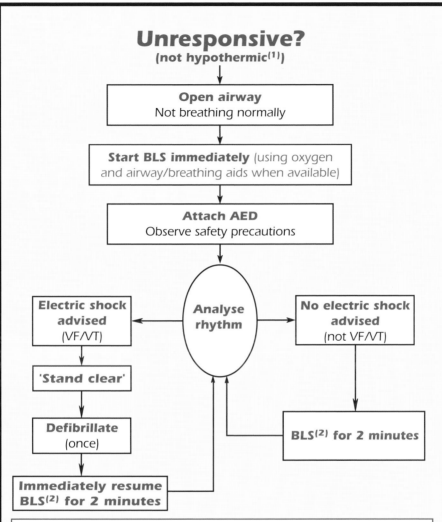

Unresponsive?
(not hypothermic[1])

Open airway
Not breathing normally

Start BLS immediately (using oxygen and airway/breathing aids when available)

Attach AED
Observe safety precautions

Analyse rhythm

Electric shock advised
(VF/VT)

No electric shock advised
(not VF/VT)

'Stand clear'

Defibrillate
(once)

BLS[2] for 2 minutes

Immediately resume BLS[2] for 2 minutes

[1] Refer to hypothermia algorithm
[2] Insert a laryngeal mask airway or intubate and cannulate.
Give 1mg epinephrine intravenously (if trained) every 5 min.

Resuscitation should be continued until qualified help arrives, the casualty shows signs of life, you become exhausted or 30 minutes of resuscitation has been unsucessful (except in severe hypothermia).

Note that each successive step is based on the assumption that the one before has not been successful.
If the casualty shows signs of life, the airway must be kept open, oxygen given and the casualty placed in the recovery position, as vomiting is likely.

Unfortunately defibrillation is of no use if the heart is in asystole or in an unconscious casualty with no pulse but with electrical complexes on the ECG. (i.e. a sudden spike of activity) This is called pulseless electrical activity (PEA) formerly called electromechanical dissociation (EMD). Successful resuscitation in these cases is much less likely; this reflects the underlying cause of the cardiac arrest. Loss of blood and ineffective breathing are examples.

Stopping resuscitation in a sudden cardiac arrest

The resuscitation guidelines acknowledge that transporting a patient (who has suffered a sudden cardiac arrest) without a cardiac output is very unlikely to result in survival. In general, if a cardiac output is not re-established on scene transporting the casualty is futile. A patient who remains in asystole after 20 minutes, despite CPR and ALS drugs, has no chance of survival. CPR can be stopped. If the casualty was initially in VF (and shocked), but is now asystolic start the 20 minutes from the last period of consciousness. Persistent VF, with the AED wanting to continue shocking, is very rare but potentially treatable and, in general resuscitation should be continued. However, in mountain rescue where the time to hospital is long and CPR impossible during the evacuation there is little chance of survival and resuscitation could be stopped after 30 minutes. (Most casualties will have reverted to asystole by this time.)

What if an AED is not available? And qualified help is unavailable?

CPR cannot be done effectively during the evacuation; a time limit has to be imposed - 30 minutes would seem reasonable. In general, children tend to be resuscitated until they reach hospital. There are a number of reasons for this including the charged emotive environment and a better chance of brain recovery. However the evidence suggests that, compared with adults, survival is no better; indeed, probably worse. If CPR does not re-establish a cardiac output in 30 minutes, there is little to be gained from continuing and resuscitation could be stopped.

The above paragraph applies to the sudden cardiac arrest only. In other circumstances, CPR may be appropriate for much longer periods as in hypothermia and drowning. In others, CPR maybe done for shorter periods, if at all, whilst a search is made for a reversible cause. For example, non-sudden cardiac arrest in a casualty suffering from trauma or illness is very unlikely to be survivable; it is best to consider a primary survey type of approach with a short period of ventilation and chest compressions whilst treatable reversible causes (for example, tension pneumothorax and hypovolaemia) are sought. Failure to respond to treatment and asystole would allow resuscitation to stop immediately.

Conclusion

Defibrillators save lives in hospital and pre-hospital settings. They will save life in mountain rescue. However the cost-per-life saved is high; cardiac arrest rarely occurs after the team arrives. Having the defibrillator in the right place, at the right time with a trained operator takes a lot of hard work. As teams do more fund raising in public places, such as car parks, the chances of being in the right place increase. Don't leave the defibrillator in the mountain rescue base!

Case Studies

These cases are fictional but were developed from several real cases. They were commissioned for *Casualty Care in Mountain Rescue* to contribute a sense of real life and to draw attention to the dilemmas that occur in rescue work.

Case 1 - Myocardial Infarction

Time and date:	18.45, Spring
Location:	30 minutes walk from a major road
Weather:	Heavy showers
Reported injuries:	Heart attack

The casualty, a 53 year old man, developed chest pain whilst coming down off the tops after a full day out. On arrival at the scene the team confirmed that the casualty had chest pain. There was no past history and he was not on any drugs. He was fully conscious, though distressed with pain. His skin was grey, cold and sweaty and he felt sick. His pulse was about 100 beats a minute and easily felt at the wrist.

The working diagnosis was a myocardial infarction. The estimated time to evacuate by stretcher and then road transport to the nearest District Hospital was two hours so a helicopter was requested at this stage. A survival tent was placed over the casualty and he was insulated from the ground by sitting him on a casualty bag. 15mg of Cyclimorph® was given intramuscularly. This relieved the pain and the casualty's colour and pulse returned to normal. After explanation and reassurance, the self-adhesive pads of an AED were placed on his chest and used to monitor the casualty's heart rhythm. 300mg of aspirin was dissolved in a 20ml of water and given to the casualty to swallow. No complications occurred. The casualty was comfortable and stable when the helicopter arrived 35 minutes later. He was flown to the hospital with a time saving of about one and a half hours.

Comments

Speed of evacuation is important as treating the casualty with thrombolytic drugs (clot-busters) improves survival. The earlier clot-busters are given the better; it has been estimated that the same urgency should be attached to getting the casualty to a place that gives these drugs as a responding to a cardiac arrest! Minutes of unnecessary delay are to be avoided. This would have been an ideal case for a helicopter to be requested as the team was activated. (The diagnosis was strongly suspected from the reporting person's mobile phone call.) Arriving together at the scene a further 30 minutes may have been deducted from the 'onset of pain to clot-buster' time; a very worthwhile improvement in the management of the casualty.

Case 2 - Sudden collapse

Time and date: 18.45, midsummer's night

Location: On a ridge 20 minutes above a cwm, and 50 minutes walk from the road

Weather: Clear evening

Reported injuries: Walking along and then just collapsed; no complaints and no signs of life at any stage

The Police activate the MR team; the Ambulance service has instructed the reporting person to start BLS and there is no rapid (<30 minutes) helicopter service. When the team leader rings the reporting person to get a location, the following information is gleaned:

> The casualty is a middle-aged man with his 12 year old son.
> The reporting person had heard the son shouting for help from the cwm.
> He and his companions had taken '15 minutes' to get to the incident site (1 km and a 300 metre ascent up the fell side).
> Confirmed 'no signs of life' and had started BLS which was continuing - BLS for 20 minutes now.

The team, with a defibrillator and doctor, arrived on scene at 19.45 by which time BLS had been carried out for over an hour. The team took over the BLS, noting the excellent technique of the reporting people. An AED was attached which, not surprisingly, showed the casualty was in asystole. Further resuscitation was stopped. The reporting people were briefed and, as one of them had built up a rapport with the casualty's son, the doctor and reporting person talked to the son. A helicopter was about to arrive and take him to the rescue base 'before it got dark'. It would then come back for his dad. Was that OK? Did he have any questions?

Comments

One can only imagine what the young lad was thinking. Children react differently to such events. Realisation is delayed and a matter-of-fact approach may be observed. All of us were uncomfortable with the situation and wondered how we should proceed. There was no chance to get his mum in the next few hours. In hospital, it is generally thought that children should not be excluded from seeing the dying and dead if they wish. During the evacuation, because of the terrain, the son had to walk past his father. We decided that we would not hide or cover the casualty but have him in a lying position with a pillow under his head and a rescuer sitting beside him. Fortunately, a team member trained in victim support met the son at the rescue base. When the doctor arrived at the base, he talked to the son again saying that his dad had been brought down from the fell too. His dad had not 'woken up' but his mum was coming.

We are accustomed to handling reporting people and adult relatives of casualties that have died. Much of the team's response in a case of cardiac arrest is to help these people, as the casualty's situation, as in this case, was beyond help purely from the time factors described above. But children? A family therapist makes the following comments.

"Children vary in their capacity to take in and manage what is happening in this sort of situation. This variability depends on: age, previous experiences of bereavements (including pets), their family's coping style for losses and the child's own personal coping style. Children are often surprisingly resilient. What the team in this situation did spontaneously, they did very well. The use of truthful but veiled language - 'he hasn't woken up yet' is helpful as a pacing strategy. Bad news shouldn't be broken suddenly to children.

Guiding principles should be to:

Establish a rapport with one person who can if possible be with the child until family members arrive.
Find out a little about the child's family, pets, school, hobbies and religious beliefs.
Information giving should be at the child's pace. It is better for realisation to dawn gradually.
It is helpful to brief the family about what the child has seen, experienced, what they have said and what they have been told. This will help the family focus on the needs of the child. It is also helpful for the child to hear that you think the child did all he could to help his Dad.

Some helpful phrases:

Was it a bit scary before anyone came to help?
What did you do to try to help Dad?
Sounds like you did all you could to help Dad.
I am impressed by what you did for Dad.
What do you think is happening to Dad?
Who are the best people for you to talk to about things?"

Case Report 3 - Sudden collapse (pre-2005 guidelines)

Time and date: 14.00, summer

Location: On the village playing field

Weather: Fine

Reported injuries: Sudden collapse of an elderly local resident at the village fete. Team fund-raising 20 metres away

Two base* team members manning the team ambulance alert the rest of the team in the rescue base 200 metres away by radio as they rush over to the scene. The casualty shows no signs of life. The team members confirm a '999' call has been made as the loudspeaker system alerts any doctors on the field. BLS is started within two minutes of the collapse. The rest of the team arrive with an AED, oxygen, airway adjuncts and the MRC drug kits. The AED is immediately applied to the casualty. A shock is advised and delivered 4 minutes after the collapse. This is unsuccessful but after the second shock a carotid pulse is easily felt and seen. Within 20 seconds the casualty attempts to take a breath. The airway is supported and oxygen given via a mouth-to-mask device. Unfortunately 1 minute later, before consciousness returns, the carotid pulse is seen to stop and respiratory efforts cease. The AED advises a shock but a series of three shocks is ineffective. Cardiopulmonary resuscitation is restarted for 1 minute. A team member trained in advanced airway support intubates the casualty and uses a bag with reservoir to ventilate the casualty with 100% oxygen. The NHS ambulance arrives just as the team start the next series of three shocks. Again these are unsuccessful. As CPR is performed again, the NHS paramedic places an intravenous cannula and gives 1mg of adrenaline. A further series of three shocks is ineffective. The defibrillator is changed. The monitor shows VF but despite different paddles and different positions the casualty remains in refractory VF. The casualty has now been in persistent VF for about 20 minutes. An air ambulance arrives with a doctor, who after checking for 'correctable' problems such as a pneumothorax, stops the resuscitation attempts and the casualty is pronounced dead.

Comments

This case illustrates exemplary (pre 2005) management. The three emergency services worked together in a seamless way and, between them, performed ALS in a timely way. The patient still died but had been given the best chance to survive with no brain damage.

There are a few points worth thinking about: The bystanders focused on the ambulance status of the team vehicle and called over for assistance. It was great that the base team members had been trained to the same standard as the fell going members and could start BLS immediately.

How much easier would it be to rush to the casualty without picking up the AED from the back of the vehicle? Like calling for help, bringing the AED to the casualty is critical.

* full team members that are non-fell going but run the MR base during callouts.

The protocol used by ambulance personnel does not allow resuscitation to be stopped in refractory VF. Where the transit time to hospital is greater than 30 minutes perhaps dignity would allow the resuscitation to stop in normal (non-hypothermic etc.) circumstances.

References

Robertson R. Sudden Death from Cardiac Arrest - Improving the Odds. *NEJM* 2000; 343:1259-1260.

Engdahl J. Outcome after cardiac arrest outside hospital *BMJ* 2002; 325:503-4

JRCALC (Joint royal colleges ambulance liaison committee). Clinical Practice Guidelines. 2004 accessed at www.nelh.nhs.uk/emergency

International Liaison Committee on Resuscitation. Special resuscitation situations *Resuscitation* 1997; 34:129-149

Thompson AT, Webb DJ, Maxwell SRJ, Grant IS. Oxygen therapy in acute medical care. *BMJ* 2002;324:1406-7

May G. The use of IV cyclizine in cardiac chest pain. BestBETs 2005. Accessed at http://www.bestbets.org

Anon. Tackling myocardial infarction. *Drug and Therapeutics Bulletin* 2000; 38:17-22

European Resuscitation Council Guidelines for Resuscitation 2005. Accessible at http://www.erc.edu/

Resuscitation Council (UK) guidelines 2005. Accessible at http://www.resus.org.uk/

Grisedale above Patterdale, Lake District

Asthma

Asthma is a very common condition with approximately 10% of the population suffering an attack at some stage in their life. However, it does not stop individuals from taking part in outdoor pursuits and is one of a few conditions that improve with altitude. Each year in the UK approximately 1500 people die from asthma; in people under the age of 40 years, many of these deaths are preventable. An acute attack of asthma is caused by airway obstruction. There are three components to this obstruction: contraction of the muscles in the walls of bronchioles (small airway pipes that lack cartilage and mucus glands, and are beyond the bronchi and lead to the alveoli); mucus plugs in small bronchi; and mucosal oedema from inflammation. The result of the narrowing of the airway and plugging of the pipes is a greater resistance to air flow and less efficient gas exchange within the lung which causes the unpleasant sensation of not being able to get enough air. The common triggers to an acute attack are:

Inhaling pollen or dust in an atopic person.

Undertaking exercise particularly in cold air.

Drugs notably beta-blockers and NSAIDs such as ibuprofen, aspirin and diclofenac.

Infection (usually viruses).

Most asthmatics control their symptoms with one or more inhalers. Usually you can tell what an inhaler does by the colour of the plastic delivery device. During an attack, a blue inhaler ('reliever') containing, for example, salbutamol is used. This relaxes the bronchioles and opens the airway.

 Occasionally, though rarely in the age groups seen in mountain rescue, ipratropium inhalers, such as Atrovent®, are used in an acute attack. These inhalers are colour-coded white.

Drugs delivered via brown or orange inhalers ('preventers') are taken on a regular basis to reduce the inflammation associated with asthma. The common 'preventers' are steroids. 'Preventers' reduce the frequency and severity of attacks but have no effect in the acute episode.

Salmeterol, a green inhaler, is a long-acting, salbutamol-type drug. Its onset of action is too slow for it to be of use in an acute attack.

Features of an acute asthma attack

The patient will complain of shortness of breath, a subjective sensation of 'not being able to get enough air'. Chest tightness and cough are frequently present. Observing the casualty, the rescuer will notice an increased respiratory rate with more time spent 'breathing out' than 'breathing in'. Wheeze (bronchospasm) is heard during breathing out (expiration). The casualty is often anxious but, unless the attack is life threatening, will be orientated in time, place and person. Speech is affected; the casualty will find it difficult stringing sentences or even words together. Rather confusingly as the attack becomes more severe, the amount of wheeze and the effort of breathing reduces. This is known as the 'silent chest'. The severity of an attack is divided into life threatening, severe and moderate. The features of these sub groups are shown in figure below.

Sub group	Features
Life threatening	Any one of the following features: Single words only 'Silent' chest Exhaustion with feeble respiratory effort Confusion or coma Hypotension SaO_2 of less than 92%
Acute severe	Any one of: Respiratory rate of greater than 25 per minute Pulse rate of greater than 110 per minute Inability to complete a sentence
Moderate	All the following features: Increase in symptoms but able to complete a full sentence Pulse rate of less than 110 per minute SaO_2 of 97% or greater

The differential diagnosis of a raised respiratory rate of 30 per minute in a non-trauma casualty by observation of the breathing pattern is outlined below.

Differential diagnosis of a raised respiratory rate		
Noisy breathing - **Asthma**		Using accessory muscles (upper arms and neck), and chest hyperinflated.
Noisy breathing - **Stridor** – laryngeal spasm, swelling or foreign body		Using accessory muscles (upper arms and neck), and face engorged.
'Panting' breathing - **Shock** blood loss/pulm. embolus		'Air hunger' - anxious; skin is cold, sweaty and white.
Hyperventilation - **Anxiety/pain**		Reassurance and distraction reduces the respiratory distress.
Key: inspiration / \ expiration · 2 seconds · ▬ extra noise		

Management

A patient with a moderate attack of asthma will frequently take extra doses of a 'reliever' and then self-rescue himself. Most calls from asthmatics for mountain rescue seem to be for mild attacks of asthma associated with other factors such as fear and exhaustion. This observation does not infer that severe or life-threatening asthma does not occur on the fells but it does seem to be rare.

Manage the patient following a 'Safety, A, B, C' approach; assessing the severity and differential diagnoses, as outlined above, as you proceed.

A - ensure the upper airway is open.

B - record the respiratory rate (and SaO_2 if possible), and start high flow oxygen via a non-rebreathing mask with a reservoir. (See below)

C - record the pulse rate.

D - record the conscious level (Is the casualty confused?) and the length of sentence between breaths. Are the sentences full, half or reduced to one or two words?

In moderate and severe asthma

Give four to six puffs of a 'relieving' inhaler (usually salbutamol) using a spacer device, such as an Aerochamber® or Volumatic®. Each

puff should be given separately and taken as soon as possible (< 30 seconds) after each activation of the inhaler; neither breathing deeply nor holding breath at the end of inspiration are needed if a spacer is used. The sequence of puffs can be repeated as needed every 10 minutes.

Nebulizer chamber

Salbutamol via an oxygen-driven nebulizer is an alternative, and has been shown to be equally effective as using an inhaler but not more so. The oxygen flow rate should be 6 - 8 litres/min. Many patients expect a nebulizer to be better than the inhaler and, of course, as the severity of asthma increases and hypoxia occurs, the addition of continuous oxygen will benefit the casualty. However, giving nebulized salbutamol to a moderate case of asthma can be counterproductive, as the side effects of tremor and palpitation will only increase the anxiety of the casualty. Careful observation should enable the rescuer to give the appropriate treatment.

Additional treatments, such as nebulized ipratropium, will usually be outside the realm of mountain rescue though on an extended rescue, oral or intravenous steroids, such as hydrocortisone, should be considered.

Maintenance note: The spacer needs periodic cleaning with water and a detergent and left to air dry to reduce the development of static charge that can affect the amount of drug delivered. Please refer to the product literature.

In life-threatening cases

The preferred method of giving the reliever is via an oxygen-driven nebulizer. The adult dose of salbutamol is 5 mg, which can be repeated after 15 minutes if needed. The team will need the necessary chamber and suitable oxygen set able to give a flow rate of at least 6 litres/min. (Below 6 litres/min the nebulized droplets are too big to penetrate deep into the lungs.) In the acute situation, ultrasonic nebulizers (powered by electricity rather than air flow) should be avoided, unless no other alternative is available, as hypoxia can worsen during the administration of the salbutamol. Oxygen therapy should be continued, the flow rate being increased to maintain an oxygen saturation of >92%. Should the casualty become exhausted, the rescuer will need to check that the upper airway is open and exclude a tension pneumothorax, which can be bilateral, by examination for surgical emphysema. The management of the tension pneumothorax is covered in the chapter on breathing. Ventilating casualties with life threatening asthma is very difficult and will usually need an advanced technique such as intubation or insertion of a laryngeal mask. In such a life-threatening attack, inhaled drugs don't get to the bronchioles. An option that would be worth trying would be giving 1 mg of adrenaline (adult dose) by intramuscular or subcutaneous injection. As adrenaline acts like a 'reliever' by opening up the bronchioles this can be very effective even in the most extreme cases. Intravenous hydrocortisone should be given, if possible, as the casualty responds to the 'reliever'. Doctors may wish to consider using ketamine as an anaesthetic and bronchodilator in these extreme cases.

Comments on oxygen therapy

Most deaths in asthma are from hypoxia, so oxygen can only be good for you! Well almost; a trial comparing 28% oxygen with 100% in moderate and severe asthma showed small but significant improvements in various parameters in the 28% group. Recent guidelines have linked oxygen therapy to oxygen saturation readings (SaO_2), aiming to keep the saturation at >92% and suggested an inspired oxygen concentration of between 40 and 60% in most cases. This equates to a flow rate of about 6 - 8 litres/min with a well fitted, non-rebreathing mask with a reservoir.

Evacuation

A mild asthma attack usually settles with rest, reassurance, a period of oxygen and extra reliever. If the casualty recovers fully, he or she can be escorted from the fell. In a remote setting a more severe attack should be taken very seriously. An early decision to call a helicopter would be appropriate.

References

Asthma. *Clinical evidence concise.* 2003. Accessed at www.clinicalevidence.com

British guideline on the management of asthma. A national clinical guideline [online]. British Thoracic Society, *Scottish Intercollegiate Guidelines Network.* 2004. At www.brit-thoracic.org.uk/c2/uploads/asthmafull.pdf

Cates CCJ, Bara A, Crilly JA, et al. Holding chambers versus nebulizers for beta agonist treatment of acute asthma. In: *The Cochrane Library*, Issue 2, 2004.

Nahum A, Tuxen DT. Management of asthma in the intensive care unit. In: FitzGerald JM, Ernst PP, Boulet LP, et al, eds. *Evidence based asthma management.* Decker: Hamilton, Ontario. 2000: p245–261

Turner MT, Noertjojo K, Vedal S, et al. Risk factors for near-fatal asthma: a case control study in patients hospitalised with acute asthma. *Am J Respir Crit Care Med* 1998; 157:1804–1809

Rodrigo GJ, Rodriquez Verde M, Peregalli V, et al. Effects of short-term 28% and 100% oxygen on $PaCO_2$ and peak expiratory flow rate in acute asthma: a randomized trial. *Chest* 2003; 124:1312–1317

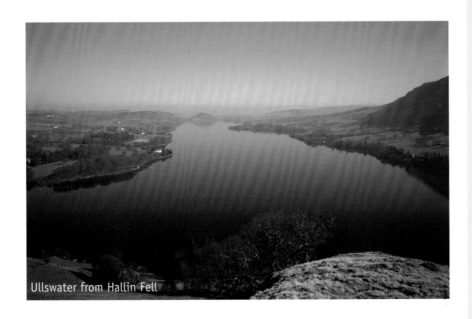

Ullswater from Hallin Fell

Seizure

A seizure, sometimes described as a fit or convulsion, is a synchronous, involuntary contraction of many of the body's muscles and is caused by a disturbance of brain function. Rescuers will come across seizures in a number of situations as outlined in the box below (likely causes in red).

Causes	Comments
Epilepsy the commonest cause; 0.5% of the population (1 in 200 people)	A specific type of seizure where the prime event is a sudden electrical discharge from the brain. Its features, such as frequency, length and precipitating factors, are highly variable. Between seizures, the person is usually normal, though often taking drugs to reduce the severity or frequency of the seizures. Many carry some form of identification, such as Med.-Alert bracelet, to help first aiders. Epilepsy varies from a short period of daydreaming (Petit Mal or 'absence') to a dramatic convulsion (Grand Mal). Sometimes an 'odd' sensation, called an aura, can warn the person of an impending seizure.
After head injury either acute or long-standing	Acute seizures need to be stopped as soon as possible to prevent the development of secondary brain damage from hypoxia.
Cerebrovascular other terms used include CVA and 'stroke'	A common cause for the onset of seizures in the elderly.
Hypoxia inadequate oxygen delivery to the brain	A failure of A,B or C. Examples include a simple faint (managed by lying down) and a cardiac arrest.
Hypoglycaemia lack of glucose; the usual energy source used by the brain	A 'hypo' in an insulin-dependant diabetic commonly causes a seizure. Treat the low blood sugar immediately.
Drugs including alcohol	Alcohol withdrawal more often than acute intoxication.
Fever and Infections	A common cause in children particularly the under 5's where almost any temperature can trigger a febrile convulsion.

A seizure starts with a sudden loss of activity followed by a fall to the ground. The body is rigid (tonic stage) for several seconds and then starts to convulse (clonic stage). Convulsions are characterised by a symmetrical shaking of the body caused by strong muscular contractions that usually last a few minutes. Involuntary passing of urine is common during the clonic stage. The patient may injure himself by biting his tongue, hitting surrounding objects or dislocating joints. After the dramatic contractions, the body becomes flaccid with consciousness slowly returning over a period of minutes. During this stage, as consciousness is regained, the casualty may become confused or even aggressive.

Status epilepticus

If the clonic stage of the seizure lasts for more than 30 minutes the patient is said to be in status epilepticus. This is a medical emergency; brain damage from hypoxia is common and death, from cardiorespiratory failure, occurs in 10 - 20% cases. Fortunately status epilepticus is rare (approximately 3 in 10,000 person years). Over half of patients do not have a diagnosis of epilepsy; the status is triggered by one of the factors mentioned above, particularly fever in children, alcohol withdrawal in young adults and cerebrovascular disease in the elderly.

Management

Most seizures in patients with epilepsy are short (less than 5 minutes) with a quick recovery, and the emergency services are unlikely to be contacted. The patient may recognise that he is about to have a seizure in which case he may have time to warn his companions and to find a safe position. During the clonic stage, the companions should try to protect the patient from further danger though restraining often results in more severe injury. When the patient stops convulsing, he should be turned into the lateral (recovery) position and the airway opened until consciousness returns (see page 19).

More prolonged or repeated seizures occurring without full recovery will result in a call to the emergency services. As we do not know if the seizure is going to stop, all calls should be treated as an emergency. Get to the casualty as quickly as possible using a helicopter, if appropriate. Of course, the seizure may well have stopped, and the casualty recovered, by the time you arrive. That's great. However, occasionally, this will not be the case, and the casualty will be entering into status epilepticus.

Managing the casualty in a clonic stage

Follow a 'Safety, A, B, C' approach though bear in mind that stopping the clonic stage of the seizure is essential. Do not wait for 30 minutes until the casualty has status. This is detrimental; treat a clonic stage actively after 5 minutes. If the seizure is triggered by a head injury, treat quicker - after 2 minutes. Give an appropriate drug or reverse the cause of the seizure as soon as possible.

A - during the clonic stage the airway is often obstructed by muscle contractions and laryngeal spasm. Attempting to overcome this with an oropharyngeal airway frequently injures the tongue and should not be attempted. If possible place the casualty in a lateral position.

B - start oxygen using a non-rebreathing mask with a reservoir at a flow rate of 15 litres/minute.

C - if trained, consider inserting an intravenous cannula. This will be very difficult in the clonic stage, as the casualty will be thrashing around.

Stop the clonic stage by either:

Giving rectal diazepam (10 mg in an adult). This is effective in about 70% of casualties though, as the drug is distributed around the body, 50% of casualties will have a further seizure. A second dose would be appropriate in these casualties.

Giving intravenous diazepam (10 - 20mg at 2 mg/min) or lorazepam (4mg at 2mg/minute, repeated, if necessary, to a total of 0.1mg/kg). Lorazepam has a number of advantages over diazepam; its efficacy at stopping seizures is slightly better, the recurrence rate is lower and the injection can be given more quickly. Though the manufacturer advises that lorazepam is refrigerated, studies have shown that it can be kept in an ambulance for 5 months without too great a loss of activity. Giving diazepam too quickly can cause hypotension.

There is an obvious reluctance to give a drug by the rectum but the alternative intravenous route takes longer particularly in unskilled hands. Intramuscular (in prolonged seizures) or buccal (in serial seizures) midazolam are other options but for most mountain rescuers, overcoming their reluctance and using the safe rectal route will be the preferred treatment option. (This may well change if buccal midazolam is licensed for use.) Remember that status epilepticus has a 10 - 20% mortality rate and hypoxic brain damage can devastate lives.

Managing the casualty in the recovery stage

Reassess A, B, C and manage appropriately. An open airway is crucial. Insert an oropharyngeal airway if tolerated, or a nasopharyngeal airway if tongue injury is apparent. Place the casualty in the lateral position and continue the oxygen. Diazepam reduces the respiratory drive; a careful check on airway and respiratory rate needs to be made until the casualty regains consciousness. This is particularly important if the seizure has been triggered by a head injury as the hypoxia and hypotension can quickly lead to secondary brain damage. Note, however, that a continuing clonic stage is much more harmful to the body and brain than not administrating diazepam. As the casualty recovers, check for injuries caused during the seizure. Shoulder dislocations can occur as well as the more usual lacerations to tongue, lips and mouth.

Evacuation

A person with epilepsy whohas had a short seizure and is fully recovered can be walked off the fell. Reassurance and not 'making a fuss' is very important, as the patient is often very embarrassed. Referring the person to hospital is not necessary; he or she could go home in the company of an adult. Clearly driving should not be allowed.

However, if the casualty is still behaving abnormally or has shaky legs evacuating on a stretcher is appropriate. All casualties treated with diazepam will require a stretcher evacuation, as the drug will cause poor coordination and dizziness for a few hours after its administration. An urgent evacuation by helicopter, if possible, would be appropriate for a casualty with an ongoing seizure or repetitive seizures (despite treatment), as well as those triggered by a head injury. Bear in mind that managing a clonic seizure or an aggressive casualty in a helicopter may be extremely difficult; the safety of the flight needs considering.

Pseudo-epilepsy

This is surprisingly common in the Accident and Emergency department; does it occur on the fells? Basically the casualty simulates a seizure as an attention-seeking behaviour. How can you tell it from the real thing? The thrashing is less well coordinated, less symmetrical and back arching and pelvic thrusting are common. The eyelids are held shut even in the flaccid stage and diazepam, in the doses described above, is poor at stopping the seizure. Injury and incontinence of urine are rare. The casualty can hear you and often contrives to observe what's going on. Preparation for rectal diazepam may be effective at stopping the behaviour.

References

Walker M. Status epilepticus: an evidence based guide. *BMJ* 2005; 331:673-677.

Marik PE, Varon J. The management of status epilepticus. *Chest* 2004; 126:582-591.

McIntyre J, Robertson S, Norris E, Appleton R, et al. Safety and efficacy of buccal midazolam versus rectal diazepam for emergency treatment of seizures in children: a randomised controlled trial. *The Lancet* 2005; 366:205-210

Wiznitzer M. Buccal midazolam for seizures. *The Lancet* 2005; 366:182-3

Coire nan Lochain, Glencoe. (2003)

Diabetes

A person has diabetes, or more correctly diabetes mellitus, if their blood glucose exceeds the normal value of 4 to 8 mmol/l. Diabetes is caused by a lack of insulin or a resistance to the effect of insulin at its main site of action - the cell membrane. Note that blood glucose and blood sugar are often used interchangeably which, though not entirely correct, is accepted in common speech; however it is preferable that we use the accurate term blood glucose.

Pathophysiology

Insulin is a hormone, produced by the pancreas, whose site of action is the cell membrane of many tissues including fat, muscle, liver and brain. Though insulin has many effects on fat and protein metabolism, its immediate action on the body's utilisation of glucose is of concern here. When we eat a meal, glucose is rapidly absorbed from the gut; the blood glucose rises and, in response to this, insulin is released. The release of insulin allows some of the glucose to move from the blood into the cells with the result that the blood glucose falls, as does the rate of insulin secretion until it is back to a low basal level. Without insulin, glucose cannot enter the cells. The liver avidly takes up glucose, where it is stored as glycogen ready to be released during periods of 'starvation'. The normal blood glucose level is between 4 – 8 mmol/l and can be easily tested with a blood glucose meter and a drop of blood as demonstrated above. Once the glucose is within the cells it is used to produce energy. Under normal circumstances some organs, particularly the brain, use glucose exclusively as an energy source. A lack of insulin leads to a higher blood glucose level and the brain has to switch to using fatty acids as an energy source.

There are a number of different types of diabetes. Older people tend to have insulin resistance, and are said to have 'late onset' or 'type 2' diabetes. However, with increasing obesity among younger people, even children are developing insulin resistance. Controlling the blood glucose level in this type of diabetes can be by diet alone, or by diet and tablets, though insulin is being used more frequently to achieve better diabetic control.

Younger people with diabetes usually have an insulin deficiency ('type 1' diabetes), and have to replace the insulin by injection. The insulin reduces the blood glucose levels, and enables the body to convert the glucose to energy. Many management regimens are available using different types of insulin (short and long acting) and daily, twice daily or multiple subcutaneous injections. Alternatively, though still rarely in the UK, an insulin infusion pump can be used.

In a diabetic patient, the normal balance between glucose and insulin can be lost much more easily than in the nondiabetic:

> Too little insulin, too much food, an additional illness or stress causes the blood glucose level to go too high (hyperglycaemia).
>
> Too much insulin, insufficient intake of food at the right time or excessive unplanned exercise causes the blood glucose level to drop too much (hypoglycaemia).

Hyperglycaemia

Hyperglycaemia occurs if the blood glucose level is greater than 8 mmol/l. The patient may not experience any symptoms; many people with diabetes can function well with levels as high as 18mmols. However, most will have some symptoms. When the blood glucose is high, too much glucose crosses the membrane in the kidneys that separates blood from urine. As the glucose crosses the membrane it takes water with it, which increases the urine volume to such an extent that dehydration (thirst, dry skin, increased pulse rate and postural hypotension - low blood pressure on standing) develops. Even though the blood is full of glucose, without insulin it cannot be absorbed into the cells. Consequently, the cells are starving for energy and have to adapt to using other sources of energy notably fatty acids. This energy usage is less efficient so people tend to lose weight over a longer period of time. Hyperglycaemia, in the long term, is not ideal, as prolonged high blood glucose levels will increase the likelihood of diabetic complications, which include painful but numb feet; blindness; skin ulcers; septicaemia; kidney and, most importantly, heart disease.

Teenagers with diabetes often rebel against their condition by denying they have it, and refuse to take their insulin injections. Some have realised that running a high blood glucose allows them to lose weight. However, they also run the risk of developing diabetic ketoacidosis (DKA).

Diabetic Ketoacidosis (DKA)

DKA occurs when the body is unable to use enough blood glucose for its energy needs. This is because of a lack of insulin. The body resorts to using fat and protein as energy sources. Unfortunately using these substances releases toxic by-products, such as ketones, into the circulation and a cycle of deterioration starts, which will eventually lead to coma and death. Ketones are used as a marker that the body is malfunctioning. High levels can be detected on the breath of the casualty as a sweet/sickly smell similar to 'pear drops' and it is usual for a person who has diabetes to test for ketones in the blood or urine if their blood glucose level is >11mmol/l for any period of time. Ketones are weak acids and the body attempts to compensate for this acidosis by getting rid of another acid, carbon dioxide, by hyperventilation (over-breathing). Vomiting is common and often used by patients as an indication that medical help is needed. Abdominal pain can be a significant feature. In DKA the brain cannot continue to function normally; the patient becomes confused and then unconscious. This sequence usually takes days but in some insulin-dependant diabetics the process can lead to unconsciousness in a few hours. Established DKA has a significant risk of death and should be treated as a medical emergency.

Management

Hyperglycaemia - Self management

A person with diabetes finding too high a blood glucose level may well try to bring the level down by giving themselves additional amounts of fast-acting insulin, together with increased fluids to minimise dehydration, and so hopefully avoid the onset of DKA. Most people with diabetes are trained to do this and are effective the majority of the time. The person is best left to their own devices – they often understand their diabetes better than anyone else.

DKA

Hospital management is almost always needed to replace the fluid (often many litres) and to restore glucose as an energy source. Under no circumstances must a casualty be given insulin until the dehydration has been corrected. To do so is dangerous. The casualty should be evacuated as rapidly as possible. In the rare situation where this is not possible, the extended management of DKA would (after consultation with a doctor) consist of intravenous fluids.

Hypoglycaemia

If the blood glucose levels falls below 4 mmol/l then the person is said to be hypoglycaemic.

Hypoglycaemia is a condition that is almost exclusive to people with diabetes. In people without diabetes, the liver is able to produce enough glucose to prevent the blood glucose falling too low. Prolonged starvation is needed to induce hypoglycaemia in nondiabetic subjects. (For example, Sir Ranulph Fiennes and Dr. Mike Stroud's unsupported crossing of Antarctica in 1992/3.)

However, when a person with diabetes injects insulin, the level of insulin follows a profile that is independent of the blood glucose. The type and quantity of insulin given and the injection site will determine the profile. If the person does not eat enough or works harder than expected, the relative excess of insulin keeps glucose moving from the blood into the cells outstripping the ability of the liver to replace it. The blood glucose falls below normal causing a 'hypo'. Note: the sufferer is almost always on insulin. It is rare for a diabetic on tablets and exceptional for a diabetic on diet alone, to go 'hypo'.

The symptoms of a 'hypo' start subtly but intensify as the blood glucose level drops. The brain is affected first so the person will become unsteady and confused. They start tripping over their feet. The behaviour of the person is commonly described as irritable, aggressive, argumentative or irrational. As the condition intensifies, adrenaline is released, the pulse rate increases and the skin becomes pale, sweaty and cold. The patient feels panicky and frequently ravenously hungry. Mannerisms such as yawning may occur, and seizures are common. Loss of consciousness follows if the patient is untreated. This sequence can evolve from start to unconsciousness in as little as 20 minutes. The blood glucose measurement will be below 2 mmol/l.

Management

Many diabetics recognize the symptoms of a 'hypo' and will take sugar to restore the blood glucose. Refuelling should be with both rapidly absorbed sugars (like glucose gels, sugar, etc.) and slow-release sugars (such as digestive biscuits). Most diabetics will then 'self-rescue' or continue their day out. Remember that a person with diabetes is continuously trying to run low blood sugar levels to minimise the adverse complications of having diabetes; it is a balancing act between too much and too little and usually works well, but sometimes other factors interfere and the delicate balance is lost. If the rescue team has been called and find, on arrival, a fully recovered diabetic, the person may well be happy to continue. This is perfectly acceptable.

A diabetic, particularly someone who frequently has a low blood sugar, may fail to recognize a 'hypo'. Perhaps the irrational behaviour or additional factors, such as a change in medication, prevents its recognition. The rescuer will need to take urgent steps to increase the blood glucose. Oral glucose is preferred if the casualty is able to cooperate and the swallowing reflex (protecting the airway) is present. Considerable skills at persuading the casualty to take sugar may be needed if irrational behaviour is present.

If the casualty is unable to cooperate or is unconscious, follow the 'Safety A, B, C' of the primary survey and then carry out a procedure to raise the blood glucose. It has been suggested that it may be possible to give sufficient buccal glucose, such as Glucogel®, rubbed into the gums, to reverse the hypoglycaemia with only a small risk of obstructing the airway. No reference explicitly stating this has been found, and the practice must be considered unsupported. An alternative, and well supported, treatment is 1 mg of glucagon given intramuscularly or subcutaneously. Glucagon is a hormone that acts by releasing the glucose from its stored form, glycogen, in the liver. Recovery from hypoglycaemia is usually quick (less than 10 minutes) and complete. Any casualty that has been treated with glucagon will need to refuel e.g. snack bar, sandwich, piece of cake etc as soon as consciousness has returned. It would be sensible to escort the casualty from the fell.

Extended Management

If glucagon does not work, first consider if the diagnosis is correct. Is there a head injury? Has the casualty had a seizure? Checking a blood glucose measurement would be useful. If the reading is less than 4 mmol/l, either repeat the glucagon or consider cannulating a large peripheral vein and giving intravenous glucose (dextrose). This needs to be done carefully as if a strong concentration of glucose is placed in the tissues outside the vein the tissue dies leaving, at best, a deep skin ulcer. For the same reason, glucose cannot be given by intramuscular injection. Rapid evacuation will be needed if unconsciousness persists.

Practicalities of dealing with the unconscious casualty

Many people with diabetes wear ID bracelets or necklaces; but many don't! Ask members of the casualty's group if they know whether the casualty suffers from diabetes. Check pockets and rucksack for sources of sugar and for equipment used by diabetics (blood glucose monitor, syringes, insulin pens, emergency details card, glucagon). Also check the tips of the fingers for signs of frequent blood glucose testing (scarring/prick marks).

If you suspect that the casualty has diabetes, your main problem is deciding if the loss of consciousness is from hypoglycaemia or hyperglycaemia. If you know how to use a blood glucose meter, that's great! However in a cold environment the blood glucose meter may not work, and finding a good source of blood can be difficult. The ear lobes are a good option. Be aware that sugar on the fingers can give a high or normal reading even when the blood level is low.

Unless you are absolutely 100% sure that unconsciousness is not due to hypoglycaemia GIVE sugar or glucagon. If you are wrong, and the casualty is unconscious from hyperglycaemia or any other problem, no significant harm has been done. Hopefully recovery (from the hypoglycaemia) will follow, and you have made a real difference to the casualty.

Diabetes, Sport and the Emergency Services

Not many years ago people with diabetes were discouraged from participating in sport. The treatment regimens were inflexible, monitoring of blood glucose rare, and the beneficial effects of exercise less well known. In addition, 'hypos' were seen as dangerous, and blanket bans were imposed on people treated with insulin from joining the emergency services. The great advances in treating diabetes, though designed to improve the long-term outlook, have had the effect that many of the old restrictions placed on diabetics can be removed. In Sport, just look at Sir Steve Redgrave to see what can be achieved. In mountaineering, the exploits of Jerry Gore leave many of us in the shade. A number of organisations can help participants with diabetes with advice and opportunities to explore the outdoors. For example MAD ("Mountains for Active Diabetics") is an international group giving advice and information on diabetes in extreme mountain sports and remote places.

A person with uncomplicated diabetes, whether or not on insulin, should not be excluded from a mountain rescue team – OK, some care needs to be taken as call-outs aren't (usually) planned but the problems should be surmountable. Restrictions on driving emergency (blue-light) vehicles remain but others, such as abseiling, are ridiculous. An open understanding and awareness between the person with diabetes and the team should benefit all.

References

Vermeulen MJ, Klompas M, Ray JG, Mazza C, Morrison LJ. Subcutaneous glucagon may be better than oral glucose for the prehospital treatment of symptomatic hypoglycaemia. *Diabetes Care* 2003; 26:2472-2473.

I am indebted to Nikki Wallis for her contributions to this section.

Nikki is an active member of the Llanberis Mountain Rescue team, SARDA Wales, and works as a National Park Warden for the Snowdonia National Park Authority. An insulin dependant diabetic herself, Nikki is founder and president of MAD. As an alpinist, participating in high altitude medical research expeditions, she has climbed all over the world and recently (2004) attempted Broad Peak in Pakistan. She can be contacted at info@mountain-mad.org

Unknown climber, Wales

Attempted suicide

Attempted suicide (sometimes called deliberate self-harm) is rarely seen on the hills. Someone who goes to the trouble of hiding themselves away is determined, and usually successful in killing himself. However, teams that get involved in urban and lowland searches may well be asked to search for a person contemplating suicide. The rescue team's first priority is to consider the safety of its members because the person may have a history of serious psychiatric illness, violence or be contemplating suicide with a weapon. In these cases it would be inappropriate for rescue teams to get involved without the Police providing security.

Deliberate self-harm is often a 'cry for help'. The intent to end their life is short-lived and passes after the act whether the mode has been an overdose of tablets or cutting their wrists. Help is often accepted with gentle persuasion. Only rarely do the powers of the Mental Health Act need to be invoked by a doctor or police officer.

Many different types of medicine can be taken, very often as a cocktail. For example, paracetamol, antidepressants, sleeping tablets and alcohol are commonly combined. It is important to try to find out how many and what quantity of each drug has been taken. Collecting packets and bottles at the scene may be the only way - the casualty may be unconscious or so distressed as to be unable to tell the rescuer. A local Accident and Emergency Department could predict the effects of the drugs and offer a management plan. Inducing vomiting is no longer favoured! In general, supportive care by applying a 'Safety, A, B, then C' approach will be all that will be needed during the evacuation of the casualty to hospital. Specific antidotes are available for some drugs: for example, naloxone will reverse the effects of opiate overdoses (heroin, methadone, codeine, cocodamol, etc.) and is often worth giving to a casualty who has attempted self-harm and is unconscious or has respiratory depression. In all cases of deliberate self-harm, the casualty will need to go to hospital for a 'checkup'. This involves both confirming the drugs taken and assessing whether the risk of suicide is significant.

Complications of Pregnancy

A pregnant woman developing abdominal pain or vaginal bleeding on the hill should be treated with urgency. In either early (< 12 weeks of pregnancy) or late (> 28 weeks of pregnancy) pregnancy immediate evacuation of the woman to hospital should be arranged. Shock is a real possibility and can develop very quickly. The amount of external blood loss may be insignificant compared with the massive life-threatening internal bleeding. The most important cause in early pregnancy is an ectopic pregnancy, which still claims lives every year.

In late pregnancy a condition called eclampsia can develop. This consists of a rapidly increasing blood pressure and seizures, including status epilepticus. Before the seizure an aura of visual disturbance and abdominal pain may develop. It is a medical emergency for both the lady and the baby.

It is comforting to know that a baby in the womb is quite well protected from most forms of trauma. The casualty can still be given morphine and Entonox® if needed for an injury.

Emergency childbirth on the hill would present quite a challenge - good luck!

Gastroenteritis

Food poisoning, or gastroenteritis, is the result of eating a pathogenic virus or, occasionally, a bacterium, such as Salmonella, E. coli, or Campylobacter. The illness can be very infectious, so pay careful attention to the washing of hands and machine-washing of soiled items. The illness starts with fever, aching joints and muscles rapidly followed by vomiting and/or diarrhoea. Most attacks are self-limiting. The main problem is dehydration, which is best treated with small sips of water or a fizzy drink. If the casualty has been unable to self-rescue, a stretcher evacuation to hospital is appropriate.

Migraine

Migraine is a particular type of headache characterized by a moderate or severe, usually one-sided, headache often associated with nausea or vomiting. The headache is usually over a temple or an eye. A period of euphoria or visual disturbance may precede the headache. This aura may allow the person to take tablets (of various types) or an injection (usually a triptan-type drug, such as sumatriptan) to stop the attack developing. Most people will self-rescue. If help is requested, there are various treatment options; the choice will partly depend on drugs already taken by the casualty and their expectations. Full dose paracetamol (1 gram), diclofenac (75mg) or aspirin (900mg) reduces the pain of the headache. An injection of cyclizine or metoclopramide (in adults), with or without one of the analgesics described above, is also effective and circumvents the problem of vomiting. Of course, the best treatment is to lie down somewhere quiet and dark until the migraine abates. In the old days, an opiate such as morphine, pethidine or codeine was added to the injection. Some patients still expect this, though clinical trials have shown its addition does not improve the resolution of the headache. Healthcare professionals try to avoid using an opiate, as addiction/ dependence can become a problem. The first attack is the most frightening and other diagnoses need to be considered particularly subarachnoid haemorrhage.

Subarachnoid haemorrhage (SAH)

Blood in the subarachnoid space (the space just above the brain surface) can occur following trauma or spontaneously. Here we consider a spontaneous SAH where, usually, an aneurysm on a surface artery of the brain ruptures. The clinical picture starts with an instant-onset, severe headache, usually over the back of the skull and the upper neck, and on both sides of the head. It is often described as like being hit by a cricket bat. Transient loss of consciousness is common and, in grave cases, consciousness is not regained. After the initial loss of consciousness, the patient often becomes irritable, confused and/or drowsy. Vomiting and seizures also occur. Examination may show that the headache intensifies with flexion of the neck (meningism). Following the initial episode of bleeding, a number of pathophysiological events can occur that worsen the casualty's outlook. These include a secondary bleed and spasm of the blood vessels supplying the brain causing ischaemia. These secondary events can lead to a relapse into unconsciousness and to respiratory arrest. This is unfortunate as the primary condition is often curable by neurosurgical clipping of the aneurysm. Many techniques have been tried (largely unsuccessfully) in hospital to prevent the secondary events, but of more importance to us is that no pre-hospital treatment has been shown to precipitate or prevent these events. As with head injury, the aim is to prevent further secondary damage from hypoxia. Manage the casualty by applying the 'Safety, A, B, C, and D' approach. Respiratory support may be required during the evacuation; if skilled, an LMA or endotracheal tube with sedation would be a good option. Given time a surprising number of patients recover spontaneous respiration but the outlook for full recovery remains bleak. The BP is often very high but artificially reducing it, as with all strokes, can be hazardous.

Drugs that 'thin the blood'

An increasing number of people are taking drugs to thin the blood. The commonest reason is to prevent heart disease and/or stroke. The person may not have suffered their first attack yet but will be taking the drug to prevent it (primary prevention). Thinning the blood refers to two distinct medical treatments and it is important to separate these. Aspirin (and, less often, clopidogrel) inhibits the activation of platelets. Their role in treatment is to prevent clumping of platelets, because a 'clump' can pass round the circulation and block small blood vessels. Aspirin also delays the initial plug that seals a leaking blood vessel but the effect is hardly noticeable. In contrast, warfarin ('rat poison') interferes with the blood's mechanism for forming a blood clot - a longer lasting mechanism for haemostasis (stopping blood leakage). The medical role of warfarin is to prevent blood clots forming in the circulation. Unlike aspirin, warfarin has a marked effect on haemostasis. Characteristically cuts will stop bleeding initially as the blood vessel goes into spasm and platelets plug the hole. However, as these two effects wane, blood leaks again. To counter this, direct pressure needs to be maintained for much longer than normal; perhaps for hours rather than the normal 10 minutes. A casualty on warfarin can lose a lot of blood from a wound and, as the casualty often has an underlying heart condition, their ability to compensate is already reduced. A casualty with a 2cm scalp laceration can bleed enough to produce shock (see page 135). It is also worth noting that intramuscular injections are contraindicated as they may cause large muscle blood clots to form. An intravenous or subcutaneous (if appropriate to the drug) injection would be a better option. Casualties on warfarin with even minor head injuries need extra observation in hospital as a delayed bleed within the skull can have devastating consequences.

References

Colman I, Brown MD, Innes GD, Grafstein E, Roberts TE, Rowe BH. Parenteral metoclopramide for acute migraine: meta-analysis of randomised controlled trials. BMJ online 2004. Accessed at doi:10.1136/bmj.38281.595718.7C

Goadsby PJ, Olesen J. Fortnightly Review: Diagnosis and management of migraine BMJ 1996; 312:1279-1283

Goadsby PJ, Lipton RB, Ferrari MD. Migraine — Current Understanding and Treatment. N. Engl. J. Med. 2002; 346:257-270

'the ethos of the mountain rescue team, with its teamwork, supportive banter and shared experiences, lessens the impact of the distress'. See page 302.

Supportive care of the injured and relatives

This book concentrates on the emergency medical care given to the injured and ill in the hills. Despite the same apparent physical injury, different casualties react in very different ways. Why is this so? The personality of the casualty, the circumstances of the injury and the amount of pain experienced are some of the factors that alter the person's behaviour. The behaviour of the rescue team also has an effect. If the incident is handled in a controlled, efficient and caring way the casualty is put at ease; the whole episode is more tolerable. This is a good 'bedside manner'. Doctors know that this results in happy, appreciative patients who get better quicker. They are also less likely to sue for damages!

Most hill-goers don't call a rescue team on a whim; the casualty may feel embarrassed, guilty, angry or frustrated. They are in a vulnerable position with little control over their destiny. Fear of the consequences of being rescued may be prominent; will the Press get their name, will they be criticized in public? Anger may be directed inappropriately at the rescue team or other members of their party. Casualties are often embarrassed at having to call for assistance and may feel everyone is making a great fuss and that nothing is wrong. The rescuer needs to take control in a firm but caring way to prevent tempers flaring. The hillside is not the place to start criticizing a hill walker's lack of waterproofs when they are hypothermic having spent three hours freezing behind a cairn on a wet day.

Remember that the casualty will be uncertain what you are doing. At each stage, explain what is happening and why. Make the casualty feel involved. This helps to reduce anxiety and increases the cooperation of the casualty. This in turn helps reduce the casualty's pain. Explain why it is necessary to have an uncomfortable cervical collar applied or why an injection is needed. The casualty must consent to any treatment or procedure; a cooperative caring approach will reduce misunderstandings.

People other than the casualty are involved in a rescue. A climbing partner, a fellow walker or someone passing by may become intimately linked with the rescue. These people are often forgotten. They may have physical problems, such as hypothermia, having sat with the casualty for some hours. They may be extremely worried for a loved one or distraught at the death of a climbing partner. They may feel guilty - 'we should have turned back when the weather worsened' or 'I should have made the belay more secure'. The words of George Mallory, written to his wife, following the death of seven porters on the 1922 Everest expedition were: 'The consequences of my mistake are so terrible; it seems almost impossible to believe that it has happened for ever and that I can do nothing to make it good'. (Mallory had led a group back to the North Col in one last attempt at the summit.) During the rush of a rescue ignoring these people is easy. Their emotions may not be recognized. Relatives and companions can feel left out. To explain to the wife of a casualty with, say, a myocardial infarct what is going on is always time well spent; it only takes a few minutes. Let people get involved with the rescue as long as they are not being placed in danger - a stretcher or rucksack carrier is always needed. Radios are indispensable to mountain rescue teams. However, don't forget that other people hear the transmissions. A climbing partner doesn't want to hear over the radio a graphic description of his companion's terrible injuries.

This is all common sense but during a frantic rescue, in difficult weather, these extras can be forgotten. Putting a patient at ease not only makes them feel better but also aids the rescue. When doctors and patients have written about their experiences of emergency medical care, they often comment on the dehumanising aspects – let's be human so the rescue is remembered for the right reasons and not as a necessary evil.

Breaking bad news

Breaking bad news on the hill or in the rescue base is one of the most challenging and least liked elements of mountain rescue. OK, it often falls to those in authority, such as the team leader, Doctor or attending Police Officer, but we all need to understand what is going on so that we can help the casualty and the team leader through a distressing part of the rescue. Let's take the scenario:

A middle-aged couple are out for a walk along a coastal path. The husband stumbles and falls over the edge. His wife sees him fall and thinks she can see him half way down the cliff but she can't get to him. The rescue team arrive, abseil down and treat the casualty as best as they can for about 20 minutes before he dies from what is presumed to be blood loss from a fractured pelvis and femur. The team leader ascends to the top of the cliff. The casualty will be evacuated by helicopter in about 15 minutes time.

These suggestions, along with those on page 273, may help when breaking the unavoidable news of the casualty's - her husband's - death.

Start the conversation as soon as practical. Ensure that the environment is safe, the person's physical needs have been addressed and that you have introduced yourself. Have another rescue person, perhaps of the same peer group as the casualty's wife (and who had been looking after her during the first aid phase of the rescue), with you. Try to minimise interruptions.

Establish what the person knows, perhaps by getting them to recount the history from a suitable point, and what they think has happened. This will allow you to establish what the person wants to know and fears most.

Pace the conversation; you can continue the chronological time frame started by the person from where 'you took over'. Remember the person is distressed so speak a little more slowly than usual, stop frequently to allow the person to react and, at suitable points, check for understanding.

Tell the truth and answer direct questions as they are asked; the conclusion will often have been guessed long before you confirm the worst but try to soften the blow with your phraseology.

If possible, allow some time for the information to sink in and then explain the practicalities from that point onwards, such as the evacuation procedure and the involvement of the Police and Coroner. Address any fears that have been flagged up earlier and ask if she has any questions.

People are sometimes reluctant to voice their desire to see and hold their loved one after death to say 'goodbye'. If the casualty can be made reasonably presentable, offer this in a sensitive and tactful way.

Return to the physical and social needs of the person. Try to humanise the situation as much as possible.

Post-traumatic stress disorder

It is important that we, as mountain rescue team members, have the willingness to confront some of our feelings. We are dealing with angry, upset and distraught people in difficult situations. We face scenes of horror and gore that many people only read about. This can be upsetting for us as well as the relatives at the scene.

Any team member experiencing problems of this nature should discuss them with fellow team members, the team leader or team doctor.

Post-traumatic stress disorder (PTSD) can occur after any major traumatic event. (Here the term 'traumatic' refers to a stressful, exceptionally threatening or catastrophic event; not just blood and gore.) It occurs in people of all ages and is common, affecting up to 25% of people experiencing a traumatic event. Rescue team members are not immune. Though training, experience, and the supportive nature of teams protect members, studies indicate perhaps 10% of rescuers develop PTSD. The main symptoms are:

PTSD symptoms	Examples
Repeated and unwanted re-experiencing the event	Flashbacks, nightmares.
Avoidance	People, situations or circumstances associated with the event.
Emotional numbness	Detached feelings, giving up, amnesia for parts of the event.
Excessive arousal	Sleep problems, irritability, poor concentration, excessive vigilance.
Depression, Drug and Alcohol abuse	Can be the alerting symptoms.
To fulfil the diagnosis the symptoms have to persist for at least 1 month and cause clinically significant distress or reduced day-to-day functioning.	

Management

For our casualties, this usually falls outside the rescue team's role. However the psychological impact of the traumatic event is lessened if survivors are offered practical, social and emotional support. This supportive care has been detailed above.

For us, the same applies. Being upset is not a sign of emotional weakness, but a natural human feeling. Fortunately the ethos of the mountain rescue team, with its teamwork, supportive banter and shared experiences, lessens the impact of the distress. Talk openly amongst yourselves, give mutual support and practical help, and accept black humour in the way it is intended. Rescuers should not feel under any pressure while involved in mountain rescue. The 'pint down the pub' is OK and even beneficial! There was a vogue for Critical Incident Stress Debriefing (CISD) where an individual was offered a short single-session debrief focusing on that person's role in the incident. This has been shown to be harmful. This differs from the 'incident debrief' that many teams carry out after a call-out. Here the group focuses on 'what went well' and 'what went less well' with the aim of learning and improving the team. Sympathetically managed this is no more than an extension of the informal debriefs in the pub and can help team members express and normalize their feelings. However, if the meeting becomes personalized, accusatory, compulsory or public, harm could follow.

From time to time one of our members will struggle to normalize after a traumatic incident. Perhaps they will suddenly give up rescue work, start drinking heavily or change their nature and become irritable or over zealous. Their family may report problems with sleeping or performance at work. A 'macho' approach - 'can't stand the heat'; etc. - by team members is extremely damaging. Significant symptoms occurring between 1 and 3 months after the incident, and all symptoms lasting more than 3 months, should be directed to their General Practitioner for assessment and help. Trauma-focused cognitive behaviour therapy and drug treatments can be effective and are available to team members via the NHS.

References

Hidalgo RB, Davidson JR. Post-traumatic stress disorder: epidemiology and health-related considerations. *Journal of Clinical Psychiatry* 2000; 61:5-13

National Institute for Clinical Excellence. Post-traumatic stress disorder. Clinical guideline 26 2005. Available at www.nice.org.uk

Persaud R. Post-traumatic stress disorder in doctors. *BMJ Careers* 2005; 86-87

Rahemtulla T, Bhopal R. Coping with the aftermath of trauma *BMJ* 2005; 330:1038-9

Mayou R, Farmer A. Trauma (ABC of psychological medicine) *BMJ 2002; 325:426-9*

Wild camping (Cairngorms with Pete. (2004)

Special circumstances

Objectives

To understand what is involved in 'extended' and cave rescue
To safely manage a diving incident
To appreciate the seriousness of suspension and entrapment
To think about the forces involved in sport
To appreciate the role of helicopters
To know a little about caring for injured animals

Extended Rescue

What is an extended rescue? Is it a rescue that lasts more than two hours; or four; or six hours? It is a poorly defined term and as a consequence the medical aspects are rarely discussed. Three areas of extended rescue are discussed in this section.

We have outlined, in the section on the primary survey, our thoughts on evacuation and the need to be constantly reassessing the casualty during this phase of the rescue. Some aspects of the care of the casualty will be more appropriate if a long pre-hospital period is expected; hopefully you picked these up!

Medical problems in extended rescues

The aim of this section is to think about preventable problems that can occur in any casualty when the rescue is prolonged. The aspects covered are care of pressure areas, food and drink and bladder function.

Pressure area care

Pressure ulcers can develop at any skin site where the blood supply is reduced. Common sites are over bony points such as the sacrum and heel. They are associated with a lot of problems and any technique that reduces their likelihood must be taken seriously. In the presence of a spinal cord injury, spinal boards, such as the KED® splint and Neil Robertson stretcher, are particularly likely to cause pressure sores. They should be removed as soon as practically possible. The time frame appears to be short (two hours) in comparison to mountain rescue evacuation times. Ideally spinal boards should be used solely for extrication of the casualty to a flat area; the spinal board can then be removed and a vacuum mattress applied.

Food and drink

It is usual to ban food and drink from all casualties until they have been fully assessed in hospital. The reason for this is that giving a general anaesthetic within four hours of liquid and six hours of food risks aspiration of stomach contents into the lungs. The resulting aspiration pneumonia has a high mortality. However, many mountain rescue casualties will be partly dehydrated and low on sugar supplies by the time they are rescued. The situation will only worsen during an extended rescue. An extreme example would be an insulin-dependant diabetic. Rescuers should use their judgement as to whether giving liquids, or even food, are appropriate. Consider whether –

> The condition of the casualty prevents oral fluids being given. This may result from the injury preventing oral intake (facial or abdominal trauma), vomiting (myocardial infarction) or unreliable swallowing (head injury with reduced GCS).
>
> Surgery is imminent. A fractured femur is usually 'fixed' during an operation within six hours of admission to hospital. This reduces the chance of a fat embolus. Open fractures usually need urgent surgical attention to reduce the risk of infection. However, consider a fell runner two hours into an event, stumbling and sustaining a fracture around the ankle. The skin is intact and there is no distortion. He or she will already be dehydrated by at least a litre of water. By the time they reach hospital perhaps ten hours after the injury they will certainly be becoming significantly short of water and simple sugars. When adequate analgesia has been achieved and the ankle has been splinted, it would be appropriate to allow small sips to drink should the casualty wish. On a cold, wet day sips of warm fluids can transform a casualty from being passive and in pain to one prepared to help themselves and whose pain has been controlled.

An alternative approach may be the insertion of an intravenous cannula and the infusion of fluid (Sodium chloride 0.9%). Here we are not talking about large volumes in a short space of time to resuscitate the casualty but the replacement of water lost before the incident and the obligatory losses that continue after. The use of subcutaneous fluids should also be considered. This involves putting a small cannula into the subcutaneous tissues, usually somewhere on the trunk, and then slowly giving sterile fluid. The same apparatus is used as for intravenous fluids. The skill required and risk of damage, to a blood vessel or the pleural cavity, is low. Though the volumes that can be given are small compared with the intravenous route, this neglected technique warrants further consideration in extended pre-hospital rescue.

Bladder function

The bladder has a limited capacity! In any seriously injured casualty the urine output after the event is going to be very small and not likely to give problems. However it is amazing how many casualties with minor injuries want to empty their bladder. Usually the request comes just after they have been strapped into the stretcher. Ask beforehand!

When does a second dose of drug need to be given?

Most drugs used by mountain rescuers are given for the relief of symptoms. Examples include salbutamol for asthma and glucagon for hypoglycaemia. In the drug section, individual drugs have their maximum doses stated. Giving a further dose depends on the symptoms returning and keeping within the maximum. Pain deserves a different approach. It is unkind to allow the analgesic effect of morphine to wear off. After a single intramuscular injection of morphine, which has reduced the pain to a tolerable level, we would expect the analgesic effect to have worn off four hours later. This may well be during the evacuation. However it is impossible to say when the next dose of analgesic should be given. Many things will have changed since the first dose was given. Positive factors reducing the need for analgesia include:

Stabilising a fracture.

Allaying the fear of the casualty.

Smoother carrying of the stretcher as the evacuation track improves.

The need for analgesia may have increased. For example, the splint on a fractured lower leg may have become too tight as the limb becomes more swollen. Rescuers should be aware of these factors and frequently reassess the need for a 'top-up' dose. A general reassessment of the condition of the casualty should be carried out before a further injection is given, paying particular attention to the foot circulation in lower leg injuries. The effort of doing this despite the delay during the evacuation is often worthwhile.

When do we need to consider the health of the rescuers?

Rescuers are not supermen or women and they can be physically and mentally over-extended on a long and difficult rescue. Individual rescuers must consider their limits and act appropriately to prevent themselves from becoming the next casualty. Likewise, those organizing the rescue must be aware and sensitive to this aspect of the rescue and try to be pro-active to prevent exhaustion. Reducing the unpleasantness of a rescue is possible and particularly important for new team members with little experience of seriously injured casualties. Returning to a scene of devastation should be avoided; there are always other surrounding teams ready to help. When many rescue teams are working at one incident, keeping individual teams together can also be beneficial.

Cave Rescue

When mountain and cave rescuers meet socially then the latter will provoke the former by alleging that their job is too easy and lacks challenge. The proof is simple - you can't fly helicopters down caves! Both tasks can be daunting but those injured down caves do face certain problems not met in situations above ground.

Confined areas

The only way out is often the way the casualty got in. This may involve forcing the body through convoluted cavities in limestone no bigger than its own dimensions and with no allowance being made for the fact that it hurts to squeeze broken bones through tight sections.

Water

The way out is likely to be along a natural watercourse. At best some immersion is likely during exit from most cave systems. At worst breathing apparatus may be needed.

Heat loss

Both mountain and cave casualties face the risk of deterioration and death from hypothermia. Cavers will not face the high wind chill and subzero temperatures of mountaineers but water is an excellent conductor of heat. Death within an hour of onset of the first symptoms of hypothermia has been described in Mendip caves in flood so the threat is ever present. Often cave rescuers have to encourage the casualty to self-rescue. This is where the 'Little Dragon' device is worth 'its weight in gold'. The effect on the morale of a chilled, previously trapped, caver who is miserable and frightened has to be seen to be believed.

Self-help, walk or carry?

Down a cave the implication of a stretcher-carry, in terms of delay and manpower logistics, is considerable particularly if the incident involves multiple casualties. A common scenario is that a caving party will be delayed due to flooding, rock fall or being lost. They are found cold, frightened and distressed. Delays of 24 hours are not uncommon. Such victims will certainly be encouraged to self-rescue. They will be given food and hot drinks, lots of encouragement, protection on even small hazards and good hauls on any vertical section but will basically have to exit under their own steam. Just occasionally a person being 'chaperoned' out as described will not cope with the exertion and be seen to deteriorate, invariably from hypothermia. Such victims should be rested, insulated, fed and evacuated, if at all possible, by stretcher.

Packaging

Due to the cave environment, the packaging requirements are rather special. Most victims will have been immobilised for several hours and have a reduced core temperature. After first aid, medical assessment and treatment, extra insulation is essential if a stretcher evacuation must follow. The exposure bag used underground must be able to provide insulation even if it is immersed in water In addition, it should not retain so much water as to significantly add to the stretcher load. Allowing the casualty to have arms and hands free is usually appreciated as it facilitates self-help through awkward sections of cave thus significantly speeding up the evacuation. Packaging should allow for this.

A neoprene bag covering the whole body including a hood for the head and sleeves without hand holes has emerged as the design of choice. After effective packaging further assessment of the casualty becomes extremely difficult. 'Un-bagging' to reassess or adjust splints will totally lose the benefits of all heat conserved. Reassessing the casualty is generally limited to verbal assessment, the carotid pulse and the respiratory rate.

Pete Allwright (BCRC)

Diving Emergencies

Recreational or sport diving is very popular with between 50,000 and 100,000 participants in the UK. There are about 12 deaths a year and 70 cases of decompression illness requiring recompression. The risk has been favourably compared with mountaineering - something I am sure we would argue against! Diving is a very specialist field and one that we cannot cover adequately in this book. Suffice to say that mountain rescue teams do get involved in diving emergencies and a few critical points, outlined below, should be understood. Of course, not all diving emergencies are related to the diving - 10% of all recreational diving fatalities are from myocardial infarction. Injury, from trauma or bites, can occur and the environment lends itself to drowning and hypothermia. For those who want to know more read on! We will confine ourselves to recreational diving at depths of less than 50 metres.

Critical points in diving emergencies
100% oxygen via a tight fitting non-rebreathing mask is essential.
Entonox® must never be used. See figure in the drugs section.
Any illness occurring within 48 hours of a scuba dive should be assumed to be decompression sickness until proven otherwise.
Transferring a casualty with suspected decompression sickness is urgent but height gains of more than 150 metres from the incident site should be avoided if at all possible.

Emergency contact numbers:
HM Coastguard via 999
Royal Navy - 0831 151523

Physiology and pathology

The weight of the column of water above the diver increases the pressure on him by one atmosphere (1 bar) for each 10 metres descended. In these situations the solid parts of the person behave like a liquid and transmit the pressure to underlying structures with an insignificant amount of compression. However any gas spaces shrink as the pressure increases so at 10 metres the volume is halved and at 30 metres quartered.

The partial pressure of any gas in a mixture, such as air, is determined by the proportion of the gas in the mixture and the absolute pressure; so if you compress air to 2 atmospheres, the partial pressure of both oxygen and nitrogen will have doubled. The volume of gas dissolved in a liquid is proportional to its partial pressure, therefore, if the absolute pressure reduces suddenly, as in an uncontrolled ascent or unscrewing the top of a lemonade bottle, the gas may come out of solution and form bubbles unless sufficient time is allowed for the transition. In divers, bubbles of nitrogen give rise to the 'bends'.

Symptoms and signs

These are different depending on whether the diving is breath-holding or Scuba.

Breath-holding diving (such as snorkelling)

The person holds his breath and dives. As he does so his chest compresses as the lung volume diminishes. His buoyancy decreases, and he may find he has to push off from the bottom or swim upwards to make progress. Hypoxia may supervene particularly if he has hyperventilated before the dive. (He has washed the carbon dioxide out of his body and removed a potent warning sign of ventilatory failure.) Drowning follows.

Middle ear barotrauma can occur even at depths of 1 metre. The pressure in the middle ear cannot be equalised with the greater pressure outside if the Eustachian tube (tube from back of the nose to middle ear) is blocked. The eardrum is damaged giving rise to pain and, if ruptured, sometimes causes acute dizziness as cold water enters the middle ear. If dizziness persists a more severe inner ear rupture may have occurred. A Doctor should assess all casualties complaining of ear pain. Pain in the sinuses, possibly with a nosebleed, and even teeth can occur for the same reasons. Rarely a similar problem occurs in the lungs resulting in pulmonary bleeding or oedema.

Scuba diving

Scuba stands for Self-Contained Underwater Breathing Apparatus. In its usual form it consists of a bottle of compressed air (at 150 bar) and two regulators. The first regulator on the cylinder reduces the pressure of the air but it is the second one on the mouthpiece that does the clever trick of reducing the inspired air pressure to that of the surrounding water. The pressure in the lungs increases in line with the outside pressure and so the lungs do not compress allowing breathing to continue, albeit at increased effort, despite the higher pressure. Breathing compressed air (about 80% nitrogen and 20% oxygen), the depth of the dive is limited by nitrogen narcosis; nitrogen is not inert, and as its partial pressure increases it acts like alcohol. The diver suffers euphoria, poor judgement, and ultimately loss of consciousness. Symptoms may start at a depth of around 30 metres and become life threatening at 50 metres. Nitrogen narcosis resolves quickly on ascent and does not give rise to residual symptoms once the diver has surfaced. (To dive to greater depths a mixture of oxygen and helium replaces air.)

So what can go wrong for a diver? There can be equipment problems too numerous to mention, and decompression illness. Decompression illness is divided into pulmonary barotrauma and decompression sickness.

In pulmonary barotrauma, either the diver has ascended too fast, held his breath or a localised area of lung becomes plugged so that when the diver ascends the air inside it expands and ruptures the lung tissue. A pneumothorax, possibly bilateral and often under tension, can result. The history is usually of sudden respiratory problems on arrival at the surface.

Decompression sickness (DCS) is a whole host of symptoms and signs that result from gas bubbles forming in the diver's blood stream or tissues. The diver will probably have ascended 'too quickly' - there are tables that divers use to calculate their rate of ascent and 'decompression stops' at certain depths, but DCS can occur even when the rules have been followed. Underwater emergencies, such as equipment problems, may prevent the diver from following a safe profile for the ascent, and induce DCS. The symptoms and signs can vary considerably - the following summary points may help.

Symptoms usually start within one hour of surfacing but may be delayed for up to 48 hours, perhaps precipitated by the decompression of the air flight home. Divers are advised not to undertake a deep dive within 24 hours of flying but, like many a climber, are often tempted to break the rules. Symptoms include:

General tiredness and fatigue, with loss of appetite.

Skin rashes and swelling; these are harmless.

Musculoskeletal pain, particularly around the shoulders and knees, is the commonest presenting symptom and is known as the 'bends'.

Neurological symptoms and signs represent a severe form of DCS. The symptoms usually develop within a few minutes of surfacing. These include headache, confusion, paralysis of one side of the body (hemiplegia) or the limbs (paraplegia), though many other symptoms and signs can occur depending on where the gas bubbles lodge. It is best to take any neurological symptom, such as pins and needles, or sign, however bizarre, seriously and institute treatment at once.

Management

Consider any illness after a dive as being potentially due to DCS. The unpredictable progression of the illness makes planning for the worst worthwhile. Recompression in a hyperbaric chamber is the best treatment so plan for this as early as possible. Know where the nearest chamber is and have a record of the emergency contact numbers (see box above). A rapid primary survey should be carried out. 100% oxygen (15 litres/minute via a tight fitting non-rebreathing mask) is essential as it encourages the elimination of nitrogen from the bubbles. Plenty of fluid by mouth should be encouraged if possible. Entonox® is absolutely contraindicated as the nitrous oxide diffuses rapidly into the bubbles and may cause them to expand. Rapid transfer to a hyperbaric chamber, usually aided by a helicopter, is critical though ideally the helicopter should ascend no more than 150 metres above the incident site so circuitous routes may need to be taken. Of course, the same applies to road transport.

Extended Management

Pneumothoraces should be specifically looked for and managed, depending on the rescuer's skill, by needle thoracocentesis. Intravenous fluids should be started.

References

Harries, Williams, Stanish and Micheli. *Oxford Textbook of Sports Medicine* 1994. ISBN 0 19 262009 6

McLatchie, Harries, King and Williams. *ABC of Sports Medicine* 1995. ISBN 0 7279 0844 8

Cordingley J. Diving Emergencies and Cave Rescue. *Mountain Rescue Magazine.* July 2004; 9:20-21

Cordingley J. Suspected decompression sickness ("the bends") in divers: General advice for cave rescue teams and doctors 2005. Available from the British Cave Rescue Council

Blast injury

I am grateful to Dr Mike Brookes (Swaledale FRO) for this section.

This is a brief summary of blast injury. Why? Three reasons come to mind:

- The rescuer inadvertently being caught up in a terrorist attack
- Rescuers responding to disasters overseas
- Civil contingency work

An explosive blast forms a rapidly expanding wave of pressure - the blast wave - which moves at supersonic speeds away from the area of detonation. The blast wave displaces air, resulting in a blast wind, which follows the original blast wave. The blast wave may shatter glass, stone or any other material in proximity to the explosion; the blast wind will then disperse the fragments, causing injury. A blast will also generate heat, which can be sufficient to cause burns or ignite other structures causing a fire hazard.

Blast injuries can be divided into:

Primary (The effects of the blast wave)

The effects of the blast wave are most noted in areas of the body where fluid and air meet, especially the ears and the lungs. Up to 50% of people involved in a blast may have some damage to their hearing. This will cause difficulties in communication at the scene. The blast wave can also cause bruising and bleeding into the alveoli of the lungs; a condition called blast lung where the alveoli fill with fluid and the casualty develops respiratory distress. A form of acute respiratory distress can follow; so all casualties must be assessed in an Accident and Emergency department. The bowel and internal organs, such as the liver or spleen, can rupture.

Secondary (Fragment injuries from the blast wind)

Flying fragments will cause a variety of injuries all over the body. Secondary injury is the commonest cause of death in blast injury. These injuries will be highly contaminated with debris.

Tertiary (The effects of the blast wind)

The blast wind will throw people against structures, resulting in fractures, contusions, and amputations. In addition, structures, such as buildings, will collapse onto people causing entrapment and compartment syndromes.

Burns

The intense energy released by the explosion can cause flash burns, which may be superficial, however there is always a risk of inhalation burns. In addition, the energy release may cause a subsequent fire with associated burns and smoke inhalation injuries.

Psychological

The majority of people involved in an explosion are psychologically unprepared. First responders will undoubtedly encounter panic and disorientation amongst the survivors. Later consequences of the blast may include post-traumatic stress disorder (PTSD).

Management

Scene safety is paramount; the risk of further blasts should be assessed particularly as terrorist bombs can be designed to lure the Emergency Services to a second device. Casualties should be rapidly prioritised using the triage system described elsewhere in this book. This is important, as often there are many walking wounded. Controlling these casualties may allow the more seriously injured to arrive at hospital before it is overwhelmed. Treatment should follow the 'Safety, A, B, C, D, E' approach. Rescuers should pay particular attention to the airway - suspicion of burns, the chest - oxygen administration, and the abdomen - intra-abdominal trauma.

References

Chaloner E. Blast injury in enclosed spaces. BMJ 2005; 331:119-120

Depalma RG, Burris DG, Champion HR, Hodgson MJ. Blast injuries. NEJM 2005; 352:1335-45

Kendrick Extraction Device ® (KED®)

Suspension Induced Shock Syndrome

('Suspension Trauma' or 'Harness Induced Pathology')

Dr Xavier Ledoux, a colleague at ICAR Medcom, first alerted me to this syndrome. He studied it in 1988 when he was a MR doctor and caver; since then it has been difficult to justify research on healthy volunteers as will become plain. Indeed, I came close to inducing it myself during a practice involving feigning unconsciousness whilst dangling on a rope. Do not try it!

I am grateful to Paul Witheridge (team leader, Cumbria Ore Mines Rescue Unit) for comments and helping with the case study.

In essence, fit, healthy men have died suddenly when suspended in a harness, and at autopsy no cause was found. Cases have been reported in Rope Access workers, cavers climbing fixed ropes and paragliders. The condition may also be identical to 'Rescue Associated Collapse' - sudden death whilst vertically winching to a helicopter usually from the sea. Of course, many people spend hours suspended in harnesses, and come to no harm. The key to developing the syndrome is **passive hanging** whether because of unconsciousness (real or feigned) or exhaustion. Passive hanging is when the legs have no muscle tone - they are relaxed and not exerting any pressure.

Physiology and pathology

Under experimental conditions, subjects tend to collapse after 15 - 30 minutes of passive hanging; sometimes with very little warning. The shortest time to collapse is 6 minutes. Although a full body harness is tolerated longer than a chest harness or waist belt, it does not protect the subject from developing the syndrome. The most likely cause of the collapse is pooling of blood in the veins of the lower limbs, which occurs when the leg muscles are not contracting and pushing blood back towards the heart. (See Circulation - a simple faint starts with the same mechanism to a lesser degree; the faint then resolves the situation!) The body's circulation is able to compensate for the reduced blood flow to the heart for some time and then, suddenly, there is no blood in the heart to pump and a primitive reflex provokes asystole - a full-blown cardiac arrest. Risk factors are said to be dehydration, exposure to the cold and immersion. An extended period of suspension, that might occur as the person becomes exhausted, may lead to toxins accumulating in the blood of the legs. Sudden release from the suspension or changes in posture can allow this blood to flow unchecked back to the internal organs. The effect is similar to that in 'crush injury', with the potential for abnormal heart rhythms (including cardiac arrest) and renal failure.

Prevention

This is a training issue but in view of the lack of appreciation of the syndrome, I would make the following suggestions:

Use manikins instead of volunteers for practising 'unconscious-casualty' lowering skills.

During rope rescues, ensure that you have, and can use, foot loops so you can stand up and use your leg muscles.

Ideally have a colleague who can help you if you become stuck or exhausted.

Consider how you are going to quickly lower a rescuer to the ground should he become symptomatic.

Symptoms and signs

The casualty suddenly collapses with no warning. No pulse will be detected; unconsciousness and respiratory arrest will follow quickly. A period of faintness and nausea with a feeling of being ill may precede collapse in the conscious.

Management

All casualties (even if uninjured) hanging passively in a harness whether unconscious or exhausted are in a life-threatening position. As soon as safety allows, the casualty must be retrieved as a matter of extreme urgency. Once brought to the ground, do not lay the casualty down. Position them with the upper body elevated, ideally in a seated position. Assess using the 'Safety, A, B, C' approach.

Those suffering from even minor symptoms must be treated with extreme caution. Do not allow them to stand or walk – keep them in the seated position for at least 30 minutes. Oxygen should be administered during this phase and the casualty continuously observed. Cautious use of intravenous fluids may be appropriate.

If unconsciousness has developed, immediately lie the casualty horizontally. Use the BLS protocol adding in adjuncts, such as oxygen and ventilation aids as they become available). If available, an AED should be attached and the heart rhythm assessed immediately. If the casualty recovers consciousness, place in the recovery position with oxygen, and do not allow the vertical position again. If there are no signs of life after 30 minutes of BLS and the AED, if available, does not advise a shock, resuscitation can be stopped as the casualty has died.

Evacuation

A casualty having recovered from minor symptoms may be fit to walk off after 30 minutes. A stretcher evacuation will be preferable for any casualty who has suffered from a period of unconsciousness. This will require a period of slowly going from the seated position to the horizontal after the 30 minutes of sitting. A helicopter evacuation, for speed, may be appropriate but winching, even on a horizontal stretcher, should be avoided.

Extended Management

Advanced airway management and epinephrine (adrenaline) may be indicated if the rescuer is trained in Advanced Life Support. An intravenous fluid bolus could also be given to a casualty that is not recovering.

Case Study

This case is fictional but was developed from several real cases. It was commissioned for *Casualty Care in Mountain Rescue* to contribute a sense of real life and to draw attention to the dilemmas that occur in rescue work.

Two relatively inexperienced climbers (late 30's) decide to climb on a quiet crag. The weather is cool and overcast. The route is harder than they expected and they struggle up the first pitch. The second pitch leads them across the face, above an overhang, and then up a steep wall to the crux. The lead climber, while attempting to place protection, falls. The second manages to hold the fall; the leader comes to a stop just below the overhang. Unable to lower to the ground, the lead climber makes a number of abortive attempts to climb the rope, exhausting himself in the process.

At this point, with rain now falling, a second party arrive; realising the seriousness of the situation, they call the police by mobile phone.

The local MR team are on scene within twenty-five minutes and quickly descend to the now cold, distressed and semiconscious casualty. They make a quick assessment and note the casualty's paleness and unusually low pulse rate but cannot find any obvious injuries.

They carry out a 'snatch rescue' with the casualty, attached by lanyards, hanging between the rescuer's legs. Once on the ground the casualty is carefully disconnected, gently laid on a stretcher and covered with a casualty bag. A full secondary survey is begun but before it is completed the casualty becomes unconscious and suffers a cardiac arrest. The team attempt resuscitation but are unsuccessful and the casualty is pronounced dead at the scene.

Comments

The casualty was suffering from advanced suspension trauma. The team should have been aware of the potential for this condition from the outset. The risk of suspension trauma in this situation was compounded by the weather and the climber's exhaustion. There was no suggestion of any other injury from the history available. Had the team followed current recommendations, and kept the casualty propped up, would the casualty have gone on to develop a cardiac arrest?

References

Millar I. Suspension Induced Shock Syndrome May 2001 http://www.alpineclub-edm.org/accidents/SuspensionInducedShockSyndrome.htm (accessed August 2004)

Paul Seddon Harness suspension: review and evaluation of existing information. HSE report 2002. ISBN 0 7176 2526 5

Entrapment

Entrapment is a rare scenario in the UK; cases have occurred both above and below ground. It can be relative (uninjured but trapped by a rock fall) or absolute (part of the casualty is trapped under a rock). It is the latter that concerns the Casualty Carer. The most common part of the body to be trapped is the upper leg. A number of problems occur:

The casualty cannot be moved to safety.

A rapid evacuation is not possible.

Assessment may be from one direction only and injured parts can be hard to get to.

It may be impossible to release the casualty without amputation. (This is extremely rare, and would present huge logistic problems in acquiring the appropriately skilled Doctor and suitable equipment. The first place to go for help would be the nearest District General Hospital.)

In most cases it will be possible to free the trapped casualty by removing the fallen object though this may take considerable time. During this period, the casualty's condition will need to be stabilised as best as possible and a robust plan should be made for a rapid evacuation once the casualty is released. Use a 'Safety, A, B, C' approach as described in the primary survey and summarised on the next page:

Safety – is it safe to approach the casualty?

A - Ensure the airway is open (with cervical spine control if appropriate).

B - Ensure the breathing is adequate and start (and maintain) oxygen at 15 litres/minute via a non-rebreathing mask with a reservoir.

C - Optimise the circulation by stopping external bleeding and starting an intravenous infusion.

An intravenous infusion is very important and a skilled practitioner should be sought if at all possible. This may be a Doctor, paramedic or a trained mountain rescuer. A thigh that has been squashed under a heavy weight has damaged tissue from the skin to the central bone. As soon as the external pressure is released, the damaged tissues swell with fluid and toxins that have accumulated in the limb enter the central circulation; the casualty can go into shock rapidly. This can be fatal if the casualty has not had intravenous fluids before and during the release. Pain relief with Entonox® and morphine will often be needed.

Compartment syndrome

In addition to shock on release, a compartment syndrome can develop at the site of crush injury. It develops within 48 hours of the injury, and is caused by the bleeding and fluid leakage into the damaged muscle. In some areas, such as the lower leg and palm side of the forearm, tough membranes called fascia enclose the muscles. As the volume of the compartment increases, the fascia does not stretch so the pressure increases. At a certain pressure, blood cannot leave the compartment; further fluid accumulates and the pressure rises further until the blood supply to the muscle is compromised. A compartment syndrome is recognised by the severe, unremitting, throbbing pain at the site of injury. Stretching the damaged tissue may increase the pain. The area is swollen and tense with red, warm, shiny skin overlying the site of crushing. The nerves passing through the crushed area are damaged causing pins and needles and, in more severe cases, numbness and paralysis of the limb. Pulses distal (further from the heart) to the injury are usually present as the main arteries are outside the main muscle compartments. If absent, the artery has often been blocked by deformity at the site of a fracture. Acute traumatic compartment syndromes are a surgical emergency requiring the release of the pressure by surgical cuts (fasciotomy) within six hours of their onset.

Maximising the oxygen delivery to the damaged tissues by counteracting shock with large volumes of intravenous fluids and high flow supplementary oxygen have been shown to be crucial in reducing both the tissue loss and medical problems, notably kidney failure, following a crush injury. Delivering a casualty as fast as possible to definitive care must be planned and carried through.

References

Vincent N. Compartment syndromes in *Oxford textbook of Sports Medicine* 1994;.ISBN 0 19 262009 6

Pearse MF, Harry L, Nanchahal J. Acute compartment syndrome of the leg. *BMJ* 2002; 325:557-8

Gardena Pass, Dolomites, Italy. (2005)

Special Sports

Horse Riding, Mountain Biking, Skiing, Hang-Gliding and Paragliding

Most casualties that rescuers encounter will have been walking, climbing or scrambling, sustaining their injury by a stumble, slip or short fall. However, some sports involve greater speeds with the potential that the body will be subject to greater forces. It is important that the rescue team members consider this and take particular notice of the mechanism of injury. The sports involved are horse riding, mountain biking, skiing, and airborne sports (hang-gliding and paragliding). These activities account for about 6% of the total number of incidents reported to the MRC. If a casualty is injured whilst taking part in one of these sports, the chances of incurring a serious injury are higher than during fell walking – see figure below. Despite this, fatalities are rare in the UK. Paragliding in the Alps has a fatality rate of 3 per 1000 pilots per year!

Category of injury	Mountain biking (n=186)	Airborne (n=86)	Fell walking (n=1090)
Fatal	5 (3%)	10 (12%)	144 (6%)
Serious	67 (36%)	49 (57%)	751 (32%)
		Based on the MRC Incident Reports, 1997 - 2004	

What injuries are likely?

The table on the next page summarises the range of injuries causing death or serious injury in 72 casualties falling from mountain bikes and 59 from airborne accidents. Lower limb injuries remain common in all these sports but the chance of a spinal injury is particularly high for those injured during airborne sports. Upper limb injuries are common in riders because the arm is stretched out when they fall to the ground. A dislocated shoulder is characteristic. Multiple injury sites occur particularly in casualties of airborne sports; care has to be taken that axial (spinal, abdominal or chest) injuries are not missed when all the attention focuses on a limb injury.

Injury sites (serious/fatal)	Mountain biking (n=72)	Airborne (n=59)
Head and facial	16	5
Spine	12	28
Chest, abdomen and pelvis	4	17
Upper limb	9	7
Shoulder girdle	11	1
Lower limb	20	17
Based on the MRC Incident Reports, 1997 - 2004		

Summary of management

Manage using a 'Safety, A, B, C, D' approach as described in sections on the primary survey. Pay particular attention to stabilising the spine.

Try not to disturb the flying apparatus and the crash site as an investigation may follow to establish the cause of the accident. Take advice from the Police.

Helicopters in Mountain Rescue

The role of helicopters in mountain rescue has expanded since our first edition. Air Ambulances (AA) have multiplied and now cover most of the country. To everyone's relief, long stretcher evacuations, at least in daylight, seem likely to disappear. However, the harmonious integration of this valuable asset has been tested by communication, control and funding issues. Hopefully these problems will be resolved nationally or locally so the casualty receives the best service.

Saving life?

Before looking at the role of helicopters in mountain rescue, let us look at the whole of an Emergency Medical System (EMS) – the infrastructure and operations designed to manage a casualty before arriving at hospital, of which mountain rescue is a tiny proportion. (Even in Zermatt, mountain rescue is only 10% of the total!) Incorporating helicopters into an EMS (forming a HEMS) should result in casualties with time-critical injuries being transported to definitive (hospital) care in minutes rather than the hours it can take by the traditional ground ambulance route. Intuitively this must save lives though proof remains elusive. The evidence suggests that getting pre-hospital critical care (see Glossary) to the casualty is the most beneficial aspect of incorporating helicopters into an EMS. Fortunately, as you will see, both the Search & Rescue (SAR) and AA have the potential to deliver the equipment and the skilled operator to the accident scene. Worldwide, helicopters operating in an EMS have two times the accident rate and 3.5 times the fatality rates of helicopters operating in other capacities. The risk factors have been documented and include pilot error, night flying and poor weather. It is reassuring that pilots in the UK are being trained in ways to combat the 'red mist' or 'adrenaline rush' we all respond to in an emergency situation.

There has been no research published on the benefits of helicopters in mountain rescue. Surely here, where the time-to-scene is reduced, where the evacuation route itself carries danger and evacuation time is slashed, there is the strongest case (and greatest chance) for showing helicopters 'save lives'. However, the helicopter accident rate must be balanced against the potential benefit for the casualty. From the MR perspective, the helicopter accident rate is reflected in the death of rescuers - a topic that has become of increasing concern to the International Commission for Alpine Rescue (ICAR). ICAR's incomplete data set, that is potentially open to bias, shows an alarming 29% of rescuers that die during a rescue operation do so in helicopter accidents; in the UK, the percentage is 20%.

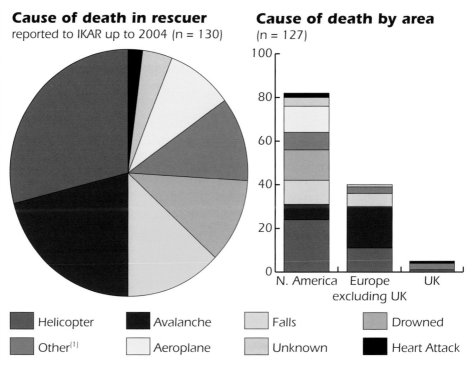

Cause of death in rescuer
reported to IKAR up to 2004 (n = 130)

Cause of death by area
(n = 127)

| Helicopter | Avalanche | Falls | Drowned |
| Other[1] | Aeroplane | Unknown | Heart Attack |

[1] hypothermia, blizzard, car accident, rock fall, rope failure

The decision to use a helicopter is not straightforward. It involves geographic information (often local), casualty data, helicopter characteristics and an appreciation of other resources. Getting the correct resource to the casualty and in the appropriate time through an integrated EMS is the only acceptable way of managing the risk. Despite this, no national guidance has been developed for the operation of air ambulances and only recently has an algorithm been published on the appropriate use of air ambulances. ICAR has published a paper on the medical considerations in the use of helicopters from the mountain rescue perspective. Critical incidents have been identified in the past and continue. Many have a common and recurring theme. From the medical perspective, these are an incomplete assessment and protection of the casualty (recently focusing on spinal care), and an understanding of the medical resources and equipment available from MR. From the operational perspective many more worrying incidents have occurred from poor communication and planning of the helicopter role and, recently, the duplicity of helicopter response.

Having both Ambulance and Police systems active at one time compounds the problem. For both SAR helicopters and air ambulances, MR operations are only a minor part of their workload and it is unrealistic that the EMS envisaged in the ICAR paper would be appropriate for all their operations. Not withstanding this, there must be an acknowledgement of the central role of MR within the EMS at all stages of the rescue. Engaging in clinical governance and multi-agency forums, as well as supporting national bodies such as UKSAR, must be the way forward. Let's keep the UK at the bottom of the rescuer's death league table!

References

Nicholl J, Turner N, Stevens K, et al. A review of costs and benefits of Helicopter Emergency Ambulance Services in England and Wales (2003). Accessed at http://www.shef.ac.uk/uni/academic/R-Z/scharr/mcru/reports.htm

Black JJM, Ward ME, Lockey DJ. Appropriate use of helicopters to transport trauma patients from incident scene to hospital in the United Kingdom: an algorithm. *Emerg Med J* 2004; 21:355-361

Tomazin I. Kovacs T. International Commission for Mountain Emergency Medicine. Medical considerations in the use of helicopters in mountain rescue. *High Altitude Medicine & Biology* 2003; 4:479-83

Search & Rescue (SAR) helicopters - a view from an experienced winch man

Mountain rescue incidents offer many challenges ranging from environmental to medical problems. Not surprisingly MRT members are required to master a wide range of skills in order to give the casualty the best possible chance of uneventful recovery. Many rescues are technically very difficult and throw up a number of obstacles, which the rescuer must overcome to achieve a successful outcome. Some of those obstacles can be potentially so time consuming that the welfare of a casualty can be seriously jeopardized. The helicopter is invaluable when time is of the essence. Helicopters are not however the panacea. MRT members should be aware of the limitations and disadvantages of helicopters. Thankfully they are relatively few. The medical qualifications of the crew are more advanced than in years past. A casualty can be monitored and treated to a high standard both on the hillside and when airborne.

Advantages

Time will always be a factor when treating a severely injured climber; the quicker a casualty reaches definitive care, the better the prognosis. Helicopters do offer rapid evacuation but only if they are involved early. It takes time to scramble a helicopter to an incident so the sooner that is done the better. Valuable time can be wasted dispatching an assessment party when the initial report suggests urgency. In such cases dispatch of personnel and a helicopter request should be made simultaneously. The helicopter can always be turned back.

A helicopter can rapidly deploy rescuers and equipment to a search area or the scene of an incident. It can also retrieve the same and thereby enable an MRT to re-equip in readiness for further calls. Unfortunately, the arrival of a helicopter should never be taken as read. Several factors influence this, most notably the weather. Other possible factors include serviceability and higher priority incidents.

Hazards

Even when on scene the helicopter can sometimes present one or two problems. The most obvious is the down wash created by such a large machine. In some situations this can be a hazard to the casualty. An unstable rock face can so easily be made more so by the small hurricane generated by the aircraft. Rescuers' equipment can also fall foul of such an environment if not properly looked after. Crews are well aware of such hazards and take every precaution to prevent such situations arising.

There will be some occasions when medical care might have to be suspended during evacuation by winch. Cardiopulmonary resuscitation (CPR) can still be administered but probably to a lesser standard. The speed of the winch however ensures minimal time in such a situation. Once on board, a high standard of paramedical care is available.

Certain medical conditions require particular consideration because of the effect of change in altitude. These are generally related to injuries to the chest especially where a tension pneumothorax is suspected. Some advanced airway management adjuncts could also be affected by altitude. For example, endotracheal (ET) tube and Laryngeal Mask Airway cuffs may need their pressure reducing. Those teams that still use inflatable splints should ensure that the winchman is given a thorough patient hand-over in order that he may properly monitor these splints throughout the flight. It is generally thought that operations at altitudes encountered by UK SAR helicopters tend to have a minimal effect on the above conditions. However crews are well aware of the potential complications.

SAR crew medical qualifications and equipment

To ensure quality casualty care the helicopter is now very well equipped with highly trained personnel and up-to-date medical equipment. Both rear-crew members possess a minimum qualification of Emergency Medical Technician (EMT - Defibrillator trained). Winchmen are required to achieve Advanced Life Support (ALS) qualifications within their first tour of duty on SAR helicopters i.e. within two years. Additionally, the majority of winchmen have attended Basic Trauma Life Support (BTLS), Advanced Trauma Life Support (ATLS) and ALS courses. In the past Northumbria Ambulance Authority and the National Trauma Training centre have provided medical training. It is now provided by a specific course run by

Specialist Medical Services. All paramedic-trained winchmen are qualified to intubate, use a Laryngeal Mask Airway, insert oro/nasopharyngeal airways, perform an emergency tracheotomy, defibrillate, cannulate and administer intravenous morphine and fluids. All SAR rear-crew are required to revalidate their qualification every three years and are expected to demonstrate a minimum level of competence set by the training staff.

The equipment carried on SAR helicopters is comparable to that on NHS Accident and Emergency ambulances. The comprehensive kit contains the minimum equipment necessary to treat life-threatening injuries. The following drugs and monitors are carried:

Drugs	Monitors
Cyclimorph® Naloxone Diazepam Heparin Glucagon Glucose 50% GTN spray Adrenaline 1: 1,000 Adrenaline 1: 10,000 Salbutamol	Laerdal FR2 Biphasic AED Propaq (ECG, NIBP, SaO_2, temperature and printer) Nelcor pulse oximeter End-tidal CO_2 detectors
	Medical gases and fluids
	Oxygen Entonox® Warm fluid (crystalloid & colloid)

Destination Hospitals

Helicopters have the ability to deliver a casualty rapidly to definitive care. However there are occasions when the destination hospital is not the one initially intended. A number of factors contribute ranging from the injury itself to the weather. The closest hospital may not always be the quickest or even the most appropriate. SAR crews take wide-ranging advice on the choice of hospital including the views of the MR Doctor and leader. However, the aircraft captain will always have the final say. He is the only person able to take into account the performance of the helicopter!

Conclusion

A SAR helicopter, whilst not always the most appropriate or able to assist, can be a valuable asset to the mountain rescuer and a life-saver to some casualties. This is made possible not just because of the unique abilities of the aircraft itself but also because of the high standard of equipment and training of the crews. A helicopter can only be effective if utilized early. It is better to request a helicopter and turn it back than not to consider one and lose a casualty.

I am grateful to Mike Holman (RAF Boulmer) for updating this section.

Air Ambulance helicopters

Within most regions of the UK, 'air ambulances' operate alongside the traditional NHS land-based ambulances. Air ambulance schemes, funded and operated by private charities, usually work in conjunction with, and are tasked by, the local ambulance control.

Air ambulances fly with either one or two pilots, usually very experienced and with a previous career flying military or police helicopters. The on-board medical staff varies from scheme to scheme, but includes paramedics, BASICS doctors, anaesthetists and Accident and Emergency doctors in training. All staff, whilst very well trained for the pre-hospital treatment of trauma, may not necessarily be familiar with or prepared for the mountain environment.

A number of different aircraft are used throughout the UK, the most common being the twin-engined Bolkow 105 DBS. The aircraft has space for two pilots and four passengers. Casualties are loaded onto the aircraft

via the tail, and there is no facility for winching. All carry a full medical kit including portable ventilator, medical gasses and patient monitoring equipment. The Bolkow 105 DBS can fly for approximately two hours and has a maximum speed of 140 miles per hour. This compares to the RAF Sea King with its crew of four, a carrying capacity of up to nineteen passengers, a maximum speed of 143mph and a radius of action of 280 miles. The Air Ambulance at 13.45m in length is considerably shorter than the Sea King at 18.9m, an advantage in the urban setting that is probably lost on the mountain side. Air ambulances, due to funding and equipment constraints, usually fly during daylight hours only and in good weather conditions.

In the mountainous regions of England and Wales, air ambulances are already working in conjunction with mountain rescue teams, and as the number of these schemes increases, this is likely to become a more common occurrence.

I am grateful to Dr Andy McAlea (Doctor for Penrith MRT and volunteer doctor for the Great North Air Ambulance) for this section.

Treating sick or injured animals

The only animals you should really deal with are dogs; either your own or those belonging to the injured party. In the event of encountering an injured horse, it is advisable that you contact the nearest available veterinary surgeon for help and advice. Your safety is an important factor as an injured or confused equine may react unpredictably and violently.

With farm animals, it is wise to contact the relevant farmer, as they will not thank you if your treatment of their animal does not comply with their own ideas.

It is prudent for each rescue base to have a telephone contact number for the nearest veterinary practice that deals with both large and small animals.

Animal restraint

The first and most important factor to consider when approaching any ill, injured or distressed animal is to establish careful restraint. This allows a safe assessment to be carried out. Fear, pain and confusion are all trigger factors for aggression in dogs. Their first instinct is to lash out and bite a stranger who, in examining or treating an injury, causes them further pain. It is therefore wise to apply a tape muzzle to every dog no matter how friendly looking it is. Use a strip of bandage material or a shoelace. Make a half hitch and, in one movement, loop this over the dog's nose whilst tightening the knot. Wrap round the nose again and tie in a bow. It is important to tie the knot very tight as dogs have extremely strong jaws and can otherwise prise the bandage open and nip you!

The dog's immediate reaction will be to use its paws to pull the muzzle off. The person restraining the dog should bear this in mind. The most successful restraint is shown on the next page with the dog held firmly and close to the person's body.

To remove the temporary muzzle safely, pull on one loose end of the bow firmly and it should release and slide off the end of the nose. Do this at arms length as instinct drives the dog to nip as soon as its jaws are released.

Common problems

Insect Stings and Bites

Most stings occur on the head and paws and often cause an acute and severe swelling. Anaphylaxis is very rare in animals. Treat with a cold compress at the site of the sting; only if very severe and uncomfortable consider giving both aspirin and adrenaline.

Sudden Onset Paraplegia

Any dog of any age, size and fitness may develop sudden onset paraplegia (loss of use of hind limbs). The cause is usually a prolapsed intervertebral disc (slipped disc). The condition is acutely painful and morphine (see below for dose) may be administered. The dog should be transported, with minimal spinal movement, to the nearest veterinary practice as soon as possible.

Seizures

These should be distinguished from syncope (fainting) episodes. A seizure will usually last two minutes, during which time the dog will lie flat on its side, with the legs either fully extended, or in a paddling motion. They may foam at the mouth or champ their jaws. When a dog faints, it lies motionless on its side and the body will be floppy in comparison. Following a two minute seizure there is often a ten minute period of complete behaviour change, during which time the dog will be very confused and disorientated; this may lead to aggression. It is best to keep a distance and keep very quiet to allow the dog to recover alone. Upon recovery the dog will seem completely normal and does not require any treatment. The dog should see a vet on itsreturn home. As in humans, any fit lasting longer than ten minutes should be considered as status epilepticus and emergency treatment started. Follow a 'Safety, A, B, C approach'. Oxygen should be supplemented via a human face mask where possible. Rectal diazepam (10mg) should be administered every 10 minutes, up to 5 times if necessary, until the nearest veterinary practice is reached. A careful eye should be kept on body temperature (normal is 37.2°C to 39.2°C). Hyperthermia is a common complication after a seizure of 10 minutes. Wetting the whole dog with cold water will help to cool the body.

Heat Stroke

This is a common condition that can occur in any dog. Dogs kept in cars on sunny days are at particular risk. It can also occur if a dog is outdoors on a sunny day with no access to shelter. Over-exertion is a rare cause in hot and humid weather conditions.

The early signs are vigorous panting, dry mucous membranes and a raised body temperature (40.5°C - 43°C). As the condition worsens, vomiting and diarrhoea commence and the dog may have a seizure. Eventually coma and then death occur.

Initial treatment ideally involves finding a place of shade or providing shelter from the sun. The dog's coat should be soaked in cold water. Cold compresses need to be applied to armpit and groin areas. Massaging the body, especially concentrating on the extremities can help the cooled blood return to the core more easily. The goal is to decrease the body temperature to 39°C in 30-60 minutes. To prevent over-cooling, treatment should be stopped when the core temperature reaches 39.5°C. Following successful treatment, veterinary attention is still indicated as organ failure can occur three to five days later.

Lameness

Look at the dog as a whole before concentrating on the injured limb as the dog may have suffered trauma and have a chest or head injury. These would take priority. If a limb is non-weight bearing then assess for signs of a fracture. If there is instability, acute pain or an obvious fracture in the lower part of a limb (elbow and below in the forelimb, stifle and below in the hind limb) then apply a support bandage. (See next page for an anatomy drawing.) If the problem is located above this, bandaging the limb is contraindicated, as the pendulum effect will aggravate the injury. However if the fracture is open (compound) then a sterile dressing should be applied and covered by a support bandage.

Lacerations

Apply a sterile dressing and then apply a pressure bandage. It is preferable not to apply a tourniquet in dogs. Bandages to paws and tails should be securely fastened with Elastoplast sticking to the fur to avoid being shaken or 'wagged' off.

Lacerations near or involving the eyes, or indeed any traumatic condition of the eye, should have a saline soaked pad applied with pressure bandage over the top - a figure of eight technique around the neck and jaw works well. The diagram above shows how an ear should be bandaged.

Morphine dose for dogs

Use to provide strong pain relief, for example in a fracture. Suitable injection sites are shown below.

For dosing without an accurate weight, it is easier to think of dogs in 4 categories: small (<10kg) e.g. terriers; medium (20kg) e.g. border collie; large (30kg) e.g. Labrador and extra large (40+kg) e.g. rottweiler.

The dose of morphine is 0.2mg/kg intramuscular or subcutaneous (Small - 1-2mg; medium - 4mg; large - 6mg; extra large - 8+mg). Higher doses lead to sedation. The peak effect is 90 minutes after an intramuscular injection.

Side effects include respiratory depression, vomiting and constriction of pupils. Do not use in case of head injury.

Case studies

No joke! The editor has done two dog rescues since the 1st edition. The first to a Grand Saint Bernard with heat stroke and the second to a terrier that fell about 100 metres. The terrier had facial injuries and would not walk. He(?) was evacuated by stretcher and transferred by car to the local Vet. Though the doctor over-diagnosed maxillary fractures (on the basis of subconjunctival bleeding with no visible posterior limit in both eyes), the vet was most impressed. The terrier made a full recovery; the owner was most grateful and the vet got the biggest cheque!

I am grateful to Elizabeth J. Allan BVetMed MRCVS for this section.

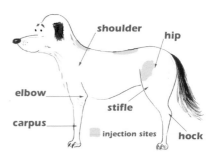

'Foot and Mouth declared'
Blackmount, Scotland. (2001)

Monitoring and the use of Drugs

Objectives
To appreciate the role of electronic monitoring of the casualty
To understand how to use a range of drugs

Monitoring: its uses in Mountain Rescue

The body is very complicated; it can tolerate many changes and threats to its survival by adapting. When is the casualty seriously compromised? We can examine the patient, but can we measure a factor that will tell us about the seriousness of the situation? Traditionally, measuring the pulse, blood pressure, respiratory rate and level of consciousness have been used to gauge the severity of injury. These parameters also tell us if our treatment is being effective. Each can be of great value but, in isolation, interpreting their importance can be complicated. For example, is the high pulse rate due to loss of blood or from pain? This simple question can be difficult to answer. On the side of a mountain, factors such as fear and the pain threshold vary considerably from one casualty to the next. Also consider the difficulties of performing a thorough examination and an accident mechanism that frequently produces multiple injuries. It is not surprising that the seriousness of the accident is often under- or over-estimated. All mountain rescue doctors have stories of being 'led up the garden path'! Can monitoring equipment help and can it be used in mountain rescue?

Monitoring equipment adds to taking a history and examining the casualty. It can never replace talking to, looking at and examining the casualty. The aim of monitoring equipment is to aid the initial assessment and to monitor the effects of our treatment. Knowing the equipment, and particularly its limitations, can be as important as the information collected. Over-reliance is a worse sin than not using it at all. Indeed electronic monitoring, as opposed to clinical monitoring of vital signs, can still be regarded as optional for most casualties. The parameters that can be measured include: blood pressure; oxygen saturation (SaO_2 by pulse oximetry); electrical activity of the heart (electrocardiogram); temperature; and end-tidal carbon dioxide concentration.

Propaq® in the 1980's – still working unlike the MAST!

Blood Pressure

Measuring the blood pressure is enshrined in medical practice. It reflects the state of the circulation. Is the pump (the heart) pumping and is there enough fluid (blood) to pump? We have seen in the chapter on the circulation that simple ideas like these are inadequate to describe the changes of shock. Having said that, a normal or high blood pressure is likely to be better than a low one, and particularly a low and falling one.

Blood pressure (BP) is measured either directly (invasive) by cannulating the artery or, more usually, indirectly (non-invasive) by compressing an artery. The pressure needed to just stop blood flow through the artery (systolic BP) and the maximum external pressure that does not cause turbulence or pressure fluctuations in the measuring cuff (diastolic BP) are measured in millimetres of mercury (mmHg). The inflatable cuff must encircle 80% of the arm as shown.

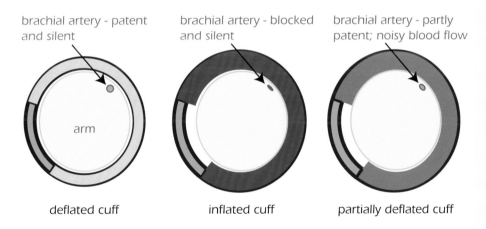

brachial artery - patent and silent

brachial artery - blocked and silent

brachial artery - partly patent; noisy blood flow

arm

deflated cuff   inflated cuff   partially deflated cuff

The BP is written: systolic / diastolic with a normal value being 120/ 80. It is usual to apply the cuff on the upper arm just above the elbow, and use the vibrations or sounds from the brachial artery. The standard hospital technique using a stethoscope is rarely practical on the fell, as external noise and exposing the arm combine to make each measurement laborious and inaccurate. An alternative method to record the systolic BP is to blow the cuff up until the radial or brachial pulse disappear (by palpation), and then slowly let the cuff down noticing when the pulse can be felt again. This is the systolic BP. (See page 107.) Modern monitors can overcome some of the problems. However kinks in the tubing are frequent and many false readings occur. To ensure as accurate a reading as possible, make sure, whichever method you are using, that the arm is straight, the cuff is applied directly onto the skin and follow the manufacturer's instructions as to where the sensor should be in relationship to the brachial artery. Wrist and finger BP measuring devices are not designed for casualties with injuries or illnesses and cannot be recommended.

There is a 'rule of thumb' that requires no equipment! If a pulse is palpable at the wrist, the systolic blood pressure is greater than 80 mm Hg. If palpable in the neck, it is greater than 60 mm Hg. There is much to recommend such a simple technique though it has been questioned in an observational study as overestimating the systolic BP and, therefore, underestimating the degree of blood loss.

What do the BP figures mean?

In the acute situation we can limit ourselves to the systolic blood pressure. A normal resting value is between 110 and 140 mm Hg. During exercise the systolic pressure often rises, perhaps to 160 or 180 mm Hg. The pulse rate also rises to around 160 beats per minute. Both return to their normal resting values within minutes of stopping. If we combine the systolic blood pressure with the pulse rate (normal resting value of 60 to 80 per minute) and history of the incident, we can start to make some tentative guesses as to what might be going on.

	Low systolic (<100mmHg)	High systolic (>140mmHg)
High pulse rate > 100 min^{-1}	Significant blood loss Other causes of shock (septic, anaphylaxis)	Pain Fear and anxiety Myocardial infarction
Low pulse rate < 60 min^{-1}	Hypothermia Heart problems 'Spinal shock'	Brain compression

Uses

Single measurements are harder to interpret than trends. A falling blood pressure and a rising pulse suggests continuing blood loss; a grave situation away from a hospital and a skilled surgeon. Figures returning to normal suggest adequate pain relief and reassurance. Traditionally, a casualty suffering from trauma with a low systolic blood pressure and a high pulse would have an intravenous transfusion started; this may be within the capabilities of mountain rescuers and is discussed further in the circulation chapter.

Limitations

Measuring blood pressure is time consuming and requires skill particularly when the systolic pressure is low. Perhaps it is only worthwhile when intravenous infusion is practical and necessary. Finding a low systolic BP in a shocked casualty emphasizes the urgent evacuation to hospital.

Conclusions

Measuring a blood pressure is an entrenched part of medicine. Integrating it into the assessment of the casualty, along with a pulse rate, remains a valuable tool. However attempts to return them to normal, in the mountain rescue setting, may lead to delay and excessive use of intravenous fluid, both of which may be harmful. Measuring BP should never delay an evacuation.

Pulse Oximetry

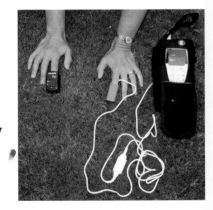

Pulse oximetry is a way of looking at the oxygen supply to the tissues. Potentially it can tell us that the oxygen intake from the lungs and its distribution around the body in the circulation is 'OK'. If the oxygen supply to the vital organs is adequate, things can't be too bad! This fundamental argument makes pulse oximetry an attractive monitoring device. In anaesthetics, and other critical care situations, it is regarded as essential. Pre-hospital uses have grown as the equipment has become smaller and more robust. Two models are illustrated above – a self-contained finger type and a larger 'remote' type. See page 351 for a price guide.

The oxygen content of arterial blood can be measured in two ways:

1) The partial pressure of oxygen in arterial blood can be directly measured. This is the most accurate method but it is not practical outside hospital.

2) When the haemoglobin in blood takes up oxygen to form oxyhaemoglobin, the haemoglobin changes colour from blue to red.

This colour change can be detected by eye. For example, the fingers develop a blue discolouration (cyanosis) when the skin circulation is slow because of cold-induced vasoconstriction. In this situation the underlying tissues have a good blood supply; the observation is of no importance. However, it is important if the central, core blood is cyanosed. The best place to look for this is the tongue. Unfortunately detecting cyanosis depends on many factors such as the ambient light and whether the casualty is anaemic (a low haemoglobin concentration). It is very difficult to detect in casualties with trauma and has largely been abandoned. However pulse oximetry uses the colour change in the blood but instead of analysing the overall colour, the electronics extract the pulsatile component of the signal. This is less than 5% of the total but gives a measure of arterial oxygen content. By the time a figure has been calculated so many assumptions and approximations have been used that the machine and probe have had to be calibrated rather than relying on basic principles.

What do the figures mean?

The read-out is a percentage of the possible total oxygen saturation (SaO_2) of the blood. Normally arterial blood is 96 to 98% saturated. Falls in arterial oxygen saturation to 90 to 93% indicate that some parts of the body, particularly the brain, are becoming short of oxygen. This may be reflected in the casualty becoming restless, agitated and uncooperative. At lower levels, the conscious level declines. (See page 86.)

Uses

A casualty with low oxygen saturation should be carefully assessed. Is the airway open? Is the breathing adequate? A falling reading can give an early warning of a problem with, for example, the airway becoming blocked. It is nice to see the oxygen saturation increase when oxygen is administered; perhaps when oxygen is in short supply the reading could be used to determine priority.

Limitations

Anything that reduces the pulsatile element of the signal predisposes to inaccurate readings. Examples are a casualty with a low blood pressure, a probe placed on a cold part of the casualty or an artefact from the probe moving on the skin. The electronics try to overcome these problems; even seeing a pulse wave on a monitor does not necessarily mean that the reading is accurate. In difficult conditions, the time to obtain a reading and to register a change can be surprisingly long. In mountain rescue, these factors often combine to prevent a useful reading being obtained. Carbon monoxide poisoning, which could occur in a smoky mountain hut, misleads the monitor entirely!

Conclusion

Pulse oximetry is a great idea. As the monitors have become smaller, it is hard not to carry one. In the casualties where knowing the oxygen saturation is most useful, the readings are least reliable.

Electrocardiogram (ECG)

The ECG is a record of the electrical activity of the heart. Not all ECGs are the same. To interpret the actual state of the heart muscle and its electrical 'wiring' a 12-lead ECG is needed. It is called a 12-lead because 12 different 'electrical views' of the heart are obtained. A simpler ECG trace, using three electrode positions, is more commonly used outside hospital. The usual position and colour of the electrodes is shown in the diagram below but this is not critical.

The information gained from a 3-lead ECG is limited to the heart rate and pattern of electrical activity. Damage to the heart muscle, such as occurs after a myocardial infarction, can be picked up but you have to be cautious not to read too much into these simple traces.

The heart rate is measured in beats per minute. Many things affect this. A short list would include exertion, pain, anxiety, blood loss, heart damage, drugs and fitness.

The pattern of electrical activity is as diverse as the number of people and the situations you record. Fortunately we are only concerned with three types of pattern as shown below. (See page 263 for further traces.)

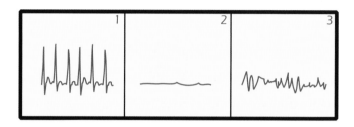

1.   Patterns with a regular spike of activity. This is part of the normal trace. It is used to count the rate. A pulse should be felt just after the spike. If not: Are you feeling in the right place? Is the blood pressure low? Is the hypothermia severe?

2.   No pattern - a straight line. This is asystole - a flabby non-contracting heart. There can be no pulse and the casualty will be unconscious. If the casualty is conscious, the monitor isn't connected properly!

3.   An irregular pattern with bizarre and random activity. This may be ventricular fibrillation (VF) in which case the casualty will be, or will rapidly become, unconscious. Shivering or movement of the electrode leads can reproduce an irregular pattern. The casualty will be conscious; do not rely on the monitor alone.

Uses

The information, taken with an appropriate assessment of the casualty, can be used to decide which is the best treatment option. This is what an automatic external defibrillator (AED) does. VF can be effectively treated with DC shock; asystole cannot.

A more controversial use would be in helping decisions as to when to stop cardiac massage. In practice, unless an underlying problem can be identified and treated, only VF has a reasonable survival rate, and then only when a defibrillator is at hand. In hypothermia, when the pulse is often impalpable, knowledge of the electrical activity can also help to direct treatment.

Limitations

Obtaining a useful trace can be difficult when the casualty is wet and shivering. The equipment is expensive and must be handled with care to prevent damage.

Conclusion

An ECG is useful, indeed essential, when resuscitation is moving to the 'advanced level', where basic skills are supplemented by the use of drugs. It has a role in supporting those difficult decisions such as when to attempt resuscitation and when to stop.

End Tidal Carbon Dioxide Concentration (ETCO$_2$)

The concentration of carbon dioxide is much higher in air breathed out than air breathed in. This difference can be detected. The type of trace seen is shown below.

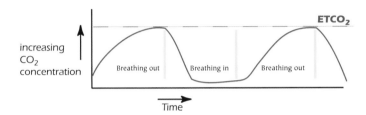

Uses

Measuring the end tidal carbon dioxide concentration can be useful in two situations.

I.   When a casualty has an endotracheal tube or a laryngeal mask in place. Detecting the higher concentration of carbon dioxide on exhalation helps to confirm that the device is positioned correctly and that the air coming out has been in the lungs, not the stomach! If the device is knocked out of position the monitor should pick this up in one breath.

2.   The ETCO$_2$ is a measure of the effectiveness of ventilation. In some situations, such as severe head injuries, it is important to maintain the ETCO$_2$ within a tight range (4.5 - 5KPa) to protect the brain from secondary damage.

Limitations

Measuring the end tidal carbon dioxide concentration is most useful when advanced airway techniques are used in extreme circumstances - a rare scenario in mountain rescue. RAF Search and Rescue helicopters carry the equipment; few, if any teams, do!

Temperature

There are many ways of measuring temperature. These range from low reading mercury thermometers, costing a few pounds, to electronic probes which can cost hundreds. Unfortunately it is not the equipment that prevents an accurate reading but the practicalities of getting to the core. (The core temperature is the one we are interested in.) Strategies tried include:

1. A low reading mercury (or digital) thermometer used in the mouth (assuming the casualty hasn't had a hot drink) to rule out severe hypothermia. The figure you measure will almost certainly be lower than the true core temperature by an unknown amount but it can't be higher. Remember to shake the mercury thermometer 'down' before use.

2. A tympanic (ear drum) probe can be used in the same way. False low readings have been disappointingly common. There are two types of 'ear canal' thermometers - the *epitympanic type* illustrated on page 236-7, which seals the ear canal and waits for its temperature to equilibrate with the surrounding tissues, and an *infrared-based* probe (as shown here), which is commonly used in hospital and by family doctors. This gives a near-instant reading but its use outside this setting has not been assessed.

3. Obtaining a rectal temperature. This is inappropriate on the fell. A reliable reading requires confirmation that the measuring device is in contact with the bowel wall and not - how do I put this? - in a large, cold lump of faeces. Team members should not perform forensic measurements at the request of the Police.

4. A temperature probe inserted deep into the nasal cavity or, if unconscious, oesophagus can give stable and continuous temperature readings. Many of the probes need to be kept in place for 9 to 12 minutes before a true reading is obtained. This is currently the only accepted strategy for decision making in hypothermia.

Uses

Obtaining a core temperature often gives surprising results and focuses the team on the management of hypothermia. Casualties can cool very quickly even in the summer. It is easy for the rescuer to forget hypothermia and neglect to insulate the casualty or take unneccesary risks by performing rapid movements of the casualty's limbs. Mild hypothermia has been associated with poorer outcomes for a whole host of conditions and should be avoided if at all possible.

Limitations

Apart from the difficulties of measuring the core temperature, there is little a mountain rescuer can do beyond insulating the casualty.

Conclusion

Temperature measurement is often of interest but is rarely practical or useful at directing treatment.

References

Ellerton JA. The Use of a portable monitor in Mountain Rescue. *Journal of The British Association for Immediate Care* 1992; 15:19-22

Deakin CD, Low JL. Accuracy of the advanced trauma life support guidelines for predicting systolic blood pressure using carotid, femoral, and radial pulses: observational study. *BMJ* 2000; 321;673-674

Berger A. How does it work? Oscillatory blood pressure monitoring devices. *BMJ* 2001; 323:919

Price guide (2006)	(£)	See page
All-in-one monitor eg. Propaq®	3-7000	10 342
ECG monitor	600	
BP monitor	1-300	
Pulse oximeter self-contained 'remote'	300 800	345 345
Temperature low-reading mecury digital epitympanic infrared	2 6 300 60	350 236 350

Phil (Eden Valley MC), Almscliffe, Yorkshire.

The use of drugs in Mountain Rescue

Fifteen years ago this topic consisted of one drug, morphine. Though it remains the most important drug, many teams now carry a whole selection of agents to treat a wide variety of conditions. Following the introduction of the MRC Drugs List in 1991 an evolving process has culminated in the MRC Drug Framework that describes the administrative and legal basis in detail. It is a shame that an outline of the Framework needs to be included in a practical manual but drug administration is often embroiled in non-clinical issues. For those amongst you who take fright, remember the clinical advantages and effectiveness of the drugs we use, and plough on for the sake of the casualty. I have also added a section on which drugs are being used, and raise a question as to a future that might surprise you!

MRC Drug Framework

This section and the description of the MRC Drug List that follows are provisional – as we go to press, the law is changing (following a lengthy campaign by Dave Allan) and the MRC Medical Subcommittee will need to revise the MRC Drugs Framework in November 2006 and May 2007. Details will be posted on the MRC website (http://www.mountain.rescue.org.uk/) and these should be read by team members wishing to use drugs as part of the treatment of the casualty.

The MRC Drug Framework has evolved over 15 years in response to the administrative and legal concerns of team members. Only in the last 2 years has it been recognisable as an entity though, in truth, it has no new features beyond what has already been announced. The Framework is shown on the next page.

The starting point, at the top, is that any team member wishing to give a drug must have a current MRC Casualty Care certificate. This came into force in 2004 in response to concerns that **only** the Casualty Care certificate tested team member's knowledge of drugs.

Drug supply, possession (in the case of Controlled Drugs) and administration are governed by the Medicines Act 1968 and Misuse of Drugs Act 1971. A good practical guide, called 'Medicines, Ethics and Practice', to the legal restrictions is available on the Royal Pharmaceutical Society of Great Britain website (http://www.rpsgb.org.uk/members/publications/socpubl.html#m).

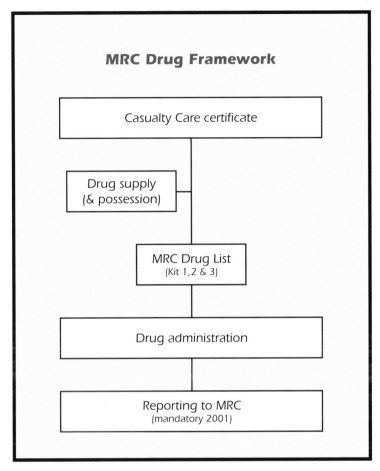

MRC Drug Framework

Casualty Care certificate

Drug supply
(& possession)

MRC Drug List
(Kit 1,2 & 3)

Drug administration

Reporting to MRC
(mandatory 2001)

By the time you read this (September 2006), the law should have changed and only drugs in the *'Prescription only'* (POM) group will require a written order from a medically-qualified doctor for the pharmacy to supply the mountain rescue team. The exception are morphine and buprenorphine where the 'morphine' Licence allows a team to directly purchase these two drugs. This rather bizarre arrangement is the consequence of the Licence. However, in practical terms, the supplying pharmacist is going to be rather nervous of dispensing morphine and usually a doctor has to act as an intermediary. If no local doctor is prepared to acquire and supply the drugs to a team then the MRC Medical Officer does this. All drugs are bought privately - an NHS prescription is not allowed - and charged to the team.

By 2007, it is envisaged that a *Casualty Care* certified team member will have the ability to administer any drug to a casualty so *'far as is necessary for the treatment of the sick or injured persons.'* The MRC Drugs List will still exist and will (I suspect) describe drugs 'approved' by the MRC Medical Subcommittee and for which the MRC has indemnity insurance. However teams with a Doctor will have more freedom as team members will be legally administering the drug directly and not on behalf of the MRC Medical Officer or team Doctor. It goes without saying that the MRC and mountain rescue teams must have robust training, supervision and clinical governance procedures in place if mountain rescue is to continue to enjoy such a privileged position. It is likely that the obligation on team members to report drug use to the MRC, via the Incident Report, will remain.

MRC Drug List

These drugs are supported by the Medical Subcommittee of the MRC and, if used correctly, are under the terms of insurance issued by the MRC. Team members with a current MRC Casualty Care certificate are encouraged to use them appropriately. The list is reviewed every three years and published on the MRC website. If necessary the list is updated through the minutes of the Medical Subcommittee. The drug list is divided into three kits:

Kit 1 Drugs carried by individual team members
Kit 2 Drugs carried by teams
Kit 3 Drugs carried by teams for use by Doctors

The initial idea was that the drugs would be physically divided into these kits, and the descriptive names indicated the people authorised to use them. However, as time has passed the distinction has become blurred and, though the concept persists, the division now often reflects a secondary characteristic of the drug. It is hard to put this into words but it involves an assessment of the drug's 'risk/benefit', level of training of the team member, the directness of the medical input and the legal implications of administration. So don't think of the kits as physical boxes; suitably qualified team members can use kit III 'starred' drugs; try to learn about the whole package of care involved in managing the casualty rather than just kit 1 and/or 2.

The analogous position of medical gases (oxygen and Entonox®), both of which are legally classed as drugs, remains to be addressed. At present (2006) the MRC supports a team member giving them to a casualty if they have been trained in their use. To place the gases in the MRC Drug List would restrict their administration to team members with a Casualty Care certificate thus depriving many casualties of their benefits.

Practicalities of giving a drug

All the drugs have been selected to be safe if used properly. Before giving a drug:

1. Check the drug is indicated (appropriate to the casualty's condition).

2. Explain to the casualty why you want to use the drug. Obtain the consent of the casualty and warn him/her of any side effects. Mentally rehearse what you are going to do if a side effect occurs. For example, if you give morphine to a casualty who is sitting up think of how you will lay them down should their blood pressure drop. Will the injuries and environment allow this? Can you make the situation safe? Have the vacuum mattress ready to place under the casualty as pain relief is achieved and before postural hypotension develops. Ensure your team members understand what is going on so they can respond quickly if necessary.

3. Check for known allergies - that is a past history of skin rash, swelling, wheeze or collapse - after administration of the drug or a closely related one. For example: aspirin and diclofenac both belong to the same group of drugs.

4. Check for contra-indications - these are specific to the drug and the condition of the casualty and can be hard to define because many are 'relative'. For example, morphine and a simple chest injury, where the use of morphine is dependent on the experience, skills and confidence of the team member. However, some are absolute, for example, Entonox® after SCUBA diving. An absolute contraindication is a ban in all situations. Rigorous thinking may need to be employed. For example, morphine is absolutely contraindicated in an asthma attack - the patient will deteriorate markedly - but not in an asthmatic (with a broken leg). Nonsteroidal anti-inflammatory drugs (NSAIDs), such as aspirin and diclofenac, cause an asthma attack in about one in ten asthmatics - so be cautious but if the asthmatic has taken these drugs in the past with no problem, NSAIDs are not contraindicated. Despite a number of sources of information, there will be times when the casualty, their condition or the circumstances are not answered by the drug list, this book or the *aide memoire* that many teams carry with their drug kits. Teams should ensure that, if a rescuer is unsure about giving a drug, advice from a doctor could be obtained rather than the casualty missing out on a beneficial treatment or an inappropriate drug given. Supplement your own resources by having a list of useful contacts such as the Accident and Emergency department telephone number and mobile phone numbers of neighbouring MR doctors.

5.   Check again; is the drug and the dose what you intend? If at all possible, talk the proposed action through with another team member and get them to check. Ampoules of morphine can contain 10 or 15 mg of morphine! Is the drug 'in date' and pristine? To calculate the correct dose, think of the strength of effect needed (the degree of pain) and the body weight. Is the casualty a child, a small adult, or a normal adult? A child is aged 12 years or less. The small adult group includes the 12 to 18 year old and elite, female fell runners - many have a similar weight to a child of 12 years old.

6.   Give the drug!

7.   Record the administration, preferably on a casualty card. The minimum information is the dose, the route of administration and the time the drug was given. For example: 300 mg aspirin given by mouth at 15.15. A note of whether the drug had the desired effect and any side effects is helpful. Drugs are not exempt from product liability so it is important to record the expiry date and batch number of the drug. This protects the team member from problems arising from giving a defective drug. The liability is passed back to the supplier and ultimately the manufacturer as long as the source of the product can be proven.

8.   You must make sure that the information about the drug's administration is passed on to the next person in charge of the medical care of the casualty. This may be the paramedic on a helicopter or ambulance, or the nurse in an Accident and Emergency department. It is indefensible not to do this verbally; it is preferable to do it in writing, again using a casualty card.

9.   Finally, the MRC needs a record of the drug administration via the Incident Report form. This has been mandatory since 2001.

Special rules for morphine and buprenorphine

It is important that a casualty receives adequate pain relief. Despite the introduction of newer drugs, morphine remains the standard analgesic for severe pain. Along with buprenorphine, it is a 'Controlled Drug'. This means that there are special rules that govern keeping, storing, destroying and documenting the use of these two drugs. An example of the type of storage facilities required in the rescue base and the team vehicle can be seen in the photographs below.

It is a rare privilege that mountain rescue teams have a specific licence from the Home Office that allows for the supply and possession of these two drugs. Not only is it a criminal offence under the Misuse of Drugs Act 1971 to contravene a condition of the licence but also many hundreds of casualties would

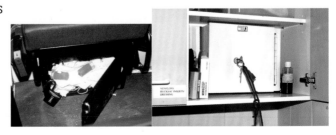

suffer if it were revoked. Team members should
ensure that they are aware of the conditions
laid out in the licence and follow them 'to the
letter'. A copy of the licence is available on the
MRC website along with a 'frequently asked
questions' document.

Routes of administration

There are many ways of getting a drug to its
site of action. A surprising number of these are
used in mountain rescue. They include:

Wilson Hey – instigator of
the 'morphine' Licence

Local – Betadine® on the skin

Oral (by mouth) – aspirin, diclofenac, Dextrosol®, cefuroxime

Sublingual or buccal (under the tongue or against the inside of the cheek -
glyceryl trinitrate (GTN), Glucogel®, buprenorphine, prochlorperazine (buccastem®)

Inhalation – Entonox®, salbutamol

Rectal – diazepam

Intramuscular -morphine, cyclizine, glucagon, adrenaline, naloxone

Intravenous – morphine, naloxone, cefuroxime

In non-emergency medical situations, most drugs are taken by
mouth. The effects on the body begin about 15 to 30 minutes after
swallowing. Tablets that can be dissolved are usually absorbed more
quickly than solid tablets or capsules. However taking a drug by
mouth is often inappropriate in the emergency situation. Pain and
stress reduce the emptying of the stomach so drugs can take a lot
longer to be absorbed. Also vomiting shortly after taking a drug and
being unable to swallow add to the problems. A more rapid onset of
action is often needed so other routes are usually preferred. Some
drugs can be absorbed through the lining of the mouth or through
the lungs. As the blood supply to these areas is high, rapid
absorption takes place. For example, sublingual GTN can relieve
angina in 10-30 seconds. An alternative method is to inject the
drug, which has the advantage that a known dose has been given
and the onset of action is rapid. The intravenous route is the best
but it is also the most dangerous. The speed of giving the drug, the
blood volume and the narrow band between being effective or
causing side effects make giving the correct dose to the casualty
difficult. Side effects and allergic reactions tend to be more severe
and can occur 'at the end of the needle'! Experience and familiarity

become very important. Acquiring these skills takes a lot of time and practice. Recently ambulance paramedics have demonstrated that they can give intravenous morphine safely, so perhaps this is something for the future particularly as safer drugs are developed. The intramuscular route, favoured by nurses for years, remains the standard for team members. Compared with the intravenous route, the onset of action of the drug is slower and smoother. Intramuscular morphine takes 7-15 minutes to give pain relief compared with 2-3 minutes when given intravenously. This is usually acceptable especially as side effects tend to be less marked. There are three problems that should be considered:

1. Absorption of the drug from muscle can be slow and erratic particularly if its blood supply is reduced. This occurs in severe shock and hypothermia. In both cases morphine is likely to be relatively contraindicated.

2. Giving the injection might damage another structure such as a nerve. Long-term damage can result. Examples include paralysis of the lower leg (sciatic nerve - buttock) and reduced muscle strength around the shoulder (circumflex nerve - shoulder). The safest site, the lateral thigh, is not always appropriate; knowing the anatomy of the other two injection sites is important. (See below.)

3. The muscle is damaged. This is usually of little importance but if thrombolysis is given later as a treatment for a myocardial infarction, a large haematoma can develop. The haematoma can be painful and may even require surgical drainage.

Intramuscular injections

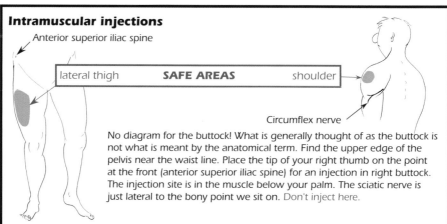

Anterior superior iliac spine

| lateral thigh | **SAFE AREAS** | shoulder |

Circumflex nerve

No diagram for the buttock! What is generally thought of as the buttock is not what is meant by the anatomical term. Find the upper edge of the pelvis near the waist line. Place the tip of your right thumb on the point at the front (anterior superior iliac spine) for an injection in right buttock. The injection site is in the muscle below your palm. The sciatic nerve is just lateral to the bony point we sit on. Don't inject here.

Draw up the drug into a syringe using a 21 or 23 gauge hypodermic needle and expel most of the air. Select a safe injection site and ensure the skin is clean – there is no need to clean the skin with an alcohol wipe but you will want a swab or cotton wool ball to press on the injection site afterwards, so use this to wipe the area. Though you can inject through layers of clothing, it is hard to be accurate; visualise the injection site if at all possible. Note that a shoulder injection is two finger widths below the bony point of the shoulder so as to avoid the circumflex nerve. Rolling up the sleeve tempts you to inject too low – go down from the neck opening. To inject the drug, use a 29mm long needle (usually 23 gauge) so that you reach the muscle. Warn the casualty and then introduce the needle perpendicular to the skin in a single smooth movement. Jabbing produces movement hence muscle damage and pain. Gently aspirate to check that the needle is not in a blood vessel and then inject the drug smoothly. If there is resistance draw the needle back slightly. Press gently on the injection site for a few minutes to minimise bruising.

Individual drugs

While every effort has been made to check drug doses in this book, it is still possible that errors have been made. Drug schedules are being continually revised and new side effects recognised. For these reasons the reader is strongly urged to consult the drug companies' printed instructions before administering any of the drugs recommended in this book. The individual drugs described here are those on the MRC Drug List, 2004-7.

Kit 1

Hypostop® (now Glucogel®) gel

Indications

Hypoglycaemia in Diabetes Mellitus. The urgency of giving glucose in developing hypoglycaemia cannot be overstated. If there is any doubt about the diagnosis give Hypostop®

Exhaustion hypothermia occurs in casualties who often have had a low calorie intake and correcting this may help the treatment of the hypothermia

Dose:

Buccal; it is possible to use, with care, in an unconscious patient, giving as much as required, though glucagon (kit 3) is an alternative

Contra-indications:

None

Side effects:

None

Use in children:

Safe to use

Aspirin

Indication

Suspected heart attack (Myocardial Infarction)

Dose:

Oral - 300mg in soluble or, preferably, chewable form immediately vomiting has been controlled

Side effects:

None in this context

Contra-indications:

A definite allergy (usually breathing problems and/or skin rash) to aspirin or another NSAID such as diclofenac and ibuprofen. The advantages usually outweigh the risk unless there is a clear history of allergy

Use in children:

Not to be used

Paracetamol

Indication

Low-grade pain (sprains, small cuts, headache, etc.)

Dose:

Oral - 2 x 500mg tablets. Repeat at 4-6 hours

Side effects:

None in the acute situation

Contra-indications:

None in the acute situation

Use in children:

5-12 years - one tablet (500mg)

Diclofenac

Indication

Moderate pain, for example an non-displaced ankle injury

Dose:

Oral - 3 x 25mg of a rapidly absorbed preparation

Side effects:

None in the acute situation

Contra-indications:

Sensitivity (Allergy) to diclofenac or another NSAID such as aspirin and ibuprofen.

Use in children:

Not to be used

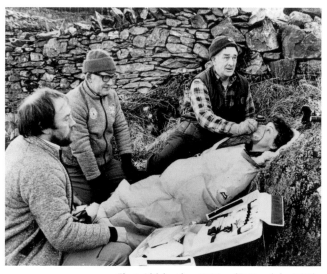

First Aid in the 1980s. (Patterdale MRT)

Kit 2

Morphine

Indication

> Moderate to severe pain. In mountain rescue practice, limb fractures and heart attacks will be the principal indications for its use. An element of euphoria may occur, and this is often a bonus. It is a Controlled Drug (see page 356)

Dose:

> Intramuscular injection - Adults 10-15mg. This may be repeated after 4 hours if required

Side effects:

> Nausea and vomiting occur in a significant number of patients. The most important step in minimising this is to keep the patient lying down and still. This is often not achievable in a rescue situation so anti-vomiting drugs are usually advised. There is a choice: Cyclizine (50mg) can be added to the morphine giving a single injection of Cyclimorph®. Concerns about the use of cyclizine in heart attacks have been investigated; on balance, Cyclimorph® remains acceptable for intramuscular injection in a mountain rescue setting. This would not be the case for intravenous use. An alternative is to use Buccastem® (see below)

> Drowsiness, respiratory depression and hypotension may develop. The initial management consists of lying the casualty flat and administering oxygen at 15 litres/minute via a non-rebreathing mask with a reservoir and, if required, artificial breathing. Naloxone (kit 3) temporarily reverses all the effects of morphine. It is preferably to give 100mcg intravenously every 2 minutes titrated to reverse the respiratory depression yet (hopefully) not fully reversing the analgesia. If this is not possible, give 400mcg intramuscularly. Naloxone should only be used when the respiratory depression is severe and after consulting with a doctor unless the situation is extreme. The naloxone dose in children is 200mcg for a 5 year-old rising to 400mcg for a 12 year old. Some teams will choose to carry morphine and naloxone together in line with ambulance trust protocol; this is acceptable and may give team members additional confidence. Where morphine maybe given intravenously, naloxone should be immediately available

Contra-indications:

> Asthma attack

> Head injury - avoid if at all possible. Do not use if there is any reduction in the Glasgow Coma Scale. Seek medical advice before administering. Should be used with caution in chest injuries particularly when the injury is severe and causing hypoxia. Seek medical help if at all possible

Use in children:

> < 5 years - consult a doctor

> 5-12 years - 3mg increasing to 7mg by the age of 12 years

Codeine phosphate

Indication

Mild to moderate pain; for example, an non-displaced ankle injury or migraine. It may be combined with paracetamol (cocodamol 30/500) for more effective pain relief

Dose:

Oral - 2 x 30mg tablets. Repeat at 4 hours

Side effects:

Nausea and drowsiness

Contra-indications:

As morphine

Use in children:

6-12 years - 1 x 30mg tablet

Prochlorperazine (Buccastem®)

Indication

For treating nausea and vomiting whatever the cause

Dose:

Buccal - 2 x 3mg tablets

Side effects:

Dystonia (abnormal muscle spasms) may occur particularly in the elderly. Rarely respiratory depression

Contra-indications:

None

Use in children:

Do not use in children

Glyceryl trinitrate spray

Indication

Treating angina, where it is very effective within minutes (and lasts for 30 minutes); it will not relieve the pain of an established heart attack

Dose:

Sublingual - 1-2 sprays under tongue. Can be repeated after 30 minutes as necessary. The spray may not work at low temperatures - keep under clothing

Side effects:

Headaches and facial flushing

Contra-indications:

Head injury

Use in children:

No indication

Povidone-iodine (Betadine® 10% in aqueous solution)

Indication

Wounds particularly when a compound fracture is suspected or where the wound is contaminated. Use of a solution gives better penetration than a spray

Dose:

Topical - apply as a soaked dressing; the maximum quantity used per casualty should be 50 ml

Side effects:

Excessive use can cause serious problems

Contra-indications:

Burns and rarely iodine sensitivity

Use in children:

Can be used

Cefuroxime

Indication

Major contaminated wounds. Antibiotics given at an early stage to such casualties, particularly a compound fracture, have been shown to reduce later complications. Should be used in any patient who will have a period exceeding four hours between time of injury and treatment in hospital. It is best given intravenously (Kit 3) but tablets may suffice if no doctor is on hand

Dose:

Oral - adults 2 x 250mg tablets. Intravenous dose is 1 x 750mg ampoule made up in water for injection

Side effects:

Unlikely with a single dose; an acute allergic reaction may occur and be life-threatening particularly when the drug has been given intravenously

Contra-indications:

A definite history of allergy to antibiotics of this type. Ask for medical advice if there is any history of antibiotic allergy

Use in children:

1 x 250mg tablet

Salbutamol

Indication

Acute asthma.

A pressurized inhaler, with a spacer device, may be effective when the patient's own system has failed to relieve symptoms or when they have forgotten it! Salbutamol nebulizer solution is an alternative for severe asthma (incomplete sentences; pulse >110; respiration rate >25 per minute or oxygen saturation <96%) when an oxygen-driven nebulizer is available

Dose:

Inhaled - 2-10 puffs of the inhaler

5mg of the nebulizer solution

Side effects:

Tremor can occur when the higher doses are used particularly in those with mild attacks

Contra-indications:

None in the acute situation

Use in children:

2-6 puffs of the inhaler

2.5mg of the nebulizer solution

oxygen-driven nebulizer

Adrenaline (Epinephrine)

Indication

Life-threatening allergic emergencies (anaphylaxis) especially in bee and wasp stings, as well as after certain foodstuffs such as peanuts

Severe life-threatening asthma where the casualty has stopped breathing

As part of Advanced Life Support (ALS) – after second shock if 'shockable' rhythm or as soon as possible if 'non-shockable' rhythm and repeat every 3 to 5 minutes during resuscitation

Dose:

0.5mg (0.5ml of 1/1000 preparation) intramuscular repeated after 5 minutes if necessary. 1mg intravenous during ALS

Side effects:

Anxiety and tremor

Contra-indications:

None for these indications

Use in children:

6-12 years - 0.25mg

1-6 years - 0.12mg

Diazepam

Indication

Seizures that are repeated or prolonged (more than 10 minutes)

Dose:

Rectal - 10mg

Side effects:

Rarely respiratory depression and hypotension

Contra-indications:

None in the acute situation

Use in children:

6-12 years - 5mg rectal

Kit 3

This kit is designed for a doctor (team or passing) to use. The contents may well vary depending on the preferences of the team doctor but some uniformity is desirable at least in the classes of drugs carried. In very rare circumstances a drug marked with a '*' may be indicated in an emergency under the direct instruction of a team doctor. The team member will have undergone extended training, usually by the team doctor, on top of *Casualty Care* training.

Indications and doses are not given as medical supervision is assumed. It is recognised that some teams may not have sufficient rescue activity to justify holding kit 3.

Glucagon injection*

Naloxone injection*

Cefuroxime injection*

Chlorphenamine injection*

Hydrocortisone injection*

Diazepam injection

Local anaesthesia

Medical gases in mountain rescue

Oxygen

Indication

> Conditions leading to hypoxia - myocardial infarction; shock; asthma; and reduced respiratory function from trauma, head injury or drugs (morphine, diazepam)

Side effects:

> None in these situations

Contraindication:

> Don't forget that oxygen supports combustion. Switch the oxygen off and remove mask when defibrillating

Using oxygen does not correct a poor airway; airway problems must be resolved if at all possible. High concentrations are required for maximum benefit. The apparatus should be capable of supplying 15 litres of oxygen per minute, and the mask should be a non-rebreathing mask with a reservoir, for example, a Hudson RCI®. This will give 100% oxygen if the mask is snugly fitted on the face. Despite the introduction of lighter weight oxygen cylinders, it is often impractical to use high flow oxygen on the fell for a long period but at least with a reservoir mask you are making the most of the oxygen you have. Rationing oxygen based on oxygen saturation of the casualty is acceptable in mountain rescue. In practical terms, oxygen is started early in the assessment of the casualty at 15 l/min. Then as things become clearer, and perhaps the oxygen saturation is measured, you can calculate what flow rate will last until the casualty is handed over to an ambulance or helicopter with their own oxygen supplies. For example, BOC Medical CD cylinders* contain 460 litres of oxygen when full. With two full cylinders, you have: 60 minutes at 15 l/min or 10 minutes at 15 l/min then 96 minutes at 8l/minute.

* - These cylinders have many practical advantages over the old steel cylinders with separate regulator. The regulator is incorporated with the cylinder and is serviced on refilling the cylinder. The contents dial is always live so you can tell in an instant if the cylinder is full. Refilling by BOC Medical is available nationally and exchanging cylinders with other users is easy and, as they can only be rented from BOC Medical, ownership is not an issue. The down side is the monthly cost (approximately £6) even if you do not use the cylinder.

They are certainly an improvement over the old steel cylinders though other suppliers have developed even lighter systems with amazing oxygen capacities; for example, Medical Gas Solutions Limited have a cylinder containing 900 litre of oxygen at about 30 pence more a month!

BOC CD oxygen (460 litres)   MGS Ltd. (900 litres)

Entonox®

Indication

Rapid pain relief during painful procedures such as during assessment and splinting of a fracture

Dose:

Inhale deeply both before and during the procedure

Contraindications:

Within 48 hours of Scuba diving

Chest injury where there is a risk of a pneumothorax

Giving the mixture in any way other than by self-administration by the casualty

Side effects:

Light headedness and dizziness

Reduced consciousness (rare)

Entonox® is a mixture of 50% nitrous oxide (a weak anaesthetic gas) and 50% oxygen. Separation of the component gases occurs at -7°C, so keep the cylinders warm with hot packs and insulation on cold winter rescues. The casualty self-administers Entonox® after instruction by the rescuer. Entonox® has a rapid onset of action, taking just 3-8 deep inhalations to reach the maximum effect. The analgesia is very good if no air is taken in with it. Hyperventilation (over breathing) adds to the effect. (Not so long ago, a general anaesthetic for a Caesarean section consisted of nitrous oxide/ oxygen and forced hyperventilation with little else!) The analgesic effect reduces very quickly when the casualty stops inhaling the mixture. Entonox® has a slightly old-fashioned, even 'primitive' feel about it. This is unfair; the modern BOC Medical apparatus based round the CD cylinder and a lightweight regulator at the mask, requiring a lower 'suck' to trigger the valve, has much to commend itself. In practical terms, it should be used as an adjunct to morphine or diclofenac, filling in before these drugs have become effective, and when pain levels increase during manipulation and splinting. It is rare for Entonox® to be an alternative to other analgesics though occasionally it can be all that is needed. In the past, Entonox® has been described as useful in casualties suspected of having a myocardial infarction (heart attack). The analgesia is good and you are giving oxygen albeit in a concentration of less than 50% (because of air entrainment). But Entonox® can suppress heart function, and it lacks other helpful features of morphine. 100% oxygen and morphine is strongly preferred for a suspected myocardial infarction.

Conclusion

Drugs are very useful in mountain rescue. Relief of pain from fractures and myocardial infarct should be a priority for every rescuer. The few drugs, used appropriately as described, will alleviate many symptoms and make the rescue more tolerable. Accurate note taking and good communication with the casualty and the hospital should avoid the following situation!

MRC drug use - What is being used and by whom?

If we take the reported drug use from three years of incident reports and analyse the data for an average year, we find:

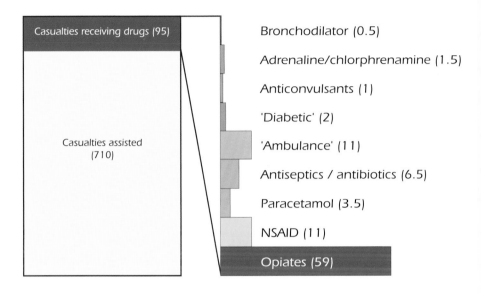

Casualties receiving drugs (95)

Casualties assisted (710)

Bronchodilator (0.5)

Adrenaline/chlorphrenamine (1.5)

Anticonvulsants (1)

'Diabetic' (2)

'Ambulance' (11)

Antiseptics / antibiotics (6.5)

Paracetamol (3.5)

NSAID (11)

Opiates (59)

About 13% of our casualties received a drug (excluding oxygen and Entonox®)

Opiates (morphine and related drugs) are the most used

A doctor or ambulance paramedic is present in over 50% of the incidents

Note - 'ambulance' refers to a NHS ambulance person giving a drug when on duty. This reflects some areas of England and Wales where the team supports the ambulance with transportation.

Of course, these figures are the result of the type of incidents, the framework and the team member's confidence in administerng drugs. They do not show need or appropriateness or unreported use. Mountain rescue urgently needs to audit their management of injured casualties so that the scale of drug use can be established. However, until we have better data, we must consider whether training team members is going to be appropriate, particularly in some areas of the country where air ambulances are becoming more active. The trend for doctors attending incidents is sadly downwards - and nearing 20% in England and Wales - so other models of care should perhaps be looked at. Would closer working with the Ambulance service remove the need for team members to spend money, time and effort in developing drug administration skills?

References

Bradshaw M, Sen A. Use of a prophylactic antiemetic with morphine in acute pain: randomised controlled trial. *Emerg Med J* 2006; 23:210-3

Dibble C. Are routine anti-emetics required with iv morphine? Bestbets accessed at http://www.bestbets.org/cgi-bin/bets.pl?record=00266

May G. The use of IV cyclizine in cardiac chest pain. Bestbets accessed at http://www.bestbets.org/cgi-bin/bets.pl?record=01054

Faddy SC, Garlick SR. A systematic review of the safety of analgesia with 50% nitrous oxide: can lay responders use analgesic gases in the prehospital setting? Emerg Med J 2005; 22:901-6

Sunset, Ullswater, Lake District (2001)

For Rescuers

Objectives

To understand the importance of blood-borne infections
To know what vaccinations are available
To give Doctors an idea of useful techniques
To understand the term 'advanced' Casualty Care

The development of the MRC Casualty Care exam

Until the end of 1977 the only First Aid training for team members was the Adult First Aid Certificate issued by either the St. John Ambulance Brigade or the British Red Cross Society. Although better than no training, the MRC considered it did not meet the needs of its members. So in 1978 the MRC approached both organisations with a view to the MRC running courses designed to cater for the "mountain" environment; eventually both organisations agreed to supply certificates endorsed "Mountain Rescue First Aid". This continued to be the best option until December 1983.

The MRC Medical Subcommittee (as we know it today) was formed in 1980, and took on the task of organising the training and examination of team members. After many meetings the committee finally accepted that the best policy would be for mountain rescue to run and examine its own courses. The post of MRC Registrar was formed in November 1983 to deal with the new courses and examinations, which were to be run every 3 years.

The first MRC Mountain Rescue First Aid course and examination took place from January to June 1984 in the Peak District and up to May 1994 a total of 1,439 certificates were issued.

During 1992 moves were made to change the terminology of "Mountain Rescue First Aid" to a more suitable term. Team members felt that the skills they were acquiring and using were far more than those of a First Aider. The term 'Casualty Care', often shortened to Cas. Care, was thought to reflect the wider range of skills and encompass non-medical aspects, such as evacuation, that are crucial to the success of a rescue. The first MRC Casualty Care course and examinations took place from February to July 1994 in the Lake District; 2,435 certificates were issued up to October 2004. On average, 250 team members are awarded certificates each year thus maintaining a pool of about 750 members with a current certificate at any one time.

The Cas. Care exam has changed considerably since 1994 as experience and knowledge has increased. A syllabus, available on the MRC web site, is produced and reviewed every 5 years. In 1999, three Medical Subcommittee members became responsible for producing the multiple-choice questions and practical exam - a thankless, time-consuming task. By January 2004, the MRC was confident enough in its examination to make holding a current Cas. Care Certificate a requirement for team members wishing to give drugs; the MRC ceased to accept other certificates as an alternative.

There may be confusion over the relationship between this book and the Cas. Care exam. The two are not the same. The book is commissioned by the MRC; it is not the exam source book. The right answers to the questions are not necessarily here, though hopefully any disagreements will be minor. There are other good sources of information and candidates are encouraged to seek a wide view of the subjects.

There is no doubt that the exam is getting more demanding. We expect our candidates to reach a standard that would be recognised as appropriate by a Doctor or paramedic sitting a Pre-hospital Emergency Care certificate. This change has been driven by the availability of *Casualty Care in Mountain Rescue* (first published in 2000, and made available to MRC members for £1!), many excellent courses and, most importantly, your ability and willingness to take on board the concepts of modern *Casualty Care!*

Birkhouse Moor, Helvellyn. (2004)

Protecting yourself and the casualty from infectious disease

When AIDS (Human Immunodeficiency Virus or HIV) came on the scene in the 1990s, treating casualties became charged with 'Will I catch it?' Team doctors were asked every other week if, how or when the disease could be contracted. The health services had the same problem and undertook a review of the risks. During this process, the concern shifted to the danger of casualties being exposed to a transmittable disease when the health professional had been infected. Fortunately avoiding transfer of infection in one direction protects against transfer in the other, safeguarding both the casualty and the rescuer. We can now look back - the AIDS epidemic has not materialised, at least in the UK, but other infectious diseases have reinforced our need to be careful and minimise the chance of infection passing between casualty and rescuer and *vice versa*. This section finishes with a related subject, picking up infection from the mountain rescue environment, and ways to minimise the risk.

Reducing transmission

We are fortunate that the serious infections that can pass from casualty to rescuer and vice versa do so by direct transfer (inoculation) of 'bodily fluids'. In our situation this is largely limited to blood and saliva. The table on the next page outlines ways of reducing the risk.

Hepatitis B

Rescuers should be vaccinated against Hepatitis B. In the UK, this brings the rescuer in line with groups like the Police and health professionals. Immunisation protects the rescuer from an infected casualty and prevents the rescuer acquiring the disease and inadvertently infecting the casualty. Vaccination involves three (0, 1 and 6 months) intramuscular injections of part of the shell of the Hepatitis B virus. This is derived from genetically modified yeast rather than the real virus and produces an antibody response that prevents the virus from getting a hold. The level of antibody is usually measured three months after the third injection to ensure that the rescuer has become immune and determine when further doses are required.

Blood-borne infections - Reducing the risk

The chance of transfer of infection depends on the:
Infectious agent - Hepatitis B is more infectious than HIV.
Quantity and type of bodily fluid - blood is much more infectious than saliva.
Type of transfer - needle-stick injury (a used needle stabs someone else) is higher risk than skin contact.
Pre-inoculation (vaccination) and post-inoculation (antiviral drugs) measures.

We can reduce the chance of inoculation by:
Avoiding contact with blood and saliva by wearing gloves.
Having a 'sharps box' ready to dispose of any used needles immediately.
Not putting the needle cover back on; the commonest cause of a needle-stick injury.
Disposing of blood-stained dressings carefully in easily identified polythene bags which are sent for incineration.
Sterilising any equipment contaminated during the rescue or, if possible, using 'single-use equipment', for example, bag and mask, face masks, etc.

We can reduce the incidence of infection, if inoculated, by:
Encouraging a needle-stick injury to bleed for a few minutes after the injury. But do not suck the blood out.
Clean the wound with Betadine® or similar antiseptic and cover the wound with a sterile dressing.
Seek expert guidance on the need for investigation and anti-viral drugs at an Accident & Emergency department as soon as possible.

HIV

Vaccination is not an option for HIV infection. Fortunately the infection rate is low. If you follow the advice on reducing the chance of inoculation and infection it is very unlikely that you will contract HIV. In the rare event of a high-risk accident, usually a needle-stick injury, expert advice is available from hospitals; sometimes, antiviral drugs are given in the immediate aftermath of the inoculation to reduce the risk of the recipient contracting the disease.

Flu

Flu, or more correctly influenza, causes epidemics during the winter. In a normal winter and with a normal flu virus, though many people suffer an acute febrile illness lasting approximately four days, the complication and fatality rate in a fit, healthy person is very, very small. The flu vaccine is reserved for those at greater risk of complications, such as the elderly and those with asthma, heart disease and diabetes. Unfortunately the vaccine only works for about a year as the flu virus itself changes ('drifts') so quickly that new components have to be added to the vaccine to keep it effective. Health professionals are offered vaccination to reduce the disruption to services and reduce the spread to their vulnerable patients. Mountain rescuers would not normally consider flu vaccination as the consequence of 'getting flu' is unlikely to disrupt the rescue service significantly. After all, in an epidemic the hills will be fairly quiet! However, with the threat of a pandemic, where the flu virus changes dramatically ('shifts') and where the fatality rate can be much higher, vaccination may be offered particularly if mountain rescue is seen as an essential service in a time of crisis. Vaccination may become the norm as mountain rescue's civil contingency role expands.

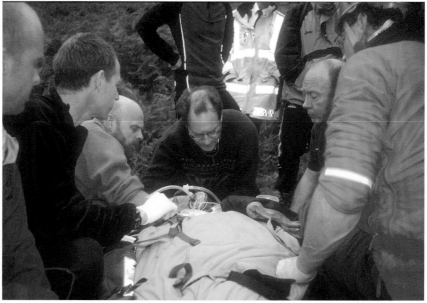

Severe head and facial injury – time for anaesthetic and intubation

Infections from the UK mountain rescue environment

Two infections deserve note:

Tetanus

Tetanus is a disease caused by an infection with *Clostridium tetani*, a bacterium that lives in soil and particularly faeces/manure. It is widespread but can only grow in the absence of oxygen (anaerobic conditions). Minor wounds when not cleaned, and particularly puncture wounds, introduce the bacteria into an area where they can multiply and produce toxins. The toxins cause muscles to contract (go rigid) and to spasm. Symptoms develop 5 to 14 days after inoculation and often start with a rigid ('lock') jaw followed by spasms, which render respiration impossible. Modern treatment has reduced the death rate at least in developed countries but prevention is far better than enduring days or weeks on a ventilator! Vaccination with tetanus toxoid is extremely effective and rescuers should ensure that they are fully vaccinated. This involves five injections in your life, usually three before you are one year old, a preschool and a school-leaving booster. If you have a very high-risk wound, the hospital may boost your immunity with an injection of immunoglobulin but this is becoming much less common.

Lyme Disease

Lyme disease is the commonest tick-transmitted disease in the northern hemisphere. It is caused by a bacterium of the spirochaete family called *Borrelia burgdorferi*. It is inoculated into a person by a tick bite. The tick has to be a particular type and infected with the bacterium; it is unknown how often a tick bite causes the disease but large regional variations exist. Originally we thought that deer ticks were the most important but this seems to be too simplistic a view - many animals can act as a reservoir, and the woodland habitat is seen as the risky environment. Fortunately the UK is in a low incidence area though cases are increasing recognised. (Central Europe is a higher risk area, and also home to Tick-borne Encephalitis (a virus infection) for which a vaccine is available.) The clinical picture of Lyme disease is very variable. The commonest presentation is a small red spot at the site of the tick bite appearing for the first time days, or weeks, after the bite. The redness spreads out slowly and starts to clear in the centre in a fairly characteristic rash called erythema migrans. The spot itself can itch a little but other symptoms at this stage are rare. The infection can spread to the joints (approximately 70% of cases), brain (up to 10%), heart and eyes, and cause long-term problems. Treatment is with antibiotics; the earlier these are taken the more effective they are at reducing the long-term sequelae. Ways of reducing the risk of Lyme disease are outlined in the table below.

Lyme disease - Reducing the risk

Avoid tick bites by:
Wearing long trousers and long-sleeved tops.

As soon as possible, remove ticks by:
Using a pair of fine-tipped tweezers, grasp the tick as near the skin as possible and pull out with an upward motion.
Do not burn-off or smother an attached tick with Vaseline®.
Using an alcohol wipe always seemed successful at loosening the tick's grasp but is not recommended now. At least the tick was drunk and incapable; after the patient had left the consulting room, it would start to crawl off the desk!

A single dose of antibiotic:
Taken within 72 hours of the bite may reduce the risk of infection. This is controversial as the studies are largely from the USA, where the infective agents are slightly different and the incidence of inoculation is much greater than in the UK. No vaccine is currently available. However, there is no doubt that erythema migrans requires medical attention.

References

Cassell OCS. Death from tetanus after a pretibial laceration. *BMJ* 2002; 324:1442-3

Stanek G, Strle F. Lyme borreliosis *The Lancet* 2003: 362;1639-1647

Outdoor Pursuits Leaflet on Lyme disease (2005). Accessible at www.bada-uk.org

Medical fitness in MR

The question of rescuers' fitness for the job is a thorny subject; one that has been discussed over the years with little enthusiasm. We are volunteers, dislike red tape and surely everyone can be given a job regardless of their fitness. Well yes, but compare ourselves with other rescue agencies like the RNLI and retained firemen where standards of medical fitness have to be met. The driving force to considering medical fitness is to minimise:

The risk of injury or illness to rescuer from the physical and mental stresses of rescue.

The chance of a rescue being disrupted by a team member's injury or illness with the consequence that the casualty suffers.

In general, the level of fitness and the way it is assessed - largely informally - can be left to the team. However, one area of mountain rescue - driving an emergency ambulance - has defined medical standards that are hard to ignore.

Langdale and Patterdale MRT, Kirkstone Pass. (1976)

National guidelines set out in the 'Medical aspects of fitness to drive' published by the Medical Commission on Accident Prevention sets out the statutory and advisory restrictions for driving all sorts of vehicles. It states: 'By convention, Group 2 standards are .. generally applied to emergency police, firemen and ambulance drivers as well as taxi drivers.'

Mountain Rescue would find it hard to argue that Group 2 (equivalent to lorries and buses) medical standards should be relaxed. So the MRC adopted the policy in 1997 leaving it to teams to arrange suitable testing of its ambulance drivers. Largely this was done by a voluntary self-declaration, perhaps with formal eyesight or blood pressure checks if needed, though some teams arranged for a formal medical for their drivers.

Since then the Driver and Vehicle Licensing Agency (DVLA) has clarified the legal position of 'Medical aspects of fitness to drive' (see http://www.dvla.gov.uk/at_a_glance/content.htm). The standards set and the responsibility to ensure that a driver is fit are left to the employing Ambulance Trust or Police Authority. Most continue to apply the Group (now Class) 2 standard, as does the MRC. This seems a good precautionary policy, if a little harsh. We must remember that driving in an emergency is recognised as a hazardous task. In the UK, over 50 people die a year from accidents involving Police emergency vehicles alone.

The medical standard is set out in the document 'At a glance Guide to the current Medical Standards Of Fitness to Drive' available from the DVLA website.

Areas of greyness around driving emergency ambulances still remain. Does the driver have to pass the higher medical standard only if he is driving to an emergency with 'blue lights' on? Some organisations have adopted a relaxed view allowing Class 1 (ordinary car) drivers to fill the vehicle with fuel or take it for service; others have been more rigorous pointing to the fact that other road users behave differently, and often erratically, even if the 'blues' are off. Teams have been left to make their own policies here.

Professional health-care providers and 'advanced' Casualty Carers in MR

What a clumsy title! I mean what does a Doctor, paramedic, specialist nurse (in Accident and Emergency or intensive care medicine) and 'advanced' Casualty Carer bring to mountain rescue? After the first edition of *Casualty Care in Mountain Rescue*, a number of Doctors asked if a supplement could be added for their benefit. Unfortunately, despite a number of attempts, this project failed to materialise. In this section, we look at what is known about the injuries our casualties suffer, the 'advanced' techniques that may be of use, the possible training opportunities and current status of 'advanced' Casualty Care.

Most mountain rescue teams have a Medical Officer, or Doctor they can call upon, for training in Casualty Care. Many teams are able to use the same Doctor's help on the hill during a call-out. However the MRC incident reports indicate that having a Doctor on a call-out has become less common and is approaching 20% of all call-outs. There should be a benefit to the casualty and the rescue team when a professional health-care provider is present on the hill to manage and treat the injured. However, it should not be forgotten that a team approach to casualty care is best, and therefore the professional should not be left alone to 'get on with it' whilst the rest of the team readies for the evacuation. The professional should be able to call upon suitably trained members of the team to assist him in this task.

Medical and nursing training varies widely. Whilst every Doctor has a basic medical knowledge, the skills possessed by a psychiatrist will differ greatly from those of an Accident and Emergency consultant. As illustrated in the following case history, a passing professional also has to contend with lack of knowledge of the workings of the MR team. He or she will not know what team members can do, nor be aware of the routine Casualty Care procedures and management plans used by the team or what extra equipment and resources they could call upon. What is in the first-aid sack? The equipment may be unfamiliar to the passing Doctor. In short, a volunteer may not be adequately experienced or qualified to take over the care of the casualty. Assisting with the casualty is 'OK' but the team should keep to its well-practised routine.

Case study: A passing doctor's story

'February 1994. With clear blue skies and the Lakeland fells looking alpine, the omens were good for a midweek half-day of snow and ice. We had just soloed up a Grade I gully, and were cramponing over perfect névé towards the back wall of the corrie to find further sport. All of a sudden, we came across a casualty. He had fallen 100 metres from the arête and had come to a halt on a small icy patch of level ground, just short of a further plunge over rocks. He would probably have been killed if he hadn't stopped where he was. We went over to offer what help we could. The situation seemed to be under control; a member of the party had already set off to alert the mountain rescue team and the third member had made the casualty comfortable. Extra clothing had been put beneath him to act as insulation. The casualty was conscious, had no head injuries, and appeared in relatively good spirits considering what had happened to him. He complained of pain in his legs and chest. As a GP, thoughts of penetrating lung injuries crossed my mind, but his breathing was satisfactory, his colour good, pulse unremarkable, and there were no visible signs of bleeding. I wondered what else I could do? He had come to rest in a recovery position so it seemed inappropriate to move him and cause more pain, and the only way I could have inspected his injuries more closely would have been to cut his clothing, and I felt it more appropriate to keep him as warm as possible. My contribution as a doctor on the scene was therefore limited to putting my Karrimat underneath him for extra insulation, and chatting to him, and his partner, for several hours until the rescue team arrived. By the time the team arrived, it was dark and I felt very cold under a cloudless sky. Undoubtedly the casualty was cooler still. With the arrival of the team, things began to happen. The casualty was made safe with ropes and belay; a tent was erected over him, with an immediate and dramatic increase in temperature. The team leader made a top-to-toe first-aid check once it was feasible to cut clothing; giving him a morphine injection, which I'm sure the team could have given just as well, assuaged my previous feeling of helplessness. He was evacuated by helicopter, and I subsequently learned that he had sustained fractures of his femur, ankle and ribs. The conclusion seemed obvious: A doctor passing the scene of a mountain incident is of no greater help than a reasonably sensible fellow climber; the rescue team working to a well-practised routine is efficient, competent, and saves lives.'

The injury patterns of MR casualties

Despite the meticulous collection of incident reports, we have very little accurate data on the injuries suffered by MR casualties. This is because incident reports generally record suspected injuries - injuries that are thought to be important during the rescue period. The actual injuries (injuries confirmed by definitive care including ones missed during the rescue) are infrequently reported. Patient confidentiality and hospital sensitivity hinder the collection of the data in many regions. The most notable recent studies that have overcome these problems are from Scotland and the western part of the Austrian Alps. Their injury patterns, of course, reflect the geography and rescue systems but make interesting reading. For example, the excellent Scottish study by Stephen Hearns shows that 3.6% of casualties suffered major trauma (head injury, spinal cord damage and chest injury) and same percentage had spinal injuries. Of the 57 casualties that died, only four (3 from trauma, 1 from hypothermia) died after the arrival of the rescue team. In the Austrian Alps, Peter Mair's group studied the records of helicopter rescues where a fall in alpine terrain was recorded. The average distance of the fall was 51.4m, so not surprisingly major trauma was common (29%). Spinal injuries, rib fractures (half also having a pneumothorax) and head injuries predominated. In this group of patients none died after the arrival of the rescue team. What conclusions can we draw?

That, most often, carefully immobilising the spine is likely to be important.

Severe head injury is less frequent in survivors.

Shock is unusual in survivors (and non-survivors in Austria).

Which 'advanced' techniques should be considered?

There must be a large 'leap of faith' if a rational list of advanced techniques is to be drawn from the studies mentioned above even before the impact of different geography and rescue systems are considered. In Patterdale (Lake District), over 20 years and about 600 rescues, I have performed very few 'advanced' techniques; these are listed below.

Technique	No.	Comments
Intubation	5	2 survivors
LMA	1	survived
Anaesthetic drugs	3	all survived
Intravenous fluids	10	all with major fractures
LA nerve block	7	femoral nerve 5; other 2
Ketamine analgesia	3	entrapment 1; reductions 2
Chest drain	1	non-survivor
Reductions	9	shoulder 3; patella 2; ankle 4
Intravenous drugs	33	analgesia 30; antibiotics 3
Suturing	1	in the Alps!

Perhaps luck, the introduction of mobile phones or better standard Casualty Care (including helicopter evacuation) account for the fall in deaths after the arrival of the rescue team over the last 20 years rather than the use of 'advanced techniques'. It is hard to know; reductions of fracture/dislocations and better pain relief have been much appreciated by the casualty at the time and, in my opinion, are the techniques most worth considering. My experience is that intubation without the use of anaesthetic drugs to facilitate the procedure has not resulted in a single survivor. Survival rates of 0.2 and 8.3% have been quoted by the London HEMS and a Danish group. Without pre-existing training in anaesthetics and Accident and Emergency medicine as well as the ordinary work at road traffic accidents it would be hard to have maintained sufficient confidence to continue with some of these techniques.

References

Christensen E, Hoyer CCS. Pre-hospital tracheal intubation in severely injured patients: a Danish observational study. *BMJ* 2003; 327:533-4

Lockey D, Davies G, Coats T. Survival of trauma patients who have prehospital tracheal intubation without anaesthesia or muscle relaxants: observational study. *BMJ* 2001; 323:141

Training opportunities for health-care professionals

These are limited and don't quite match the profile of MR if you include a mountaineering element. The following list is not exhaustive but gives a flavour of what is available.

The Pre-hospital Emergency Care certificate and the Diploma in Immediate Care are centred on road traffic incidents and medical emergencies. There is no mountaineering component.

The Emergency Care for Mountain Rescue (ECMR) course - a five and a half day course run in Snowdonia by a MR Doctor and, in Scotland, the British Association of Ski Patrollers courses are more specifically designed for adverse environments and are open to a wide range of participants including team members wishing to develop 'advanced' skills.

Expedition Medicine courses will vary as to their rescue and mountaineering content.

Finally, the Diploma in Mountain Medicine (UIAA/ICAR accredited, University of Leicester) is a multi-week course lasting a year with significant mountaineering, altitude and travel components. It is most attractive to Doctors (not exclusively) that travel abroad either as a trek or expedition Doctor. A speciality rescue module can follow the standard diploma but has so far only been run once - in Argentina!

'Advanced' Casualty Care

This is a term used to describe Casualty Carers that have had advanced or extended training and, as a consequence, have become skilled at additional (usually) invasive techniques. The MRC Medical Subcommittee circulated a paper in 1998 outlining its views on the subject. The nucleus of the extended training is a greater grasp, understanding and experience of casualty care. Through a more accurate assessment, a clearer diagnosis can be made thus facilitating a more effective management plan. Most of the management will still be at a 'standard' level but some skills, such as inserting a Laryngeal Mask Airway or endotracheal tube, giving appropriate drugs intravenously and reducing dislocations may be appropriate depending on the type of rescues performed, the medical input and the isolation of the MR team. Criteria for the selection of Casualty Carers have been defined by the MRC and incorporated into those of individual teams. The Patterdale MRT criteria are shown below.

Patterdale MRT Advanced Casualty Care Group Criteria for membership
Member of a mountain rescue team for at least five years
Has sat and passed at least two recent Casualty Care certificate exams
Better than average marks in the MCQ part of the exam
Endorsement of the Team Leader and Team Doctor(s)
Attends at least 9 out of the 12 Doctor-led teaching sessions each year
Should sit the ECMR or equivalent course and maintain certification
Keeps a log of practical procedures
Undergoes an annual review/appraisal by the Team Leader and Team Doctor(s)

The number of Casualty Carers operating at this level is small and, as all operate with a Doctor monitoring and supervising their performance, separate certification has not been deemed necessary. Working in this way 'advanced' Casualty Carers are currently covered by the MRC liability insurance (2006).

References

Hearns S. The Scottish mountain rescue casualty study. *Emerg Med J* 2003; 20:281-284

Hohlrieder M, Eschertzhuber S, Schubert H, Zinnecker R, Mair P. Severity and Pattern of Injury in Survivors of Alpine Fall Accidents. *HAMB* 2004; 5:349-355

Rammlmair G, Zafren K, Elsensohn F. Qualifications for Emergency Doctors in Mountain Rescue Operations in *Consensus Guidelines on Mountain Emergency Medicine and Risk Reduction* edited by Elsensohn 2001 ISBN 88 884 29 00 X and accessible on the ICAR website (www.ikar-cisa.org)

Welch E. Medicine in the mountains. *BMJ Career Focus* 2004;328:57. Accessible at http://careerfocus.bmjjournals.com/search.dtl

Hearns S. Mountain rescue medicine. *BMJ Career Focus* 2000; 321 (suppl): s2. accessible at http://careerfocus.bmjjournals.com/search.dtl

'Advanced' techniques

These invasive techniques have been of benefit in MR. The purpose of their inclusion here is to encourage Doctors to consider acquiring the skills to perform them.

Femoral nerve block

Fractures of the shaft of the femur do occur in isolation but often there is a history of a tumbling fall and anxiety over other injuries particularly to the head and spine. In such cases giving adequate analgesia with morphine can be compromised because of concern over the side effects of morphine. A well-performed femoral nerve block can give a high degree of pain relief within 5 minutes thus facilitating splinting, and reducing the need for morphine. The technique is simple, quick to do and safe if the main complication of an accidental, intravascular bolus injection of lidocaine is avoided.

Exclude allergy to local anaesthetics. An intravenous cannula and a small dose of intravenous morphine are sensible preliminary steps.

Draw up lidocaine (lignocaine) 1% 10ml (100mg) into a syringe and attach a 5cm 22-gauge needle

The casualty should lie flat and the major landmarks identified.

Place your index finger of your non-dominant hand on the femoral artery just below the inguinal ligament

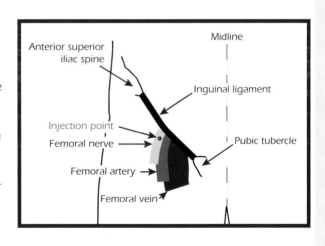

Clean the skin, and then insert the needle just lateral to the artery at a 45 degree angle advancing it in a cephalad (towards the head) direction. Minimal resistance is felt, sometimes as the needle penetrates the femoral fascia resistance decreases - a good sign that the right depth has been reached. Paraesthesia may be elicited over the anterior thigh though this is unusual in the casualty with pain. At a depth of 3 to 4 cm, carefully aspirate to exclude intravascular placement, and then inject the lidocaine at this point; again there is minimal resistance. If no paraesthesia had been elicited, inject perhaps 5ml of lidocaine, and then withdraw the needle to the subcutaneous tissue before advancing again in a different direction to create a fan of anaesthetic. Usually the fan needs to be extended towards the artery, as the first advance has been understandably cautious with the pulsatile artery seeming very close! Do no more than 3 advances.

Complications are rare. Puncture of the femoral artery is easily recognised by spontaneous flash back of blood into the syringe or on aspiration. Withdraw the needle without injecting any lidocaine, and apply firm pressure for about 10 minutes. The procedure could be tried again but is often abandoned. Neural injury, neuritis and infection are very rare complications. However carefully the procedure is carried out, accidental, intravascular bolus injection of lidocaine is always possible though is very rare. The casualty quickly shows signs of lidocaine toxicity - tingling of the tongue, light-headness, seizures, coma and cardiovascular collapse with increasing toxicity. Facilities to treat these complications should be at hand - oxygen, benzodiazepine and adrenaline (epinephrine).

More experienced Doctors may be confident to extend the technique by using larger volumes and larger quantities of lidocaine, approaching the quoted maximum of 3mg/kg body weight, to increase the block of the obturator nerve and femoral cutaneous nerve. They have no need for this book!

Dr. Theo Weston and Dave Freeborn (team leader) – "the next Landrover is going to have a flat carrying bed for the stretcher." And the colloid infusion is looking a bit dated! Patterdale MRT (early 1990s)

Case Study - Ketamine and reduction of a fracture/dislocation of ankle

This case is fictional but was developed from several real cases. It was commissioned for *Casualty Care in Mountain Rescue* to contribute a sense of real life and to draw attention to the dilemmas that occur in rescue work.

'One winter's afternoon, while descending from a good day out walking, a man in his mid 50s fell awkwardly on an icy patch on the main path leading off the mountain. His friend phoned on his mobile for help and when the Rescue Team arrived approximately 45 minutes later, the Casualty Care trained rescuers found that he was in severe pain from his right ankle and foot, which was clearly dislocated being deviated laterally and posteriorly. Intramuscular Cyclimorph® 15mg was immediately administered along with almost continuous use of Entonox®. The boot and sock were removed and a pulse found. However, the skin appeared white and stretched over the distal end of the front of the tibia and the pain continued unabated. The lower leg was immobilised in a vacuum splint and the evacuation from the hill was commenced. However, half an hour later, two hours since the accident, the descent was stopped as the casualty's pain was so intense and he had used two bottles of Entonox®! The Team Doctor arrived, reassessed the ankle, identified the fracture/dislocation and determined that a peripheral pulse was barely palpable. There were still at least a couple of hours to go before the casualty would reach hospital. A decision to reduce the fracture/dislocation was made; one that the casualty agreed to readily!

An intravenous cannula was inserted.

A monitor to measure BP, oxygen saturation and pulse was applied and the patient given oxygen.

Intravenous midazolam (2mg) was given (to reduce the chance of emergence phenomenon) followed by intravenous ketamine (30-40mg) administered.

The patient became 'lightly anaesthetised' (asleep). The ankle was disimpacted by pulling posteriorly and then reduced back into its normal position by pulling down. There was a reassuring clunk!

Five minutes later the casualty woke up asking when the procedure was to be commenced but feeling significantly more comfortable. The pulse returned, the foot was re-immobilised in the vacuum splint and the evacuation continued with not one further puff of Entonox® being needed.'

Comment

An ankle injury is the commonest injury that is likely to be encountered by Mountain Rescue Teams; trained Mountain Rescue personnel can easily treat most. However, occasionally the injury is a fracture dislocation of the ankle. The urgency of the situation may not be fully appreciated by those who have no experience of such injuries. Even if the seriousness of the condition is recognised by the team member, they may feel that they are not in position to help. If this is the case and no qualified health professional is available, then immediate evacuation by helicopter should be considered.

Ketamine

Ketamine has been around since the 1960s and to this day is still being regularly used in some under-developed countries as the main anaesthetic drug. It has recently begun to receive greater attention and is being used more frequently in the pre-hospital setting. It is a very safe drug having both analgesic and anaesthetic properties. The best description of its actions, at an anaesthetic dose, is 'complete analgesia combined with only superficial sleep' - a unique state! It can be given intramuscularly or intravenously. As an analgesic, it is given intravenously in a dose of 0.5mg/kg. As an anaesthetic, the dose is 1-2mg/kg. Ketamine's effects commence within 30-60 seconds and, following a single dose, last about 10-15 minutes. If anaesthetic properties are still needed after this time further aliquots of 10-20mg can be given to maintain anaesthesia. Ketamine can also be given intramuscularly in a dose of 10mg/kg to produce a period of anaesthesia, lasting for 15-25 minutes, though as with any drug given intramuscularly in trauma cases, absorption may be variable. The cardiovascular system is stimulated and respiration is not suppressed significantly. The gag reflex is maintained to a greater extent than other anaesthetic drugs. Some increase in salivation is experienced and should be watched for especially if there is an airway problem. Extraneous muscular movements are common particularly nystagmus (a rapid eye movement). There is also a rise in intracranial pressure (ICP) though this is matched by a rise in mean arterial blood pressure; in head injuries, the better oxygenation from airway and breathing control, and better blood pressure have to be balanced against the effect of a raised ICP. Hypertension, penetrating eye injury and a history of hallucinations are contraindications to its use. The main side effect of ketamine is severe hallucinations and vivid dreams, which occur in a number of people but which can be minimised by the administration of 1-2mg of midazolam. A quiet, dimly lit recovery area minimises the emergence phenomena but is unlikely to be achievable in the MR setting.

In summary, ketamine is a drug with unique properties that can be of immense value in pre-hospital care.

Reducing a shoulder dislocation

Dislocations are associated with fractures of the humerus and neurological, notably axillary and musculocutaneous nerve, damage. Early reduction is thought to be beneficial though I could find no supporting literature in terms of reduced nerve damage, reduced rehabilitation times or improved functional results. It is said that reduction is easier because muscle spasm has not set in; certainly, the casualty becomes almost free of pain and is able to assist himself. This may be of overriding importance in a rescue incident. However, attempted reduction in the presence of a fracture may be detrimental, the analgesia/anaesthesia required may cause problems, and, of course, pre-manipulation radiograms are not obtained so sorting out 'when the fracture occurred' may become unpleasant. Despite these concerns, in-the-field reduction is accepted if done by a suitably qualified person. (ICAR)

So how do I approach a casualty with shoulder pain following a fall? When do I reduce a shoulder?

Firstly do the clinical findings fit the picture of an anterior dislocation? The pain should be intense; the arm should be slightly abducted and externally rotated from the body and resist any adduction. The external contour of the shoulder should confirm an empty glenoid without any local bony tenderness or swelling. Reference to the uninjured side is often helpful in muscular individuals. If these features are not all present, consider a fracture of the humerus (with or without a dislocation), acromioclavicular separations or a posterior glenohumeral dislocation. A fracture with a dislocation is much more likely in the elderly and in high speed injures such as car accidents - similarly, other injuries implying high forces would make me cautious at attempting a reduction.

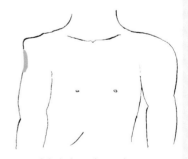

I test the function of the axillary and the musculocutaneous nerve by presence of sensation over the deltoid insertion ('Admiral's patch') and lateral border of the forearm.

Admiral patch numbness

Next, I would consider the safety of giving adequate analgesia/anaesthesia. Yes, incidents have been described using no analgesia, Entonox® and intra-articular lidocaine but most often some analgesia/anaesthesia is given. An intravenous benzodiazepine (to obtain muscle relaxation) with or without a small dose of opiate would be my preferred option though, in the recurrent dislocation or cooperative casualty, I have found an opiate alone successful. Are the facilities to cope with side effects from the drugs available, particularly respiratory depression (oxygen, bag-and-valve equipment and airway adjuncts) with benzodiazepines? When was the last meal? Is the casualty allergic to any drugs?

And what technique would I use? The simple answer is any with in-line traction as often this is the only component that is needed. The key is maintaining the traction until the casualty's shoulder muscles relax (fatigue) enough. So once applied the traction must be continued until the shoulder is reduced or attempts abandoned. Forced manipulation and direct axillary pressure are frowned on. I will describe two techniques; the first I have not used but can see me using, and the second I have used many times, without failure, since it was recommended by ICAR in 1998.

1) Stimson manoeuvre

Lay the casualty face down (prone) on a trolley/table. The affected limb is hung over the edge and about 4 kg weight hung from the hand. The casualty must relax the shoulder muscles and, hey presto, the shoulder pops back in. How useful for 'self rescue' if the casualty can get into the right position! Analgesia does not seem to be necessary; indeed you would need to be cautious with giving a benzodiazepine, as it would be difficult to treat respiratory depression in this position.

2) ICAR recommended

With the casualty in the sitting or semi-recumbent position, reassure him that you are not going to move the arm. Firstly apply traction along the axis of the casualty's upper arm by grasping just above the elbow. If it is the casualty's right shoulder that is dislocated, use your left hand. When the traction has been applied for a minute or two, the casualty should lie down - try not to move the shoulder at this stage, just maintain the traction. The rescuer now changes grip without releasing the elbow hold until the change is completed. With your free hand (right in this case) gasp the casualty's right wrist. Slowly extend the casualty's elbow to straight and take over the in line traction on the upper arm. You can now release your elbow grasp, and, if you like, apply a two handed grasp at the wrist. Explain that you are slowly going to abduct the shoulder to almost 90 degrees and also elevate the arm to about 45 degrees from the coronal plane (floor surface). The shoulder pops in often with an audible clunk; the casualty's pain disappears, and you breathe a sigh of relief. The key to success is constant traction that never decreases, reassuring the casualty and getting them to relax the shoulder muscles particularly when the shoulder partially returns only for muscle spasm to overcome your traction, and taking time - 5 or even 10 minutes is not unusual.

With the shoulder reduced, splint the arm across the body as external rotation of the upper arm, particularly when the casualty is still partially anaesthetized, may undo your work. Many casualties will be evacuated by stretcher though if circumstances dictate self-evacuation may be necessary. However all casualties need to be seen at an Accident and Emergency department for two reasons - firstly to have a 'x-ray' to confirm reduction and exclude any fractures and, secondly, to access the rehabilitation services.

Further thoughts

Analgesia

Methoxyflurane inhaler - an inhalational anaesthetic used in the same way as Entonox® giving almost immediate pain relief.

This is a small device that could replace Entonox® and would be particularly useful in confined-space rescue. Oxygen can be administered (8 litres/min) at the same time giving approximately 50% oxygen. The Penthrox™ inhaler (picture below) is reportedly used extensively in Australian pre-hospital emergency care.

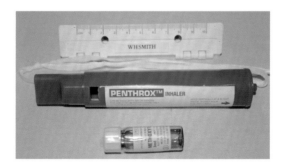

Methoxyflurane was withdrawn from the UK because of renal failure after prolonged (16 hour) use. Smells like glue sniffing!

Intranasal diamorphine may be as effective as an intravenous opiate. It is reported to have a good safety profile when used in Accident and Emergency departments for children and teenagers with suspected fractures. There are no published studies in adults but then many of my patients do it daily! It would be politically difficult to change the MRC's 'morphine' Licence.

Intravenous fluids - hypertonic solutions

A bolus of up to 4ml/kg body weight of hypertonic saline (7.5%) with or without dextran 70 is safe and comparable to isotonic solutions in haemorrhagic shock. The small volume (about 250ml) benefits the rescuer (easier warming, bolus technique) and though better outcomes were hoped for, these have not been substantiated in clinical trials except in cases of severe closed head injury. Hypertonic solutions are rarely used in the UK and are expensive. Are we using too much volume anyway?

Pelvic splints

Closed unstable pelvic fractures have a mortality of between 10 and 27%, and of those that die, 42% die from persistent haemorrhage. Definitive care involves resuscitation, orthopaedic fixation and angiographic embolisation (= blocking the bleeding arteries by inserting a catheter in them and then injecting a substance to form a thrombus). The patient often has other life-threatening injuries including haemorrhage into other cavities. Stabilisation and reducing the pelvic volume are early goals, which are thought to reduce the amount of bleeding though there is no published evidence of a survival benefit. Commercial pelvic splints are available but most papers report using a sheet wrapped round the pelvis and clamped or tied tight - a technique that MR could easily adopt! In addition to the vacuum mattress, this is probably the best we can do now that medical anti-shock trousers (MAST) / pneumatic anti-shock garments (PASG) have fallen from use. Using an *inverted* KED® has been suggested for a number of years, though with no documented reports or cases personally known to the author, it is hard to recommend it. Many of the casualties may well need the KED® on the right way!

Closed oxygen systems

Allows very small volumes of oxygen to be used whilst giving 100% oxygen. Cylinders last hours rather than minutes! Most appropriate with an LMA or endotracheal tube to ensure a closed system; if not, the mask on the casualty's face must be airtight, which is hard to achieve. The systems are becoming more robust and portable. Monitoring (FiO_2 and $ETCO_2$) would be essential. See http://www.wenoll.de/ for an example of the type of equipment currently available.

References

Femoral nerve block

McGlone R, Sadhra K, Hamer DW, Pritty PE. Femoral nerve block in the initial management of femoral shaft fractures. Archives of Emergency Medicine. 1987; 4:163-8

Fletcher A K, Rigby A S, Heyes F L, Ken Koval. Journal Of Bone and Joint Surgery 2004; 82:441

Levine J, Triner WR, Lai SY. A randomized controlled trial comparing femoral nerve block to intravenous morphine in isolated femur fractures. Academic Emergency Medicine 2003; 10:469

Ketamine

Wood PR. Ketamine: Prehospital and in-hospital use. Trauma 2003; 5:137-140

Porter K. Ketamine in pre-hospital care. EMJ 2004; 21:351-354

Clinical Effectiveness Committee of the British Association for Emergency Medicine. Guideline for ketamine sedation in emergency departments (2005). Accessed at http://www.emergencymed.org.ukCousin MJ, Mazze RI. Methoxyflurane Nephrotoxicity JAMA 1973; 225:1611-6

Shoulder reduction

Kocher MS, Feagin JA. Shoulder injuries during alpine skiing. American Journal of Sports Medicine 1996; 24:665-9

Marx RG, Scott D. Sideline orthopaedic emergencies in the young athlete. Pediatric Annals 2002; 31:60-72

Forster H, Zafren K. Treatment of shoulder dislocations ICAR recommendation number 9 1998; Consensus guidelines on mountain emergency medicine and risk reduction ISBN 88-884-29-00-X. Accessible at http://www.ikar-cisa.org

Harries M, Williams c, Stanish W, Micheli L. Oxford Textbook of Sports Medicine 1994. ISBN 0 19 262009 6

Further thoughts

Kendall JM, Reeves BC, Latter VS. Multicentre randomised controlled trial of nasal diamorphine for analgesia in children and teenagers with clinical fractures. BMJ 2001; 322:261-265

Heetveld MJ, Harris I, Schlaphoff G, Balogh Z, D'Amours SK, Sugrue M. Moore FA, McKinley BA, Moore EE. The next generation in shock resuscitation The Lancet 2004; 363:1988-96

Hemodynamically Unstable Pelvic Fractures: Recent Care and New Guidelines. World J.Surg. 2004; 28:904-909

Qureshi A, McGee A, Cooper JP, Porter KM. Reduction of the posterior pelvic ring by non-invasive stabilisation: a report of two cases. Emerg Med J 2005; 22:885-6

Crawford I. The prehospital use of pneumatic anti-shock garments. Accessed at http://www.bestbets.org/cgi-bin/bets.pl?record=00090

Final thoughts

Yes, a pair of scissors!

Don't forget mountain rescue is not about operating in a well ordered environment. The basics are what you need to know, and need to do well. After 397 pages and 20+ years of rescuing, are these the greatest step forward?

Index